UNIX™ – The Complete Book

A guide for the professional user

Jason J. Manger

SIGMA PRESS
Wilmslow, England

© 1991, Jason J. Manger

All rights reserved. No part of this publication may be reproduced, stored in a retrieval system or transmitted in any form or by any means, electronic, mechanical, photocopying, recording or otherwise, without prior written permission of the publisher.

In this book, many of the designations used by manufacturers and sellers to distinguish their products may be claimed as trademarks. Due acknowledgment is hereby made of all legal protection.

Typeset and Designed by Sigma Hi-Tech Services Ltd, Wilmslow, UK

Cover Design by Anchor Design, Wilmslow, Cheshire

First published in 1991
Sigma Press, 1 South Oak Lane, Wilmslow, Cheshire SK9 6AR, UK

First printed 1991

ISBN: 1-85058-219-X

British Library Cataloguing in Publication Data
A CIP catalogue record for this book is available from the British Library

Printed by: Interprint Ltd, Malta

Preface

Whilst writing this book, I have found that many people are referring to UNIX as a world standard. This is not strictly true: we have to distinguish between a standard UNIX system, and a UNIX version. I assume that most people are referring to the latter. UNIX, like many other systems, is still being produced by several different manufacturers, and thus the trend in the development of UNIX is a tendency away from the standardization process.

So what has all this got to do with you, the reader of this book and possible end-user of UNIX? You should be aware that the word ''UNIX'' is frequently used to classify all the UNIX and UNIX-like products that are now available (although there is an actual UNIX system, which is the trademark of Bell Laboratories). Other manufacturers therefore have to choose a different name for their ''UNIX'' products.

Because there are many different types and *flavours* of the operating system, parts of what you have learnt about UNIX on one machine may be very different on another. Of course, there are many similarities between the majority of UNIX systems, and where these occur they will be pointed out. Commands and naming conventions tend to alter from version to version, therefore most commands in this book have descriptions about the versions from which they originated.

Establishing a unified version of UNIX has been a major problem for some time, but there are the de-facto UNIX systems, namely those produced by AT&T (American Telephone & Telegraph - the US equivalent to British Telecom in Britain), and IBM.

This book is based on two modern systems: SunOS - Sun MicroSystems' UNIX, versions 3 and 4 (Berkeley orientated), and Xenix, Microsoft's UNIX - based on System V UNIX. Gould/Encore UTX/32 UNIX (Berkeley oriented) has also been used in many of the examples. Extracts from other leading UNIX manufacturers have been included where relevant, and the use of Berkeley UNIX is prominent.

This book is aimed at the reader who has experience of at least one computer operating system, such as PC/MS-DOS. If you have never used UNIX before, this will help you to get started. All the topics are presented and explained in an in-depth manner. The aim is to bring you up to date with today's UNIX systems, and to allow you to become immediately effective in a modern environment. The topics are backed up by real examples, and there are exercises at the end of the most important chapters, so that you can see how well you are progressing. Solutions are also provided.

If you are a student, then you may know that UNIX is becoming more widely used in Colleges, Polytechnics and Universities. Some material in this book is gathered from under-graduate courses in Computer Science, including topics on shell programming, and the software tools philosophy behind the UNIX System.

However, if you are already working in a UNIX environment, you should find the chapters on Shell-programming, Security, Systems Administration and Communications useful. There are full syntax descriptions for each command, with detailed definitions and explanations, along with information about the various files that are processed by the commands in question.

By its very nature, UNIX is a large and complex system, and many subject areas overlap into others. If you are interested in one particular aspect, such as Systems Administration, look for a Chapter devoted to that subject area. If you do not find a relevant Chapter, use the subject index to look up entries that may be embedded in other topics.

Jason Manger

CONTENTS

1

Introduction to UNIX

UNIX has existed for over twenty years. The history of UNIX makes interesting reading but is only covered briefly here. It is a large, and somewhat cumbersome system in many respects, but it must not be ruled out because of this. If you are interested in how the system began, start here – otherwise go straight to Chapter 2.

1.1 The Origins of UNIX

UNIX is the name of a computer operating system, the trademark which is owned by Bell Laboratories. But UNIX is not just one system – it is a generic name given to a family of related systems. The following brief history may help you understand its development.

In the late 1960s, Bell Laboratories were involved in the development of an interactive multi-user system called 'Multics'. In 1968 increasing problems with this system led the Computing Science and Research Department of Bell Laboratories to withdraw from the project. This took place between 1968 and 1969.

Staff working on the Multics project decided to search for a new system. This began in 1969 and K. Thompson, D. Ritchie and R. Canaday designed a file structure for the new operating system that was finally to become the structure found in the UNIX systems of today. Also during 1969, Thompson had developed a space simulation program called 'Space Travel'. The system was hard to control, because of severe machine limitations. It had originally been written under the Multics project on a GE-645 time-sharing computer system.

Thompson then started using a PDP-7 series computer, and he and Ritchie re-wrote Space Travel to run on the new computer. Thompson also started to implement the older Multics file-system onto the new PDP-7 computer, followed by a set of smaller utility programs necessary for file-handling such as file copy mechanisms.

This was the first 'porting' of the UNIX system: the movement of an existing system to a new make of computer. In 1970, Brian Kernighan suggested 'UNIX' for the name of the new system. The origin of the word UNIX has caused great discussion to take place. Many people believe it was named after the earlier Multics system.

Kernighan and Ritchie had already developed the C language. This was very flexible, and the new UNIX system was nearly all written in C, apart from the code for the Kernel, which was written in assembler. Because of this, UNIX was very machine independent, and hence portable. This is probably one of the main factors that has made UNIX such a world-wide success.

During the first few years of 1970, the UNIX system was still pretty much a private matter for Bell Laboratories, and it was not until the mid 1970s that UNIX was released to the academic world. Thompson acted as a visiting Professor at the University of California at Berkeley, where he had introduced UNIX to the Computer Science department. Bell Laboratories supported the promotion of the UNIX system in this way, and agreed to promote it in both the United States and Europe.

UNIX was intended to be used in a program development environment, but there are probably two main factors which popularised it in the commercial arena. Up to 1980, UNIX had been taught in many Colleges and Universities both in the United States and in Europe., and had practically dominated parts of many Computer Science courses (especially on the theme of operating systems).

The new graduates who entered the job market, and who were trained on UNIX, favoured it as a computer system and made their views known to their employers. These graduates had now worked their way into senior data-processing positions. They alone now made the decisions to install UNIX systems in their organisations, not only because of its advantages, but because it was the system that they had been taught during their earlier education, and with which they felt most confident.

Another event that contributed to the introduction of UNIX into the commercial environment was the break-up of the AT&T, and the separation of Bell Laboratories from it. Bell Laboratories were no longer constrained by AT&T, and hence UNIX could now be promoted in the commercial arena.

1.2 UNIX the Standard?

So what are the possibilities of a UNIX version becoming a real industry standard? Unlike other operating systems such as MS-DOS, which are controlled by a single system vendor, UNIX is spread amongst hardware vendors, UNIX software companies, and AT&T itself. UNIX System V has been termed the foundation standard which other UNIX systems would have to conform to. Many commercial UNIX systems in the organisations of today are found to be System V orientated.

There are now so many different types of UNIX and UNIX-like systems, that the very process of a standard version is somewhat hindered, if not shattered entirely. This is caused by competitors who continue to release their own enhanced versions (or flavours) of the UNIX system, in order to capture a share of this now huge market.

System V version 4.0, has recently been released. This combines three popular UNIX systems: Xenix – Microsoft's version of UNIX, which is popular in the Personal Computer world; System V, the older foundation system; and Berkeley UNIX. All three of these UNIX systems were used in the writing of this book.

2

Communicating With UNIX

In order to 'converse' with UNIX, a few fundamentals have to be explained. If you are already proficient with the use of a computer terminal, then you can overlook this Chapter.

Communicating with UNIX is through a terminal. A terminal normally consists of a visual display unit (VDU), and a keyboard. The keyboard is the main input device to be used when communicating with the UNIX system.

UNIX is an interactive system. This means that you supply UNIX with instructions (which are typed in at the keyboard), which are then sent to the system for processing. When these have been processed, the results are made available to you.

Because the UNIX system is interactive, it is also known as a full-duplex system. The keyboard allows you to enter commands, so that UNIX can process them. Nearly all the keys on a typical keyboard are printable alphabetic characters (a character being a single letter or digit). However, apart from the normal printable characters, there are what is termed control characters. These are non-printing characters. Some examples of non-printing characters are the ones generated by the DEL and cursor movement keys found on a typical keyboard. In interactive mode, such as in a session with UNIX at a terminal, you cannot normally make use of all the cursor keys because your commands are typed in on a single line. On some systems the left and right cursor keys (the keys ← and →) can be used to amend the command-line. The command-line in our context is the line that contains the current UNIX instruction to be executed. An exception is when you are using a screen editor.

Probably the most important key on the keyboard is the RETURN key (also known as the ENTER key). This key must be pressed after you have entered a UNIX command. If you type in a command and wait for a response, you will be out of luck. UNIX will probably wait until the end of mankind, or until the system is turned off – whichever happens first.

2.1 The Dumb Terminal

Terminals are normally one of two types. The first type is called a dumb terminal. Dumb terminals are simply terminals that do not have any processing power, and hence they are only used as a two-way communications device with the host computer system.

2.2 The Intelligent Terminal

The other type of terminal is the intelligent terminal. These have additional processing power. The important fact to note is that intelligent terminals can download information from the UNIX system, and can store that information locally on a storage device attached to the terminal, such as on a hard-disk storage device.

Intelligent terminals also alleviate the amount of processing that the main computer system has to perform. Most personal computers can be used as terminals via a technique known as terminal emulation. Personal computers used in this way are also known by the name 'smart terminals'.

2.3 Standard Terminal Systems

Computer terminals are slightly different from personal computers in the way that characters are displayed, and how control characters are interpreted. Luckily, there are already some standard terminal emulations in existence. The VT100, and later VT200/300 series terminals are already industry standards in their own right (VT stands for video, or virtual terminal).

The VT family mentioned above were originally manufactured by DEC (Digital Equipment Corporation), but you may see the terminal type VT100 used in many other terminal and terminal emulation systems. The basic VT100 terminal could be considered to be in the dumb terminal class since it lacks additional processing power, however DEC have produced intelligent terminals also. The VT200 range, for example, includes some intelligent terminals, and the Rainbow 100 (now extinct) is another good example of an intelligent terminal. Most of Digital Equipment Corporation intelligent terminals have local storage facilities and additional processing power to enable them to run other computer software locally.

2.4 Identifying a Terminal

How do you know whether a terminal is dumb or intelligent? By definition, intelligent terminals have additional processing power. This additional processing capability may take the form of an internal storage device. If this is the case, the terminal will have to house the device inside its casing, which in turn makes the terminal larger.

However, some terminals have additional processing power in the form of additional circuitry. This circuitry is becoming more and more compact. If the terminal that you are using is a PC, such as an IBM AT or clone computer, then it has extra processing power, for example additional storage facilities, memory circuits, and the like. These are normally housed in the system-unit of the device concerned.

Many organisations are already using PCs as "smart" terminals via the use of special terminal emulation software. This is an attractive option, since the terminal device can not only be used to communicate with the main host computer system i.e. a UNIX system, but can also be used to run other applications software, such as those available under the MS-DOS operating system.

2.5 UNIX and the Terminal

The terminal is one of the many devices that interacts with the UNIX system. UNIX recognises the terminal you are using by an individual name. This name takes the form of the letters tty and then a number and/or letter combination. The letters "tty" stand for "teletype" which is an aged synonym for the word "terminal".

The number which is part of the identification code for a terminal sometimes relates to the number of terminals that the host UNIX system can support. For example, if a UNIX system had twenty user terminals installed, then any of the terminal identification codes in the range tty0 through tty19 may be valid (note that 0 is valid in most UNIX configurations).

Terminal codes vary from manufacturer to manufacturer, and you may find that some UNIX systems employ complete alphabetical identification conventions such as ttya, ttyp, and to confuse matters further, a mixture of both i.e. ttyp1.

Another terminal name is used on many UNIX systems – the 'console'. The console terminal is used by the Systems Administrator. This is frequently used to monitor the terminals on the current UNIX system (and therefore all the actions taken by every user of the system). It is also the terminal on which changes to the day-to-day running of the UNIX system are normally made.

It is important to note that UNIX can support a wide variety of terminals. The topic of computer terminals and the UNIX system are examined in more detail in later chapters.

3

UNIX – The Multi-User System

UNIX is a multi-user system, meaning that more than one user at any one time can access the facilities of the host system. A typical UNIX installation may have a hundred or more users. The possibility of all of these communicating with UNIX at any one time depends on the amount of terminals installed, and the configuration of the host system. Most UNIX systems have many more registered users than terminals.

3.1 Shared Resources

Since UNIX is a multi-user system it can share its resources. UNIX does this by allocating a time period to each user on the system. This time period is sometimes known as a time-slice When there are many users all accessing or processing data at one time, UNIX will switch between each user of the system very quickly (almost unnoticeably on most occasions).

When UNIX processes a task, the main aim is to try and complete it. This depends on how much processing is needed, and what priority the task has been allocated. If the task is long and complex, UNIX may leave the task and come back to it after it has dealt with another that is also awaiting attention. This switching process is known as multi-tasking, and a major part of the UNIX system management is concerned with processing the various tasks from each terminal. The sharing of resources is an integral part of any multi-user system, as is the use of time-slice allocations and multi-tasking facilities.

3.2 Networking

All multi-user systems are networked. The advantages of networking are enormous. For example, data is not duplicated, it is stored centrally in a mass storage device, and peripherals, such as printers and disk-drives, can be accessed by all users.

3.3 Network Types

Networks are mainly classified by their shape and size. The shape of a network, or the way in which the user terminals are interconnected, falls under the heading of network topologies (examined later). There are therefore two main factors that define the type of network – its shape and size.

3.4 The Size Factor

The size of a network depends on the number of users and their whereabouts (in a geographical sense). In this section we will examine the two main types of networks, according to their physical size.

3.4.1 LANs and WANs

Networks are divided into two main categories, largely determined by their geographical sizes. The two network types considered here are the local and wide area networks (LANs and WANS) respectively. A LAN (Local Area Network) is a series of connected devices (i.e. personal computers or workstations) distributed over a small geographical area. LANs have data rates up to 10 Megabits per second (greater data-rates are achieved with fibre-optic technology, such as FDDI – Fibre Distributed Data Interface).

A WAN (Wide Area network) is concerned with the interconnection of devices over a wide geographical area. The public switched telephone network (PSTN) is a good example of a WAN in everyday use. WANs typically extend over distances in the region of up to 1000 Kilometres. Many existing WANs have data rates approaching 100 Kilobits per second. The newer digital netwotk technologies, such as ISDN (Integrated Services Digital Network) allow for an increase in data-rates (typically in the order of 144 to 2048 kilobits per second – basic and primary rate ISDN).

3.5 Network Topologies

We will examine four main types of network topologies, their advantages and disadvantages.

3.5.1 The Star Network Topology

The central node of a star network normally does all of the work of transmitting the data between each terminal, hence the intelligence of this system normally lies in the central node alone. Peripheral nodes need less intelligence, giving a cheaper system overall. The one main disadvantage with the star topology, is that if the central node fails, the entire network breaks down.

3.5.2 The Ring Network Topology

Ring network topologies have intelligent nodes (or terminals) spread evenly over the network, hence central control is no longer necessary. Most Ring networks have one monitoring station (normally a node in the network itself). This takes care of any errors in the transmission of data. Transmission of data around this type of network is normally one-way, although some Ring network systems can be configured for data transmission in either direction.

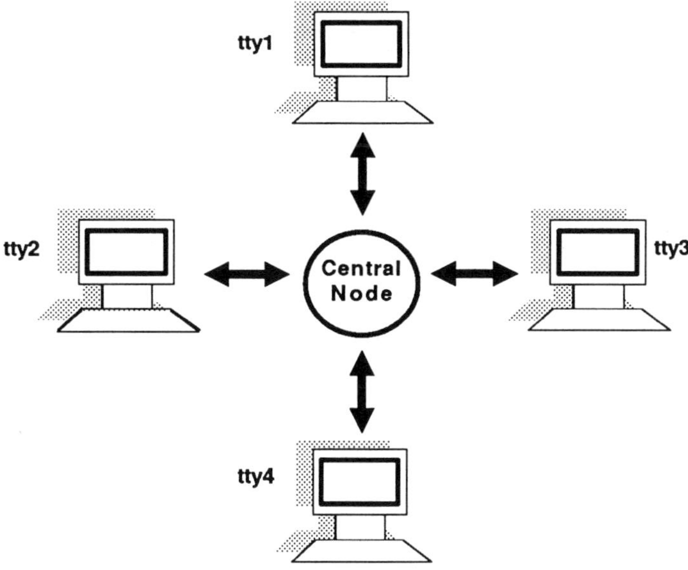

Figure 3.1 Star network Topology with four nodes

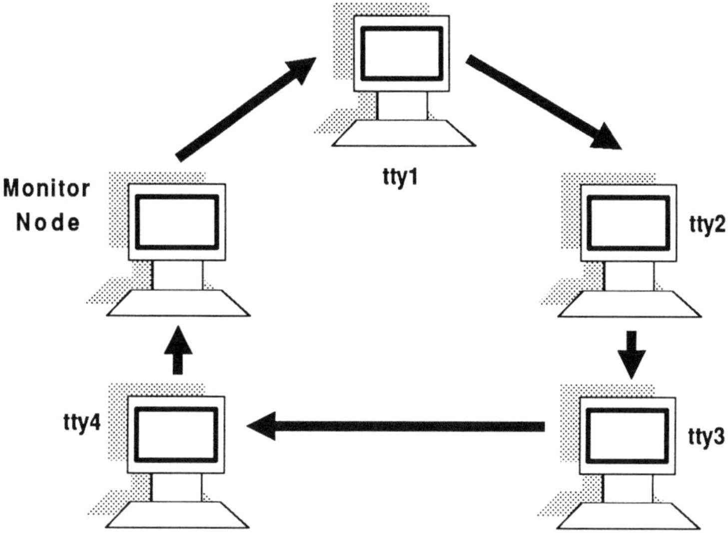

Figure 3.2 Ring Network Topology

3.5.3 Bus Network Topology

The Bus network is easily identified since it simply consists of one bus and terminators at both ends (see Figure 3.3). Devices in the network (a terminal is an example) send data and a device address along the bus. All devices quickly examine the data to look for the address, just in case it corresponds to them. This type of network is a "passive" network, which means that the devices on the network listen for data addressed to them.

When a device wants to transmit data over the network, it "listens" to determine if the network is busy (i.e. if any data is being transmitted). When the network goes quiet for a brief moment, the device will transmit its information. The intelligence in this type of network topology lies in the individual nodes (terminals) themselves. They must have the necessary intelligence to recognise an address, so that they can receive information, and also determine when it is safe to send a particular message (to avoid a network collision). This type of network is normally used in probabilistic systems, using a protocol such as CSMA/CD over a LAN (described in section 3.9.5).

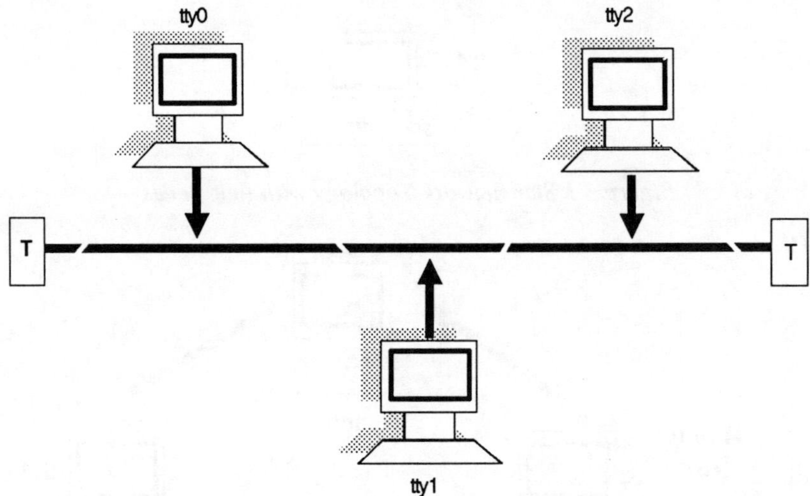

Figure 3.3 Bus Network Topology

The main advantages of this type of network topology are the ease of installation and expansion. Another advantage of this system is that a break in the main bus that isolates one or more devices may not cause a total network breakdown. The disadvantage of this type of network topology is cost, since the system relies on the fact that each node in the network will have a certain amount of intelligence.

3.5.4 Loop Network Topology

The Loop network topology is similar to that of the Ring network, except that all messages on the network must pass through an intelligent controlling node. This sends periodic empty messages around the network. A device can either pick up the empty message body that has been transmitted, and use it to send a new message to a recipient on the network using a unique destination address, or a device can *poll* each device on the network.

Polling is the task of constantly asking a device (at regular intervals) whether or not it needs attention (e.g. to send a message over the network etc), and is discussed in more depth in the next section. An advantage of this system is the low cost of implementation. Since intelligence lies in one specific area only, the other peripheral devices cen be purchased much cheaper. A major disadvantage is the reliance on the intelligent controller node. If this breaks down, the whole system will fail, and communication across the network would be impossible. Another disadvantage lies in the throughput rate of the system. These types of systems tend to have low data transmission speeds, and hence the data throughput is somewhat restricted.

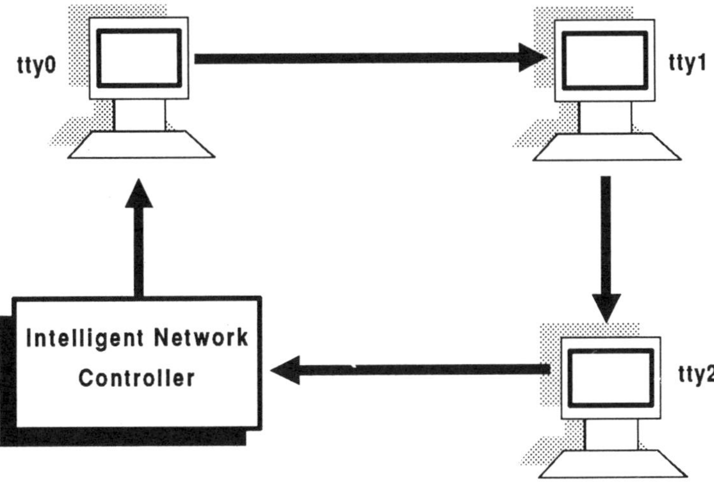

Figure 3.4 The Loop Network Topology

3.8 Network Sharing and Access Methods

We mentioned earlier that the topology of a system is not really an accurate description. For example, a Ring topology can look like a Star, and a Bus topology can look like a tree-shaped network topology. The later sections of this Chapter will examine some of the most popular access and sharing techniques used in the networking of computer systems, such as CSMA/CD (see section 3.9.5).

3.8.1 Polling

We met the term *polling* in an earlier section. This requires a node with considerable intelligence to ask the other nodes in the network if they need attention. Polling systems are very CPU intensive. The master node which polls the other nodes in the network can consume a considerable amount of processing time. Also, the node being polled might not need attention in the first place. Nevertheless the system will still poll all the nodes in the network. Priority mechanisms may be set up so that a heavily used node can get more access to the network than the others.

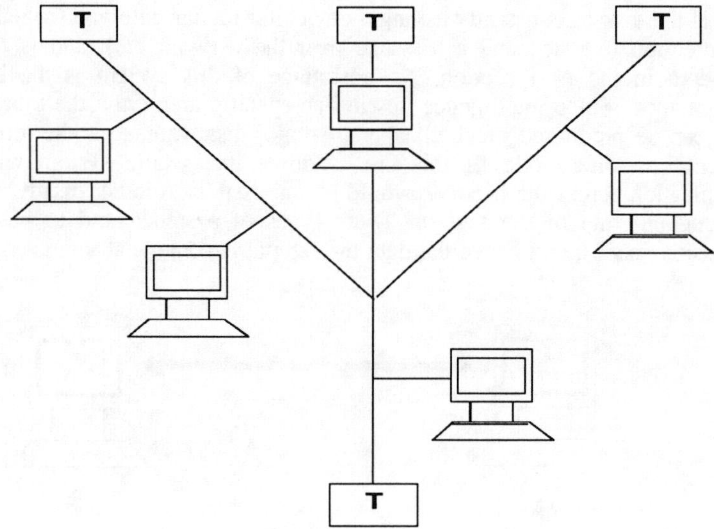

Figure 3.5 Bus as a Tree

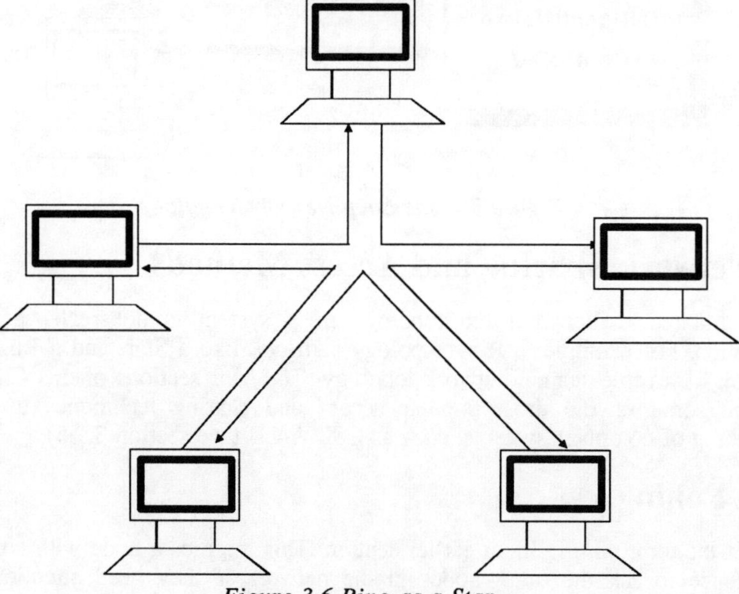

Figure 3.6 Ring as a Star

The more logical alternative would be to allow the device that needed attention to poll the master node for attention. This would save valuable processing time, since only genuine requests would be serviced.

3.8.2.1 The Ethernet Connection

Ethernet is a standard in its own right (IEEE 802.3). It is used extensively in LAN systems world-wide and is a specification that describes how computers and data systems can be connected. It encompasses the *physical* and *data link* layers of the OSI standard .

Networks can be configured in a variety of ways. The way in which a network is constructed is termed its *topology* as we have seen already in section 3.5. The discussion here focuses on the methods currently undertaken to construct simple network topologies and examines some of the hardware devices that are required in order to achieve a working configuration.

All devices (PCs, Workstations, printers etc.) are connected into an Ethernet cable and each will have an Ethernet controller device into which the Ethernet cable passes (these are sometimes card-based – see later). Each device has a unique Ethernet address so that it can be uniquely identified. The basic components of any Ethernet system are described here, and shown diagrammatically in Figure 3.7.

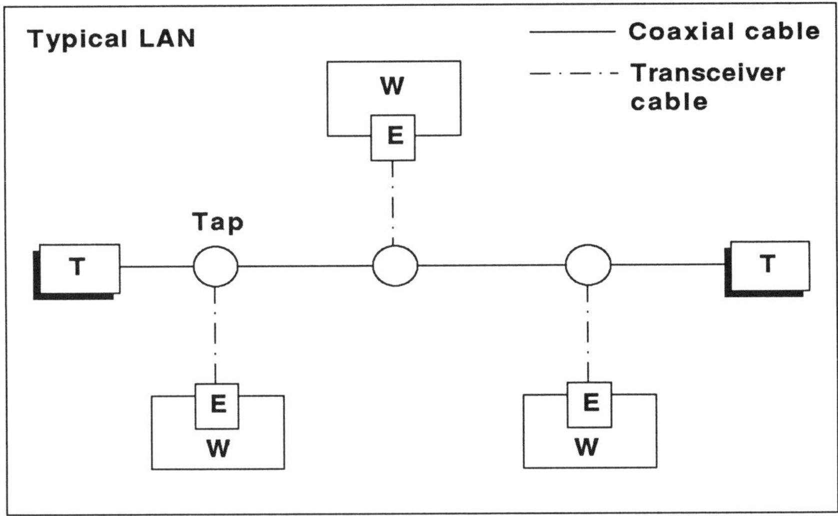

Figure 3.7 A typical LAN configuration

- ❑ **Ethernet controller** This is installed inside the device in question, and it handles the incoming and outgoing data to and from the machine. A unique Ethernet address in encoded in the Ethernet controller.
- ❑ **Transceiver cable** ("drop cable") This piece of cable media connects the Ethernet controller into transceiver *tap* devices that connected to the Ethernet coaxial cable. A multiplexing device may optionally be used here.

- **Coaxial cable** This forms the backbone of the Ethernet network. All devices in the network are attached into this cable through transceiver *tap* devices which are positioned on the coaxial cable. The maximum length of the cable segment is approximately 1500 meters.
- **Terminators** These devices are positioned at the end of the main coaxial cable segment. They are used to terminate the main cable segment.

LANs are used to link a series of devices in a limited area – perhaps within a single building. The sequence of actions that a workstation has to undertake to make a file transfer between itself and another machine involves:

- The user at a particular workstation issues a command to the operating system to specify that a file is to be transferred to another machine;
- The operating system will copy the file to the destination machine as a series of datagrams (or as a *virtual circuit* – a dedicated connection between two parties for the duration of their communication). The datagram/virtual-circuit software will then decompose the actual information (a byte stream) into a series of *packets* for transmission across the network;
- The packets are passed to the controlling Ethernet software (an Ethernet *driver*);
- The Ethernet software copies the various packets into an area of memory known as a *buffer*, and then informs a controlling device to send out the information on the network. The controller "listens" on the cable to sense the existence of any other passing packets and when the line is free, it transmits the information;
- The destination machine receives those packets which are addressed to it (via an Ethernet address attached to the packets) passed through the *data link* layer of the ISO stack. The various packets are decoded and interpreted accordingly.

Other LAN devices

There are many other devices that LANs use. The most common devices are the **repeater**, **router**, and **bridge**:

A *repeater* is a device utilised at the *physical* layer of the ISO protocol. A LAN can be expanded in size through use of repeater devices, since their function is to allow different coaxial Ethernet segments (*backbone* segments) to be connected together. A physical LAN consists of a series of Ethernet segments connected by repeater devices. Repeater devices regenerate the data signals when two Ethernet segments are connected together, thus extending the overall size of the network.

A *bridge* is an device used at the *data link* level. Bridges copy data selectively between different Ethernet cable segments (of the same type). A bridge device filters traffic on a network, conditionally passing data to another cable segment. Because a *selective* mechanism for packet passing has been introduced, network traffic can be reduced on individual cable segments. The IEEE have defined a bridge standard (IEEE 802.1) which encompasses the MAC standards (media access control). Bridges come in many forms:

A *local bridge* is a single physical unit that physically joins two networks.

A *remote bridge* configuration consists of two *half bridges* that connect two LANs over a point-to-point link or via public data network (such as a WAN). An example of this is a remote bridge to connect two remote LANs via the PSDN/CSDN (Packet Switched Data Network/Circuit Switched Data Network). This is done by using a protocol stack that maps MAC – Medium Access Control (LAN based protocols) to a WAN-based protocol such as HDLC (High Level Data Link Control – an OSI data-link based protocol). MAC and HDLC are encapsulated within each other, and passed from network to network accordingly.

A *router* (also known as a **gateway**) is a device that simply forwards packets from a LAN to another network. The forwarded packets may be passed to a network of a different type. Routers are often comprised of two Ethernet controller devices, one to communicate with each LAN. Routing tables are used in a router device to allow it to direct packets onto the correct network.

Routing tables can be kept up-to-date using a *routing protocol*. During the forwarding process, a packet's destination address is examined, upon which the relevant routing table in the routing device is examined to try and find a match. If a successful match is made, the forwarding process is quite simple. In the case where an address is not found, the router may choose to broadcast (or flood) the network, so that the packet has a better chance of reaching its destination.

Routers can also be used to extend LANs (i.e. between different parts of a building) in much the same way as a repeater device, although one must distinguish between the two, since in reality they provide different services. Router devices can also be used to pass data from a local area network to a wide area network. Figure 3.8 illustrates two LANs joined by a router device. LAN configurations using the Internet protocols require that an IP (Internet Protocol) network number be assigned to each workstation and router device.

A typical **/etc/hosts** file is shown below (after the router device has been added to the network):

```
# LAN 1 128.16.8     Ethernet - Personnel department
#
IP Addresshost name
-------------------
128.16.8.10     wombat
128.16.8.5      merritt
128.16.8.4      orinda
128.16.8.3      coliseum
# LAN 2 128.16.9     Ethernet - Sales department
#
128.16.9.6      mithras
128.16.9.12     wombat2
```

The **/etc/hosts** file contains the IP (Internet Protocol) addresses of all workstations and router devices. A router device is strange in that it has two unique names. This is because for the network software to work properly, the router must have a unique host name for each interface. In this case machines on both networks can address the machine by its primary name (*wombat*), while it is possible for the administrative user to tell the difference between the two host names.

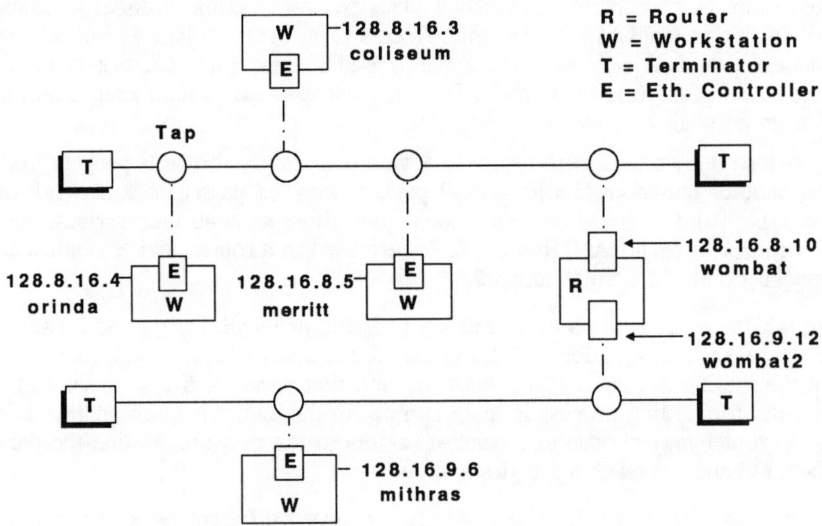

Figure 3.8. Two LANs joined via a router device

Network Card Products

If you are purchasing a network product which is card based (e.g. Western Digital's PC EtherCard PLUS system for LANs), then each terminal must have a card installed inside its casing.

The card fits into an expansion slot inside the computer's vacant expansion slot. A network card product normally has two main interconnection ports. This allows the network card to interface with either a Thin Ethernet system or a rugged Ethernet system. Figure 3.9 illustrates a network in which some Ethernet controller cards have been joined to a series of drop cables (to allow connection into the LAN backbone segment). The Thin Ethernet cabling will be plugged into the connection top socket interconnection. The second port, a 15 pin D-type connection, is used to connect the rugged Ethernet cable, again depending on the size of the network.

One end of the drop-cable that was described earlier will be attached into the card, and the other end will be attached to the Ethernet cable segment. The attachment will be made through a medium attachment unit (MAU) when a terminal is to be inserted into the network, i.e. into the spine or the ribs of the network.

If the spine breaks away to a rib section, the attachment must connect to an MAU first, but it will then be diverted to a repeater device; The Ethernet line will be a thin type, allowing more than one terminal to be joined together in a form of sub-network.

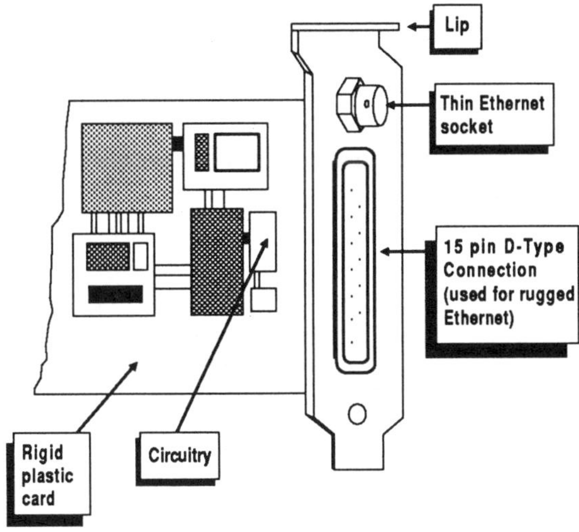

Figure 3.9. A Typical Network Card.

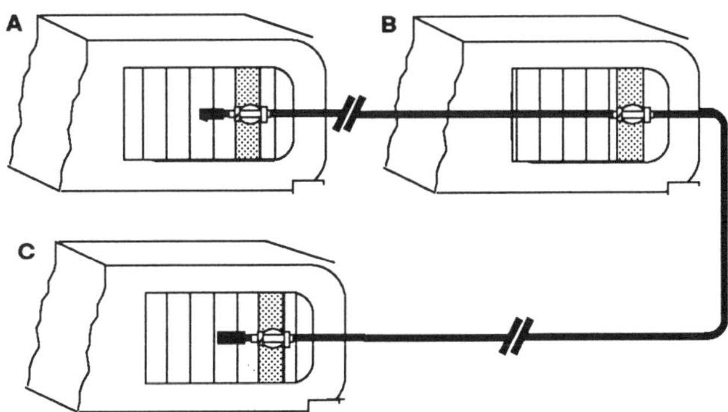

Figure 3.10 A Typical Thin Ethernet Connection Route

Assume that machines A, B and C (in Figure 3.10) are connected into an Ethernet network. Machines A and C have terminator devices attached, hence they are the last machines on the cable. Machine B illustrates how a connection is made to a machine, and out to another. The ability to link machines in this manner is very useful, since terminals can be disconnected from the network without breaking the Ethernet line, hence the network is still operational.

Machines can be separated by a T-connector. The T-connector is also known as a standard BNC connector. T-connectors of this type are commonly used to link thin

Ethernet cables together. Linking up the more rugged Ethernet cables normally requires the use of special connectors: an MAU transceiver/connector device will be used for each cable connection in the network. Network cables are normally marked at special intervals so that MAU devices can be attached. The terminal usually interfaces into the MAU device using a standard 15 pin D-type connector (the network can then be allowed to continue).

3.8.3 Token Passing

This technique is often used in Ring networks to ensure that a node can gain access to the network. Normally the transmitting node will send a message that will pass through one or more nodes in the network (when trying to reach the recipient). This is not always the case, and it is possible to implement a system whereby particular nodes can access messages more frequently than others.

The token is the actual packet of information in our context. It continually passes around the network. When a node wants to send data to another node, the sending node must grab hold of the token as it passes by. Once the passing token has been caught, the node fills the token with the appropriate data. The token contains individual compartments, the largest compartment normally being reserved for the actual data which is to be received and processed by the recipient node.

The only drawback with the token passing method is that only one node can send data at any one time. The empty slot-ring network configuration overcomes this by allowing packets of data to circulate around the network. All the nodes monitor the progress of this packet. When a node wants to transmit data, it simply grabs the empty packet, and fills it with the necessary information. Token passing systems are normally very inefficient when traffic through the network is unevenly balanced.

Token passing systems are more complex than CSMA/CD. They are also more costly to implement, since node intelligence is required. Individual node intelligence is required because nodes must be able to recognise messages addressed to them. Token passing normally results in predictable message-transmission times. In a ring topology, the sending node is also the receiving node for acknowledgement purposes.

In a bus topology, a complex algorithm is sometimes employed to establish what is termed a virtual-ring, giving the impression that the bus is a ring topology. Such systems normally require a significant amount of additional computational power. The Token Ring method is in itself a recognised standard, the IEEE 802.5 protocol, so its importance cannot easily be overlooked.

3.9 Networking with UNIX

This part of the chapter is concerned with UNIX networking and communications.

Protocols

This section introduces some of the most up-to-date and relevant protocols in the UNIX arena. These include:

- X-Windows/X Protocol
- PC-NFS/NFS – Network file system
- TCP – transmission control protocol
- IP – Internet protocol
- UDP – user datagram protocol
- TELNET – remote terminal protocol
- FTP – file transfer protocol

What is a protocol?

A protocol is a set of formal rules that controls how hardware and software systems interact together within a network to control the flow of information. The flow of information may pass between local processes (on the same network), or between different networks. The development of UNIX over the past two decades has led to the development of many new communications protocols.

3.9.1 PC-NFS

PC-NFS (Network File System) is a distributed file system protocol from Sun Microsystems, also noted for their **SunOS** version of UNIX (based on Berkeley v4.2 UNIX) which is also one of the systems to be included in the new "unified" System V Release 4.0 version of the UNIX operating system. PC-NFS was developed for use in a UNIX and Personal Computer (PC) environment, the goal being to allow PCs to access UNIX files stored on a Sun file-server machine. Two main design goals for NFS (which equally apply to PC-NFS – NFS's smaller brother) were:

- To permit access to a remote file system (with access speeds comparable to that of a local disk);
- Transparent access to files, treating them in the same way as remote files (transparency has not been achieved totally in PC-NFS);

PC-NFS is not a networking system, neither is it an operating system. NFS is a piece of software that interacts with the host network system. The PC-NFS system makes remote file access transparent (files may in fact be situated on another machine). NFS thus acts as system which handles client requests for certain pieces of information (such an individual file, or a complete file-system).

Users can mount file-systems in a fashion similar to the mounting of a file-system under the UNIX system (see section 11.9.1). PC-NFS allows UNIX directory structures to be accessed and maintained through the MS-DOS operating system. The user can thus traverse a UNIX file-system from within MS-DOS, using the *cd* (change directory) command.

PC-NFS works by allowing some terminals on a network to be designated as servers, while others are designated as clients (RFS shares this principle also – see section

2.2.2). A client can mount parts of a UNIX file-system which can either be local or remote to the current workstation (or PC, etc). Client machines request services from the server e.g. to mount a file-system, or to access a file etc.

PC-NFS does have drawbacks. One is the problem of file formats. ASCII ("plain-text" files) files can be accessed and interchanged without any major problems. MS-DOS applications can be run from some UNIX systems (such as **SunOS** UNIX) using a dedicated utility, although users will not be able to run a MS-DOS executable file (i.e. a .EXE or .COM file) from within UNIX (and vice-versa), since UNIX and DOS are entirely different systems.

PC-NFS provides some MS-DOS commands which emulate UNIX commands. These utilities normally have similar names, and in some cases the same names, which can be confusing for the user. PC-NFS also provides some file transfer utility programs (accessed from MS-DOS) which enable users to transfer MS-DOS files to a host UNIX system, although standard MS-DOS copy commands can be used to copy files to a virtual drive.

Virtual drives are used heavily in the PC-NFS system. MS-DOS users access different disk-drives using drive identifier letters (in the range A-Z, although not all of these are used in reality). Under PC-NFS, the user can mount UNIX file-systems from MS-DOS using a NET USE command followed by a drive identifier letter and then a fully-qualified path- name (see Chapter 7 for more details on path-names) of the UNIX directory area that is to be accessed through the drive letter concerned. The directory (from the UNIX file-server) is then grafted onto that particular drive identifier. While the user can select existing drive-letters (to access a hard or floppy-disk from MS-DOS), selecting a drive letter used by PC-NFS will allow the user to access a UNIX directory area that was specified earlier in the NET USE command with that drive letter.

Another drawback of PC-NFS lies in the file naming conventions between itself and the partner operating system, here MS-DOS. MS-DOS allows a user to refer to a file using a maximum of 12 characters, whereas most UNIX systems allow the user to use more than 12 characters. MS-DOS and UNIX also have their own conventions with regards to file-naming (with reference to just how and what a file can be named, i.e. which characters can and can not be used in a file-name). If PC-NFS encounters a file-name that was valid under UNIX, but not from MS-DOS, PC-NFS would alter the file-name accordingly. Truncation of UNIX file-names will be carried out by PC-NFS if a file name is too long for MS-DOS. PC-NFS also has the habit of inserting characters into UNIX files accessed through MS-DOS.

The use of virtual drive access through NET USE (see later examples) commands, coupled with some of the naming problems detract from the claims that PC-NFS operates transparently. However, the NFS/PC-NFS systems continue to be very popular, and offers a great deal of flexibility for the internetworking of the MS-DOS and UNIX systems.

PC-NFS commands

The PC-NFS system provides the user with commands that can be executed from

DOS. A few of these commands are examined in this section. The reader may have noticed that some PC-NFS utilities emulate UNIX commands. Commands for the support of Yellow Pages facilities (**YP**) are also provided on some UNIX systems (see section 2.2.6), as are commands to transfer files to and from DOS to UNIX (such as **FTP** the file transfer protocol).

The NET command

The NET command is used to access all of the PC-NFS services. This includes the mounting of UNIX file-systems onto DOS virtual drives. For a full list of options that can be used in conjunction with the **NET** command, simply type **NET** at the DOS prompt. Mounting a UNIX file system is probably the most important command available, since it is the one major feature provided by the PC-NFS system. The NET USE command is used for this purpose, and the syntax is:

```
NET USE drive: \\hostname\path [/SHARE] [/READONLY]
```

For example, to mount the part of a UNIX file-system called /usr/STUDENTS/john onto the DOS virtual drive **E:** type, at the DOS prompt:

```
C:\>NET USE E:\\sun\usr\STUDENTS\john /SHARE
```

Accessing the DOS drive E: would now allow access to the UNIX file-system area **/usr/STUDENTS/john.** Note that the directory level separators under UNIX use the / character while under PC-NFS (DOS) the \ symbol is used (although they have the same meaning in this context). The **/SHARE** and **/READONLY** options in the **NET USE** command allow a file-system to be mounted in an openly accessible mode (/SHARE), or on a read-only (non-writable mode) using the /READONLY option.

Also note that the user must know the host name of the server on which a file-system is mounted. The UNIX command **hostname** can be used to find this information out (so log into UNIX first to get the necessary information).

To get a list of all the currently mounted file-systems (on the current machine), and the virtual drive identifiers that access them, type **NET USE** with no arguments:

```
C:\>NET USE
Drive  Filesystem                   Tsize  Kbytes Used   Avail  Capacity
E: /SH \\sun\usr\STUDENTS\john      8192   95072  93456  1616   98%
O: /SH \\sun\usr\STUDENTS\fred      8192   14848  8304   6544   55%
D: /RO \\sun\ibm                    8192   16092  9084   7008   54%
C:\>
```

As can be seen from the above example, **NET USE** shows a list of all the currently mounted file-systems, their virtual drive letters, the mode in which the file-system area was mounted (/**SH** – shared, /**RO** – read only), the file-system area which has been mounted, the total size of the file-system (commonly measured in blocks), the number of kilobytes that the file-system area can contain, kilobytes actually used up, the number of available kilobytes, and finally the capacity used (in percentage terms).

The previous example also shows that three UNIX file-system areas have been mounted, and that two of them are mounted in a shared mode, whereas the **\\sun\ibm** directory has been mounted in a read-only mode. This was most probably mounted through an administrative procedure since users are not allowed to update information on the drive. This particular set-up is common where single packages are made accessible on a large capacity disk-drive (DOS compatible) which is to be accessed by multiple users (this saves replicating copies of the same software on each users machine). In this case the **\\sun\ibm** directory is a DOS compatible disk that contains a series of DOS application packages (or a collection of customised PC packages etc). UNIX executables (binary files) cannot be executed from under DOS (due to differences in internal file formats), therefore access to a DOS compatible disk is common in such situations to increase software availability.

Another option that can be used with the **NET** command is the keyword **NAME.** This keyword will make the user's host workstation display some information about itself, including the name of the current machine, and the user's *login name*, UID and GID (from the /etc/passwd file). The example below illustrates this:

```
C:\>NET NAME
The name of this system is triton, and its IP address is
192.9.200.28
It is in the Yellow pages domain noname, for which there is no YP
server.
The authentication server is sun (192.9.200.1).
NFS030I : No gateway is currently defined.
You are logged in as Fred, with UID 87 and GID 23.
It is Thu May 23 14:34:09 1991, GMT
C:\>
```

There are many other **NET** commands. A full list of **NET** keywords can be summoned by entering the command **NET** (on its own) at the DOS prompt.

3.9.2 RFS

The RFS protocol allows users of one host machine to access files and data on a remote machine. RFS boasts transparent access to remote files i.e. the user simply thinks that the file(s) in question are local to the host system.

The RFS scenario is one of a number of machines, each which has a *resource* (some data) that other machines may want to access remotely. Using RFS terminology, a machine will *advertise* its resource(s) and, as in NFS, the machine requiring the resource will mount the resource (or *graft* it) onto one of its own directories in its file-system, thus accessing the data required. This mounting process is transparent to the user. As in the NFS protocol, RFS uses *server* and *client* machines. In some systems, the larger UNIX machines act as server machines for smaller client machines, thus allowing them to run different applications.

RFS maintains data integrity and consistency through file and record locking. Files are continually kept track of (all of the information regarding the accessing of such files by client machines is logged, or *audited* by the system). Considerable processing is required by the RFS system to ensure that this information is accurate.

In the event of a system crash, the RFS system must ensure that the network does not suffer a delay in its response time because of locks (locks are mechanisms that stop multiple updates on a file) that still exist on important files. RFS must also ensure that machine crashes do not lead to total network degradation. Other mechanisms have been provided for RFS to overcome such problems. Some server machines in a network act as a source of additional resources, which contain information regarding the names of backup server machines.

3.9.3 TCP/IP

TCP/IP (Transmission Control Protocol/Internet Protocol). TCP/IP is very relevant to UNIX networking, and its use is widespread in many of the larger UNIX systems. TCP/IP was developed in the United States to address the problems of wide area networking (WAN) systems. Research into TCP/IP began with the Department of Defense (DoD) in the 1970s, who needed to internetwork separate packet switched networks into much larger networks (typically WANs).

DARPA (Defence Advanced Research Project Agency) sponsored research projects into the TCP/IP system for use on DARPA's network, called ARPAnet. TCP/IP followed a layered approach similar to that of the OSI model (discussed later in the Chapter), although at the time when TCP/IP was being developed, OSI was still very much in the design stage. There are three main layers in the TCP/IP network protocol:

❑ Host-to-host communication Layer;

❑ Network interface layer;

❑ Application layer.

The layered ISO stack protocol model is similar to TCP/IP in many respects. In the OSI context the ISO transport layer would roughly correspond to the TCP/IP Network interface layer and the ISO transport layer would correspond to the host-to-host communications layer of the TCP/IP model. Layers five and six of the ISO stack (the application and presentation layers) would roughly compare with the last TCP/IP layer, namely the applications layer.

The Network interface layer of the TCP/IP protocol supports the IP protocol (Internet Protocol). The IP protocol (which is part of the main TCP/IP protocol) supports a wide range of data communication standards, such as those laid down by the Institute of Electronic Engineers (IEEE), for example the IEEE 802.3 (Ethernet) standard is supported, as is the 802.5 Token Ring standard (all part of the MAC – Medium Access Control suite of standards).

The IP protocol handles the delivery of *datagrams* across the host network. A datagram in our context could be thought of a packet of information, each which is made up of a series of *fields*. A complete IP datagram structure is illustrated in Figure 3.11. The *IHL* field contains the length of the Internet header information. The *TOS* field (type of service) allows datagrams to select special services such as low delay etc. The *flags* field is altered to indicate a fragmented datagram, and the *offset* field is used to show where the fragmented information was fitted into the original datagram.

The *type* field indicates the type of protocol being used (**1** for **IP**). The *source* and *destination* fields contain IP addresses of the form *n.n.n.n*, e.g. **128.16.9.3**. The *padding* bits at the end of the datagram are used if the data packet is not "filled" to an exact 32 octets.

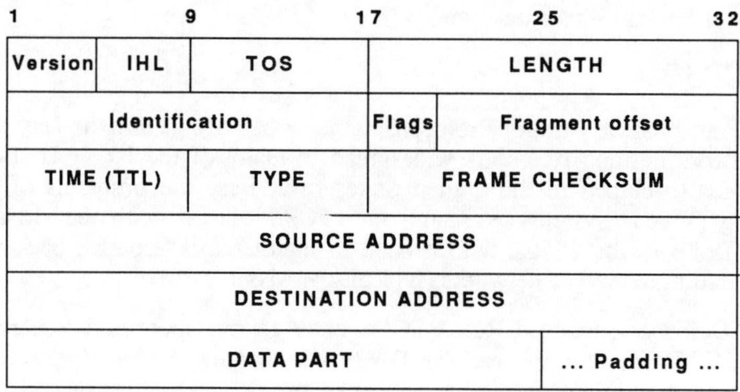

Figure 3.11. Example Internet Datagram (version 4 IP)

The IP protocol also looks after the *routing* of the datagrams across a host network, much in the same way as the transport layer in the OSI model does. The host-to-host communications layer in the TCP/IP protocol also supports other data communication protocols, such as UDP (discussed briefly below) and TCP.

UDP (User Datagram Protocol) is what is termed a broadcast protocol. It allows application programs to access an extended version of the IP protocol. Like some other protocols, UDP cannot guarantee that a datagram (or packet) will be received by the recipient. The sender of the packet will also not be notified about damaged or corrupted packets. This is basically a consequence of the *connectionless* (CL) operation of UDP (no connection establishment, just data transmission, in essence).

TCP provides a solution to the previous problem just described. It establishes a *virtual circuit* (operational in a CO – connection orientated mode) which is a more reliable two-way link. This provision is established so that messages can arrive in the correct order, and to ensure that they are complete. Figure 3.12 illustrates the layered structure of the TCP/IP protocol.

The FTP and TELNET protocols

FTP (File Transfer Protocol), and the TN (Telnet Login) virtual terminal service use the TCP protocol which lies below these two services. The TFTP (Trivial File Transfer Protocol) and NAME (Name Serving Facility) use the UDP datagram protocol. The TCP/IP lowest level protocols shown in Figure 3.12, such as 802.5 (Token Ring) and 802.3 (Ethernet) are only two of many such protocols that the Internet Protocol (IP) supports. Many others are available such as: 802.4 MAPS, and T1 (WAN), which can link into other data networks. The TELNET and FTP protocols are dealt with again in more detail later in this chapter.

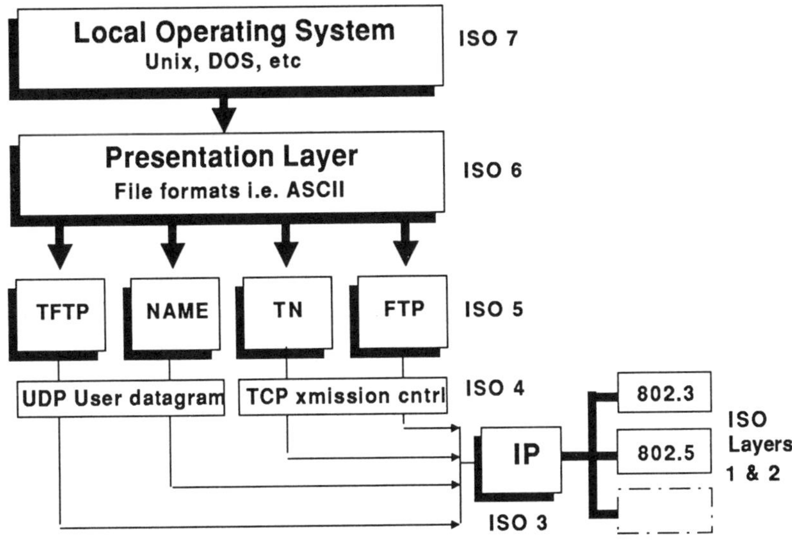

Figure 3.12 The layered structure of the TCP/IP protocol

3.9.4 The OSI model

The OSI standard has been at the centre of much protocol development. The model uses a seven layer approach. The topmost layer is the application using the services of the OSI protocol, while at the lowest level we encounter the physical medium on which data travels i.e. an Ethernet. The OSI model is comprised (fundamentally) of two parts:

❑ A set of service definitions;

❑ A set of protocol specifications.

The lower layers (layers 1 to 4) of the OSI *stack* are used for host-to-host interconnection, while the upper layers (layers 5 to 7), relate to the interworking of the application processes within each host system. The *service definition* for each of the seven layers in the OSI model defines just what services are provided by that layer (the service provider) to the layer that lies immediately above it (the service user). The *protocol specification* will indicate how a particular service will actually be provided by defining a set of rules (the protocol) of how data is exchanged between the service provider and the peer entity. The seven layers of the OSI ISO *stack* are shown in Figure 3.13.

The structure of the ISO protocol stack offers some degree of flexibility in allowing designers to implement their software protocol systems. It is possible for some applications to bypass some layers altogether, so that they can interact directly with other layers in the ISO stack. Sun microsystems, for example, uses a mixture of different protocols at each level according to their needs. This is shown in Figure 3.14.

ISO Layer	FUNCTION
Application	Defines network services
Presentation	Concerned with data presentation
Session	Responsible for the actual communications link
Transport	Connects processes at different locations
Network	Provides addressing of machines on the network
Data Link	Responsible for bit level operations (i.e. grouping)
Physical	Actual hardware link used for data transmission

Figure 3.13. The ISO protocol model

ISO Layer	RPC based services	Non-RPC services
Application	NFS, YP, mount	TFTP, RLOGIN etc.
Presentation	XDR	Bypass layers
Session	Remote Proc. Calls (RPC)	
Transport	TCP, UDP	TCP, UDP
Network	IP	IP
Data Link	Ethernet controller	Ethernet controller
Physical	Ethernet cable	Ethernet cable

Figure 3.14. ISO Protocol stack in SunOS UNIX

At the *application* layer, the various user applications (or services) can be found. These include (for SunOS) protocols such as **NFS** (Network File System), **YP** (Yellow pages naming service), and the mount daemon. These services are termed **RPC** (Remote Procedure Call) based services (a standard mechanism for communication between two *remote* programs). Other services that are available to users as application programs include **tftp** (trivial file transfer protocol – similar to **FTP**), **rlogin** (the remote login program), and **telnet** which are all application programs in their own right. These applications are however, not RPC based.

When data transfer (or reception) begins, information passes through each layer of the ISO stack until it is received at the destination (or *peer* entity). For example, a user issuing a **mount** command to mount a remote file-system would invoke the necessary command, whereupon the request would start to be processed at layer 7. It (the request) would then pass through the lower layers of the ISO stack (gaining information as it passes through each layer) until it reaches the physical layer at the bottom of the stack.

At this stage the request would be travelling over a physical connection (e.g. cable), and it would enter the peer entities stack. At this point the original request would travel up the stack on the peer entities machine, whereupon its header would be stripped. Finally the information would be conveyed in an appropriate form to the recipient process.

XDR (eXternal Data Representation) is a protocol which, in our example, exists in the presentation layer of the ISO stack. The purpose of **XDR** is to translate (or convert) data from different hardware devices into a compatible form so that the recipient can interpret the information correctly. The actual specifics of **XDR** are covered in section 2.2.8. In our scenario an item of information passing through the *presentation* layer would be translated into **XDR** format as it headed towards the peer entity via the lower layers. Once the **XDR** encoded item of data reaches the presentation layer in the peer machine, it is decoded accordingly.

The *session* layer in SunOS contains the necessary RPC (Remote Procedure Call) functionality. RPC based services such as the **NFS** protocol will use this layer accordingly, although non-RPC based services (such as **telnet**) will bypass this layer. The RPC services use a fixed program number as their addressing method. Non-RPC based services use an identifying *port* number as a means of addressing themselves.

At the *transport* layer we will find protocols such as **TCP** (Transmission Control Protocol) and **UDP** (User Datagram Protocol). The UDP protocol is a *connectionless* (CL) datagram based transmission services. **TCP**, however is a reliable *connection-orientated* (CO) service. Their addressing method is again a *port* number. The services that bypass the session and presentation layers communicate directly with the transport layer, as can be seen from Figure 3.14. It is the *nature* of a request that will normally determine whether **TCP** or **UDP** are used. A request will enter the transport layer as a sequence of bytes. Both **TCP** and **UDP** can fragment and reassemble data that is too long to fit into the predefined sizes that are imposed by the protocol. The reassembly process is undertaken by the corresponding peer entity layer (and vice-versa). In SunOS **NFS** requests are handled by UDP, while simple print requests are handled by **TCP**. In our scenario (where a user has issued a **mount** request), the request would be handled by the **UDP** protocol.

At the *network* layer the **IP** (Internet Protocol) protocol is found. The IP addresses of all host machines and networks which are known to a particular server are defined in the file **/etc/hosts**. Typical addresses are of the form *n.n.n.n* i.e. 128.16.34.2. The **/etc/networks** file also describes the addresses of many other network devices.

At this stage of processing (in the ISO stack), the address of the recipient will now be known. The network level based protocols can now establish a connection between a process on one machine to another process on another machine (peer machine). In our scenario with the **mount** request, a **UDP** datagram packet, on reaching the network layer, will be passed to the **IP** protocol, which routes the message to its destination.

At the *data link* layer, information will be prepared ready for transmission on the physical link. Ethernet software is normally responsible for the bit organization of the source message and will attach header information to it, so that it can be referenced at the destination data link layer. If a recipient process is not available locally (on a local network) the message will be sent to a router on that local network, which will then be responsible for relaying the message to the appropriate network. A **mount** request at this layer will be formatted to Ethernet specification (i.e. an Ethernet address will be added to the message).

Once an item of information reaches the *physical* layer, it will be sent out (probably through a transceiver device) into the network. The message will then be received by a controller or routing device.

SunOS enables individual programs to treat network communications in a manner similar to that of UNIX file-handling primitives (such as **read**() and **write**() etc), known as *sockets* (discussed later in section 3.10). Sockets allow programs to communicate with each across a network on a local and/or remote basis.

3.9.5 CSMA/CD (IEEE 802.3)

CSMA/CD (Carrier Sense Multiple Access with Collision Detection) makes up the IEEE 802.3 standard. It is a protocol (for use on Ethernet based systems) that allows individual stations to access the network on a contention basis. Before a station can transmit any information, the CSMA/CD protocol checks to see if the network is busy. If so, the station will not transmit its data until the network is quiet (until a route is free for the transmission). The carrier sense multiple access (CSMA) part of the protocol ensures that collisions can be kept to a minimum. If a collision occurred, the station transmitting the information stops sending any more data and issues a signal on the cable medium to all other stations (a type of broadcast message) so that the collision to can be brought to their attention. The original station then waits for a specific period of time (known as a *back off* period) before retransmitting the same information.

The 802.3 standard was itself taken from the Ethernet standard. This, however, does not mean that the two systems are identical. The 802.3 standard uses a length indicator (LI) field that stores the length of a particular packet (in bytes/octets). Ethernet also uses the same field (same position), although its meaning is slightly different. Ethernet refers to this field as the *type* field. Other differences occur in the actual lengths of some fields. Ethernet has a 48 bit address field, whereas the 802.3 allows 48 and 16 bit fields. A gradual movement away from the Ethernet field format (towards a 802.3 format) is taking place, although problems still exist (data corruption being a particular problem here).

3.9.6 The Yellow Pages (YP) naming service

The *yellow pages* (YP) service is a distributed network look-up service used primarily on Sun based UNIX systems. A *database* is maintained, which all machines can access and query. The concept of *naming* is a difficult one, especially when attempting to define the concept. The use of naming allows a system's configuration (machine names and locations, etc.) to gradually change without disrupting the overall service, thus making administration easier.

The information that is of use to a process is vast. For example, the naming service may map **IP** addresses to actual machine names, perhaps providing the physical whereabouts of a particular machine. One common use of YP on UNIX systems is to replicate the **/etc/passwd** file (see section 11.2.1 for more information on the **/etc/passwd** file) over a group of servers to facilitate logging-in a group of users in a network.

The files that are accessed are referred to as *YP maps*. These are replicated on several machines known as *YP servers*. Each YP server runs a service that a client can access. The actual YP server that replies to a client's request is unimportant since the information will be identical across all YP servers (or at least it should be).

The problems of manipulating and sharing files through protocols such as **NFS** has led many naming and identification problems (some within the confines of the SunOS version of UNIX). The YP service is not common to just the Sun UNIX environment. Many other manufacturers have developed their own implementations to solve naming problems.

A *YP map* is an ordered collection of *key* and *value* pairs. For example, the map file **/etc/hosts.byname** contains a list of the machine host names in a particular UNIX domain. The actual host names are the key values, while the value elements contain Internet addresses of the various host machine names. This service can be useful for locating certain hosts on a network, and a client process may call on a YP server to retrieve such information.

All YP maps have a *map name* which is used by processes to access the YP map. The majority of YP maps are obtained from existing files in the UNIX file system, such as **/etc/passwd**, **/etc/group** and **/etc/hosts**. A *YP domain* is a set of named YP maps located in a particular directory of the UNIX file system (commonly in the directory **/var/yp**). This holds all of the YP map files for a particular YP server. Maps are normally made available to network clients by servers. There are two types of servers: a *YP master* and a *YP slave*.

The master server updates the maps of the YP slaves. Maps are therefore always modified on a master YP server, otherwise discrepancies may occur. The YP service offers the user a series of commands that can be used for editing and configuration. These commands also perform certain administrative tasks for the YP service. The most common Yellow Pages commands are listed below:

makedbm Takes an input file as argument, and converts it into a pair of **dbm** encoded files, which can be used as YP maps. **Makedbm** can also be used to decode map existing files so that the key-value pairs can be examined. Use a standard UNIX editor to edit or examine a *decoded* file, such as **ex**, or **vi**.

ypcat Display the entire contents of a YP map. It should be used in the case where you are not concerned about a server's version number. In order to request a specific server, a utility such as **rlogin** (remote login) should be used to log in on a particular YP server, and then use **ypcat** accordingly.

ypfiles Describes the internal file structure of a YP service.

ypinit Creates the necessary map files from the files in the **/etc** directory (such as **/etc/group**, **/etc/hosts** etc). **Ypinit** should also be used to configure the master and slave YP servers.

yppoll Asks a **ypserv** daemon for any information that it has about a YP map.

yppush Requests each of the **ypserv** processes within a particular domain to transfer a YP map. It is run on a master YP server machine most commonly.

ypserv This is the YP map server daemon that listens for incoming client requests. This daemon must be running on all designated YP server machines on the network.

ypset Instructs a **ypbind** process to get YP services for a particular domain from a named YP server machine.

ypupdated Daemon process that is used to update YP information. It is commonly started by the daemon **inetd** (originally from a file such as **/etc/rc.local**). This utility will normally refer to the file **/var/yp/updaters**, in order to determine those YP maps which should be updated and how to go about changing them. The facility only operates in a *secure* RPC mode.

ypwhich Allows the user to see which YP server a particular host is accessing. **Ypwhich** can also be used to see which YP server is a master of a YP map.

ypxfr Moves a YP map from one YP server machine to another. Can be used interactively or can be explicitly handled using the Cron (*clock daemon*). Refer to section 11.11.1 for detailed information on the Cron facility.

3.9.7 XDR – eXternal Data Representation

XDR (eXternal Data Representation) is a standard for representing data in an architecture-independent manner. **XDR** itself is a DDL (Data Description Language) and interacts with a C library package. **XDR** services are implemented on a particular server machine (most probably at the *presentation* layer of ISO stack), whereupon a host entity can convert information to and from the **XDR** format.

The UNIX **XDR** library is used to encode and decode data in and out of the XDR format using a set of standard C procedures. There are two different types of procedure. The first is *stream* based (nothing to do with the AT&T Streams mechanism coincidentally). The second is used to convert data to and from the streams. Such procedures are known as *filters*. An **XDR** stream is an interface to a particular item of data (such as a file). Data can be stored in the **XDR** format to disk, so that a process reading the data will be able to decode it correctly (working on the assumption that it has access to the necessary **XDR** decoding procedures).

XDR streams are used with only one type of filter. There are three types of stream in **XDR**: standard input/output; record; memory.

The standard i/o stream connects an **XDR** filter to a standard C input/output file. The memory stream connects a filter to a block of memory that may be shared by more than one process (used in datagram based services, since a memory stream can write data to buffer memory areas).

A record stream is used where data items are placed in a delimited (record) format. This is particulary useful for virtual-circuit based protocols since the filter should be able to identify any data that is to be transmitted.

3.9.8 X Windows and the X-Protocol

X Windows, or just **X**, is a windowing system which supports device-independent graphics. breaking with tradition, **X** allows virtually any style of user interface to be built through use of its facilities. The unusual aspect is that is built around an asynchronous protocol rather than the more common procedure-call interface. It can be implemented in a wide variety of computer languages (C is notable), and can be run on a variety of host operating systems (UNIX systems being prominent). The **X** system is now a *de facto* standard and has been supported by a wide variety of UNIX manufacturers. Standardising the graphical interface on UNIX machines will help to solve many of the incompatibility problems of graphical-based software.

The **X** system operates is said to operate in a *client-server* context. The concept of a server is slightly different from other applications that are given the same name. In **X**, the *server* comprises in a workstation (including the mouse device, keyboard and display). A *client* in this context is an application that is running in the **X** environment. Clients send requests (commonly *drawing* and *information* requests) to server entities, and the server sends back similar information (such as error reports etc). Clients may exist locally or remotely on a particular server machine.

The server in an **X** environment is not based remotely, only locally to the host machine. There may be many clients running on a particular server, and a single client can interact and communicate with several server machines.

X clients are programmed using a variety of client-programming libraries. The libraries available are implemented in the C and Lisp languages. These currently allow for the creation and manipulation of all **X** resources, including window creation, manipulation, keyboard and mouse manipulation, and event handling. *Xlib.h* (C library) offers a limited set of facilities for basic interface design, such as simple menu creation, and mouse interaction interfaces (events, etc).

The file **/usr/lib/X11/Xlib.h** (system dependent location) contains all of the available *Xlib* function primitives. As a C program header, file it can be included in any C program (**X** client source-code), whereupon the various *Xlib* functions can be called to manipulate the necessary resources that the programmer requires.

Some incompatibility problems arise when one or more different **X** libraries are used and mixed together. The OSF/Motif library (primarily used for the fast prototyping of X-based interface applications – complex menus, mouse control, dialogue boxes and user input through the keyboard and mouse devices etc.) is compatible with *Xlib*, although strange results have been known to occur (minor incompatibilities in window displays etc). A higher level (object based) library known as the *Xt Intrinsics* is used to build user interface components called *widgets*. Several preprogrammed widget kits are available to the programmer (the *Athena* widget set is an example).

The X protocol

The **X** protocol was designed to operate in an asynchronous mode (asynchronous models are *non-blocking* – they allow the user to deal with multiple events). The network on which **X** operates could be a protocol such as **TCP/IP**. The *Xlib* library uses *sockets* (Berkeley-based UNIX systems). Server processes are normally implemented for more than one type of underlying protocol, to facilitate the simultaneous communication with multiple clients that exist on more than one network. The most common network protocols for **X** servers are **TCP/IP** and **DECnet.**

X Packet types

The **X** protocol uses four different packet types:

Event packets originate from a server and are directed to a client. The packet contains information about an action or the effect of a previous action. This packet is used the most widely to get information to a client. Event packets are held in a 32 octet structure, and are queued by the client if too many are generated to be dealt with at any one time.

Request packets are sent from a client to a server process. They contain requests for a variety of drawing directives, window size requests and the like. Request packets can be of any size that is a multiple of 4 octets.

Reply packets are sent from a server to client process. The **X** system does not answer all requests with a reply (many requests were designed not to generate replies, such as drawing requests). The reply packet can be a minimum 32 octets in length (it has to be a multiple of 4 octets if greater than the 32 octet minimum limit).

Error packets are similar to *event* packets except they are treated slightly differently by client processes. Errors are send to a specific error-handling service by the client programming library. Error packets have a minimum size of 32 octets (and like the event packet, have to be a multiple of 4 octets if larger). The use of 4 octet multiples simplifies the implementation of the protocol on machines that use 16 or 32 bit boundaries (which is common in many architectures).

Client-server graphical Xlib applications

This section introduces some of the programming concepts used in an *Xlib* environment. Attention is focused on the concept of drawing pixel-based images. The reader may wish to read section 2.3 on Berkeley *sockets*, since this is the IPC mechanism used within the programs examined in this section. The **X** Window system provides the user with a series of library routines that allow **X** client applications to be built. The *Xlib* (C based) library is the most fundamental library, and will be used for the programming applications throughout this section, and in our discussion generally.

The Window system can create and manipulate rectangular areas of the screen known as *rasters* (groups of pixels – the most atomic part of any graphical image that can be shown on a workstation screen). The **X** system represents these raster areas in three separate ways: Bitmaps; Pixmaps; and Images.

Bitmaps can be: text file information for loading into a bitmap type of pixmap (see below) or a pixmap with a series of pixel values limited to just one bit (0 or 1).

Pixmaps are resident to the workstation) in which the user can issue a variety of drawing requests. An *image* is a structured data object that represents the contents of raster areas. All may seem very similar, although these are many differences in the ways that each is created and manipulated under *Xlib*. This section is confined to just *pixmaps* and *bitmaps*, and how they can be created and incorporated into an **X** client application to send graphical images over a network (typically a LAN) between client and server programs.

The *Xlib* library has a variety of different procedure calls for the creation, conversion and manipulation of pixmap and bitmap rasters. We can only attempt to cover a few of the most commonly used *Xlib* calls in this section.

Pixmaps

A *pixmap* is a rectangular raster area onto which an application can draw. Pixmaps are not directly visible on the workstation screen, but are firstly assembled in memory, and then made visible by copying them into portions of the screen (into areas known as *windows*). During the process of creating a pixmap, three items of information must be supplied by the user. These are the *depth*, *size* (width and height), and a *screen* identifier.

All pixmaps share the above characteristics, and each of them are now examined. The depth of a window defines the number of *planes* (number of bits per pixel) in the pixmap that you are defining. The depth of the pixmap will determine the types of images that you can draw into the pixmap, and what can be done to the pixmap.

Pixmaps that have a depth of one (as have the pixmaps in the programs in this section) are called *bitmaps*. The window area into which your pixmaps will be copied (so that they become visible) should have a depth **equal** to that of the window.

The size of the pixmap is measured by its width and height. All pixmaps must be given fixed (positive) dimensions. The pixmap and window sizes can be different, so that pixmap images can be drawn into different areas of a window. The dimensions of a pixmap cannot be altered once the pixmap has been created in an application. Dimensions are specified as **[x,y]** coordinates in the calls that create them (**x** and **y** are measured in **pixels**).

The screen identifier represents the screen to be associated with a pixmap. Workstations can have multiple screens, and it is quite possible to display pixmap images on one or more such screens. It is therefore necessary to use a screen identifier (a simple character string) to represent the screen that is to be used for a particular pixmap operation. In a single screen environment (which is assumed here) the problem of writing to multiple screens does not arise.

Creating pixmaps

The **XCreatePixmap()** call is the most fundamental call used to create a new pixmap. The syntax of the call is:

```
pixmap_id = XCreatePixmap(display, drawable, width, height, depth)
```

where **pixmap_id** is the *resource identifier* of the newly created pixmap, *display* is a pointer to a *Display* structure (found in the header file *Xlib.h* – this is used to hold the specific data for the pixmap's manipulation), *drawable* specifies the screen the pixmap is on, *width* and *height* are the dimensions (in pixels) of the pixmap, and *depth* is the number of bits per pixel (1 for bitmap manipulation). The *drawable* parameter is particulary important since it is the resource identifier of a previously created pixmap or window (see next section).

The programmer must mention the correct variable definitions for the necessary pixmap to be created. These definitions should be placed before the **XCreatePixmap()** call is made preferable in the same procedure section as the call itself, for simplicity. The complete definition for an **XCreatePixmap()** call is as below:

```
Display *display;      /* pointer to Display data structure */
Drawable drawable;     /* screen pixmap is located on */
unsigned int width;    /* width of the pixmap */
unsigned int height;   /* height of pixmap */
Pixmap pixmap_id;      /* resource id for this pixmap */
...
pixmap_id = XCreatePixmap(display, drawable, width, height,
depth)
```

Creating windows

A *window* is an area into which text or graphics (such as pixmaps) can be copied. The window will be created in a particular style, according to the type of **X** library being used. Most windows have a toggle area that can be used to enable or disable the window i.e. to hide it or make it visible. This facility is accessed through use of a mouse device that is clicked on the toggle area. Once a window has been hidden from view, a window identifier *icon* will appear. This is clicked on with the mouse to make the window visible again (likewise, the icon can also be used to toggle the window in and out of view). The intensity of the icon indicates if the window is in use or not.

The **XCreateSimpleWindow()** call can be used to create a simple window area (another call, **XCreateWindow**, is used in much the same way, but it takes more parameters, and can be given some extra characteristics. The syntax of the **XCreateSimpleWindow()** call is:

```
w = XCreateSimpleWindow(d, parent, x, y, width, height, b_wid,
border, bck).
```

where **d** is the display pointer, **parent** is the name of the parent in which this window will be created (probably another window), **x** and **y** are the positions of the new window (in pixels) i.e. the position on the screen where the window is to be drawn, **width** and **height** are the dimensions of the window area, **b_wid** is the border width of the window (in pixels), **border** is the border colour, and **bck** is the background colour.

The **w** variable is a window resource identifier, and must be kept for subsequent pixel operations that use this window to *draw* into. The complete **XCreateSimpleWindow** call in a program could look like this:

```
Display *d;
Window parent;
Window w;
int x, y;
unsigned int width;
unsigned int height;
unsigned int b_wid;
unsigned long border;
unsigned long bck;
...
w = XCreateSimpleWindow(d, parent, x, y, width, height, b_wid,
border, bck);
...
```

Creating pixmaps from data

Pixmap structures can also be created from raw data. The **XCreateBitmapFrom-Data()** call can be used for this purpose. This creates a one-plane bitmap which can then be loaded with a bitmap image. Bitmap resources can be incorporated into a program in a number of ways, including the raw bitmap data created by the user using the UNIX editor tool, **bitmap**.

This utility is invoked with the width and length of the bitmap (in pixels) that you wish to create. These are provided by the utility in the form of an onscreen *bitmap matrix* and you create your picture by filling in pixels until you are satisfied with the end result, whereupon you can save the file to disk. The file that is created can be then imported into a C program and used to create a pixmap.

The **XCreateBitmapFromData** can be used with the resulting bitmap file (created using the **bitmap** utility) in a simple server program (the server is sent the bitmap data, and processes these to form a pixmap which can then be drawn into a window). If you examine the bitmap file, you will see that the contents are nothing more than a series of hexadecimal digits (0x is the prefix given to a hexadecimal digit in C), encapsulated in a one-dimensional array (of no fixed size, note):

```
...
static char bitmap_bits[] = {
0xff, 0xff, 0xff, 0xff, 0xff, 0xff, 0xff, 0xff, 0xff, 0xff, 0xff,
0xff, 0xff, 0xff, 0xff, 0x7f, 0xfe, 0xff, 0xff, 0xe1, 0xff, 0xff,
0xff, 0xff, 0xff, 0xff, 0xff, 0xff, 0x7f, 0xfd, 0xff, 0xff, 0xee,
0xff, 0xff, 0xff, 0xff, 0xff, 0xff, 0xff, 0xff, 0x7f, 0xf9, 0xff,
0x7f, 0xf6, 0xff, 0xff, 0xff, 0xff, 0xff, 0xff, 0xff, 0xff, 0x7f,
0xf3, 0xff, 0x7f, 0xf6, 0xff ...
};
```

These hexadecimal values could easily be sent over a socket connection (to be discussed in section 3.10) to a server process, which could then create the necessary pixmap using the "raw" bitmap data. The **XCreateBitmapFromData()** call would be specifically used for this purpose, and we will examine a pair of programs that do just this. The name of the array in the above C code excerpt is taken from a filename argument given to the bitmap utility. For example, if we invoked bitmap with the name **mybits**, the resulting bitmap file would have the array name implemented as **mybits_bits** (the suffix **_bits** is given by the system). Of course, we could change this to any name we require at will. The **XCreateBitmapFromData()** call has the syntax:

```
my_pixmap = XCreateBitmapFromData(display, drawable, data, width,
        height)
```

where **display** is a pointer to a Display structure and **drawable** specifies which screen the pixmap is on; **data** is the actual bitmap data for the pixmap, **width** and **height** are the size dimensions of the newly created pixmap (measured in pixels). The entire definition to be included in a potential X client using this call is thus:

```
Display *d;              /* Pointer to an Xlib Display structure */
Drawable drawable;       /* screen the pixmap is actually on */
char data[];             /* Character array containing bitmap data */
unsigned int height;     /* pixmap dimensions */
unsigned int width;
Pixmap my_pixmap;        /* created pixmap's resource identifier */
...
my_pixmap = XCreateBitmapFromData(d, drawable, data, width, height);
...
```

In the first program example below, you may wish to create your own bitmap (and import this into you final client program) since the amount of typing to reproduce this bitmap is rather large. Use the command: **cc filename.c -lX11 -o executename**, to compile the programs.

Program Example 1 – X Client (client program)

```
/*
 * XClient.c
 *
 * A simple client program to transmit a series of bitmaps
 * to a server process. The server will get the bitmap(s)
 * and display them once fully retrieved.
 *
 * (c) J. Manger
 *
 */

#include <sys/types.h>
#include <sys/socket.h>
#include <sys/stat.h>
#include <netinet/in.h>
#include <netdb.h>
#include <stdio.h>
#include <strings.h>

#define END                      0xdd
#define BUFFER                   1024   /* Size of input buffer */
#define MYPORT                   2001

/*
* Actual bitmap data taken from a file using bitmap(1X)
* These frames form a simple moving face (the file
* "/usr/include/bitmaps/sorceress" - which may be available
* on your UNIX system - was used for this purpose
* (this file was edited to show how the eyes and mouth can
* be animated. Users may wish to find this file and
* include it here - since there is a lot of typing!
*/

static int frame1_bits[] = {
0xfc, 0x7e, 0x40, 0x20, 0x90, 0x00, 0x07, 0x80, 0x23, 0x00, 0x00, 0xc6,
0xc1, 0x41, 0x98, 0xb8, 0x01, 0x07, 0x66, 0x00, 0x15, 0x9f, 0x03, 0x47,
0x8c, 0xc6, 0xdc, 0x7b, 0xcc, 0x00, 0xb0, 0x71, 0x0e, 0x4d, 0x06, 0x66,
0x73, 0x8e, 0x8f, 0x01, 0x18, 0xc4, 0x39, 0x4b, 0x02, 0x23, 0x0c, 0x04,
0x1e, 0x03, 0x0c, 0x08, 0xc7, 0xef, 0x08, 0x30, 0x06, 0x07, 0x1c, 0x02,
0x06, 0x30, 0x18, 0xae, 0xc8, 0x98, 0x3f, 0x78, 0x20, 0x06, 0x02, 0x20,
0x60, 0xa0, 0xc4, 0x1d, 0xc0, 0xff, 0x41, 0x04, 0xfa, 0x63, 0x80, 0xa1,
0xa4, 0x3d, 0x00, 0x84, 0xbf, 0x04, 0x0f, 0x06, 0xfc, 0xa1, 0x34, 0x6b,
0x01, 0x1c, 0xc9, 0x05, 0x06, 0xc7, 0x06, 0xbe, 0x11, 0x1e, 0x43, 0x30,
0x91, 0x05, 0xc3, 0x61, 0x02, 0x30, 0x1b, 0x30, 0xcc, 0x20, 0x11, 0x00,
0xc1, 0x3c, 0x03, 0x20, 0x0a, 0x00, 0xe8, 0x60, 0x21, 0x00, 0x61, 0x1b,
0xc1, 0x63, 0x08, 0xf0, 0xc6, 0xc7, 0x21, 0x03, 0xf8, 0x08, 0xe1, 0xcf,
0x0a, 0xfc, 0x4d, 0x99, 0x43, 0x07, 0x3c, 0x0c, 0xf1, 0x9f, 0x0b, 0xfc,
0x5b, 0x81, 0x47, 0x02, 0x16, 0x04, 0x31, 0x1c, 0x0b, 0x1f, 0x17, 0x89,
0x4d, 0x06, 0x1a, 0x04, 0x31, 0x38, 0x02, 0x07, 0x56, 0x89, 0x49, 0x04,
0x0b, 0x04, 0xb1, 0x72, 0x82, 0xa1, 0x54, 0x9a, 0x49, 0x04, 0x1d, 0x66,
```

```
0x50, 0xe7, 0xc2, 0xf0, 0x54, 0x9a, 0x58, 0x04, 0x0d, 0x62, 0xc1, 0x1f,
0x44, 0xfc, 0x51, 0x90, 0x90, 0x04, 0x86, 0x63, 0xe0, 0x74, 0x04, 0xef,
0x31, 0x1a, 0x91, 0x00, 0x02, 0xe2, 0xc1, 0xfd, 0x84, 0xf9, 0x30, 0x0a,
0x91, 0x00, 0x82, 0xa9, 0xc0, 0xb9, 0x84, 0xf9, 0x31, 0x16, 0x81, 0x00,
0x42, 0xa9, 0xdb, 0x7f, 0x0c, 0xff, 0x1c, 0x16, 0x11, 0x00, 0x02, 0x28,
0x0b, 0x07, 0x08, 0x60, 0x1c, 0x02, 0x91, 0x00, 0x46, 0x29, 0x0e, 0x00,
0x00, 0x00, 0x10, 0x16, 0x11, 0x02, 0x06, 0x29, 0x04, 0x00, 0x00, 0x00,
0x10, 0x16, 0x91, 0x06, 0xa6, 0x2a, 0x04, 0x00, 0x00, 0x00, 0x18, 0x24,
0x91, 0x04, 0x86, 0x2a, 0x04, 0x00, 0x00, 0x00, 0x18, 0x27, 0x93, 0x04,
0x96, 0x4a, 0x04, 0x00, 0x00, 0x00, 0x04, 0x02, 0x91, 0x04, 0x86, 0x4a,
0x0c, 0x00, 0x00, 0x00, 0x1e, 0x23, 0x93, 0x04, 0x56, 0x88, 0x08, 0x00,
0x00, 0x00, 0x90, 0x21, 0x93, 0x04, 0x52, 0x0a, 0x09, 0x80, 0x01, 0x00,
0xd0, 0x21, 0x95, 0x04, 0x57, 0x0a, 0x0f, 0x80, 0x27, 0x00, 0xd8, 0x20,
0x9d, 0x04, 0x5d, 0x08, 0x1c, 0x80, 0x67, 0x00, 0xe4, 0x01, 0x85, 0x04,
0x79, 0x8a, 0x3f, 0x00, 0x00, 0x00, 0xf4, 0x11, 0x85, 0x06, 0x39, 0x08,
0x7d, 0x00, 0x00, 0x18, 0xb7, 0x10, 0x81, 0x03, 0x29, 0x12, 0xcb, 0x00,
0x7e, 0x30, 0x28, 0x00, 0x85, 0x03, 0x29, 0x10, 0xbe, 0x81, 0xff, 0x27,
0x0c, 0x10, 0x85, 0x03, 0x29, 0x32, 0xfa, 0xc1, 0xff, 0x27, 0x94, 0x11,
0x85, 0x03, 0x28, 0x20, 0x6c, 0xe1, 0xff, 0x07, 0x0c, 0x01, 0x85, 0x01,
0x28, 0x62, 0x5c, 0xe3, 0x8f, 0x03, 0x4e, 0x91, 0x80, 0x05, 0x39, 0x40,
0xf4, 0xc2, 0xff, 0x00, 0x9f, 0x91, 0x84, 0x05, 0x31, 0xc6, 0xe8, 0x07,
0x7f, 0x80, 0xcd, 0x00, 0xc4, 0x04, 0x31, 0x06, 0xc9, 0x0e, 0x00, 0xc0,
0x48, 0x88, 0xe0, 0x04, 0x79, 0x04, 0xdb, 0x12, 0x00, 0x30, 0x0c, 0xc8,
0xe4, 0x04, 0x6d, 0x06, 0xb6, 0x23, 0x00, 0x18, 0x1c, 0xc0, 0x84, 0x04,
0x25, 0x0c, 0xff, 0xc2, 0x00, 0x4e, 0x06, 0xb0, 0x80, 0x04, 0x3f, 0x8a,
0xb3, 0x83, 0xff, 0xc3, 0x03, 0x91, 0x84, 0x04, 0x2e, 0xd8, 0x0f, 0x3f,
0x00, 0x00, 0x5f, 0x83, 0x84, 0x04, 0x2a, 0x70, 0xfd, 0x7f, 0x00, 0x00,
0xc8, 0xc0, 0x84, 0x04, 0x4b, 0xe2, 0x2f, 0x01, 0x00, 0x08, 0x58, 0x60,
0x80, 0x04, 0x5b, 0x82, 0xff, 0x01, 0x00, 0x08, 0xd0, 0xa0, 0x84, 0x04,
0x72, 0x80, 0xe5, 0x00, 0x00, 0x08, 0xd2, 0x20, 0x44, 0x04, 0xca, 0x02,
0xff, 0x00, 0x00, 0x08, 0xde, 0xa0, 0x44, 0x04, 0x82, 0x02, 0x6d, 0x00,
0x00, 0x08, 0xf6, 0xb0, 0x40, 0x02, 0x82, 0x07, 0x3f, 0x00, 0x00, 0x08,
0x44, 0x58, 0x44, 0x02, 0x93, 0x3f, 0x1f, 0x00, 0x00, 0x30, 0x88, 0x4f,
0x44, 0x03, 0x83, 0x23, 0x3e, 0x00, 0x00, 0x00, 0x18, 0x60, 0xe0, 0x07,
0xe3, 0x0f, 0xfe, 0x00, 0x00, 0x00, 0x70, 0x70, 0xe4, 0x07, 0xc7, 0x1b,
0xfe, 0x01, 0x00, 0x00, 0xe0, 0x3c, 0xe4, 0x07, 0xc7, 0xe3, 0xfe, 0x1f,
0x00, 0x00, 0xff, 0x1f, 0xfc, 0x07, 0xc7, 0x03, 0xf8, 0x33, 0x00, 0xc0,
0xf0, 0x07, 0xff, 0x07, 0x87, 0x02, 0xfc, 0x43, 0x00, 0x60, 0xf0, 0xff,
0xff, 0x07, 0x8f, 0x06, 0xbe, 0x87, 0x00, 0x30, 0xf8, 0xff, 0xff, 0x07,
0x8f, 0x14, 0x9c, 0x8f, 0x00, 0x00, 0xfc, 0xff, 0xff, 0x07, 0x9f, 0x8d,
0x8a, 0x0f, 0x00, 0x00, 0xfe, 0xff, 0xff, 0x07, 0xbf, 0x0b, 0x80, 0x1f,
0x00, 0x00, 0xff, 0xff, 0xff, 0x07, 0x7f, 0x3a, 0x80, 0x3f, 0x00, 0x80,
0xff, 0xff, 0xff, 0x07, 0xff, 0x20, 0xc0, 0x3f, 0x00, 0x80, 0xff, 0xff,
0xff, 0x07, 0xff, 0x01, 0xe0, 0x7f, 0x00, 0xc0, 0xff, 0xff, 0xff, 0x07,
0xff, 0x0f, 0xf8, 0xff, 0x40, 0xe0, 0xff, 0xff, 0xff, 0x07, 0xff, 0xff,
0xff, 0xff, 0x40, 0xf0, 0xff, 0xff, 0xff, 0x07, 0xff, 0xff, 0xff, 0xff,
0x41, 0xf0, 0xff, 0xff, 0xff, 0x07, 0xaa, 0xdd};

static int frame2_bits[] = {
0xfc, 0x7e, 0x40, 0x20, 0x90, 0x00, 0x07, 0x80, 0x23, 0x00, 0x00, 0xc6,
0xc1, 0x41, 0x98, 0xb8, 0x01, 0x07, 0x66, 0x00, 0x15, 0x9f, 0x03, 0x47,
0x8c, 0xc6, 0xdc, 0x7b, 0xcc, 0x00, 0xb0, 0x71, 0x0e, 0x4d, 0x06, 0x66,
```

```
0x73, 0x8e, 0x8f, 0x01, 0x18, 0xc4, 0x39, 0x4b, 0x02, 0x23, 0x0c, 0x04,
0x1e, 0x03, 0x0c, 0x08, 0xc7, 0xef, 0x08, 0x30, 0x06, 0x07, 0x1c, 0x02,
0x06, 0x30, 0x18, 0xae, 0xc8, 0x98, 0x3f, 0x78, 0x20, 0x06, 0x02, 0x20,
0x60, 0xa0, 0xc4, 0x1d, 0xc0, 0xff, 0x41, 0x04, 0xfa, 0x63, 0x80, 0xa1,
0xa4, 0x3d, 0x00, 0x84, 0xbf, 0x04, 0x0f, 0x06, 0xfc, 0xa1, 0x34, 0x6b,
0x01, 0x1c, 0xc9, 0x05, 0x06, 0xc7, 0x06, 0xbe, 0x11, 0x1e, 0x43, 0x30,
0x91, 0x05, 0xc3, 0x61, 0x02, 0x30, 0x1b, 0x30, 0xcc, 0x20, 0x11, 0x00,
0xc1, 0x3c, 0x03, 0x20, 0x0a, 0x00, 0xe8, 0x60, 0x21, 0x00, 0x61, 0x1b,
0xc1, 0x63, 0x08, 0xf0, 0xc6, 0xc7, 0x21, 0x03, 0xf8, 0x08, 0xe1, 0xcf,
0x0a, 0xfc, 0x4d, 0x99, 0x43, 0x07, 0x3c, 0x0c, 0xf1, 0x9f, 0x0b, 0xfc,
0x5b, 0x81, 0x47, 0x02, 0x16, 0x04, 0x31, 0x1c, 0x0b, 0x1f, 0x17, 0x89,
0x4d, 0x06, 0x1a, 0x04, 0x31, 0x38, 0x02, 0x07, 0x56, 0x89, 0x49, 0x04,
0x0b, 0x04, 0xb1, 0x72, 0x82, 0xa1, 0x54, 0x9a, 0x49, 0x04, 0x1d, 0x66,
0x50, 0xe7, 0xc2, 0xf0, 0x54, 0x9a, 0x58, 0x04, 0x0d, 0x62, 0xc1, 0x1f,
0x44, 0xfc, 0x51, 0x90, 0x90, 0x04, 0x86, 0x63, 0xe0, 0x74, 0x04, 0xef,
0x31, 0x1a, 0x91, 0x00, 0x02, 0xe2, 0xc1, 0xfd, 0x84, 0xf9, 0x30, 0x0a,
0x91, 0x00, 0x82, 0xa9, 0xc0, 0xb9, 0x84, 0xf9, 0x31, 0x16, 0x81, 0x00,
0x42, 0xa9, 0xdb, 0x7f, 0x0c, 0xff, 0x1c, 0x16, 0x11, 0x00, 0x02, 0x28,
0x0b, 0x07, 0x08, 0x60, 0x1c, 0x02, 0x91, 0x00, 0x46, 0x29, 0x0e, 0x00,
0x00, 0x00, 0x10, 0x16, 0x11, 0x02, 0x06, 0x29, 0x04, 0x00, 0x00, 0x00,
0x10, 0x16, 0x91, 0x06, 0xa6, 0x2a, 0x04, 0x00, 0x00, 0x00, 0x18, 0x24,
0x91, 0x04, 0x86, 0x2a, 0x04, 0x00, 0x00, 0x00, 0x18, 0x27, 0x93, 0x04,
0x96, 0x4a, 0x04, 0x00, 0x00, 0x00, 0x04, 0x02, 0x91, 0x04, 0x86, 0x4a,
0x0c, 0x00, 0x00, 0x00, 0x1e, 0x23, 0x93, 0x04, 0x56, 0x88, 0x08, 0x00,
0x00, 0x00, 0x90, 0x21, 0x93, 0x04, 0x52, 0x0a, 0x09, 0x80, 0x21, 0x00,
0xd0, 0x21, 0x95, 0x04, 0x57, 0x0a, 0x0f, 0x80, 0x67, 0x00, 0xd8, 0x20,
0x9d, 0x04, 0x5d, 0x08, 0x1c, 0x80, 0x07, 0x00, 0xe4, 0x01, 0x85, 0x04,
0x79, 0x8a, 0x3f, 0x00, 0x00, 0x00, 0xf4, 0x11, 0x85, 0x06, 0x39, 0x08,
0x7d, 0x00, 0x00, 0x18, 0xb7, 0x10, 0x81, 0x03, 0x29, 0x12, 0xcb, 0x10,
0x00, 0x30, 0x28, 0x00, 0x85, 0x03, 0x29, 0x10, 0xbe, 0xf1, 0x1f, 0x20,
0x0c, 0x10, 0x85, 0x03, 0x29, 0x32, 0xfa, 0xe1, 0xff, 0x27, 0x94, 0x11,
0x85, 0x03, 0x28, 0x20, 0x6c, 0x81, 0xff, 0x01, 0x0c, 0x01, 0x85, 0x01,
0x28, 0x62, 0x5c, 0x03, 0xff, 0x00, 0x4e, 0x91, 0x80, 0x05, 0x39, 0x40,
0xf4, 0x02, 0x3c, 0x00, 0x9f, 0x91, 0x84, 0x05, 0x31, 0xc6, 0xe8, 0x07,
0x00, 0x80, 0xcd, 0x00, 0xc4, 0x04, 0x31, 0x06, 0xc9, 0x0e, 0x00, 0xc0,
0x48, 0x88, 0xe0, 0x04, 0x79, 0x04, 0xdb, 0x12, 0x00, 0x30, 0x0c, 0xc8,
0xe4, 0x04, 0x6d, 0x06, 0xb6, 0x23, 0x00, 0x18, 0x1c, 0xc0, 0x84, 0x04,
0x25, 0x0c, 0xff, 0xc2, 0x00, 0x4e, 0x06, 0xb0, 0x80, 0x04, 0x3f, 0x8a,
0xb3, 0x83, 0xff, 0xc3, 0x03, 0x91, 0x84, 0x04, 0x2e, 0xd8, 0x0f, 0x3f,
0x00, 0x00, 0x5f, 0x83, 0x84, 0x04, 0x2a, 0x70, 0xfd, 0x7f, 0x00, 0x00,
0xc8, 0xc0, 0x84, 0x04, 0x4b, 0xe2, 0x2f, 0x01, 0x00, 0x08, 0x58, 0x60,
0x80, 0x04, 0x5b, 0x82, 0xff, 0x01, 0x00, 0x08, 0xd0, 0xa0, 0x84, 0x04,
0x72, 0x80, 0xe5, 0x00, 0x00, 0x08, 0xd2, 0x20, 0x44, 0x04, 0xca, 0x02,
0xff, 0x00, 0x00, 0x08, 0xde, 0xa0, 0x44, 0x04, 0x82, 0x02, 0x6d, 0x00,
0x00, 0x08, 0xf6, 0xb0, 0x40, 0x02, 0x82, 0x07, 0x3f, 0x00, 0x00, 0x08,
0x44, 0x58, 0x44, 0x02, 0x93, 0x3f, 0x1f, 0x00, 0x00, 0x30, 0x88, 0x4f,
0x44, 0x03, 0x83, 0x23, 0x3e, 0x00, 0x00, 0x00, 0x18, 0x60, 0xe0, 0x07,
0xe3, 0x0f, 0xfe, 0x00, 0x00, 0x00, 0x70, 0x70, 0xe4, 0x07, 0xc7, 0x1b,
0xfe, 0x01, 0x00, 0x00, 0xe0, 0x3c, 0xe4, 0x07, 0xc7, 0xe3, 0xfe, 0x1f,
0x00, 0x00, 0xff, 0x1f, 0xfc, 0x07, 0xc7, 0x03, 0xf8, 0x33, 0x00, 0xc0,
0xf0, 0x07, 0xff, 0x07, 0x87, 0x02, 0xfc, 0x43, 0x00, 0x60, 0xf0, 0xff,
0xff, 0x07, 0x8f, 0x06, 0xbe, 0x87, 0x00, 0x30, 0xf8, 0xff, 0xff, 0x07,
```

```
0x8f, 0x14, 0x9c, 0x8f, 0x00, 0x00, 0xfc, 0xff, 0xff, 0x07, 0x9f, 0x8d,
0x8a, 0x0f, 0x00, 0x00, 0xfe, 0xff, 0xff, 0x07, 0xbf, 0x0b, 0x80, 0x1f,
0x00, 0x00, 0xff, 0xff, 0xff, 0x07, 0x7f, 0x3a, 0x80, 0x3f, 0x00, 0x80,
0xff, 0xff, 0xff, 0x07, 0xff, 0x20, 0xc0, 0x3f, 0x00, 0x80, 0xff, 0xff,
0xff, 0x07, 0xff, 0x01, 0xe0, 0x7f, 0x00, 0xc0, 0xff, 0xff, 0xff, 0x07,
0xff, 0x0f, 0xf8, 0xff, 0x40, 0xe0, 0xff, 0xff, 0xff, 0x07, 0xff, 0xff,
0xff, 0xff, 0x40, 0xf0, 0xff, 0xff, 0xff, 0x07, 0xff, 0xff, 0xff, 0xff,
0x41, 0xf0, 0xff, 0xff, 0xff, 0x07, 0xaa, 0xdd};

static int frame3_bits[] = {
0xfc, 0x7e, 0x40, 0x20, 0x90, 0x00, 0x07, 0x80, 0x23, 0x00, 0x00, 0xc6,
0xc1, 0x41, 0x98, 0xb8, 0x01, 0x07, 0x66, 0x00, 0x15, 0x9f, 0x03, 0x47,
0x8c, 0xc6, 0xdc, 0x7b, 0xcc, 0x00, 0xb0, 0x71, 0x0e, 0x4d, 0x06, 0x66,
0x73, 0x8e, 0x8f, 0x01, 0x18, 0xc4, 0x39, 0x4b, 0x02, 0x23, 0x0c, 0x04,
0x1e, 0x03, 0x0c, 0x08, 0xc7, 0xef, 0x08, 0x30, 0x06, 0x07, 0x1c, 0x02,
0x06, 0x30, 0x18, 0xae, 0xc8, 0x98, 0x3f, 0x78, 0x20, 0x06, 0x02, 0x20,
0x60, 0xa0, 0xc4, 0x1d, 0xc0, 0xff, 0x41, 0x04, 0xfa, 0x63, 0x80, 0xa1,
0xa4, 0x3d, 0x00, 0x84, 0xbf, 0x04, 0x0f, 0x06, 0xfc, 0xa1, 0x34, 0x6b,
0x01, 0x1c, 0xc9, 0x05, 0x06, 0xc7, 0x06, 0xbe, 0x11, 0x1e, 0x43, 0x30,
0x91, 0x05, 0xc3, 0x61, 0x02, 0x30, 0x1b, 0x30, 0xcc, 0x20, 0x11, 0x00,
0xc1, 0x3c, 0x03, 0x20, 0x0a, 0x00, 0xe8, 0x60, 0x21, 0x00, 0x61, 0x1b,
0xc1, 0x63, 0x08, 0xf0, 0xc6, 0xc7, 0x21, 0x03, 0xf8, 0x08, 0xe1, 0xcf,
0x0a, 0xfc, 0x4d, 0x99, 0x43, 0x07, 0x3c, 0x0c, 0xf1, 0x9f, 0x0b, 0xfc,
0x5b, 0x81, 0x47, 0x02, 0x16, 0x04, 0x31, 0x1c, 0x0b, 0x1f, 0x17, 0x89,
0x4d, 0x06, 0x1a, 0x04, 0x31, 0x38, 0x02, 0x07, 0x56, 0x89, 0x49, 0x04,
0x0b, 0x04, 0x11, 0x70, 0x82, 0xa1, 0x54, 0x9a, 0x49, 0x04, 0x1d, 0x66,
0x00, 0x00, 0xc2, 0xf0, 0x54, 0x9a, 0x58, 0x04, 0x0d, 0x62, 0x01, 0x0f,
0x44, 0xfc, 0x51, 0x90, 0x90, 0x04, 0x86, 0x63, 0xc0, 0x3f, 0x04, 0xef,
0x31, 0x1a, 0x91, 0x00, 0x02, 0xe2, 0xe1, 0x78, 0x84, 0xf9, 0x30, 0x0a,
0x91, 0x00, 0x82, 0xa9, 0x00, 0xc0, 0x84, 0xf9, 0x31, 0x16, 0x81, 0x00,
0x42, 0xa9, 0x03, 0x00, 0x08, 0xff, 0x1c, 0x16, 0x11, 0x00, 0x02, 0x28,
0x03, 0x00, 0x08, 0x60, 0x1c, 0x02, 0x91, 0x00, 0x46, 0x29, 0x06, 0x00,
0x00, 0x00, 0x10, 0x16, 0x11, 0x02, 0x06, 0x29, 0x04, 0x00, 0x00, 0x00,
0x10, 0x16, 0x91, 0x06, 0xa6, 0x2a, 0x04, 0x00, 0x00, 0x00, 0x18, 0x24,
0x91, 0x04, 0x86, 0x2a, 0x04, 0x00, 0x00, 0x00, 0x18, 0x27, 0x93, 0x04,
0x96, 0x4a, 0x04, 0x00, 0x00, 0x00, 0x04, 0x02, 0x91, 0x04, 0x86, 0x4a,
0x0c, 0x00, 0x00, 0x00, 0x1e, 0x23, 0x93, 0x04, 0x56, 0x88, 0x08, 0x00,
0x00, 0x00, 0x90, 0x21, 0x93, 0x04, 0x52, 0x0a, 0x09, 0x80, 0x01, 0x00,
0xd0, 0x21, 0x95, 0x04, 0x57, 0x0a, 0x0f, 0x80, 0x27, 0x00, 0xd8, 0x20,
0x9d, 0x04, 0x5d, 0x08, 0x1c, 0x80, 0x67, 0x00, 0xe4, 0x01, 0x85, 0x04,
0x79, 0x8a, 0x3f, 0x00, 0x00, 0x00, 0xf4, 0x11, 0x85, 0x06, 0x39, 0x08,
0x7d, 0x00, 0x00, 0x18, 0xb7, 0x10, 0x81, 0x03, 0x29, 0x12, 0xcb, 0x00,
0x7e, 0x30, 0x28, 0x00, 0x85, 0x03, 0x29, 0x10, 0xbe, 0x81, 0xff, 0x27,
0x0c, 0x10, 0x85, 0x03, 0x29, 0x32, 0xfa, 0xc1, 0xff, 0x27, 0x94, 0x11,
0x85, 0x03, 0x28, 0x20, 0x6c, 0xe1, 0xff, 0x07, 0x0c, 0x01, 0x85, 0x01,
0x28, 0x62, 0x5c, 0xe3, 0x8f, 0x03, 0x4e, 0x91, 0x80, 0x05, 0x39, 0x40,
0xf4, 0xc2, 0xff, 0x00, 0x9f, 0x91, 0x84, 0x05, 0x31, 0xc6, 0xe8, 0x07,
0x7f, 0x80, 0xcd, 0x00, 0xc4, 0x04, 0x31, 0x06, 0xc9, 0x0e, 0x00, 0xc0,
0x48, 0x88, 0xe0, 0x04, 0x79, 0x04, 0xdb, 0x12, 0x00, 0x30, 0x0c, 0xc8,
0xe4, 0x04, 0x6d, 0x06, 0xb6, 0x23, 0x00, 0x18, 0x1c, 0xc0, 0x84, 0x04,
0x25, 0x0c, 0xff, 0xc2, 0x00, 0x4e, 0x06, 0xb0, 0x80, 0x04, 0x3f, 0x8a,
0xb3, 0x83, 0xff, 0xc3, 0x03, 0x91, 0x84, 0x04, 0x2e, 0xd8, 0x0f, 0x3f,
```

```
0x00, 0x00, 0x5f, 0x83, 0x84, 0x04, 0x2a, 0x70, 0xfd, 0x7f, 0x00, 0x00,
0xc8, 0xc0, 0x84, 0x04, 0x4b, 0xe2, 0x2f, 0x01, 0x00, 0x08, 0x58, 0x60,
0x80, 0x04, 0x5b, 0x82, 0xff, 0x01, 0x00, 0x08, 0xd0, 0xa0, 0x84, 0x04,
0x72, 0x80, 0xe5, 0x00, 0x00, 0x08, 0xd2, 0x20, 0x44, 0x04, 0xca, 0x02,
0xff, 0x00, 0x00, 0x08, 0xde, 0xa0, 0x44, 0x04, 0x82, 0x02, 0x6d, 0x00,
0x00, 0x08, 0xf6, 0xb0, 0x40, 0x02, 0x82, 0x07, 0x3f, 0x00, 0x00, 0x08,
0x44, 0x58, 0x44, 0x02, 0x93, 0x3f, 0x1f, 0x00, 0x00, 0x30, 0x88, 0x4f,
0x44, 0x03, 0x83, 0x23, 0x3e, 0x00, 0x00, 0x00, 0x18, 0x60, 0xe0, 0x07,
0xe3, 0x0f, 0xfe, 0x00, 0x00, 0x00, 0x70, 0x70, 0xe4, 0x07, 0xc7, 0x1b,
0xfe, 0x01, 0x00, 0x00, 0xe0, 0x3c, 0xe4, 0x07, 0xc7, 0xe3, 0xfe, 0x1f,
0x00, 0x00, 0xff, 0x1f, 0xfc, 0x07, 0xc7, 0x03, 0xf8, 0x33, 0x00, 0xc0,
0xf0, 0x07, 0xff, 0x07, 0x87, 0x02, 0xfc, 0x43, 0x00, 0x60, 0xf0, 0xff,
0xff, 0x07, 0x8f, 0x06, 0xbe, 0x87, 0x00, 0x30, 0xf8, 0xff, 0xff, 0x07,
0x8f, 0x14, 0x9c, 0x8f, 0x00, 0x00, 0xfc, 0xff, 0xff, 0x07, 0x9f, 0x8d,
0x8a, 0x0f, 0x00, 0x00, 0xfe, 0xff, 0xff, 0x07, 0xbf, 0x0b, 0x80, 0x1f,
0x00, 0x00, 0xff, 0xff, 0xff, 0x07, 0x7f, 0x3a, 0x80, 0x3f, 0x00, 0x80,
0xff, 0xff, 0xff, 0x07, 0xff, 0x20, 0xc0, 0x3f, 0x00, 0x80, 0xff, 0xff,
0xff, 0x07, 0xff, 0x01, 0xe0, 0x7f, 0x00, 0xc0, 0xff, 0xff, 0xff, 0x07,
0xff, 0x0f, 0xf8, 0xff, 0x40, 0xe0, 0xff, 0xff, 0xff, 0x07, 0xff, 0xff,
0xff, 0xff, 0x40, 0xf0, 0xff, 0xff, 0xff, 0x07, 0xff, 0xff, 0xff, 0xff,
0x41, 0xf0, 0xff, 0xff, 0xff, 0x07, 0xaa, 0xdd};

struct sockaddr_in sin,
dst;

main(argv)
char *argv[];
{
 FILE *fptr;
 register int c;
 int n=0, i ,s, len;

 /* Create a socket */

 s = socket(AF_INET, SOCK_DGRAM, 0);

 if (s < 0) {
   printf("Error: Cannot create socket.\n");
   exit(1);
 }

 /* Fill in the sockaddr_in structure ... */

 bzero((char *)&dst, sizeof(dst));
 dst.sin_addr.s_addr = INADDR_ANY;
 dst.sin_family = AF_INET;
 dst.sin_port = htons(MYPORT);

 /* Connect our end to the socket */

 bind(s, (char *)&sin, sizeof(sin));
```

```
/*
** Send bitmap(s) to server...
*/

while (1) {

for (n=0; frame1_bits[n] != END;) {
    sendto(s, &frame1_bits[n], sizeof(frame1_bits[n]), 0, &dst,
                    sizeof(dst));

    n++;
}

for (n=0; frame2_bits[n] != END;) {
    sendto(s, &frame2_bits[n], sizeof(frame2_bits[n]), 0, &dst,
                   sizeof(dst));

    n++;
}

for (n=0; frame3_bits[n] != END;) {
    sendto(s, &frame3_bits[n], sizeof(frame3_bits[n]), 0, &dst,
                  sizeof(dst));

    n++;
}

}
}
```

As can be seen from the previous client program, the basic concept of sending a bitmap image to a server is quite straightforward. The **bitmap** utility is used to create an image to the requirements of the user. This is then saved, and imported into the client program. The actual transmission of the bitmap data is done using a **sendto()** call. Notice how the bitmap data array has an *end-of-data* marker, so that we can determine just how many data items (hexadecimal digits) we are sending to the server (the marker is defined as the constant **END** at the start of the program). The client program terminates when it has sent all bitmap data items. The number of bytes sent is displayed.

The server program will receive the incoming bitmap data, and store it an array (byte by byte). The server then creates a window, assembles a bitmap (pixmap of depth 1) using the **XCreateBitmapFromData()** call, and draws it into the window previously created for the user to see. The bitmap in this example is a simple drawing of a face (this is animated by **sending** a series of slightly different (modified) bitmap data. The user can create bitmaps of increasing complexity at will using the **bitmap**(1X) utility.

```
/*
* XServer.c
* This server receives bitmap(1X) files over a socket
* connection (i.e. between two machines) and animates
* the incoming images to show how movement can be
* achieved.
*/

#include <errno.h>
#include <sys/time.h>
#include <stdio.h>
#include <strings.h>
#include <X11/Xlib.h>
#include <X11/Xutil.h>
#include <X11/Xatom.h>
#include <sys/param.h>
#include <sys/time.h>
#include <signal.h>
#include <unistd.h>
#include <sys/types.h>
#include <sys/socket.h>
#include <sys/stat.h>
#include <netinet/in.h>
#include <netdb.h>
#define END 0xffffffaa /* End of data value */
#define NO(p) (p)0
#define MAXLINKS 16
#define XRES 1
#define YRES 1
#define XSIZE 40
#define YSIZE 40
#define XDELTA 1
#define YDELTA 1
#define MAX_DISPLAYS 1
#define MYPORT 2001 /* Port Number */
#define bitbuffer_width 75
#define bitbuffer_height 75
#define bitbuffer_x_hot -1
#define bitbuffer_y_hot -1

static char buf[BUFSIZ], bitbuffer[BUFSIZ];
int column=1 , byte_count=0;
int i, s, ns, len, c, z=0, p=0, ok = 0, lw, lh, lw2, lh2;

char *a_name = "Susan";

unsigned int status;
extern errno;
struct sockaddr_in sin, from;

typedef struct _disp {
 Display *Dp;
```

```
 GC Gc;
 Window Win1;
 Pixmap Px;
        Pixmap bit_map;
       char *name;
} disp;

unsigned int depth;

disp displays[MAX_DISPLAYS];

int ndisplays = 0;
int currentdisplay = 0, previousdisplay = 0;
int errors = 0;

int X_res = XRES,
    Y_res = YRES,
    x_origin = 230, /* Origin for window display */
    y_origin = 200,
    border = 5,
     Fontid,
    Y_tim = 220, /* Height and width of our window */
    X_log = 650,
    Y_log = 1;

char Next[128];

int xdelta = XDELTA;
int ydelta = YDELTA;
int rate = 4, steps = 4;
int X_dir = -1; /* Initial directions */
int Y_dir = 0;
int dx=XRES, dy=YRES, odx = -1, ody = -1;

/*
* Functions ...
*
*/

StartX(d)
disp *d;
{
Window                     w;
Display                    *Dp;
XWMHints                   myhints;
Window                     Win1;
XSizeHints                 hintsz; /* Hints for WManager */
GC                         Gc; /* Graphics Context */
Pixmap                     Px;
Pixmap                     bit_map;
char                       *name;
```

```
if (ok == 0) {

/*
** Open a display on Workstation ...
*/

if ((Dp = XOpenDisplay("")) == NO(Display *)) {
printf("Cant open display");
exit(-1);
}

d->Dp = Dp;
depth = XDefaultDepth(Dp, 0);

/*
* Find the parent window ...
*/
if ((w = RootWindow(Dp,0)) == NO(Window)) {
printf("Orphaned Window\n");
exit(-2);
}
if ((Win1 = XCreateSimpleWindow(Dp, w, x_origin, y_origin, X_log,
Y_tim, border, 5)) == NO(Window)) {
printf("Cant create Window\n");
exit(-3);
}
d->Win1 = Win1;
Gc = XDefaultGC(Dp, 0);
d->Gc = Gc;
XSetFunction(Dp, Gc, GXxor);
XSetPlaneMask(Dp, Gc, AllPlanes);
}
ok = 1;

/* Create a bitmap from array data ... */

bit_map = XCreateBitmapFromData(Dp, Win1, bitbuffer, bitbuf-
fer_width, bitbuffer_height);
XCreatePixmap(Dp, bit_map, bitbuffer_width, bitbuffer_height,
depth);
d->bit_map = bit_map;

myhints.icon_pixmap = NULL;
XSetWMHints(Dp, Win1, &myhints);
XSetStandardProperties(Dp, Win1, a_name, "RT V/T/G", bit_map,
NULL, 0, &hintsz);

name = d->name;

XMapRaised(Dp, Win1);
XFlush(Dp);
```

```
show(); /* Show the image */
}

/*
* Copy our pixmap into our window ...
*/

CopyAt(d, dx, dy)
disp *d;
{
Display *Dp = d->Dp;
Pixmap Px = d->Px;
GC Gc = d->Gc;
dx = dx % X_res;
dy = dy % Y_res;
}

show()
{
int odx, ody;
disp *dp;
static int update = 0;
previousdisplay = currentdisplay;
odx = dx;
ody = dy;
dx += xdelta * X_dir;
dy += ydelta * Y_dir;
if (dx < 0)
dx += (ndisplays * X_res);
if (dy < 0)
dy += (ndisplays * Y_res);
currentdisplay = ((dx/X_res) % ndisplays);
dp = &displays[previousdisplay];
XFlush(dp);
if (previousdisplay != currentdisplay) {
XFlush(dp->Dp);
XSync(dp->Dp, 0);
}

XClearWindow(dp->Dp, dp->Win1);

XCopyPlane(dp->Dp, dp->bit_map, dp->Win1, dp->Gc, 1, 1, X_log,
Y_tim, 10, 10, 0x01);

dp = &displays[currentdisplay];
CopyAt(dp, dx, dy);

XFlush(dp->Dp);
XSync(dp->Dp, 0);

p = 0;
}
```

```
main()
{
 char c, *cp;
 int i, n;
 Display *Dp;
 ndisplays = 0;

 s = socket(AF_INET, SOCK_DGRAM, 0);

 /* Fill in the sockaddr_in structure ... */

 sin.sin_addr.s_addr = htonl(INADDR_ANY);
 sin.sin_family = AF_INET;
 sin.sin_port = htons(MYPORT);
 bind (s, (char *)&sin, sizeof(sin));

 len = sizeof(from);

 if (s < 0) {
    printf("Error: Cannot bind to socket.\n");
    exit(0);
 }

 /* Generate a buffer for all incoming bitmap (hex) data ... */

 p = 0;

 while(1) {
 recv(s, buf, sizeof(buf));

 if (buf[0] == END) {
                    if (ndisplays <= 0) {
                         displays[0].name = NULL;
                         ndisplays++;
                    }

          xdelta *= steps;
          ydelta *= steps;

          for (i = 0; i <ndisplays; i++)
               StartX(&displays[i]);

               }
               else {
                    bitbuffer[p] = buf[0];
                    p++;
               }
   }
 }
```

3.10 IPC and UNIX 4.2 BSD sockets

This section introduces some of the fundamental concepts of interprocess communication (IPC) in a UNIX environment. The use of client-server applications is heavily used in many UNIX environments, and the use of sockets as an IPC mechanism will allow the reader to develop simple client-server applications.

3.10.1 The basics

The topics discussed in this section are relevant to the 4.2 Berkeley System Distribution (BSD) version of the UNIX operating system. The C program excerpts were created and compiled in an *Ultrix* Berkeley UNIX environment. The reader is expected to be familiar with the C language, as all examples and code fragments are written in this language.

The model for *interprocess communication* (IPC) in this section is confined to the use of sockets. Basically, this involves the development of client-server programs which initiate connections with each other across a network (a LAN environment i.e. a departmental Ethernet was the development environment for all programs in this section) whereupon data can be exchanged between processes.

An important part of the 4.2 BSD version of UNIX is the provision of IPC facilities that can be utilised at the programming level by the user. *Sockets* allow programs to communicate locally or remotely in a manner that is similar to the standard C functions provided for the reading and writing of files. A socket is the fundamental agent through which allows processes to communicate with each other. Sockets are said to exist within a particular *domain.* The domain is an abstraction in itself. Domains are used to group together all those processes which utilise sockets as an IPC mechanism, and we will return to this point later. Sockets are also said to have *properties.* Such properties include those features of the socket which are unique to a particular system, such as naming.

Socket domains

Most socket operations are performed in the same domain, although it is quite possible to communicate with processes external to a particular domain. In such cases, where we cross boundaries, it may be necessary to perform some conversion or translation process to avoid ambiguities between the different systems. UNIX 4.2 BSD supports two domains: Internet and UNIX

The Internet domain is used for those systems which adhere to the DARPA communication protocols (which are heavily used in the US i.e. the TCP/IP protocol). The UNIX domain, whose socket implementations are very similar to the Internet domains, are used to access localised machine protocols i.e. those local to a specific local domain.

Differences between these two domains may not seem too apparent at first, and is best illustrated through use of a program utilising the different domains (this should make the differences more apparent to the reader). In general though, the reader can think of UNIX domain sockets as "scaled-down" versions of their Internet partners. The facilities offered by the two domains mentioned differ widely and they will significantly alter the way in which the programmer implements a system based around the use of IPC socket mechanisms.

Socket types

There are a number of different socket *types* for use within an application. Sockets are categorised according to the type of communication qualities that they possess. A fundamental assumption is that processes normally only communicate through sockets of the same type. Communication through different socket types (as through different domains) is quite possible, although this will depend on the underlying protocol being used (i.e. TCP/IP etc). This section considers two different types of socket (although others exist). These are: Stream Sockets (SOCK_STREAM); and Datagram sockets (SOCK_DGRAM).

Stream sockets provide a reliable, sequenced, and unduplicated bidirectional communications path (or stream) between processes. *Datagram* sockets also provide a bidirectional communications path between cooperating processes, although the service itself can be unreliable i.e. data in a different order than was originally specified, duplicated, or even lost. Datagram sockets, as the name suggests, tend to exhibit the characteristics of some packet switched networks such as those found on Ethernet based networks.

Creating a socket – socket()

At this stage, we will start to introduce some of the programming concepts to utilise sockets. All sockets are initially created using the *socket()* call. This call returns an integer value corresponding to the state of the socket connection i.e. successful creation (normally > 0) or failure (commonly < 0). The syntax of the *socket()* call is:

```
s = socket(domain-name, socket-type, protocol)
```

Where **s** is an integer value used to capture the state of the socket connection. This is done so that we can provide an error message to the user if a socket connection could not be created (see below). The parameter **domain-name** is the domain name of the socket required. This is **AF_INET** for DARPA based protocols i.e. TCP/IP, and **AF_UNIX** for the local UNIX domains.

Skeletal program example 1 – Creating a socket

```
main()
...
int s;
...
 s = socket(AF_INET, SOCK_STREAM, 0);

  if (s < 0) {
    fprintf(stderr, "socket(): cannot create connection\n");
    exit(3);
}
```

The **socket()** call illustrated in the preceding code extract would create a stream socket with a TCP-based protocol providing the underlying communications. Likewise, to create a datagram based socket, we would replace SOCK_STREAM with SOCK_DGRAM. The **protocol** parameter in the **socket()** call allows the programmer to select a specific protocol for the underlying communication process that will be used for the socket connection. In the Internet domain the protocols that are available to the programmer are defined in the C header file **<netinet/in.h>**. A number of predefined library functions exist for the socket services, such as the protocol required. The procedure **getprotobyname()** is a common routine for the direct selection of a particular protocol. It is used in the following way:

```
my_protocol = getprotobyname("tcp");
s = socket(AF_INET, SOCK_STREAM, my_socket->p_proto);
```

This code extract stipulates the use of a TCP service as the underlying communications protocol for a stream socket connection (although we could use others, e.g. UDP). The -> notation is a way of indirectly referencing a C structure (a data structure that contains a sequence of different parameter elements all grouped into one entity). The parameter **p_proto** (a variable holding the protocol number of a specific protocol) is one such element in a structure returned by the **getprotobyname()** procedure. In earlier examples we specified **0** as a protocol number (this normally allows the system to choose an appropriate protocol for us). Socket failures can be caused for many reasons. An unknown protocol, or failure to set up the connection for the socket are examples of why a socket call may fail. A specific error is returned in the case of failure. They can be captured by the user so that more specific error messages can be issued, as in the example below:

Skeletal program example 2 – catching specific socket errors

```
main()
int s;
...
s = socket(AF_INET, SOCK_STREAM, 0);
switch (s) {
     case ENOBUFS:
          fprintf(stderr, "socket(): out of memory\n");
          exit(6);

     case EPROTOTYPE:
          fprintf(stderr, "socket(): No supporting protocol\n");
          exit(7);
}
```

Binding to a socket

Binding is the name given the process whereby a socket is named. The binding process allows a process to reference the socket you have created, and therefore to allow them to connect to the "end" of your socket connection. No data may be received on a socket that has not been bound. The **bind()** call has the syntax:

```
bind(socket, name, length)
```

where **s** is the created socket (created with the **socket()** call – as we have seen earlier). The **name** parameter is a simple character string which will be interpreted by the supporting protocol. The **name** parameter is most commonly set as the address of a structure identifier. This particular structure is called **sockaddr_in** and it should be defined near to the top of any client-server application that you are building (see below). This structure will be "filled in" by the programmer. The **length** parameter is an integer value representing the size of the **sockaddr_in** structure.

Skeletal program example 3 – code for server program

```
struct sockaddr_in sin;
...
main()
...
int s;
...
 s = socket(AF_INET, SOCK_STREAM, 0);

 if (s < 0) {
     fprintf(stderr, "socket(): cannot create connection\n");
     exit(3);
 }
...
 bind(s, &sin, sizeof(sin));
```

As we will see, it is normally the server program that must bind to a socket. Note the use of the **sizeof()** function in the extract above. This standard C function returns the size of the object given to it, here **sin** – which references (addresses) the **sockaddr_in** structure throughout the program.

Establishing a socket connection

Once a socket has been bound (using the **bind()** call) a *connecting* process (any process that knows of that socket) may start data transmission. Before this can be done however we have to show a "willingness" to accept data over the socket. This is done by the **connect()** call. The **connect()** call is nearly always used by the client program. A client program requests the services of a server program by connecting to it, and then *listening* for data over the connection. The syntax for the **connect()** call is:

```
connect(socket, server-name, sizeof(server-name))
```

where **socket** is our created socket, and **server-name** is the address identifier of our variable that addresses the **sockaddr_in** structure.

Skeletal program example 4 – code for client program

```
struct sockaddr_in sin;
...
main()
...
int s, i;
...
s = socket(AF_INET, SOCK_STREAM, 0);
if (s < 0) {
fprintf(stderr, "socket(): cannot create socket connection\n");
exit(3);
}
...
i = connect(s, &sin, sizeof(sin));
```

Notice here how the **connect()** call has been called with the same parameters as the **bind()** call in the server program. The **connect()** call has also been assigned to the value **i** (an integer). This has been done so as to allow us to capture any return code from the **connect()** call if it fails. We can then issue an error message by simply testing the value of **i** (< 0 for an error, and > 0 for success normally). There are many connection errors, including the case where a host refused the connection, or if a route to a host was unavailable etc (the errors ECONNREFUSED and EHOSTUNREACH are commonly returned respectively in this case).

For a server process to receive data over a socket, it must listen for incoming data from the client program. This is done using the **listen()** call, with the syntax:

```
listen(socket, queue-length)
```

where **socket** is the socket identifier, and **queue-length** is an integer value representing the maximum number of outstanding socket connections that will be queued awaiting acceptance by a server process. If a connection is requested while the queue length is at its maximum the connection will not be aborted. Instead, the message that initiated the request will be discarded by the system. This is done so that a server is given time to make room in its connection queue while the client process retries the request for a connection.

Once a socket is in its "listening" mode, a server process may accept a connection to allow data transfer. This is done using the **accept()** call. The syntax is:

```
accept(socket, structure-address, length)
```

where **socket** is our socket identifier, and **structure-address** is another address variable that is used in conjunction with the **sockaddr_in** structure. There are therefore two address identifiers that are used in most server programs: one for the *binding* process, and one for the *accept*ing process (both in the *server* program).

The **accept()** call is what is termed a *blocking* call, – that is, a call to **accept** will not be allowed to return (or terminate) until a connection is available or until the process is interrupted.

Also note that a process cannot indicate that it will accept connections from only one specific individual. It is possible to achieve this by accepting the connection, seeing who it is, and then if you do not want to exchange data with the individual, to close down the socket, thus ending the link. Figure 3.15 illustrates the concepts of creating, connecting, binding, listening and accepting a connection.

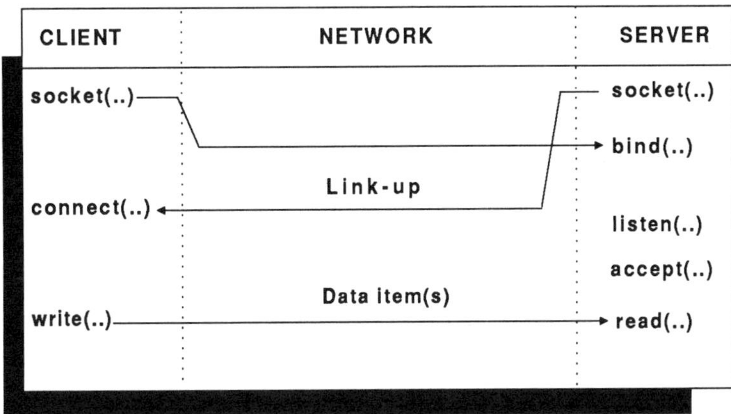

Figure 3.15. Client-server interactions

Data Transfer

Once connection establishment has taken place, data transfer can start. There are two function calls for this purpose, **read()** and **write()**. The **read()** call allows us to receive data *from* a process, while **write()** allows us to send some data *to* a process. The syntaxes of the two function calls are:

```
read(socket, buffer, sizeof(buffer))
write(socket, buffer, sizeof(buffer))
```

where **socket** is the socket identifier integer, and **buffer** is the store of data we are going to send (such as an array, or a character etc). We must specify the size of the data object we are reading/sending to/from a process. This is done by the use of the **sizeof()** call, but the user can place direct integer values in its place i.e. if we knew we were transferring single characters, the number **1** could be substituted. If the data object is of an arbitrary size, it is obviously safer to use **sizeof()**.

Sockaddr_in revisited

We now come to the **sockaddr_in** structure and the addressing parameters that reference it. When we require a connection there are a number of settings that have to be established by the user. A number of these are placed in a C data-structure known as **sockaddr_in**. We cannot reference this structure directly, so we assign to it an addressing parameter (a pointer) so that we can refer to it. This has a form similar to:

```
struct sockaddr_in sin;
```

where **sin** is our addressing parameter. The **sockaddr_in** structure is expected to hold at least a few values to ensure our socket session runs smoothly. These values include the *port number*, the socket *family*, and the *addressing* mechanism of the socket to be used. The full **sockaddr_in** structure is defined in a C header file (normally <sys/socket.h>), and this will be included in our client/server programs(s) using a **#define** directive. The complete definition of the **sockaddr_in** structure is:

```
struct sockaddr_in {
                short sin_family;     /* Address family */
                short sin_port;       /* 2 octet port number */
                long sin_addr;        /* 4 octet IP address */
                char sin_data[8];     /* unused here */
};
```

As can be seen from this structure definition, the **sin_addr** structure component is using the IP address (remembering that IP is the Internet domain protocol, part of the TCP/IP protocol – see section 2.2.3). In the Internet family of protocols transport addresses are 6 octets in length, 4 octets for the Internet address, and 2 octets for the port number.

The programmer must assign values to the first three values of the **sockaddr_in** structure to start a socket session. This is normally done after we have created a socket (and tested for any socket creation errors) by assigning direct values to the structure addressing parameter (here **sin**), for example:

```
sin.sin_addr.sin_addr= INADDR_ANY;
sin.sin_family       = AF_INET;
sin.sin_port         = MY_PORT;
```

where **MY_PORT** is a constant (defined using a **#define** constant at the start of the program). The value for **AF_INET** is system provided and represents the socket family being used (**INternET** domain). The value for **INADDR_ANY** represents a wildcard value for the address of the socket connection. This will be provided automatically if INADDR_ANY is specified.

3.10.2 Header files and compilation notes

A number of special header files have to be included in your program(s) at the time of compilation. These are commonly: **<netinet/in.h>**, **<sys/socket.h>**, **<netdb.h>** and **<sys/stat.h>**. A number of the more obvious header files such as **<stdio.h>** and **<sys/types.h>** will have to be included so that the normal string processing and input-output functions can be used. The compiler command that will have to be issued is normally of the form:

```
$ cc myfile.c -lX11 -o executename
```

where **file.c** is the source file-name to be compiled, and **executename** is the name of the executable file produced as a result of compilation. If the **-o** and **executename** are omitted, the resulting executable image will be placed in a file called **a.out.**

The programs in this section require the server process to be run first. The server can then listen for data accordingly. Start the client program after starting the server. If you are using a windows-based system such as X-Windows, open a separate window for the client and server and execute in the same order as mentioned. If you only have access to one terminal (why on earth are you developing client-server programs?) execute the server as a background process i.e. with the **&** (ampersand) metacharacter, for example:

```
$ myserver &
```

and then run the client program, and the server should respond, although the output may appear strange. If you are working in a networked workstation environment where each machine is configured separately, you may have to use the **rlogin** (remote login command) to log in onto another particular machine, so one machine runs a server, while the other runs a client. The file **/etc/hosts** normally contains a list of machines that you may **rlogin** into. For example, you may access another machine and type:

```
$ rlogin orinda
... etc ...
$ myserver
```

At your original machine you would start your client normally (after the server is running). The name of the remote machine is *orinda* in this small example.

Program example 1 – Simple client program

```
/*
**
** Client.c - (c) Jason Manger
**
** Simple client program to send data (characters) to the
** server process server.c. This program creates a socket,
** connects with the server process and then accepts user
** data which is sent to the server process.
**
*/

#include <sys/types.h>
#include <sys/socket.h>
#include <sys/stat.h>
#include <netinet/in.h>
#include <netdb.h>
#include <stdio.h>

#define MY_PORT 2001 /* Our port number. This is duplicated */
                     /* in server program, so it can latch on */

struct sockaddr_in sin;

main()
{
int i, s;
 s = socket(AF_INET, SOCK_STREAM, 0);
```

```
if (s < 0 ) {
    fprintf(stderr, "socket(): error creating socket.\n");
    exit(2);
}

sin.sin_addr.sin_addr = IANNDR_ANY /* Wildcard address */
sin.sin_family = AF_INET;
sin.sin_port = MY_PORT;

i = connect(s, (char *)&sin, sizeof(sin));

if (i < 0) {
    fprintf(stderr, "connect(): error connecting to server\n");
    exit(3);
}

printf("%s: Enter data then RETURN (CTRL-C = exit):\n", argv[0]);
/* Loop infinitely getting some data ... */

while (1) {
    c = getchar(); /* Get a character from keyboard */
    write(s, &c, 1); /* Send a character to server */
}
}
```

Program example 2 – Simple server program

```
/*
**
** Server.c - (c) Jason Manger 1991
**
** Simple server program to receive data (characters) from the
** client process client.c. This program creates a socket, binds
** an address to it, and then listens over the socket connection
** for client data.
**
*/

#include <sys/types.h>
#include <sys/socket.h>
#include <sys/stat.h>
#include <netinet/in.h>
#include <netdb.h>
#include <stdio.h>

#define MY_PORT 2001 /* Our port number - will be duplicated */
                     /* in server program, so it can latch on */

struct sockaddr_in sin, from;

main()
{
int i, s, t, ns, len;
```

```
s = socket(AF_INET, SOCK_STREAM, 0);

if (s < 0 ) {
     fprintf(stderr, "socket(): error creating socket.\n");
     exit(2);
}

sin.sin_addr.sin_addr = IANNDR_ANY /* Wildcard address */
sin.sin_family = AF_INET;
sin.sin_port = MY_PORT;

t = bind(s, (char *)&sin, sizeof(sin));

if (t < 0) {
     fprintf(stderr, "bind(): error binding to socket\n");
     exit(3);
}
listen(s, 5);
len = sizeof(from);
ns = accept(s, &from, &len);

if (ns < 0) {
     fprintf(stderr, "accept(): Error accepting connection.\n");
     exit(4);
}

printf("%s: Waiting for incoming data:\n\n", argv[0]);

/*
** Loop infinitely reading client data ...
*/

while(1)
     {
     i = read(ns, buf, 1); /* read some data from client */

     if (i < 0) {
          fprintf(stderr, "connection interrupted.\n");
          exit(5);
               }
     else
          printf("%s", buf); /* Print the client data */
}
}
```

These two programs form a simple *echo server* implementation. A UNIX utility called **write** allows two users to communicate with each other (see section 10.21.1). This system works in a very similar way to the programs above, except that two way communication (server → client, client → server) is allowed. This can easily be implemented in the programs above by building the client and server facilities into both programs. This is common in many acknowledgement systems where single processes both send and receive data over a network.

3.10.3 The client-server model

The client-server is widely used in many distributed programming situations. These systems are built in an asymmetric form, as can be seen from the program examples (and from Figure 3.15, which neatly shows the interactions of the client and server processes using socket IPC). This section briefly introduces some of the other important concepts behind client-server applications.

The *rules* or *conventions* used by the client/server are more formally known as a *protocol*. This defines how a service is implemented, and the conventions that make up the protocol in the client/server model are implemented in both client and server.

The client-server model is an asymmetric protocol, although symmetric protocol models may also be built. In the asymmetric model, one process is the *master* while the other is termed the *slave*. An example of a symmetric protocol is **TELNET** (remote terminal protocol), which allows a user (from one site) to establish a connection a **TCP** connection to a *login server* at another site, and thus login to a remote system. The client process communicates with a **TELNET** process on the user's local machine, which then transfers data to a remote **TELNET** server, and the remote application then accepts data. This is shown in Figure 3.16.

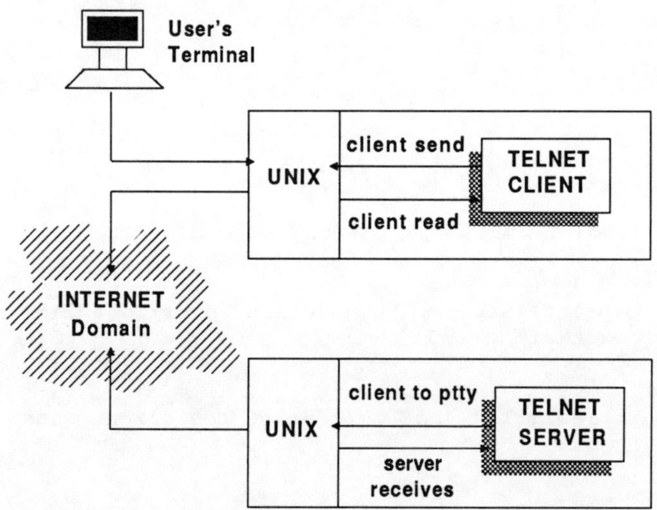

Figure 3.16. Data transfer between two TELNET processes

In order to make the actual link between a process and the **TELNET** protocol transparent, the concept of a *pseudo terminal* is introduced (**pseudo tty**). A pseudo terminal is not a real terminal device (although many appear alongside existing terminals in the /**dev** directory of any UNIX system). They are implemented as if they were real terminal devices, though in reality they are implemented as software. The transparency offered by the pseudo device often leads to an application that does not know of the existence of the pseudo device, although it is communicating through it. Such applications treat the pseudo (software) device as hardware.

An example of a asymmetric protocol is the file transfer protocol **FTP**. The **FTP** protocol allows users to log in to a remote UNIX computer system, and then use the system as if it were their own host system (in reality, only a limited subset of the normal UNIX commands are available to the user). **FTP** is used to transfer files (normal ASCII files, or more complex files, such as binary executables, i.e. applications) from a remote machine to a local machine. **FTP** also allows third parties to join a session i.e. to engage in file transfers. In such a case one machine initiates a file transfer between two remote machines. The operation of **FTP** is more complex than that of the **TELNET** protocol. Firstly, TCP uses two **TCPs**, one for data transfer and one for signalling. The **TELNET** protocol is used by **FTP** for signalling purposes. This is done because **TELNET** has an authorization scheme to allow only registered users to transfer files, thus increasing the overall security of the system.

The terms *client* and *server* are generic terms and are used in both symmetric and asymmetric protocols. Server processes in 4.2 BSD UNIX are accessed at "well known" Internet addresses and/or UNIX domain names. The concept of well-known addresses has its disadvantages in that services that *move* i.e. which are relocated to another machine etc. cannot be found by client processes. In this case a mechanism known as a *binder* is used (although many other names are used, including *naming servers*). These systems act on the client's behalf to locate a particular service.

Address binding in the Internet domain

Address binding is explained in more detail in this section so that some of the complexities can be understood. Processes are bound by an *association* in the Internet domain. An association in this context consists of a local and remote address, and a local and remote port number. Addresses of all the host machines in your local network (and perhaps some remote networks also) should be available for viewing in the **/etc/hosts** file. Port numbers are allocated from each Internet protocol. Associations themselves are unique, and these should be no duplicates.

The **bind()** call specifies half of an association, while the **accept()** and **connect()** calls complete the association process (supplying the other half of the sockets' association). The association process is therefore seen to be completed in two separate stages. Many potential problems arise at this stage. For example, the two-stage association process could violate the uniqueness requirement for a particular association. Because a host may reside on more than one network, it is not practical to assume that processes will know their local port and address values.

It is possible to bind a port number to a socket and leave the local address unmentioned, as we have already seen in our server program. This can greatly simplify the coding process, although our code could not be considered to be truly portable since we have defined explicit port numbers as manifest constants, and both the client and server processes must know the common port number.

The concept of a *wildcarded* local address has already been seen in our small client/server programs. The **INADDR_ANY** manifest constant (defined in the **<netinet/in.h>** header file, is used to make the system interpret the address as *any valid address*, so we leave the work to the system where addressing is concerned. A socket that has a wildcard local address may therefore receive incoming messages that are directed to the specified port number, and which is also addressed to any (using the wildcard notation) of the possible addresses that are assigned to a particular host.

A port number can also be left unspecified. In this case it will be set to zero (0) i.e. **sin.sin_port = 0**. If a port number is set to zero the system will select an appropriate port number value for it automatically. The port numbers 0 to 1023 are reserved for privileged users, so an error will result if one of these numbers is selected by a user other than the super user (**root**, or a user with **root** status). The use of restricted ports was originally to allow processes executing in a secure environment to implement an authentication scheme based on the originating process, port and address values.

Datagram sockets

Another type of socket is the **datagram** (SOCK_DGRAM) socket. The advantage of datagram sockets is that we can send "broadcast" messages over a network i.e. messages will be distributed to all hosts even though the message may not even be addressed to them.

The datagram mode of operation tends to place a high load on the network (since all hosts will service the incoming data packets). The ability to send broadcast data packets in such a manner is therefore restricted to the Super User. However, the user can make use of a connectionless mode of operation through datagram sockets by *anchoring* the socket connection between two processes i.e. between the client and server programs. Requesting a datagram socket is quite simple, requiring a simple redefinition of the **socket()** call (see below). Beware though, that different read and write calls must be used in order to utilise datagram sockets.

Example 5 – Datagram socket creation

```
...
s = socket(AF_INET, SOCK_DGRAM, 0);
...
sin.sin_addr.s_addr = INADDR_ANY;
sin.sin_family = AF_INET;
sin.sin_port = MY_PORT;
...
bind(s, (char *)&sin, sizeof(sin));
...
dst.sin_family = AF_INET;
dst.sin_addr.s_addr = INADDR_ANY;
dst.sin_port = DESTN_PORT; /* locally defined constant */
```

The code fragment above shows how a datagram socket is created, along with the necessary value assignments to the **sockaddr_in** structure. Note the use of the addressing variables **sin** and **dst**. The **sin** value has been used in accordance with earlier conventions, whereas the **dst** variable is addressing the message we are going to send. The new calls to initiate the sending and receiving of data are called **sendto()** and **recvfrom()** respectively. The syntax descriptions for these two calls are:

```
sendto(socket, buffer, length, flag, pdestination, plen)
recvfrom(socket, buffer, length, flag, pdestination, plen)
```

where **socket** is our socket identifier variable, **buffer** is the data object we are going to send e.g. an array or a single character, **flag** is an integer value allowing us to specify the mode of operation for the data transfer, **pdestination** is the addressing parameter to a **sockaddr_in** structure for the outgoing message, and **plen** is an integer representing the length of the **sockaddr_in** structure addressed by **pdestination** (a **sizeof()** function can be used here for convenience).

The **flag** parameter is usually zero, although a non-zero value will allow extra facilities to be used during data transmission, such as the ability to send data without routing information being applied to the outgoing packets. A value of 0 will normally be used in the majority of **sendto()** calls. The **recvfrom()** call has the same syntax as **sendto()**, as can be seen from the syntax description. The **flag** parameter can take non-zero values for the reception of out-of-band data (use SOF_OOB constant here), or the ability to preview incoming data. This can be a useful mechanism and is used to preview *unread* information, that is, the data from the next **recvfrom()** call applied to the current socket will return the data that was previously previewed. Use (SOF_PREVIEW here). Check the manifest constant definitions on your system since they do tend to change between system.

Closing down a socket connection

Once a data transfer session has been completed, and a socket is no longer required, a call known as **close()** can be used. The **close()** call has the syntax:

```
close(socket)
```

In the case where a stream socket is being used (SOCK_STREAM) the process sending data to the process closing down the socket connection will try to continue transferring its data. In doing this, the data will be discarded if the data transfer continues for too long. If a process wants to discard such *pending* data the **shutdown()** call can be specified. It has the syntax:

```
shutdown(socket, flag)
```

where flag can normally take the integer values 0, 1, or 2. A **flag** value of 0 means that the process shutting down the socket connection (receiver) is not interested in any pending data (therefore the connection is *torn down* immediately). A **flag** value of 1 corresponds to the situation where no more data will be sent, and a value of 2 corresponds to the situation where no data is to be sent or received. Any queued data that a process is about to send will be lost (discarded) if the **shutdown()** call is applied to an existing socket connection.

3.10.7 Signals

In the small client-server programs already illustrated, there are no **close()** or **shutdown()** calls in the code. This is because the code has been structured simply to allow just transmission and reception of data. There is no way (in these programs) to signal the end of data transmission, since data is read by continuously accepting data from the keyboard. To overcome this problem, we can use a signalling mechanism to capture a specific event (such as an interruption from the user via the keyboard).

The header file **<signal.h>** should be included in the case where a signal is to be captured. Many signals are catered for in the UNIX system, although just one will concern us in this elementary introduction to 4.2 BSD socket IPC, namely the interrupt signal. This signal can be *captured* using the **signal()** call, and is generated most commonly by the keypress <Control-C>. It is called the SIGINT signal (or interrupt signal).

The **signal()** call is used with a constant value (defined in the file SIGNAL.H) that corresponds to the signal that is to be caught. Once the signal has been caught we can act on it. In our context we want to shut down our socket connections gracefully (perhaps even send a message to the recipient telling it of the intention to quit etc). The **signal()** call has the syntax:

```
signal(signal-type, handle)
```

where **signal-type** is a constant name i.e. SIGINT, as defined in the header file **<signal.h>**, and **handle** is the name of a C function that will be invoked when the signal is detected. This may be a simple void function (a function that does not return a value). The example code extract below illustrates how we can detect for the Control- C (interrupt signal SIGINT), and shut down our socket connection.

Example 6 – Capturing a SIGINT signal

```
#include <signal.h>
...

my_handle()
{
 int s;
 system("clear"); /* Clear screen; OK on most UNIXs */

 printf("Interrupt detected, closing down socket ...\n");

 shutdown(s, 0);
 close(s);
 exit(3);
}
...
main()
{
 ...
 signal(SIGINT, my_handle);
 ...
```

Of course, it is possible to shutdown our socket connections in a more *structured* way. In the code extract below, we can loop infinitely while testing for incoming data with a **recvfrom()** call. If the call returns a value less than zero (reception error), we can terminate the loop using a **break** statement (we do not use an **exit()** statement here since we would exist in an ungraceful way i.e. without shutting down our connection in an orderly fashion). The **break** statement will allow us to reach code that will eventually shut down the socket:

Example 7 – Structured solution to the shutdown of a socket

```
...
main()
...
 while(1) {

   /* Receive some data ... */
   if ((n = recvfrom(s, buf, my_len, 0, &dst, sizeof(dst)) < 0) {
      fprintf(stderr, "Error receiving data over socket.\n");
      break;
   }
   ...
   ...
   }

   shutdown(s, 2);
   close(2);
   exit(1);
 }
```

3.11 Questions

1. Name the two principal socket types for inter process communication using BSD sockets.
2. What is a protocol?
3. Name the seven layers of the OSI standard (in order, if possible).
4. In the "Yellow pages" naming service, define the following terms: YP map; YP client; YP Server
5. Name three packet types used in the X protocol.
6. Explain some of the concepts behind the PC-NFS protocol.
7. How are OSI and TCP/IP similar with respect to each other?
8. The OSI model can be said to comprise of two fundamental parts. What are these?

9. In the context of the Xlib X-Windows library, define the following terms: Bitmap; Pixmap; Window

10. Name and describe two fundamental components of a Local Area Network (LAN).

A Login Session with UNIX

4.1 Introduction

In this chapter we will learn how to identify ourselves to the UNIX system, a process that is known as logging in. If you want to continue learning about UNIX at the interactive level please read Chapter 6 after you have completed this chapter. If you cannot see the word ''login :'' on your VDU screen read section 4.2 below, otherwise proceed to section 4.2.1 now.

4.2 Logging In

To log in, you need access to a terminal connected into the host UNIX system. Because most systems tend to have their own initial screen displays, possibly offering a choice of one or more computer systems, there is no standard login screen, before you are communicating with UNIX.

If your terminal is not forthcoming with a greeting message, wake it up by pressing the RETURN key a few times. If this fails try turning the terminal on and off and start again. If this fails then it may be time to contact the systems administrator. If you do not have a Systems Administrator, you may have a problem. Before you call the Administrator or head for the manual, check that your terminal is on-line (a feature common to some terminals, which have a set-up key to allow you to set certain terminal characteristics). If you have now solved this problem, read on.

The only problem is that there is no standard way to wake a UNIX system up. You may have to key in a few options or you may be lucky and get in first time. The key word to look for on your screen is login:.

Login is actually a program that allows you to identify yourself to the UNIX system. If UNIX knows you, then you will be let in, in which case you can start reading the rest of this book. If you cannot log in, you cannot make use of UNIX. End of story. We assume that you have the login message on your terminal. On the next page we will examine a typical log-in session, and some partial screen displays will show you just what to expect.

4.2.1 User names

Figure 4.1 illustrates a typical login screen. At this stage UNIX requires you to enter a user-name. Your user-name should have been allocated to you by your systems administrator. If you are lacking a user-name, but are in an administrative capacity, refer to the section on adding new users in Chapter 11 – Systems Administration.

A user-name can be a mixture of upper- and lower-case characters as in the example below. This can help to distinguish users of the same name e.g. john and John. UNIX is a case-sensitive system, so remember that ''jim'' is not the same as ''Jim''.

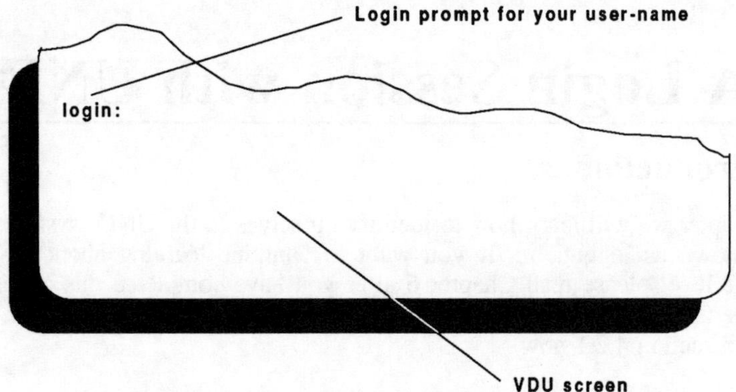

Figure 4.1 A typical login screen

When you see the login: prompt, enter your user-name and press the RETURN key. You must press RETURN to tell UNIX that you have entered some information, here your user-name. Figure 4.2 illustrates this event. Notice the UNIX password prompt.

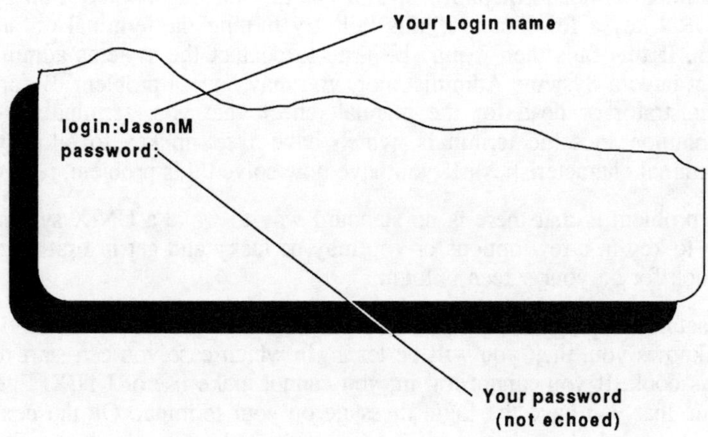

Figure 4.2 Typical login screen and password prompt

Once you have typed in your user-name, the password: prompt will appear. If you are using UNIX system for the first time, it is common to find that you do not have a password at all. This can be checked by pressing the RETURN key at the password prompt.

If you have not been allocated a password, a screen will appear similar to that in Figure 4.3. Not allocating a password to your account is not the best of ideas, even if you are a new user. Moan at your administrator about this. A good systems administrator will normally allocate a temporary password, temporary in the sense that it can be changed once you log in. This password is sometimes taken from a list of common words i.e. from a dictionary. These words are sometimes stored in a file in the UNIX system.

Temporary passwords should only be known to the systems administrator, who allocated them. They act as a safety mechanism to stop anybody else from logging in, other than the user who can prove his or her identity. Remember that if you do not have a password, anybody can log in as you.

4.3 Typical login messages

All UNIX systems display messages. Some messages appear when you log in and are normally stored in a file on the system. When UNIX detects that you have logged in, it either displays the message concerned, or a message exists for your attention.

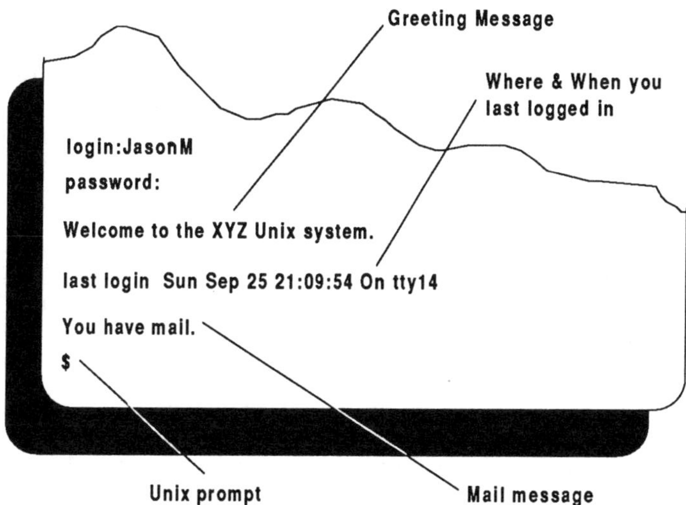

Figure 4.3 A completed UNIX login session

4.3.1 Message of the day (motd)

It is common for UNIX systems to display a message of the day file (motd file) to every user that logs in, although some systems leave this blank. In our example, the message of the day tells that we are indeed using UNIX, although the type of UNIX isn't actually shown. The name of the company, XYZ, is also shown. The motd file is discussed in Chapter 11 – Systems Administration.

4.3.2 Last login message

This message tells you the last time you logged in, and the name of the terminal that you used. UNIX stores all the times and dates of all the users who log in – so watch out, the big UNIX brother is watching you!

The last login message is useful since you can see if anybody has logged in with your user-name. This of course is only of any real use if you have a reliable memory. If you use UNIX infrequently it is doubtful that you will be able to remember just where and when you logged in last.

As mentioned, the login times and dates etc, are all stored on the system. Nearly all such files can be examined, depending on how security conscious your systems manager is. This data is collected because it is, supposedly, useful for examining the workloads of the system e.g. do these peak? Whether this data is useful for such purposes is debatable.

The process of recording all of this information is called *system accounting*, and this topic is examined in some detail in the Chapter 12 – UNIX Security, section 12.8 *Monitoring and Accounting Utilities*.

4.3.3 Mail messages

All UNIX systems have an electronic-mail system which allows users to send messages to each other across a network. The only problem is that the user, who you are sending the message to, may not be logged-in. UNIX gets over this problem by storing incoming messages in a type of mail-box. This mail-box is scanned every time you log in, and UNIX notifies you if there are recent messages to be read, hence the message "You have mail".

The whole process of mailing messages to each other is a somewhat strange concept, since most users will probably communicate orally anyway, and since most terminals are grouped together locally i.e. in a LAN environment. However, the advantages of electronic-mailing systems are enormous.

Firstly, take the concept of remote sessions, where users are accessing a UNIX network through a terminal which is not local to the system where they are logging in. In this situation, the E-mail system would be very useful, since the users may not meet frequently, or they may never even meet at all, hence a sort of pen-pals relationship would occur. Since both users access the same UNIX network, they will be notified of any new mail that awaits their attention.

Herein lies the main problem with E-mail systems: user participation. Some users are reluctant to read their mail, some users don't want to read their mail, and sometimes, users don't even know how to read their mail.

The UNIX electronic-mail facility is very large, and very powerful. Other smaller commands are available under UNIX to send messages directly to users. In this sort of system, a two-way link is established between the two users, and they can communicate directly. For more information on such communication systems, read Chapter 10 – UNIX Communication facilities.

4.4 The UNIX prompt

A prompt simply means that the system requires input i.e. it is prompting you for input. Such a prompt mechanism is common to all interactive computer systems, including MS-DOS, VAX/VMS and so on. The most common UNIX prompt is simply a dollar sign ($). On some Berkeley versions of the UNIX system i.e SunOS, the prompt is sometimes a percent sign (%).

You may even see a prompt character preceded by the name of the host system, like the prompt 'sun%', which some SunOS UNIX versions use. However, the $ sign is probably the most common UNIX prompt in existence, and we will use it throughout this book. Whenever you see the $ prompt, UNIX is awaiting your next command. The UNIX system is very subtle, and in most cases the only guarantee that a UNIX instruction was successfully accomplished, will simply be the return of the UNIX prompt on a new line.

4.5 Where have we actually logged into?

Because UNIX is a multi-user system, there has to be a place for storing the information belonging to each user. This 'place' is called a directory. A directory is simply a place where information can be kept together in one area, like a telephone directory that contains information regarding people's names, addresses and phone-numbers. In a typical UNIX system, there are probably hundreds of directories. Each user of the system will have a directory, while other directories will be reserved for the UNIX system itself.

When you first log in, you are initially placed in your home directory. Directories are discussed in the next chapter in more detail.

5

The UNIX File-system

5.1 Introduction

In this chapter we will explore the UNIX file-system which manages all the data stored on the system's mass-storage devices. We will look at the UNIX logical file organisation, showing how it stores and structures information, and at the physical organisation of the file-system, examining the way in which files are laid out on a typical storage device. Slightly more advanced topics towards the end of the chapter include file access mechanisms and file ownership.

5.2 Features of the UNIX file-system

Amongst the many features of the UNIX file-system, four main aspects stand out:

Hierarchical structure: The UNIX system organises its files using an upside-down hierarchical tree structure. All files will have a 'parent' file, apart from a directory called the 'root' directory, which is the parent of all files on the system. This hierarchical component also adds to the dynamic flexibility of the file-system.

Structureless files: Files are also said to be structureless, since the utility that creates the file normally dictates the internal format of that file.

Dynamic file expansion: The file-system structure is dynamic (greatly influenced by the hierarchical tree structure); that is to say, its size is not determined by any rule other than the amount of disk-storage that it is available on the system. A file's size can be changed at will by the user, at any time.

Security: Files are protected using file ownership mechanisms. These allow only a specific class of user to access certain files.

5.3 Overview of the file-system

Information in a UNIX system is stored in individual files. A 'file' is simply a collection of information, such as a letter, or the complete text for a book. UNIX imposes no rules about what a file should contain; a UNIX file simply occupies disk space on a mass-storage device. UNIX has many different types of files, the most common being ordinary files and directory files.

5.4 Directory Files

Directory files are the key to the hierarchical nature of the file-system, and UNIX was one of the first operating systems to implement such a structure. The hierarchical aspect improves access times, although care must be taken when structuring the file system i.e. if the file-system is not carefully planned, gradual deterioration in the speed of the system can result.

A directory is a special sort of file. It can contain ordinary files or additional directory files. With directories, the user has complete flexibility in grouping files in a meaningful way. A UNIX directory must have a name, normally of up to fourteen characters. These characters may be upper or lower case, or a mixture of both.

5.4.1 Path-names

A route to an individual file is called a path-name. In UNIX we find ourselves constantly referring to file-names, and because these files may be stored in different directories (as in the file-system previously shown) we need an accurate naming convention in order to locate them.

A typical UNIX file-system will have many levels in its hierarchy. Figure 5.1 illustrates a hierarchy with just two levels. A path-name is simply a list of directories grouped side by side.

5.4.2 Fully qualified path-names

A fully qualified or full path-name is the route to a file that starts from the root directory. The root directory, as we have seen, is the directory through which all files are linked; it is the parent directory of all files ('parent' meaning the directory file that lies immediately above the file in question).

The file-system hierarchy in Figure 5.1 has two levels. If we wanted to know the full path-name of the ordinary file ''L'' (on the bottom level) we would have to trace this file back up the tree to the root directory.

Each level in a UNIX path-name is represented by a slash (/). The root directory is one level because files lie beneath it, for example the directory file 'left'. Since this file is a directory file, there is thus another level to count. The file we require is called 'L', and it lies within the 'left' directory.

The file 'L' is not a directory, so there are no further levels to count, and hence there are only two levels in this tree (note the two '/'). Hence the full path-name for the file 'L' would be:

```
/left/L
```

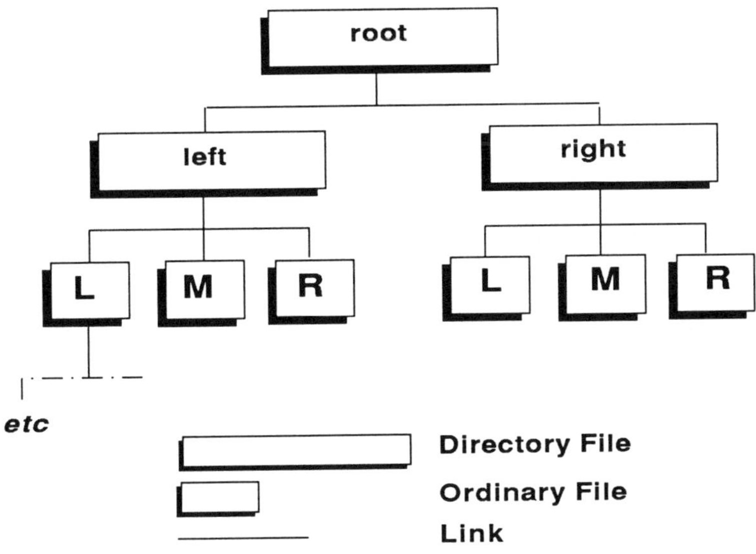

Figure 5.1 Typical File Hierarchy

Many common errors are found here. The root directory is not actually called 'root', but '/'. You could create a file named 'root' but it would not be the same as '/', which is the real root directory. The real root directory has no parent files i.e. there are no further levels above the root directory. Some people describe the root directory as a link to itself for this very reason. Figure 5.2 illustrates the use of '/' as a directory level separator, and also as a naming convention for the root directory.

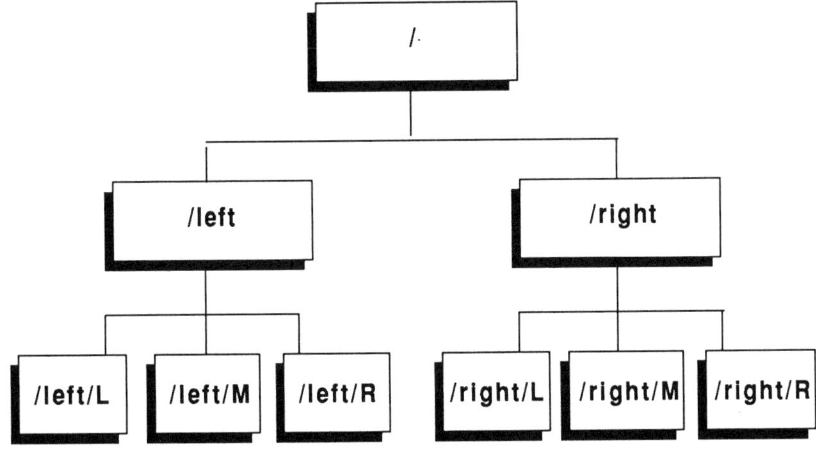

Figure 5.2 Typical File hierarchy with full file path-names

The following examples will give you a better understanding of Figure 5.2.

Full path-name examples

/ The full path-name Root directory of the root directory, the parent of all files.

/left The full path-name for the directory called **left**. This is a directory that exists inside the root directory.

/left/L The full path-name of the ordinary file called **L**. It resides in the directory file called **left**, which itself resides in the root directory. All the files here reside in the root directory.

/L Does not exist in this structure.

/right/R The full path-name of the ordinary file called **R**. It resides in the directory called **right**, which is just below the root directory level.

5.4.3 Partial path-names

When you work with UNIX, you will always be in a directory. The directory that you are working in is called the 'current working directory'.

Looking at Figure 5.2, let us assume that we are in the directory '/' which is the top level directory i.e. the root directory. If we wanted to refer to the file '/left/L' we would not have to use the whole name '/left/L' since we are already in the '/' directory. Instead we would only have to refer to the name 'left/L', because the root directory is our current working directory.

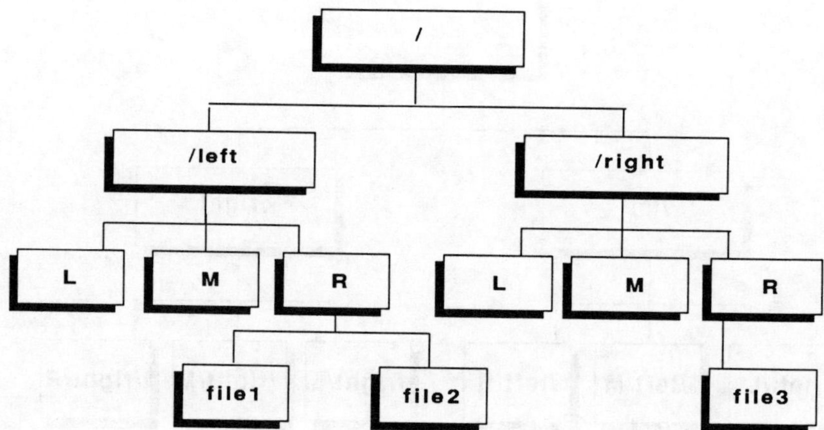

Figure 5.3 Extended version of Figure 5.2

Partial path-name examples

Assume that the current working directory is **/left**:

/R/file2 The partial path-name of the ordinary file called **file2**.

/left/R/file2 The same file as above, but we have entered the full path-name. We don't need the **/left** here, as the current working directory is already **/left**.

5.4.4 Path-name summary

In summary, the partial path-name is a shorthand notation. It omits the initial slash and directory names up to and including the working directory. A full path-name is simply a path to an individual file that starts from the '/' (root) directory.

5.5 Linked files and i-nodes.

Unlike some other operating systems that have hierarchical file-systems (such as MS-DOS systems), a UNIX file can have more than one name. A single UNIX file may also be identified in more than one directory. This is done by the use of multiple links to the file.

UNIX assigns a unique number to every file that is created in the file-system, and this is called an i-node number. Every file on the system must have one i-node (a unique number). Figure 5.4 illustrates the use of i-nodes for files that only have one link, i.e. files that are only known by one name (files are linked under UNIX via the use of the command 'ln').

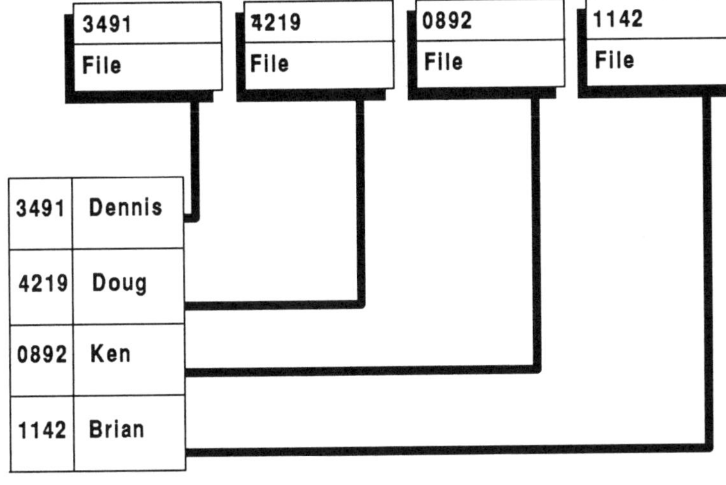

Figure 5.4. A typical UNIX directory with i-node links

Since UNIX can also have multiple links, a file can appear in more than one directory. Once the directory is entered, the link is followed and the user finishes up inside that directory (remembering that only one file has a unique i-node number means that both these files are the same).

The thing to remember is that the file is not duplicated – this would be a waste of disk-storage space, and would take longer to process. The key thing is, we are talking about the links to a single file, and where the links originate from doesn't matter.

This ability to link files is very useful, since different people can access the same file from different areas in the file-system. Figure 5.5 illustrates the concept of linked files. Here we have two directories, the directory on the left of the diagram contains one file whose i-node number links it to one individual file. On the right-hand side of the diagram we see another directory. This directory contains two links to the same file, since the i-node number is shared.

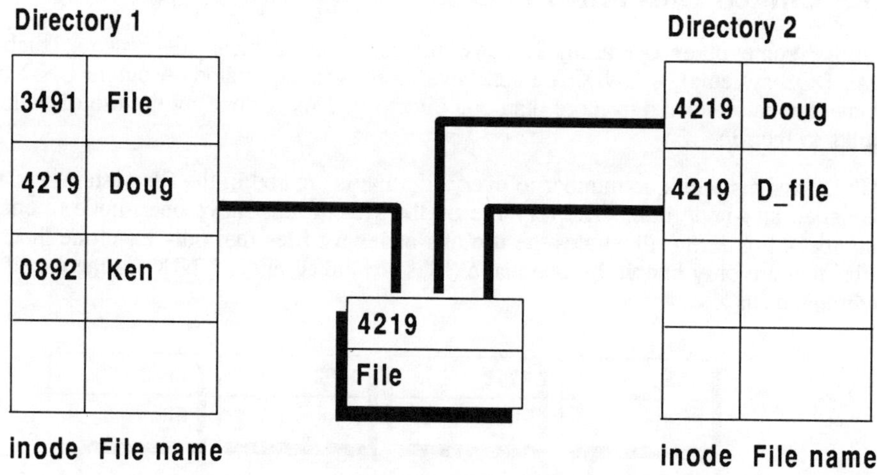

Figure 5.5 One file with multiple directory entries

If we take a look at a typical file-system, we can demonstrate how the file-system would look, when a linked file exists. In Figure 5.6 the ordinary file '/left/file2/link_file' is accessible from two directories, namely the '/left/file2' directory and the '/right/link_dir directory'. There are hence two full path-names for this one file.

5.6 Ordinary files

An ordinary file consists of a sequential series of bytes, which occupy disk-storage space. An ordinary file is different from a directory in that a directory allows layers of files to be built up. It therefore constitutes a 'leaf node' in the context of the tree-structured hierarchy, around which all our diagrams are based.

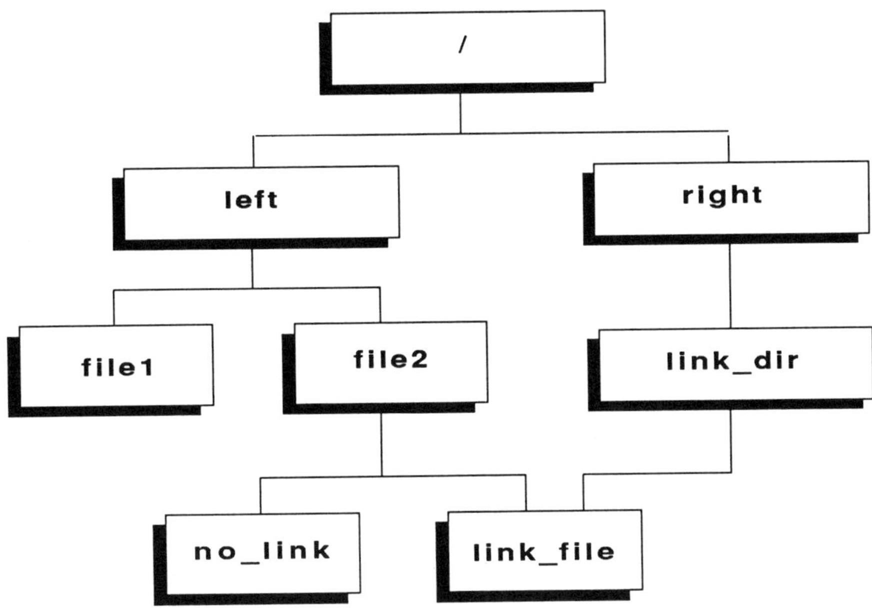

Figure 5.6. Hierarchy with two directory entries for one file

We mentioned earlier that UNIX imposes no rules regarding the internal format of an ordinary file. Ordinary files are created using text editors. UNIX supplies these editors as standard, and they can be found in various directories in a typical UNIX file-system. There are other ways of creating files, which will be discussed later.

For now though, we can think of an ordinary file as a group of characters. UNIX is not worried about the internal file structure; this type of file is structureless, which is a major advantage of the UNIX system. An ordinary file could contain text from a word-processing package, or it could contain something more complex, like a program written in the language of the Shell.

5.7 Special files

Special files are those that refer to devices such as terminals, printers, and other peripherals. The concept of a computer device as a file does seem rather strange, but it is a key advantage where device independency is concerned. All of the UNIX devices are stored in a directory called **/dev**, which resides immediately below the root directory.

5.8 File characteristics

All files have a number of characteristics that UNIX maintains automatically for the user. We have met a few already, for example the name of the file, and its location in the file-system using full path-name notation. Other information that is maintained by UNIX is:

❑ Location of the file (using the path-name convention)

❑ Size of the file (in bytes; one character is one byte)

❑ Link count (as an integer i.e. a whole number)

❑ Owner of the file (simply the owner's user-name)

❑ Time and date of creation and modification

❑ Security details (users who can access the file)

5.8.1 File security mechanisms

When you create a file, you automatically become the owner of that file. UNIX has a security mechanism called file ownership that dictates which files a user can access. We will examine this later, but first let us look at the access allocated to a file. The word access is a very loose term. Accessing a file in the simplest sense means simply to examine the contents of the file. However access is also available in other ways.

File ownership and permissions

UNIX supports three types of access to a file, and assigns a single letter to each of type of access, given here in the square brackets:

❑ Read access [r]

This allows the user to examine a file's contents. The file can be displayed and copied etc.

❑ Write access [w]

This access allows the user to alter and modify the contents of a file. A user can also delete a file if write permission is permitted on a file. The ability to both amend and delete a file are treated synonymously by UNIX.

❑ Execute access [x]

As mentioned earlier, files can contain a diverse amount of information, including programs i.e. Shell scripts or C source-code. When a file is "executed", the instructions held in that file are performed.

The UNIX system mainly consists of executable files called utilities. These utilities are stored in predesignated directories on the file-system. All of the access types just described can be granted and denied to three types of user:

❑ The owner/user of the file (you) [u]

❑ Group owners of the file (people like you) [g]

❑ Other users of the system (anybody else) [o]

The letters in the square brackets notation denotes how UNIX refers to each type of user in the system. These concepts are explained in more detail in Chapter 12.

5.8.2 Access permissions on directory files

The access permissions just described work slightly differently on directory files. Write [w] access on a directory file allows users to add files to that directory. Read [r] permission on a directory allows the user to list the files in that directory, and finally execute [x] permission on a directory allows a user to make that directory the user's current working directory.

The owner of the directory file has access permissions to read, write, and execute all the files in his or her own directory, except for the parent file.

5.8.3 Home directory access and permissions

Here we discuss the access and file ownership permissions that are assigned to your home directory, the directory in which you log initially.

Access permissions on parent files

All files, apart from the 'root' directory, have a parent directory. The 'root' directory (/) is the parent directory of all files on the system.

When you log in, you are placed in your home directory, a part of the overall file-system. Your own 'root' directory is the directory in which you are immediately placed after you have logged in. Note though, that your personal root directory is not called '/', the name '/' being reserved for the real root directory which lies at the very top of the file-system.

It should be said that each user will perceive the file-system slightly differently. We refer to a user's personal root directory as the directory in which they are first placed in upon logging in (see Figure 5.7).

UNIX refers to the parent file as '..' (two periods). The parent file is always a directory, and it exists in the level immediately above your current working directory. The use of a parent directory, and more importantly the use of the '..' notation, allows you to move upwards in the file-system (towards the root directory '/'). Moving down implies moving into directories that exist at a lower level.

If your parent directory contains the directories of other users, of which you are one, you probably find that the permission on the parent directory (..) is set so that you do not have permission to alter/delete files that exist at a higher level, for obvious reasons.

If you were working in the directory '/library/report/sales', then the parent directory would be '/library/report'. However, if your current working directory was '/library' then the parent directory would be the '/', the root directory, since it lies immediately above the 'library' directory.

Home directories in a typical file-system

Figure 5.7 illustrates a typical file-system structure that is used in some UNIX systems. It may be used in an academic environment where staff and student files must be distinguished. In this diagram, the staff have their own directory, as do the students. The dotted line area shows where the files belonging to user 'mark' are stored.

The root directory for **mark** is the directory '/staff/mark/', and all his files lie below this directory. We can also see that mark has structured his files into a miniature hierarchy in his own directory area.

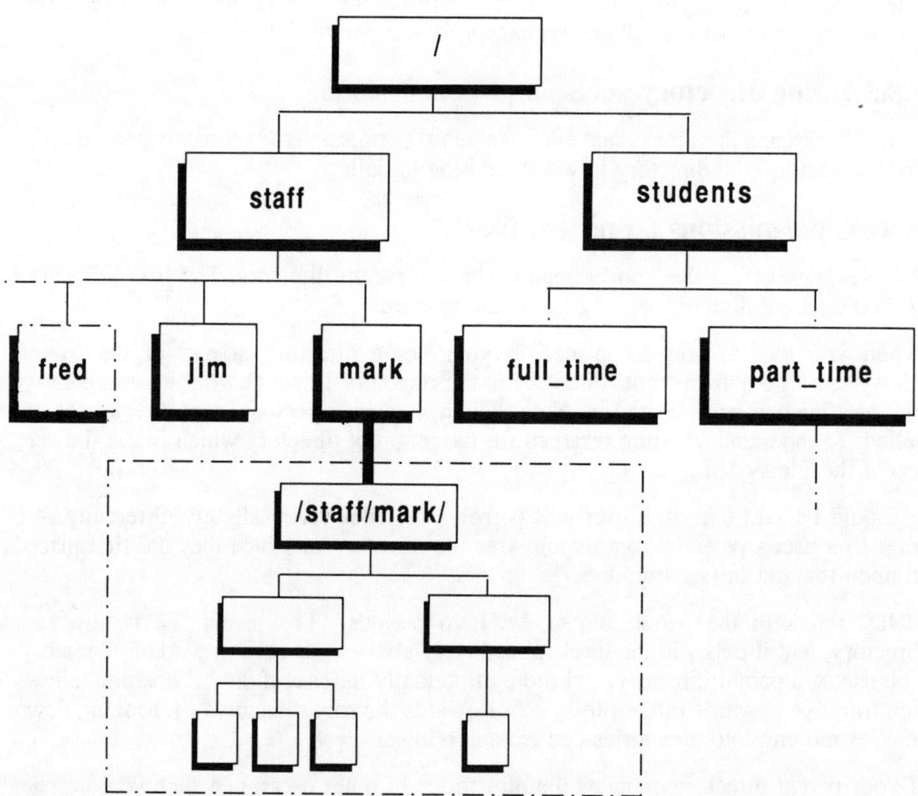

Figure 5.7 Home directory area for /staff/mark and his files

Removable disks and mounted file-systems

UNIX file-systems can become very large, especially where a large number of users have to be registered. In Figure 5.7 we see a file-system that was used in an academic environment, where staff and students have their files stored on the system.

UNIX systems can perform what is called a *mount* of the file-system. The process of mounting a file-system allows the systems manager to join different file-systems together to form one main hierarchy. Nearly all UNIX systems have at least one permanent non-removable hard disk as a principal source of mass storage.

A file-system called the root file-system is stored on such a device. This contains a smaller file-system, onto which other file-systems can be mounted. The user files (or directory areas) for all users of the system can be mounted separately from transportable disk media. UNIX systems commonly have removable disk devices so that the disk(s) can be taken away and stored safely.

The process of un-mounting a file-system is to remove a mounted file-system. The disk with the mounted file-system should not be removed until the file-system concerned has been un-mounted. Removable disks will have a file-system of their own, with a root directory as its top level directory. The mounting process is normally done by the systems manager when the UNIX system is started up, or bootstrapped. The advantages of mounted file-systems are not overwhelmingly apparent, but some examples are given below, along with the disadvantages of such a system.

Advantages of mounted file-systems

(i) The systems manager may want to deny access to a certain group of files before a certain time of the day. This may be done to alleviate pressure on the system. The systems manager may mount this system in a low system usage period.

(ii) Some files may be sensitive in terms of their security. The systems manager may therefore decide to mount such files at certain time periods, in order to improve security.

(iii) There is flexibility over the structure of the file-system. The systems manager could change the file-system quite easily by mounting other available file-systems. This would be less time consuming than altering a file-system that was contained on only one mass storage device such as on a non-removable device.

Disadvantages of mounted file-systems

(i) More and more application programs are making use of removable disk media for personal storage. The user now finds that the system must be fed disks so that the appropriate devices can mount different file-systems. Problems occur when the application's program cannot decide which device the file-system was mounted from, therefore it normally found that most users have to mount their disk file-system before running the application concerned.

(ii) Security is also a problem. It has been known for users to mount file-systems that contain special utilities to which only the systems manager normally has access. These various utilities have had their permission modes set to by-pass the security of the existing system. Figure 5.8, illustrates the concept of a mounted file-system.

You may notice a slight problem in with the file-system in Figure 5.8, namely the existence of a second root directory. We said earlier that to have two root directories would be completely unacceptable. UNIX gets over the problem of the second root directory problem by making the file-system's root directory 'transparent' to the user who passes straight through it, only accessing the files that lie beneath it.

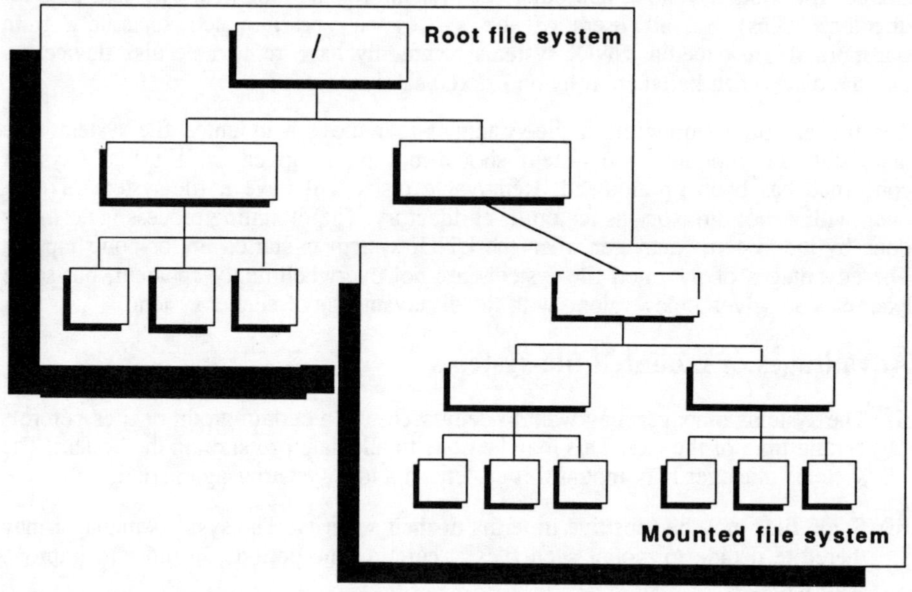

Figure 5.8 A typical mounted file-system

5.8.4 The standard UNIX file-system

UNIX uses the hierarchical file-system to organise its own files. There are many standard directories that you will find on all UNIX systems, and these are briefly discussed in this section.

A quick note on super-users

Super-users are granted absolute access to the whole UNIX system. They can carry out certain administrative tasks, such as starting up and shutting down the system, and intermediate tasks such as mounting file-systems and generally ensuring the smooth running of the system.

The super-user has the login name of 'root', an apt name since the super-user's home directory is '/', the root directory. The super-user's password is probably the most guarded secret on the system, and many good hacks have been carried out by obtaining it. The use of a user-name that matches a UNIX system directory is not uncommon, we will see other users who are less powerful than root, and who are also an integral part of any UNIX system. Chapter 11 examines the concept of super-users and privileged users in more detail.

Interesting system directories

This section examines some of the most important directories on the UNIX system. The directories given here are common to most System V, Xenix and Berkeley implementations of the UNIX system. On the next few pages we will examine twelve system directories that are common to the majority of UNIX systems.

The / directory

The '/' directory is the called the root directory, The '/' directory is known as the super user's directory. The user who logs in as **root** will be placed in '/' initially. The number of directories that are kept in / depends on the system in use, and the types of file-systems that are mounted. The root directory resides on a mass storage device (the root file- system), and is not normally mounted.

The /bin directory

The '/bin' directory contains essential UNIX utilities that all users will have to use at some time or another. The word 'bin' stands for binary, hence this directory contains binary files. A binary file is the product of a compiled C source-code program. The process of compilation speeds up the execution of such utilities.

Binary files are executable files. The common majority of UNIX utilities are all binary files, although some utilities are Shell scripts i.e. individual UNIX commands. Shell scripts are also executable, but they are not binary files. In this context, UNIX just executes a Shell script sequentially as a series of individual UNIX commands. Hence a Shell script is referred to as a type of interpreted language, the opposite of a compiled version. '/bin' is normally part of the root file-system.

The /dev directory

The '/dev' or device directory is where all the devices are kept. UNIX treats devices such as printers, disk-storage devices, terminals, and even areas of the computer's memory as a file. The files in '/dev' are termed special files, since the file types are neither directory or ordinary. The '/dev' directory will contain a file for each device on the network, so typical entries are file-names such as tty1, tty2 and so forth. '/dev' is also part of the root file-system. The files in '/dev' contain information which is common to all files such as file creation and modification dates, and file permission codes etc.

One important to thing to note about the '/dev' directory is that there are no file sizes. Instead, there are included what are known as *major* and *minor* device numbers. The major number encodes the type of device being referred to, while the minor number distinguishes between possible instances of the same device.

For example, the terminal **/dev/tty6** and **/dev/tty5** may be two ports on the same terminal controlling device, hence the two files would have the same major numbers, but different minor numbers.

Block and Special devices

File types in the '/dev' directory are not ordinary or directory as we have come to expect. Instead the type of file is either **character special** or **block special.** Disk and tape devices are all block special devices. All other devices are character special devices. These include terminals, printers, and even raw memory (these files are commonly named **/dev/kmem** and **/dev/mem** respectively).

A character device is simply a device from which characters are read. A block device is a device that is used only for the file system and can only be accessed by users via standard input/output requests such as for using the various UNIX utilities.

Block devices are divided into measures called blocks. A block is a unit of storage that is used to hold the i-node entries of a file or files. The position of these blocks is dictated by the i-node itself, or through a system called indirect-addressing. More details of the use of blocks and i-nodes can be found in *Chapter 6 The Physical File Structure of UNIX*.

The /etc ('et cetera') directory

The '/etc' directory, which resides at the root level, is a directory that contains various administration utilities together with other special system files that allow the host UNIX system to start up properly at bootstrap time.

Utilities for the handling of the system's terminal devices are stored in '/etc', as are the lists of all the registered users of the system, including you. The message of the day file (motd) can also be found in '/etc'. This file is displayed at login time, and is useful for displaying important system messages to users.

The /tmp directory

This directory is used for files that have a short life expectancy (temporary files). All users normally have permission to store files in the '/tmp' directory. The contents of this directory are normally deleted when the UNIX system starts up.

The /usr directory

This directory is fairly common on nearly all UNIX systems. It is the 'user' directory, which is commonly (but not necessarily) the parent directory for most of the everyday users of the UNIX system. Typically, '/usr' will contain many directories, one for every user of the system.

Because many systems cater for a lot of users, it is not uncommon to find additional user directories such as **u1**, **u2**, **u3**, or **usr1**, **usr2**, etc. This convention may also be used because file-systems may be individually mounted.

The /usr/adm directory

This directory is part of the '/usr' directory just mentioned, which is the parent directory of '/usr/adm'. The 'adm' stands for 'administrative' in this context, hence the '/usr/adm' directory, contains administrative utilities for use by the systems administrator, although most users will not be able to access them.

Accounting files that record user movements can also be found in this directory (see Chapter 11 Systems Administration).

The /usr/bin directory

The '/usr/bin' directory acts as an overspill for the '/bin' directory already described. It tends to hold binary file utilities that are of more use to normal users, whereas '/bin' contains utilities that could be considered more important to the end-user. Then again, this varies from system to system.

The /usr/games directory

This directory, as the name suggests, contains information about the many UNIX games that are available. On the whole, they tend to be incredibly boring, but there are a few that are worth a look, such as the addictive hack and nethack games.

The /usr/man directory

UNIX has quite a few on-line help facilities, of which 'man' is one. **Man** is the UNIX manual feature, a small UNIX utility program, that enables access to information on all UNIX utilities.

Approximately five thousand pages are available for viewing using the man utility. Information is included about all the UNIX commands that are available on your system, so get reading.

The /usr/src directory

This is a directory that contains the source-code for many of the binary utilities mentioned so far. Some UNIX sites keep the source code for hundreds of programs so that they can make their systems more flexible.

Site independent code can also be generated, and minor alterations to source-code to meet the purposes of the host UNIX system can be made.

All the source-code is written in a high-level language called C. These source-code programs are then compiled for speed, and are then placed in the various system directories, such as '/bin' for use by us. This process is sometimes referred to as the *installation of the executables.*

Other directories

In addition to those directories mentioned above, there are numerous other directories on all UNIX systems. The types of directories that you will come across will depend on the system that is being used, and the facilities that it includes.

You may also try to note changes in the file-system of your UNIX system. Many systems continually change, through the process of 'upgrading' the system. One thing that most serious UNIX users like to do, is to keep up-to-date listings of the main directories in a file-system, and then compare them at frequent intervals. When an upgrade occurs, or the systems manager installs some new executables, you can note the change, and conduct a quick examination.

All of these facilities are very simple to learn and use and all the necessary UNIX commands to carry out such tasks will be shown to you in the appropriate chapter. In this case you would need to read Chapter 7 on the UNIX Shell.

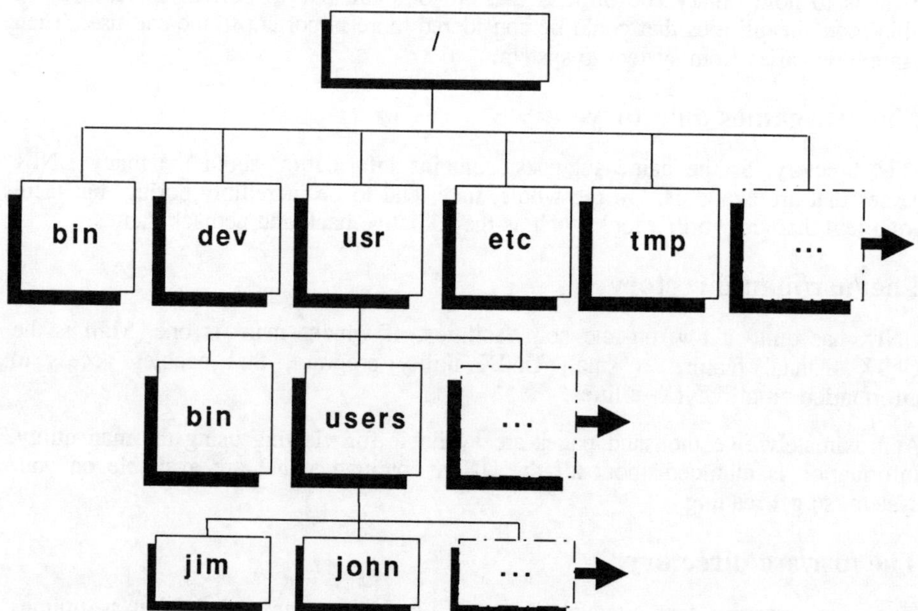

Figure 5.9 Typical 'standard' UNIX file-system with user directories included

5.9 Questions for Chapter 5

1. Explain what a parent file is.
2. Which file is the parent of all files?
3. What is the difference between the location of the two files /usr/john/file and /usr/john/file/?
4. What are the three types of user classification that can be used when setting the access protection on a file(s)?
5. Explain the difference between a 'mount' operation and an 'un-mount' operation?
6. List two disadvantages of mounted file-systems?
7. What is a file-system?
8. Explain the use of major and minor numbers?
9. In whichdirectory are the various system devices held?
10. Give the name of the directory whose contents are normally deleted at system-startup time.
11. What is a path-name?
12. Explain the difference between a partially qualified path-name and a fully qualified path-name?
13. What is the current working directory?
14. Explain what an i-node is.
15. How do character devices and block devices differ?
16. What is the root file-system?
17. List three access attributes that can be assigned to a file.
18. What is the special notation for a parent directory?
19. List three features of the UNIX file-system.
20. What do we mean by a structureless file?

6

The Physical File Structure of UNIX

6.1 Introduction

This short chapter deals with the physical elements of the UNIX file-system, including i-nodes and disk file organisation.

6.2 Overview

The UNIX file-system structure is a randomly addressable collection of characters. The maximum size of the file-system is simply the size of the disk-storage device that supports it. **Deitel [1]** defines the size of a UNIX file-system to be in the region of about one billion characters.

The file-system itself is contained on disk devices that can be found in the '/dev' directory. These disk devices are normally composed of blocks (512 bytes each). The more modern System V versions of the UNIX system use 1-Kilobyte sized blocks (1024 bytes each). Figure 6.1 illustrates a typical structure of a file-system.

6.3 Disk Blocks

A disk is broken down into four zones:

- ❑ The boot block.
- ❑ The super block. This contains the size of the disk being used, and its boundaries i.e. the allocated disk-space already used.
- ❑ The i-list. The i-list simply contains a list of i-nodes.
- ❑ The free-list (a list of unused blocks).

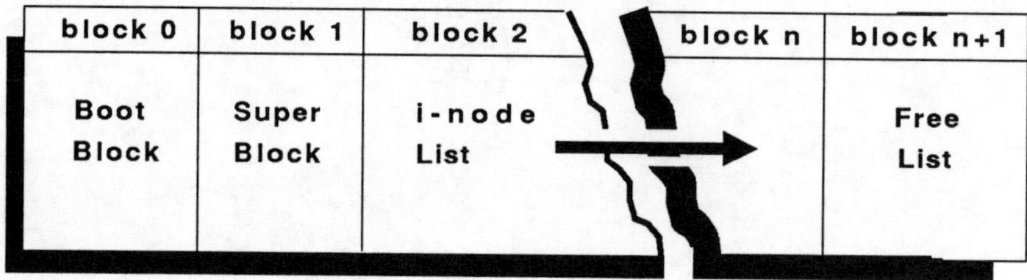

Figure 6.1 Overall structure of a typical file-system

6.4 Disk Blocks

6.4.1 The boot block

The boot block is block zero of the disk concerned. This is normally the first track of the disk, and it contains the bootstrapping program. This program is normally a standalone utility that is used to bring the UNIX system into operation.

The kernel of the UNIX operating system is sometimes contained in the file /unix. This is read from disk into the computer's memory at boot time. Before the kernel is loaded into memory, a program called /boot is read. This contains instructions in the form of a program that tells UNIX how to load the kernel.

6.4.2 The Superblock

The superblock is block 2 of the disk file-system. It contains information regarding the whole disk file system. It typically contains the actual size of the disk (the total number of blocks that make up that device), and the number of blocks that have been allocated to it for the i-nodes in the system. It also contains the address of the next list of unused data blocks (this may involve stepping over some existing data blocks that are already allocated).

6.4.3 The i-list

The *i-list* (i-node list) is probably the largest part of the file-system, since one i-node will be allocated to every file on the system. The actual number of i-nodes that can be stored is calculated by taking the total number of blocks, and then dividing this by the number four (the number of regions in the file-system). Of course the actual disk space size must be taken into consideration, to make sure you do not run out of disk-space.

For example, a disk device with 20,000 blocks will give 5,000 i-nodes i.e. 20,000 divided by 4. Since the number of i-nodes is 5,000, the number of possible files that could be created is also 5,000. Five thousand files may seem quite considerable, but waste of disk space is a continual problem. Disk space is lost because of the size of individual files created on the system. For example, System V uses a block size of 1 Kilobyte. If the average size of file created on the system is about 4 Kilobytes, the system will run out of i-nodes when only 50% of the block space is used!

Another problem occurs when the average size of an individual file tends to be on the large side. Here a problem can occur because the block limit becomes exhausted. This may happen even if there may be hundreds or possibly thousands of i-nodes left unused in the file-system. The solution to the problem of allocating the appropriate amount of blocks is really only achieved through experience.

It is good idea to check the average file size on a particular system, and then carry out the calculation, dividing the number of available blocks by the average file size. It is also beneficial to allocate more blocks than were initially calculated (if they are available) as a safety precaution.

6.4.4 The Free-list

The free-list is simply an area that is made up of unused data blocks. The free list area contains the addresses of these free data blocks. Figure 6.2 illustrates this concept. In our diagram 'pointers' are used to link the free data blocks. The individual i-nodes can be seen along the top, in a horizontal direction.

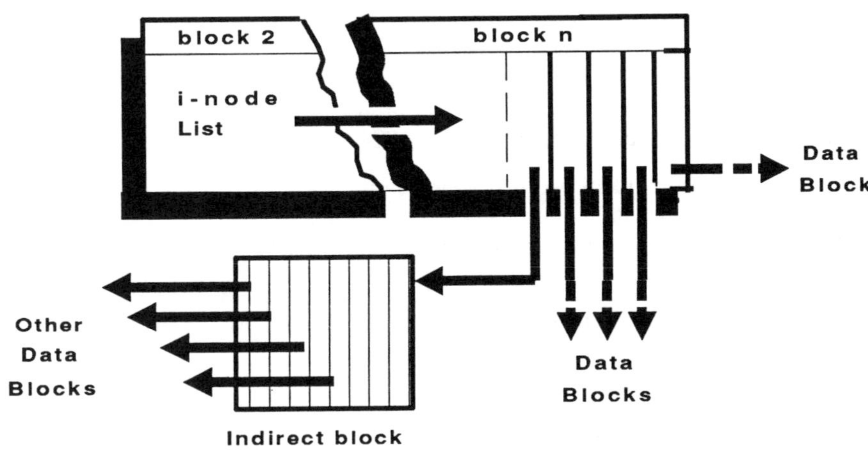

Figure 6.2. The concept of an indirect block

Individual data blocks may also hold 'indirect blocks'. Indirect blocks are used because the individual links from an i-node may be fully allocated. Thus, indirect blocks are used to address other free data blocks.

6.5 I-node structures and more

A typical i-node contains seven main elements:

- ❑ Owner's group identification
- ❑ Owner's user identification
- ❑ File type
- ❑ Protection information
- ❑ Date of file creation
- ❑ Date of most recent access/modification
- ❑ Pointers to individual data blocks/indirect blocks

6.5.1 Directories and I-nodes

The i-node contains much more information than an actual directory entry does. A typical directory will normally hold information about the file in the form of a name (up to 14 characters in length), and a unique i-node number.

Directories are only really acting as mapping devices. They simply provide UNIX with a means of locating the address of file through the i-list. When a user refers to a file, UNIX simply searches for that file in its file-system by the path-name supplied. Once it finds the directory, it notes the i-node number, and then jumps to that particular i-node entry which is stored in block 2 of the file-system (in the i-list).

Once UNIX finds the i-node in the i-list, it follows the pointer from that i-node to the data block indicated. This eventually leads to the required data. The first ten blocks of data in this file can then be read (a maximum of 5120 bytes if you are using a non-system V UNIX system), or a maximum of 10240 bytes (just over 10 Kb) if you are using System V, which commonly uses a 1024-byte block size.

Block 11 is the indirect block we mentioned earlier. It is used if the i-node becomes full with links to other data blocks. This block contains the addresses of the next 128 data blocks in the file-system (on a 512 bytes per block system), if they are allocated.

Data block numbers 12 and 13 also act as blocks which refer to yet more data blocks. This entails three levels of indirect addressing i.e. an address of an address which finally leads to the address required.

6.5.2 Internal File Structure

We have talked about the structure of a disk device in a broad sense, but what about the file itself? There are no rules dictating how a file's internal structure should look – hence the term structureless files. However, there is one type of file organisation used by UNIX: this is simply a sequential organisation, a group of bytes side-by-side. Individual bytes in a file are identified by their position, relative to the beginning of the file. Figure 6.3 illustrates a typical framework for this type of file.

Unlike UNIX, many operating systems organise files into records of a finite length, known as fixed-length records. This sort of structure has many disadvantages, one of which is the clash between the structure of files created by the user and the structure imposed by the disk device. For example, most of us will not even think about the organisation of a disk when we are typing in a document, but the host operating system will have to take this into account.

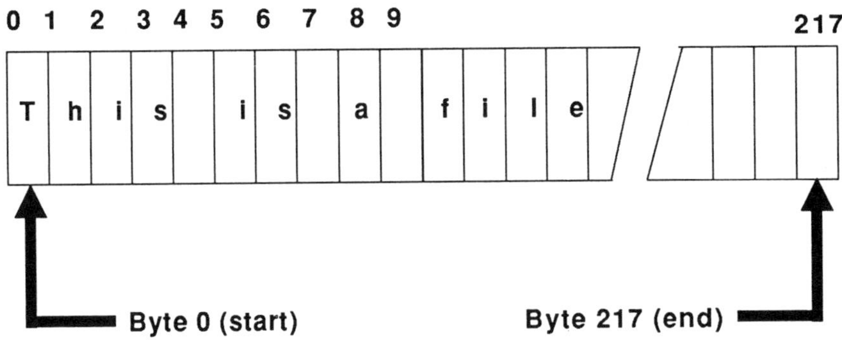

Figure 6.3 UNIX file organisation

The program which accesses the data that the user is working on will have to translate the requirements for the access of pieces of individual data into requests for areas of the disk being used i.e. requests for disk records. UNIX overcomes this problem by eliminating record structure, and using a file that is simply groups of sequential bytes (which are typically 217 bytes in length).

6.5.3 Disk Storage Organisation

We have briefly talked about disk blocks already. This section extends the concept of file access *via* i-nodes, and indirect addressing techniques. We understand UNIX files to be dynamic. They can grow as large as there is disk space available, and they can also contract in size. The UNIX file-system is hierarchic in structure, as is the organization of the disk storage area; however, the latter normally only goes to about five layers (whereas the actual file-system can be much deeper).

We also understand that UNIX organises its disks into areas of typically 512-byte blocks (noting that this figure is commonly 1024 bytes on the System V implementation of UNIX). These blocks may be scattered in what is termed a non-contiguous area. This is an area in which the files are not stored sequentially and it happens simply because the disk area (or rather, the superblock) is being constantly updated by the operating system.

The i-node of a typical file also stores the links to the first ten blocks of a file (using a 512 byte block) along with the other information mentioned in section 6.5. An i-node is normally resident in the computer's memory (for purposes of speed), hence only one disk access is normally needed to retrieve these blocks of information. This in turn implies that UNIX tends to favour the processing of shorter files, than longer ones. Once a file is determined to be larger than 10 blocks, a method known as indirect addressing is employed, where UNIX refers to an indirect block, as already seen in outline in Figure 6.2. Figure 6.4 extends this concept.

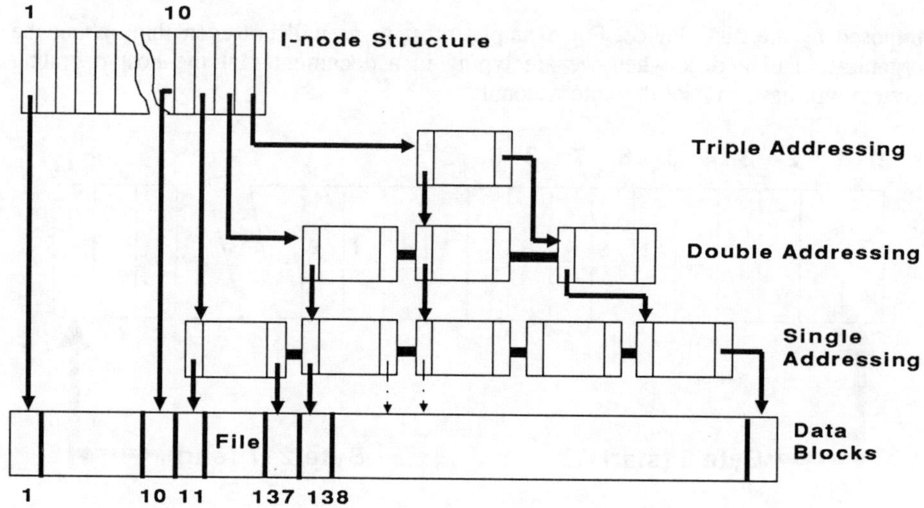

Figure 6.4. Extended Version of Figure 6.2

The method of indirect addressing allows the UNIX system to handle larger files. UNIX System V uses a 1024-byte block size (1 Kb), which allows disk access to transfer twice as much information, hence less input/output activity. Other versions such as Berkeley UNIX, use a 4096-byte block size (4 Kb). This results in a much more efficient disk access rate, and hence input/output activity is kept to a minimum.

6.7 Questions for Chapter 6

1. What is the advantage of a 1024-block system over a 512 block-system?
2. Name the one UNIX system in this chapter that uses a block size that exceeds 1024 bytes?
3. Why are "indirect" blocks used?
4. What is an indirect block?
5. UNIX files are termed "dynamic". Why is this?
6. What is the maximum size of a UNIX file-system?
7. Name the four regions of a typical disk.
8. What is the superblock?
9. Name five pieces of information held in an i-node.
10. What is an i-node?
11. What is significant about the boot block?
12. What does non-contiguous mean in the context of file storage?

7

The UNIX Shell and Utilities

7.1 Introduction

This chapter introduces the user to the UNIX shell, the command interpreter. The shell is the most widely used utility program on all UNIX systems since it is from the shell that UNIX receives its instructions. The shell is the key to the interactive nature of the UNIX system. This chapter also introduces a few of the most frequently used UNIX commands that can be issued from the shell.

7.1.1 Shell Features

In this first section of Chapter 7, we will discuss the features that the UNIX shell offers the user. These features will be explained in separate sections later.

- *Interactive Environment:* The shell allows the user to create a dialogue between the user and the host UNIX system. This dialogue lasts until the user ends the session.

- *Shell Scripts:* It is the shell that has the facility to be 'programmed'. The shell contains internal commands which can be utilised by the user. Shell scripts are groups of UNIX commands strung together and executed as individual files. The shell is itself a program, except that it is written in C.

- *Input/output redirection:* UNIX commands can be instructed to take their instructions from files, and not from the keyboard. The shell also allows the user to place the output of UNIX commands into a file and not on the screen of the terminal. Output can also be redirected to other devices, such as to a printer or even another terminal on the network.

- *Piping Mechanisms:* UNIX supplies what is called a 'pipe' facility that allows the output of one command to be used as input in another UNIX command. The UNIX file-system contains many utilities that are useful for such purposes. They are designed for piping in mind, although in reality the majority of UNIX commands were designed to be strung together in a pipe.

- *Metacharacter facilities:* Apart from the normal characters found on a keyboard, i.e. letters and digits, the shell provides the use of what are called metacharacters. These allow the user to apply selection criteria when accessing files, for example the user could access all files that begin with the letter 'm' They also help to speed up the selection of files and can be used in UNIX pathnames.

- *Background processing:* True multi-tasking facilities allow the user to run commands in the background. This allows the command to be processed while the user can proceed with other tasks. When a back-ground task is completed, the user is notified. For example, the user could request UNIX to search the whole file-system for a particular file. This task would in theory take quite a long time while every directory on the system is scanned for files matching the name you specified. This would be a good example of when to use the background facilities. Multiple background jobs are possible on nearly all systems.

- *Customised Environment:* The shell is your working environment. Facilities are available by which the shell can be customised for your personal needs.

Some UNIX systems supply many different shell environments. An example is the 'C-Shell' which has been developed with C programmers in mind.

7.2 The Interactive Shell

The shell is a program that is continually running during your session with UNIX. In this short section we cover some of the features of the shell.

7.2.1 Terminating the Shell

Terminating the shell makes UNIX sever the communications route from the host computer to your terminal, the process of logging yourself out. The control keystroke **<ctrl-d>** will nearly always terminate your shell although it is common for some UNIX systems to intercept this keystroke, and insist that you supply a UNIX command to log yourself out.

The **<ctrl-d>** keystroke generates an ASCII end-of-file code. UNIX actually treats your whole UNIX session as the opening and closing of a file, where the shutting of the file implies the end of the communications link (a log-out).

Figure 7.1 illustrates the 4 steps involved in a typical user session with the UNIX shell. Firstly the user has to log in, a two-way interaction, since UNIX asks the user for a user-name, and the user responds with a password. Second, the shell prompts the user for input, a one-way communication from the shell to the user. Third, the user enters a command be processed at the shell prompt. Finally, the command is processed, and shown back to the user, again a two way interaction. At this stage the user either logs-out (using **<ctrl-d>**), or the user can enter another command. This process continues, until the user chooses to log out.

7.2.2 Command Structure

The UNIX prompt is the place at which all UNIX commands are entered. Nearly all

UNIX commands have a common structure which dictates how that particular command will operate.

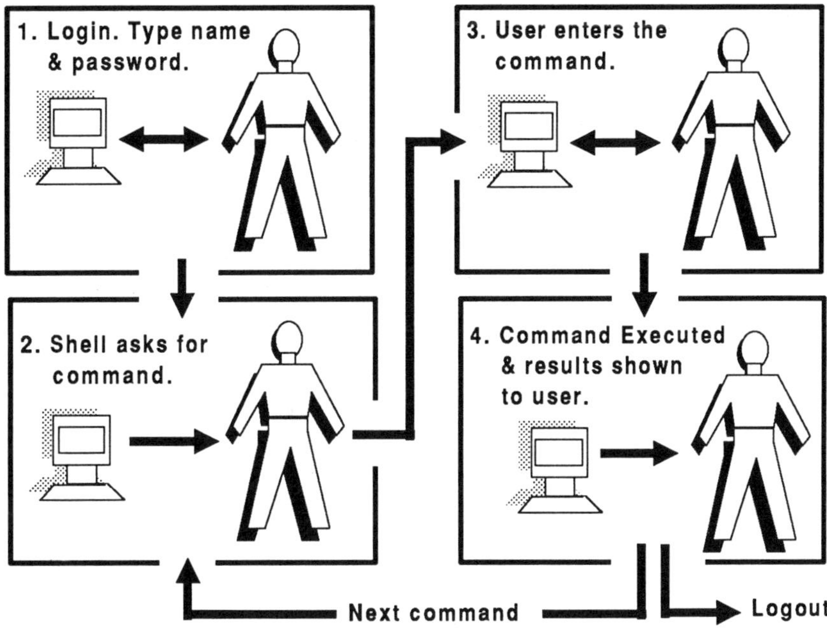
1. Login. Type name
& password.
2. Shell asks for
command.
3. User enters the
command.
4. Command Executed
& results shown
to user.
Next command
Logout

Figure 7.1 A typical session with the Shell

Figure 7.2 illustrates a typical command line. The command line will firstly consist of a UNIX command name, the name of a UNIX utility, followed by a list of options which control how the command will work, and what sort of output it will produce. Finally there is an argument – the data which is to be processed by the command.

An argument is most commonly a filename, although some commands do not require a filename as an argument, and some do not even require any arguments at all. Commands without arguments simply imply which data they are processing, and what output is required. Some UNIX commands can also accept multiple arguments. In such a case the arguments are normally typed in next to one another, separated by a blank space.

7.2.3 Default arguments

As shown in Figure 7.2, a UNIX utility is executed by typing its name on the command line, followed by an option list, and then an argument. Some UNIX programs can run without an argument, but still refer to a file without any mention of it on the command line.

This is because some UNIX utilities have the ability to default to a particular filename. This file is normally specified in the source code for the utility concerned i.e. it is embedded in the compiled version of the file (the binary version). Typical examples are the various accounting utilities on many UNIX systems, which without arguments simply default to a predefined file on the file-system that contains the correct data to be processed.

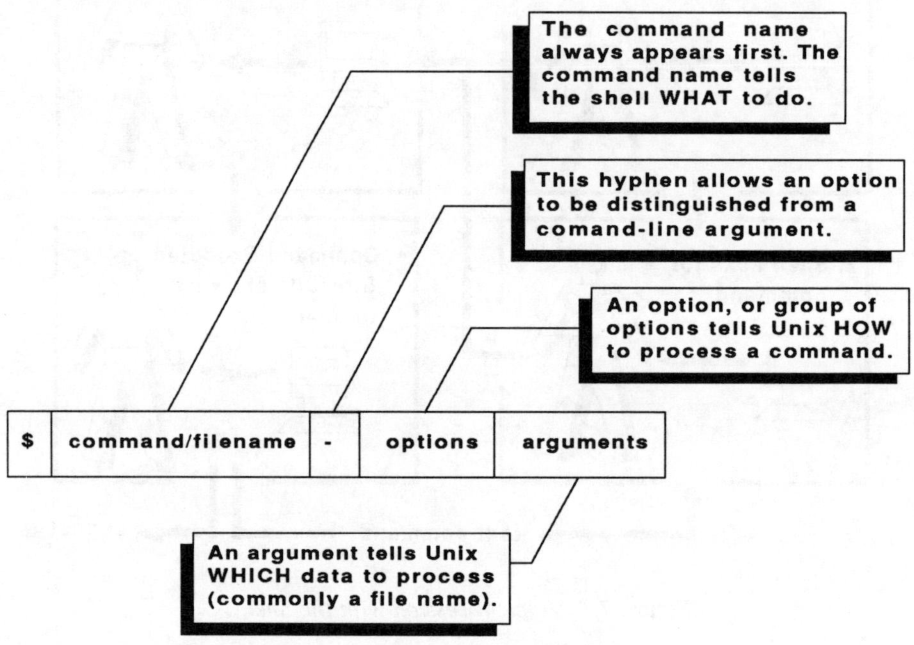

Figure 7.2 A Typical Command Line

7.2.4 The Standard input, output and error files

When a file is executed from the shell, the shell runs the program and simultaneously assigns the executing program to what are termed 'standard' files. These standard files are:

- The standard input file from where a program takes its input data.
- The standard output file which will receive the output of the utility program.
- The standard error file which will receive any error messages that are generated by the utility program.

By default, all three files are assigned to the user's terminal. This is because the system assumes that the standard input file is the user's terminal device. The user, logically, supplies input through the keyboard. However, the user could rightly specify that input should arrive from a file.

If the standard output file is also the terminal device, then the output of a program will go to the screen of the terminal device, which again seems the appropriate place. However, you could send the output to a multitude of output devices such as a printer or even another user's terminal screen (if you have the necessary write-permission on that person's device).

The standard error file is also, by default, the user's terminal device. This is so that any errors that may occur can be displayed on the user's terminal, upon which the appropriate action may be taken. However, if we wanted to, we could make any occurring errors go to a file for later examination, or to another device. The standard file assignments are shown below in Figure 7.3:

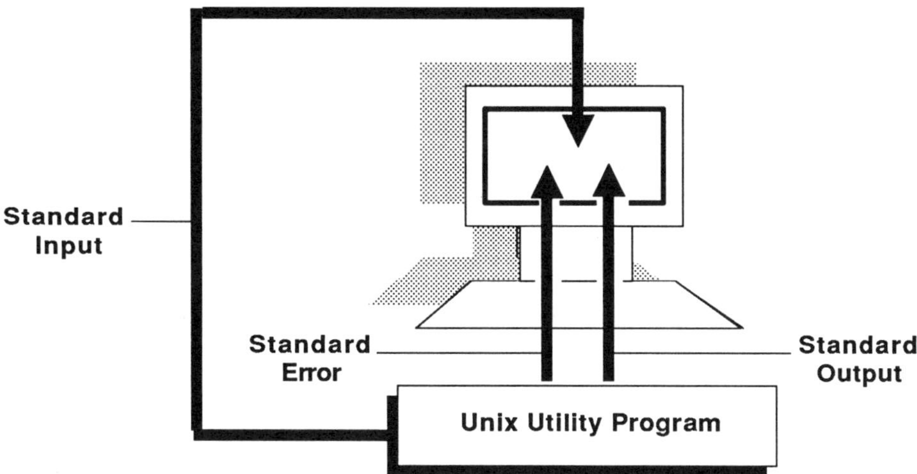

Figure 7.3 Default settings for standard files

7.3 General file utilities

In this section, we will examine some of the most fundamental file handling utility commands which are essential to every UNIX system. These commands appear frequently in the later chapters of this book, where the more complex file manipulations are described.

These commands have been chosen because they are common to the majority of UNIX systems, including System V, Berkeley Systems Distribution (BSD), Ultrix and Xenix, etc.

The following commands are covered in this section: **cd**, **pwd**, **cat**, **passwd**, **file**, **rm**, **cp**, **rmdir**, **ls**, **touch**, **mkdir**, **tty**, **mv**, **sort**, **tail**, **grep**, **wc**, **time**, **mesg**, **mail**, and **who**. Brief syntax descriptions of the commands concerned are also given. The [ ] brackets denote optional command parts. Essential (compulsory) command parts are enclosed in angle brackets (< >).

7.3.1 Cd – change the working directory

Syntax

cd [*pathname of directory*]

Description

Cd is the UNIX command that changes the current working directory (**cd** being an abbreviation for change directory). **Cd** is used to allow the user to move up and down through the file-system hierarchy. Moving 'up' involves moving into directories that are nearer to the root directory, the highest level being the root directory itself. Moving downwards through the file-system is achieved by entering directories that lie beneath the directory where you are currently working.

The syntax description states that the pathname of the directory where you want to move to is optional. This is because **cd** used on its own (i.e with no arguments) simply makes the new directory the home directory where you logged in originally.

Apart from normal directory names, for example, **/tmp, /dev** the **cd** command recognises two other special directory names, namely **'.'** and **'..'**. The double dot notation tells UNIX that we want to make the current working directory the parent of the directory we are currently in. The single dot notation is simply another name for the current working directory i.e. if we were in the directory **/usr/john/mydir**, then **'.'** would also hold the value **/usr/john/mydir.**

The single dot directory name is not commonly used with **cd**, since you do not achieve anything by continually moving into the same directory. Its use is more apparent in other utilities shown later in this chapter.

Fully and partly qualified pathnames can be used with the **cd** command. If a directory in a **cd** command does not contain an initial slash, i.e. a '/' sign, UNIX assumes that you want to move into a directory which is relative to the current directory.

For example, if our current working directory is **/usr/john**, and we want to move into the directory **/usr/john/file/dir1**, we would use **cd file/dir1**. When a pathname has an initial slash, **cd** assumes that the user wants to move to a directory relative from the root directory.

Examples for use with Figure 7.4:

$ **cd /**	Moves us into the root directory
$ **cd /dev**	Moves us into the /**dev** directory
$ **cd .**	Same place again.
$ **cd /dev/**	The same place again.
$ **cd /ul/link**	We have moved into a linked directory. The current working directory is now **/usr/users/mike.**
$ **cd /dev/..**	This pathname refers to the parent of /**dev**, which in this case is /.
$ **cd ..**	Does not exist if we are in the / directory.

$ **cd tmp** Works if we are in the / directory since **/tmp** and **tmp** are the same if the current working directory is /.

$ **cd** Takes us back to our initial login directory.

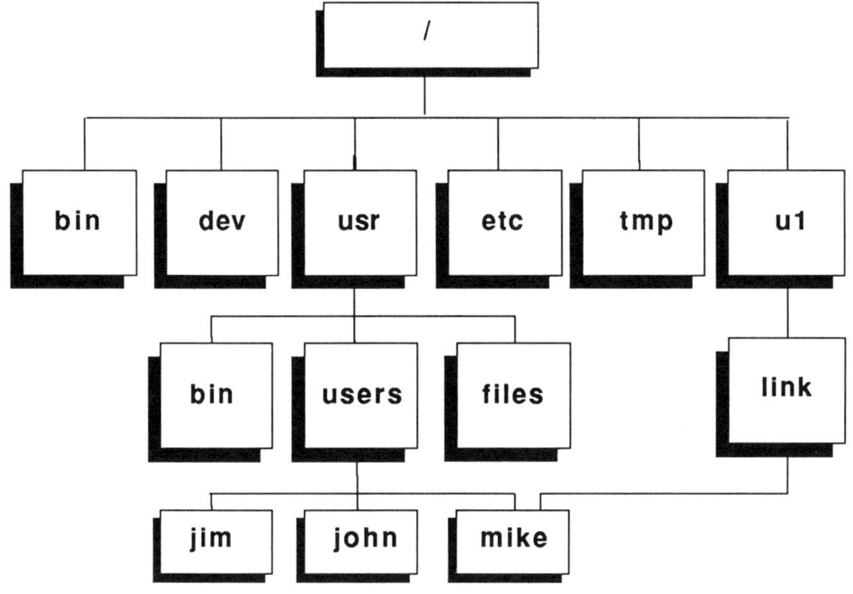

Figure 7.4 An example file-system

Common error messages

Invalid directory The directory you specified does not exist in the file-system.

Permission denied Execute permission has been disabled on this directory, hence you cannot make it your working directory.

7.3.2 Cat – concatenate files

Syntax

cat [*<filename 1>* .. *<filename n>*]

Description

Cat is a UNIX utility that is used to display the contents of an ordinary file. **Cat** can however, be used with other files, but the files that you are trying to display may appear as gibberish, and since non-ordinary files tend to contain a multitude of control characters, your terminal may lock-up in the process.

Cat should only be used with plain-text ASCII files, which are plentiful on any UNIX system. For example, shell-script files are plain ASCII files since they are groups of shell commands. From the syntax description we can observe that **cat** can work with one or more input files, hence the name concatenate. Concatenation (or simply catenation) is the process of joining pieces of data, such as simple character strings. UNIX takes this a step further, and allows the user to concatenate whole files (which in reality are only groups of character strings anyway).

The syntax description also implies that **cat** can be used without any arguments. If you type **cat** on its own, **cat** will read from the standard input file (see section 7.2.4). You could, at this stage proceed to type in the names of a few files, and then signal that you want them to be processed.

Since the standard input is associated with a file (the standard input file), we could send an end-of-file code to cat, to tell it to process the files i.e. a **<ctrl-d>** keystroke. Once this has been done, **cat** has no further input, so it simply proceeds to display the files. Use **<ctrl-c>** to interrupt the program, or **<ctrl-z>** if appropriate.

A typical computer terminal can only display between 23 and 25 lines, and hence large files that are being displayed tend to shoot up the screen at an unreadable rate. To solve this problem a keystroke called **<ctrl-s>** exists. This allows you to freeze and un-freeze the screen. Some VT100 emulation terminals have a hold screen key, which is utilised though use of the F1 key. Slightly more advanced terminals have a set-up screen (accessed using the F3 key on some VT models) which allow the user to alter the screen scrolling rate.

Examples

Example 1

The concatenation of the ASCII password file **/etc/passwd**.

```
$ cat /etc/passwd
root:IgHdHIL3Zqj0U:0:1:Super User:/:/bin/csh
mftadmin:gszsEC3cojrS6:0:1:Operator:/:/bin/csh
daemon:*:1:1::/:
sys:*:2:2::/:/bin/csh
$
```

Example 2

The concatenation of the two files:
/etc/passwd – which resides in the **/etc** directory, and
old_passwd – which resides in the current working directory.

```
$ cat /etc/passwd old_passwd
root:IgHdHIL3Zqj0U:0:1:Super User:/:/bin/csh
mftadmin:gszsEC3cojrS6:0:1:Operator:/:/bin/csh
daemon:*:1:1::/:
sys:*:2:2::/:/bin/csh
root:AZ4qj0DzIS:0:1:Super User:/:/bin/csh
mftadmin:gEdaDsCq3LjW:0:1:Operator:/:/bin/csh
$
```

Example 3

Example of the concatenation of a file whose name is typed in as the standard input.

```
$ cat
/etc/passwd
<ctrl-d>
root:IgHdHIL3Zqj0U:0:1:Super User:/:/bin/csh
mftadmin:gszsEC3cojrS6:0:1:Operator:/:/bin/csh
daemon:*:1:1::/:
sys:*:2:2::/:/bin/csh
$
```

Common messages

can't open *<file>* Cat cannot find the file named *<file>*. Check your spelling and the location of the file that you have specified.

<file> : **permission denied** The file you are trying to look at has its read-permission turned off. You must have the necessary read-permission to access this particular file.

7.3.3 File – verify contents of a file

Syntax

file [filename-1] [filename-2] .. [filename-n]

Description

The **file** utility returns a message indicating a guess concerning the contents of the file(s) concerned. The **file** command is useful, since there will always be a time when you don't know what a file contains. An example is the situation when you want to display the contents of a file using **cat**, but are reluctant to do so because it may result in a mass of gibberish.

The **file** command takes as input, the names of one or more files whose contents are then analysed. **File** then returns a description of the files in the order in which they were originally given. Since the main argument to the **file** utility is itself a filename argument, full or partially-qualified pathnames can also be used (see the later examples). A filename without a preceding '/', is assumed to exist in the current working directory, whereas files with just a preceding '/' are assumed to exist relative to the root directory of the file-system.

If no arguments are given to **file**, it simply drops into standard input mode, where it can either be interrupted, or given arguments in the form of individual filenames line by line. The **<ctrl-d>** code will terminate the standard input, and **file** will proceed as normal with the arguments that have been supplied as the standard input. The following examples illustrate some of the different types of data that the **file** command can recognise.

Examples

Example 1 – A linked directory:

```
$ file /ul/link
/ul/link : link to /usr/users/mike
$
```

Example 2 – A normal directory:

```
$ file /ul
/ul : directory
$
```

Example 3 – An executable (binary file):

```
$ file /bin/ls
/bin/ls : pure executable
$
```

Example 4 – A Shell-script:

```
$ file /etc/rc
/etc/rc : Shell-script
$
```

Example 5 – An ASCII file:

```
$ file /etc/passwd
/etc/passwd : ASCII text
$
```

Example 6 – Multiple input on one line:

```
$ file /etc/wtmp /etc/rc
/etc/wtmp : data
/etc/rc : Shell-script
$
```

Common messages

can't open <*file*> The argument <*file*> that you gave cannot be found. Check the pathname of the arguments and the spelling.

<*file*> : permission denied The file that you are trying to examine, has its read-permission disabled.

7.3.4 Cp – copy files

Syntax

cp *<source file1>* .. *<source file n>* *<destination file>*

Description

Cp is the UNIX file copy utility. It allows the user to make an exact copy of a file, which is then stored under a different name.

From the syntax, we can see that one or more arguments are required for the source filename(s). All the arguments are files in the **cp** command, the first one (or more) is called the source file, and the last argument is called the destination file. The source-file(s) can reside in the current directory, or they can reside in another directory on the file-system. The use of fully and partly qualified pathnames allows the user to specify the location of the file(s) in question.

The destination filename can also be a fully or partially-qualified pathname, so the user can copy the contents of a file in the current directory into another directory. In this case the destination name would include the pathname of the destination file (see the examples later). The user can, if desired, use full or partially-qualified pathnames within both arguments.

It is also important to note that the i-node number of the new file (the destination file) will be different from the source file, even though it is an exact copy. The **cp** command can also be used to copy one or more source files into a directory because a directory is a single file; it is a special sort of file however: a file area where we can store yet more ordinary and directory files.

Cp does not allow directory names to be included as a source filename, it only copies files at the first level of the hierarchy (see the errors section for an example).

Examples

Example 1

```
$ cp letter1 letter2 letter3 /usr/john/letters
$
```

This command copies the ordinary files **letter1**, **letter2**, and **letter3** into the directory called **letters** which resides in the directory **/usr/john**. The command here contains three source filenames, and one destination name. The source filenames are assumed to be in the current working directory, hence the missing pathnames on the files. The destination file (here a directory) is referred to by a fully-qualified pathname.

Example 2

```
$ cp letter1 letter2 letter3
$
```

This command contains two source filenames and one destination name. The files

letter1 and **letter2** have to be directories, since **cp** will not allow directories to be specified in a source filename. If we assume that **letter3** is not a sub-directory (noting that this command would work if the current working directory had a directory called **letter3** within it), where do the contents actually go? In fact, both the source files are concatenated together (see **cat** above), and are placed in the file **letter3**. If we examined the file **letter3** using **cat** (assuming this file was in ASCII format) we would indeed find that the two files have been joined.

Example 3

```
$ cp file file2
$
```

This is the simplest form of the **cp** command, a copying of one file to another, creating in the process a duplicate image of the file under a different name.

Example 4

```
$ cp letter1 /dev/lp1
$
```

This may appear a rather strange command, but is still perfectly valid. Here we are copying the ordinary file **letter1** (the source file) to a device file **/dev/lp1**. The destination file in this case is not a directory, or even another ordinary file, but an actual device (a line printer in this case – one of many special files contained in the **/dev** directory).

Assuming that the write-permission to the **/dev/lp1** file is enabled, this would simply allow us to print the file out.

Example 5

```
$ cp letter1 ..
$
```

This example uses the parent directory notation for the destination name. In this case the ordinary file named **letter1** will be copied into the directory immediately above the current working directory where this command was entered. The filename can stay the same in this case, because the copy will reside in a different directory on the file-system.

Example 6

```
$ cp /usr/users/jim/letter .
$
```

This command allows the user to copy the ordinary file **letter**, which resides in the directory **/usr/users/jim** into the current working directory, hence one copy of the file will be now be available in each two different directories. This example demonstrates the use of the **.** notation, which refers to the current working directory (**/usr/users/john**); which is where the copy is to be stored, in this example.

This command is faster than having to type the two equivalent commands given below. We have assumed that the necessary read-permission for the file **/usr/users/jim/letter** is granted.

```
$ cp /usr/users/jim/
$ cp letter /usr/users/john
$
```

Common messages

cp : source file directory The source filename that you have specified is the name of a directory, which is not allowed.

<file> : **permission denied** The file you are trying to copy has its read-permission turned off.

can't open *<file>* The argument *<file>* cannot be found. Check the spelling of any arguments, and also check for any pathname mistakes.

7.3.5 Ls – list files command

Syntax

ls [*-option letter(s)*] [*<filename 1>* .. *<filename n>*]

Description

The **ls** command lists the files in a specified directory. If the directory name is not specified, **ls** simply lists the contents of the current working directory by default. Ls is probably one of the most useful commands on the entire UNIX system, since it allows you to examine the contents of a directory. The **ls** command, by default, sorts the directory contents into alphabetical order. Where multiple arguments are presented to **ls**, it normally processes the ordinary files first, followed by any directory files (if they exist).

When a directory is specified as an argument, **ls** lists the contents of that directory, followed by any additional information requested in any options that may also be supplied. When an ordinary file is passed as an argument, **ls** simply prints the filename followed by any additional information that was requested using one of the option letters.

Ls is one of the many UNIX commands which gives the user a plethora of different options. These options affect what is actually displayed by the command, and the way in which it is presented. The options that we are going to explore in this section are **-l**, **-a** and **-A** respectively. The **ls** command given on its own produces an output similar in format to Figure 7.5. This illustrates the listing of a typical directory. As mentioned earlier, **ls** sorts (by default) all directories in an alphabetic order, and files are listed as such in a left to right manner. Figure 7.5 shows eleven such files. The only disadvantage of the basic **ls** command, is that it is lacking detailed information. This detailed information is supplied by the options that can be used with the **ls** command.

Figure 7.5 Output of an ***ls*** *command without any options*

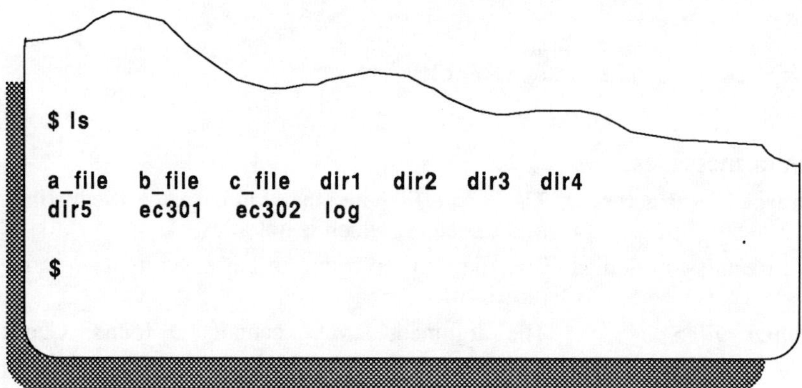

$ ls
a_file b_file c_file dir1 dir2 dir3 dir4
dir5 ec301 ec302 log
$

The ls -l command

The **-l** option of the **ls** command is used to give a *long* listing of the files in a directory – typically, an eight-column line of information about each file. This includes:

❑ The type of file (special, ordinary, or directory)

❑ The permissions for the file (for owner, group and others)

❑ The number of links to the file (for multiple entries)

❑ The user-name of the owner of the file (here jim)

❑ The size of the file (in bytes)

❑ The date the file was last changed

❑ The time the file was last changed

❑ The name of the file (up to fourteen characters)

A typical **ls -l** directory listing the files included in Figure 7.5 is shown in Figure 7.6.

Listing Explanation

The first column of an **ls -l** command contains 10 characters and the initial character always refers to the type of file concerned. Directories are flagged with the letter 'd', ordinary files with a single '-' (hyphen).

Ordinary files which are linked to more that one directory (also known as symbolic links) are flagged with the letter 'l' (the name of the linked directory is also given). UNIX flags block devices with the letter 'b', and character devices with the letter 'c'.

The next 9 characters of the first column represent the permissions associated with the file. Three characters are associated with three different types of user on the UNIX system, namely the user (login owner), the group, and lastly all other users. Figure 7.7 illustrates the file permissions for the owner of the file, group users, and other users of the system.

```
$ ls -l

-rwxrwxrwx 1 jim    1043 Sep 15 12:09 a_file
-rwxrwxrwx 1 jim    1983 Sep 15 13:51 b_file
-rwxrwxrwx 1 jim    1431 Sep 16 15:01 c_file
d rwxrwxrwx 1 jim   1121 Oct 11 12:16 dir1
d rwxrwxrwx 1 jim   1432 Oct 11 15:16 dir2
d rwxrwxrwx 1 jim   4441 Oct 11 13:11 dir3
d rwxrwxrwx 1 jim   5521 Oct 11 14:34 dir4
d rwxrwxrwx 1 jim   5612 Oct 11 16:34 dir5
-rwxrwxrwx 1 jim    1252 Nov 1  14:06 ec301
-rwxrwxrwx 1 jim    1614 Nov 1  16:05 ec301
-rwxrwxrwx 1 jim    2210 Nov 1  14:02 log
```

Figure 7.6 Typical ***ls -l*** *listing*

As described in section 4.8.2, the three permission letters **r**, **w**, and **x** show just 'what' the user can do to the file i.e. read from it, write to it, or execute it. In Figure 7.6 the user has allowed everyone to access his files, since the 'rwx' combination has been set for all users of the system. This means that any user could alter or amend, or even delete the contents of any of the files here, a potentially dangerous situation. Changing the permissions on such files is discussed later in Chapter 12 – UNIX Security.

Examples

Example 1

```
$ ls -l
Total 2
drwxrwxr-- 1 john   1034  Jan 14  14:04   a_file
-rwx------ 1 john    453  Jan 15  12:01   script1
$
```

This example of a long directory listing shows two files (the 'Total 2' message shows the total number of blocks for the listed files – assuming the block size is 1024 bytes on a System V machine, the user has used 1024 x 2 = 2048 bytes of disk space). The files are all owned by the user named **john**. The first file is called **a_file**, it was created on the January 14 at 2.04 pm (note the 24 hour format). The file is a directory, and the total size of the files contained within it totals 1024 bytes.

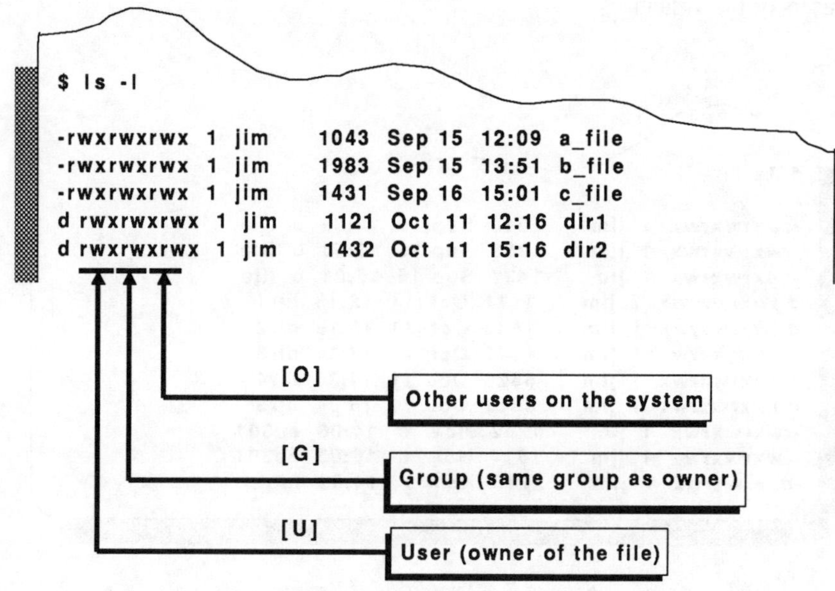
$ ls -l
-rwxrwxrwx 1 jim 1043 Sep 15 12:09 a_file
-rwxrwxrwx 1 jim 1983 Sep 15 13:51 b_file
-rwxrwxrwx 1 jim 1431 Sep 16 15:01 c_file
d rwxrwxrwx 1 jim 1121 Oct 11 12:16 dir1
d rwxrwxrwx 1 jim 1432 Oct 11 15:16 dir2
[O]
Other users on the system
[G]
Group (same group as owner)
[U]
User (owner of the file)

Figure 7.7 File permissions

The permissions that have been set allow the owner (**john**), to read, write and execute the file (noting that execute in this context means that the owner can make that directory his current working directory).

The owner can also read the directory, and add new files to the directory. All other users can only read from the directory i.e. they can examine its contents (using an **ls** command, for example), but cannot make it their working directory (for this they need execute permission). The users in the same group as **john** can also access the files in nearly the same way as **john** can. We say nearly, since we have to remember that **john** is the owner of the file, therefore the actions that can be performed on the file are slightly restricted i.e. other users cannot remove all trace of the file from a directory, although they could erase the contents.

The file has one link, therefore it appears in only one directory, in this case the current directory. The second file is called **script1**, and again it is owned by user **john**. It is an ordinary file, and **john** has permission to read, write and execute the file. Because the file is executable, this implies that it is a program file. The name of the file also implies that the file is a shell script.

The group and other users have no access at all to this file, so they cannot read, write or execute the file. Finally, the file is 453 bytes in length, and it has one link, which tells us that the file only appears in one directory – the current directory being examined.

Example 2

```
$ ls -l
Total 2
-rwxrwxr-- 1 john   1024 Jan 14 14:04  file1
---------- 1 john    453 Jan 15 12:01  file2
$
```

This example again shows two files, both of which are ordinary files. They are both owned by **john**, and both have only one link. The permissions dictate the following. The file called **file1** can be read by the owner (**john**), the group users, and any other users of the system. However, only the owner and group users can write to the file i.e. alter it. All users can execute the file, apart from the users who are outside the group (and those who are not the owner of the file).

The second file is named **file2**, and it is owned again, by **john**. The permissions on the file indicate that no users of the system, including the owner, can read, write or execute the file. In this case **john** must have rescinded the permissions on his own files (either by mistake, or on purpose). However, since **john** is the owner of the file, he can override such protection, to delete the file, for example.

Example 3

```
$ ls -l /dev/tty14
Total 1
crw--w--w- 1 jim 1, 3 Sep 12 18:12 tty14
$
```

This **ls** command has one argument, namely a filename which consists of a fully-qualified path to the file **/dev/tty14** – a terminal device file. The left-most character indicates the type of file. A terminal is a character special device, so UNIX has displayed the letter 'c' here.

The permissions indicate that the owner can read and write from the terminal, but he cannot execute it. This seems logical, since a terminal is not an executable program, hence neither is the file **/dev/tty14**. The group and other users of the system can write to the terminal. This implies writing on the standard output (the VDU screen of the terminal). These permissions allow these users to display messages on your screen.

These messages could be transmitted to your device using a UNIX utility, or they could redirect the standard output of a command to your terminal. Input/output redirection is discussed later in this chapter. This example also illustrates the major and minor numbers associated with the terminal device (see the subsection entitled

Interesting system directories in section 5.8.4 for more information on major and minor numbers).

Terminal ownership

The last example also tells us that the terminal is actually owned by the user who logged in to it. When a user is not logged in, his terminal is normally owned by 'root', for protection reasons. However, if this condition were to persist after the user has logged in, what would happen? This would depend on the protection settings on the terminal, and the default values are: `crw--w--w-`. So, in this situation, only **root** can read and write to the terminal, while the users in root's group and all the other users of the system can only write to this particular terminal. Assuming that the user's name is not **root** and they are not a super user, because the owner of the terminal is **root**, then the user (or any users in the same group as **root**) will not have permission to read from the device, rendering it useless – to converse with UNIX the user must be able to read from as well as write to a terminal. To solve this problem, UNIX makes the current user the owner of his terminal, to ensure there are no permission problems concerning reading and writing to the device. Now the default permission settings (**crw- -w- -w-**), as applied in Example 3 above, allow user 'jim' as the owner (and a non-super user) to read and write to his terminal.

Examining the /**dev** directory will actually show you who is logged in, by examining the user-names who own the terminal (note that finding out whether 'root' was logged in this manner is a bit harder, because ownership remains the same). Another UNIX command will allow you to see who is logged in to the system, and this is discussed later.

Another question that arises is the ability to delete your own terminal. You may be asking yourself how can you delete a terminal? But take the example where you log in (say with user-name **jim**) and become the owner of the terminal as we have seen already. The protection attributes in /**dev** for your terminal may tell you the following:

```
crw--w--w- 1 jim 1, 3 Sep 12 18:12 tty14
```

Surely this means you can delete your own terminal (since write-permission is enabled, and you are the owner)? Actually this is not the case, since write-permission on the /**dev** directory will not normally be available to you, even though the actual terminal is owned by yourself. Remember that to write to a file, you must have write-permission on the directory that contains it.

The ls -a option

The **-a** option of the **ls** command is used to list all the files in the current directory, or of another directory when using a partly or fully qualified pathname. By all files we mean the entries for directory files, ordinary files, special files and 'hidden' files. Hidden files have filenames that start with a period (full stop) – they are also known as 'dot files' or 'period files'. All UNIX systems make use of hidden files; some contain shell scripts which can be automatically executed when you log in, while others have more subtle actions. Those which are recognised by the UNIX system (i.e. hidden files which have a special meaning to the shell), are nearly always placed in your login or 'home' directory; this is where UNIX expects to find them.

Ls -a is used to reveal hidden files. You could, if you wanted, create your own hidden files, just by creating a file with a name that begins with a period. Creating such files is the subject of later chapters, but for now you should just know that they exist.

Two other directories contain a period as the first character in their filenames, namely '.' and '..'. A normal **ls** command will not list such files, and neither will a **ls -l** command. Some UNIX systems have a **-A** (capital A) to stop the printing of the '.' and '..' files in a **ls** command. You check this option by typing the command **ls -A** at the shell prompt.

Example 4

```
$ ls -a
. .. .profile a_file b_file c_file
$
```

This command asks the shell to list all the hidden and non- hidden files in the current directory. The current directory is assumed because no argument has been supplied. Some people insist that arguments and options are really the same thing, that is, they are all arguments to the command, however for our understanding arguments normally tell the command *what* information to process, and options tell commands *how* to process the information.

This example lists the hidden files '.' and '..' which are in all directories on the system (apart from '..' which has no significance in the root directory area). The file **.profile** has a special meaning to the shell, and is discussed later.

Example 5

```
$ ls -la
Total 2
drwx------ 1 john   1056  Sep 10  13:34  .
drwxr--r-- 1 root 154232  Nov 27  12:03  ..
-rwxrwxr-- 1 john   1031  Jan 14  14:04  .login
$
```

This example needs a bit of explaining. Firstly we have requested for two options to be used with the command, which is quite possible when using looking at the syntax description. Options like this can be given as above, or individually i.e. **ls -l -a**, although the first method is faster. We have not used any filename arguments so the command will default to the current working directory.

The command in this example is requesting a list of all the hidden and non-hidden files (**-a**) in a long format (**-l**). Note that the order of the options is not important i.e. **-la** and **-al** are the same. Three files are shown in the example above. The first is the

'.' directory, the current working directory. The size of the file is simply the size of all the files in the current directory (noting that a directory file actually takes up a few bytes of disk space).

The second file is '..', the parent directory. This directory is owned by root, and the permissions allow us only to read the contents of the directory immediately above us (for security reasons – i.e. so we cannot amend or delete the files above us). The parent file is naturally large, since it may contain hundreds of files.

The third file is a hidden file called '.login'. The file .login, as mentioned earlier, has a special meaning to the shell. This file normally contains a few UNIX commands to allow the user to personalise their entry to the system, with a greeting message, for example. The protection attributes on this file look a bit dubious, since group users can update the contents of the file.

Example 6

```
$ ls -lA
Total 1
-rwxrwxr-- 1 john 1031 Jan 14 14:04 .login
$
```

This example shows the use of the **-A** option. It is the same as the **ls -la** command except that the '.' and '..' files are excluded from the listing.

Common messages

ls : permission denied	You do not have the necessary permission to read the current directory.
no such directory	The argument you supplied to **ls** could not be found.

7.3.6 Mkdir – make a directory file

Syntax

mkdir [<*directory-name 1*> .. <*directory-name n*>]

Description

The **mkdir** command creates directories, as specified by the user. The files '.' and '..' for the directory are created automatically by the **mkdir** command.

The **mkdir** command has no options, only filename arguments. This argument can be one or more files which are to be newly created directories. **Mkdir** can be used with partially or fully-qualified pathnames. This allows the user to create a directory somewhere else in the file-system (using a fully-qualified pathname). By default a newly created directory is created relative to the current directory. The directory you are working in will therefore be the parent of the directory being created.

Examples

Example 1

```
$ ls -l
Total 1
drwxr--r-- 1 john 1031 Jan 14 14:04 dirl
$ mkdir dir2
$
```

In this example we have taken a hypothetical directory, and listed it (using **ls -l**). This initially includes one file, which from the listing can be seen to be a directory file called 'dirl'. The user then types the command **mkdir dir2** which creates a new directory. The new directory has no pathname, therefore it is created relative to the working directory (which we assume to be **/usr/users/john**). If we now type:

```
$ ls
```

we would see that the directory listing has now changed to

```
Total 1
drwxr--r-- 1  john   1031  Jan 14  14:04  dirl
drwxr--r-- 1  john   1031  Jan 14  17:01  dir2
$
```

Figures 7.8 and 7.9 illustrate the file-system before and after the new directory in the last example was created.

Example 2

Mkdir can also be used with fully and partly qualified pathnames, as in the example below. Assume that the current working directory is **/usr**.

```
$ mkdir /usr/users/john/dir3
```

This command will only work though, if the user has write-permission on the directory in which the new directory is to be placed. Since you are the user 'john' you will most definitely have write-permission on your own directory, hence the command will succeed.

Example 3

An example of another command that you may want to try typing in is:

```
mkdir /hello_to_you
```

This command will fail, unless you are the super user who can create directories in anyone's directory. This fails because you do not have the necessary write-permission into the '/' directory. Try taking a look at the permission on the '/' directory by doing an **ls -a** /. Look for the '.' entry, and you may find that the protection attributes are `drwxr--r--root`.

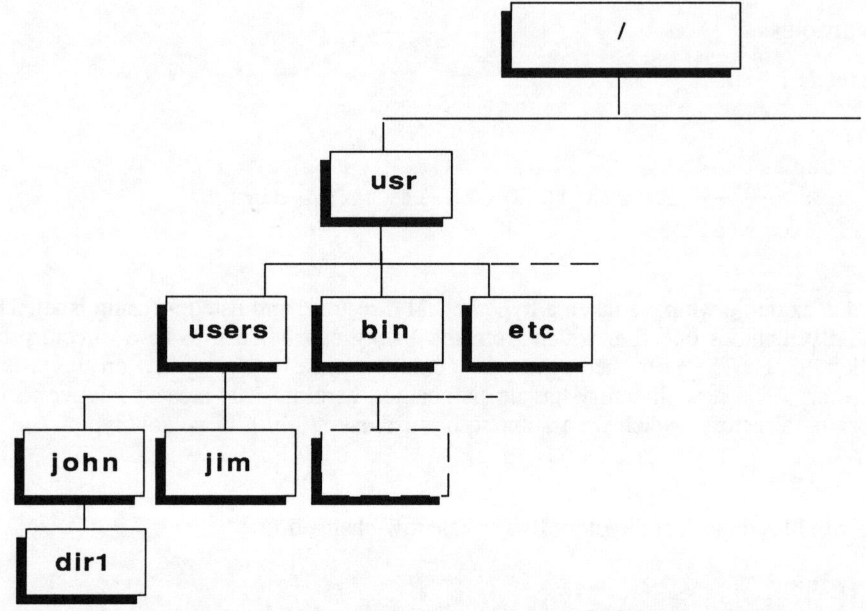

Figure 7.8 File-system before the new directory was created

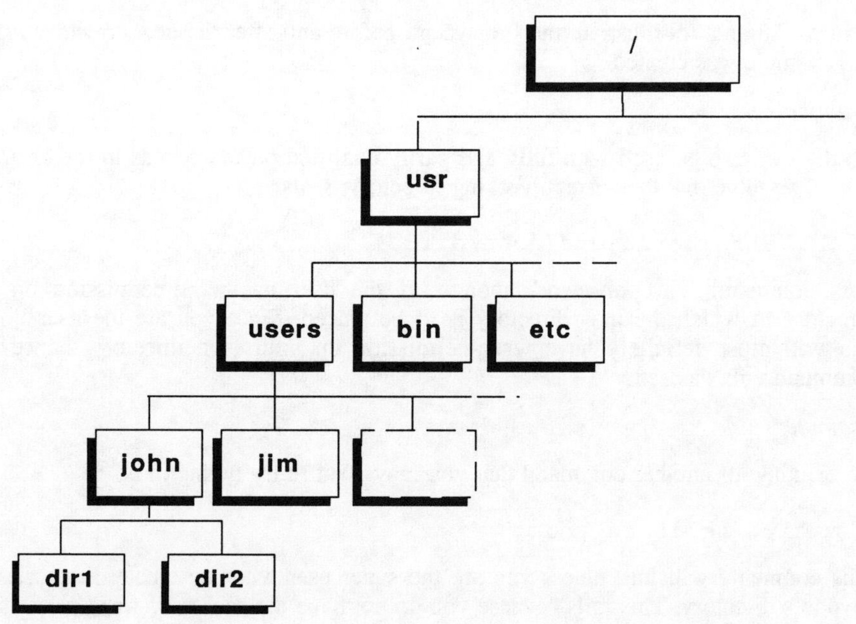

Figure 7.9 File-system after the new directory was created

Example 4

Mkdir can also handle multiple file arguments, as is demonstrated below. Assume that the current working directory is **/usr/users/john.**

```
$ mkdir dir3 dir4 dir5 dir6
```

This command creates four new directories at the level where you are currently working. If, after typing in the last few commands, we looked at the file-system, we would see one similar to that shown in Figure 7.10 below.

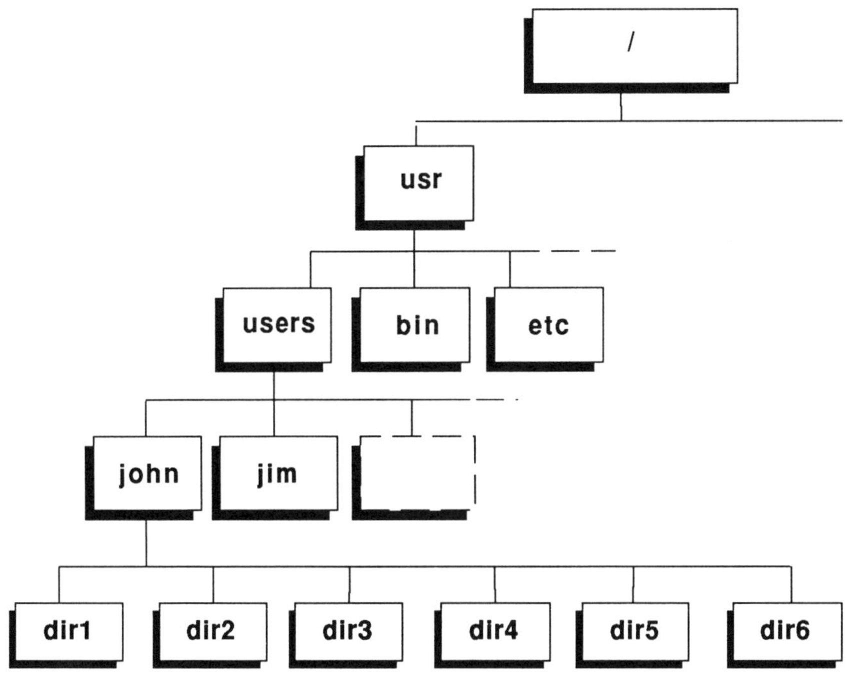

*Figure 7.10 File-system after example **mkdir** commands*

Common messages

permission denied — You do not have permission to create the directory since write-permission in the current directory is denied to you.

<file> : **cannot create** — The directory you are trying to create already exists, or the name you have supplied is invalid. May be permission problem on working directory (see above).

7.3.7 Mv – move files

Syntax

mv [*-options*] <*filename 1*> .. <*filename n*> <*new filename*>

Description

Mv is the UNIX utility that allows the user to move (rename) files. **Mv** simply changes the name and/or the location of the file, leaving the contents unchanged. It has two main options. We are going to examine one of these in this section, the **-i** option.

Mv can be used to move files that contain full or partially-qualified pathnames. Files without pathnames are assumed to be in the current directory. Files with an initial /, are assumed to be relative to the root directory. **Mv** is a powerful command; it can move any type of file, including directory files (see the examples later). In such a case, the files will keep their original names. Files in a directory that have duplicate names will be replaced (a potential disaster). This is where the **-i** is used.

The **-i** option is used to prompt the user to replace a file (when such a replacement will take place). The prompt is normally a **?** (question mark). This is called the interactive mode of **mv** (the safe mode). The user enters 'y' to replace the file, or 'n' to abort the replacement of this particular file.

Also note that any other reply apart from 'y' will be taken as a negative reply.

Examples

Example 1

```
$ ls -l
Total 2
-rwx------ 1 john   1021  Sep 14  13:34   file
-rwxr--r-- 1 john   1031  Nov 1   12:03   file2
$ mv file2 file3
```

The command in this example moves the file called **file2** to the new filename **file3** (effectively renaming the file). File3 will be an exact copy of **file2**, although **file2** no longer exists. We can verify this by typing **ls -l** to see the directory entry for th erenmaed file (for this example, assume the current date to be 1st December).

```
$ ls -l
Total 3
-rwx------ 1 john   1021  Sep 14  13:34   file
-rwxr--r-- 1 john   1031  Nov 30  12:03   file2
-rwxr--r-- 1 john   1031  Dec 1   14:14   file3
$
```

Example 2

This example illustrates the moving of files between *directories*. Assume that the current working directory is **/usr/john**, and that directories **dir1** and **dir2** exist in this directory, as shown below:

```
$ ls -l
Total 1
drwx------ 1 john   1016  Sep 1   13:34   dir1
drwx------ 1 john     23  Sep 1   13:34   dir2
$
```

Assume the contents of **dir1** are the two files – **file1** and **file2**, as shown below:

```
$ ls -l dir1
Total 1
-rwx------ 1 john    591  Jun 4   12:01   file1
-rwx------ 1 john    505  Jun 2   12:12   file2
$
```

And that the directory **dir2** contains a single file called **file3**:

```
$ ls -l dir2
Total 1
-rwx------ 1 john 12 Jun 7 12:17 file3
$
```

Then the command:

```
$ mv dir1 dir2
```

would move **file1** and **file2** into the file **dir2**, which can be shown to now contain the following files:

```
$ ls -l dir2
Total 1
-rwx------ 1 john    591  Jun 4   12:01   file1
-rwx------ 1 john    505  Jun 2   12:12   file2
-rwx------ 1 john     12  Jun 7   12:17   file3
$
```

So directory **dir2** now contains all the files that were originally in **dir1**, and **dir1** is now empty. This is because **mv** actually moves the files to a new location and does not emulate the command **cp** (copy files) discussed earlier – although the whole process could be though of as a copying of the source files to a destination file and then deleting the source files. We can verify the contents of dir1, as below:

```
$ ls dir1
$
```

Example 3

For the last example in this section, let us take the following scenario. The login directory of person **/usr/john** contains two files: an ordinary file called **a_file**, and a directory file, called **dir1**. We verify this using ls -l:

```
$ ls -l
Total 1
-rwx------ 1 john    591 Jun 4   12:01   a_file
drwx------ 1 john    505 Jun 2   12:12   dir1
$
```

The command:

```
$ mv a_file dir1
```

would move the ordinary file called **a_file** into the directory **dir1**. The previous occurrence of **a_file** has now disappeared, and the directory **/usr/john** contains a single file, namely **dir1**. We can verify this using **ls**:

```
$ ls
dir1
$
```

If we examine **dir1** we see that the file **a_file** has appeared within it. The files **b_file** and **c_file** were already in existence in this directory, so the listing for this directory will be as illustrated below:

```
$ ls dir1
a_file b_file c_file
$
```

If the file **a_file** had already existed in this directory, the replacement would have overwritten the file **a_file**. To make sure this didn't happen we could have used the command:

```
$ mv -i a_file dir1
mv : a_file?y
$
```

In this case **mv** detects that a file will be overwritten in the destination directory, hence it prompts us for confirmation of the replacement. Here the letter 'y' (yes) was entered to confirm the action, and hence the replacement of the file named **a_file**.

Common messages

mv: permission denied The read-permission has been disabled on file you are trying to read. The source or destination files may be the cause of the problem. Remember, that write-permission is needed to move files into a directory and read-permission is needed to access a file for moving. Check all permissions.

mv: cannot access *<file>* The file you are trying to move does not exist. Commonly a problem with source files, but could be an error when the destination argument is a directory i.e. a directory that does not exist. Check all pathnames in this case.

7.3.8 Pwd – print working directory

Syntax

pwd

Description

The **pwd** command displays the user's current working directory. **Pwd** is one of the commands that requires no user arguments or options. **Pwd** returns a fully qualified pathname indicating the location of the current directory in the file-system.

Example

```
$ pwd
/usr/users/john
$ cd /bin
$ pwd
/bin
$
```

Common messages

none

7.3.9 Passwd – change password file information

Syntax

passwd [*-options*] [*user*]

Description

Passwd is a utility that allows the user to change their current password. The password file is a plain ASCII file, and it resides in **/etc** directory, hence its full pathname is **/etc/passwd**. This file is common to all UNIX systems, and it contains critical information about each user of the UNIX system, of which the password is only one piece of information. The **/bin/passwd** program is a binary executable file, and should not be confused with **/etc/passwd**.

Most **passwd** utilities have two options. These options are not discussed here. For more details concerning the password file, see sections 11.2.1 to 11.5 in Chapter 11. In this section, we are confined to simple explanations and examples of the **passwd** utility.

The **passwd** command has one main argument, namely a user-name. This user-name must exist in the **/etc/passwd** file if the command is to work (see common messages). If a user-name argument is not specified, then **passwd** changes the password of the person who is currently logged in. Only the super user can use the user-name argument, unless the user-name argument is the name of the person currently logged in with that name.

Passwd will not change the user's password unless the old password is typed in first. New passwords must be typed in twice for verification reasons. A user who forgets a password cannot ask the systems manager for that password to be revealed. All the systems manager can do is reissue a new password, using the **passwd [user]** command.

The options that can be used with the **passwd** command allow the user to change other information in the **/etc/passwd** file. Examples of this are changing the user's login shell, or the alteration of the user's name and other personal details stored in the **/etc/passwd** file.

How to alter the **/etc/passwd** file is discussed in detail in Chapter 11 – Systems Administration (section 11.2.6 describes how a new user can be added to the **/etc/paswd** file). Numerous other examples of the manipulatio and use of the **/etc/passwd** file can be found in Chapter 11, sections 11.2.1 to 11.5.3.

Examples

Example 1

```
$ passwd jim
Changing password for jim
Old password:<your old password>
New password:<your new password>
Retype new password:<your new password>
$
```

This example will work only if the user issuing the **passwd** command is **jim** (see below). If the user does not log in under the name **jim** then this command would fail. Only the super user can change the password of any user on the system. The user's old password is typed first; this authenticates that the user issuing the command is the person in question and should a user forget to log out, it prevents someone else attempting to issue the **passwd** command at their terminal to try to change the password.

The old and new passwords are not echoed on the screen, just in case somebody is looking over your shoulder. This is a compulsory feature, and is also used when you initially log in. The user has to retype the new password, so verify it, and to make sure that the user remembers the new password. The shell returns the **$** prompt to indicate that the password has been changed. The user should then log out, and log back in again to test the new password.

Example 2

```
$ passwd john
must be logged in as root
$
```

This example shows a common message (messages change from system to system), that indicates that you must be logged in as **root** to change another user's password, which is the action being attempted here.

Example 3

```
$passwd
Changing password for jim
Old password:<your old password>
New password:<your new password>
Retype new password:<your new password>
old and new passwords do not match
password unchanged
$
```

This example illustrates the mistake a user makes when the old and new passwords do not match. UNIX simply issues a message indicating the mistake, and the password is left unchanged.

Common messages

must be logged in as root	You are trying to change another user's password, and to do this you must be logged in as root (the super user).
old and new passwords do not match	Typing mistake made when typing old and new passwords.
password incorrect	The first password you entered was incorrect.

7.3.10 Rm – remove files

Syntax

rm [*-options*] *<filename-1>* .. *<filename-n>*

Description

Rm is the UNIX utility that deletes (or removes) ordinary file(s) from a specified directory. In this section, we are only going to examine the **-r** option. Firstly though let us note a few other important facts about **rm** in general.

To remove a file or group of files, you must have write-permission on the file(s) concerned. If your current working directory is write-protected, then **rm** will not allow you to delete any file in that directory (note also that individual file permissions are ignored when the whole directory is protected in this manner).

Files that are owned by a user, but whose write-permission has been taken away can still be deleted by the owner (in the case where the current directory is not protected that is). This is because UNIX recognises you are the owner, and anyway **rm** has been programmed to recognise the owner of the file(s) concerned, so that problems like this can be overcome. In such cases **rm** will prompt for the user to confirm the deletion (see the examples later).

Rm can also be used to delete entire directories contents by recursively removing the entries in that directory (whether they are directories or ordinary files).

Examples

Example 1

```
$ ls -l
Total 3
-rwx------ 1 john   1021  Sep 14  13:34  file
-rwxr--r-- 1 john   1031  Nov 30  12:03  file2
-rwxr--r-- 1 john   1031  Dec 1   14:14  file3
$ rm file
$ ls -l
Total 2
-rwxr--r-- 1 john   1031  Nov 30  12:03  file2
-rwxr--r-- 1 john   1031  Dec 1   14:14  file3
$
```

This example illustrates the use of **rm** to delete a single file. The second **ls -l** command verifies the deletion.

Example 2

```
$ ls -l
Total 2
-rwxr--r-- 1 john   1031  Nov 30  12:03   file2
-rwxr--r-- 1 john   1031  Dec 1   14:14   file3
$ rm file2 file3
$ ls
$
```

In this example the last two files in the directory are to be removed. We use two arguments separated by a space (which is syntactically valid in this and other similar UNIX commands). We verify that the directory is now empty by using **ls** to show us its contents, and we can now see that all files have been deleted, or have they? Well, the answer is 'no', because there are two files that can never be deleted with **rm**, namely '.' and '..', the current and parent directory files. This is because **rm** cannot delete directories, although it can delete their contents.

Example 3

```
$ ls -l
drwxr--r-- 1 john 1031 Nov 30 12:03 j_dir
$ rm j_dir
rm : j_dir directory
$
```

This example shows just what happens when an attempt is made to try to delete a directory file. **Rm** simply issues a message indicating that the file is a directory, and the file in question remains intact. **Rm** can be used to delete directory files, when used with the **-r** option (to be discussed shortly).

Example 4

```
$ cd
$ pwd
/usr/john
$ cd /etc
$ rm passwd
rm: passwd not removed
$
```

This command would be a potential disaster if the password file **/etc/passwd** was unprotected. The file **/etc/passwd** should always be owned by **root**, and have the permissions **-rw-r--r--**. These permissions dictate that only normal users i.e. non super-users can read the file, whereas root can read or write to the file at will. The example illustrates the attempt to delete a file that does not belong to the current user. We can verify this because the permission settings on the file indicate that root is the owner. In such a case **rm** tells us that the file was not removed.

```
$ rm ..
cannot remove ".."
$
```

This command tries to delete the parent directory of the directory you are currently working in. If this command was allowed to be executed, you would find yourself floating in limbo, not a very desirable place to be. Deleting such files is the subject of the **rmdir** command (to be examined shortly).

Example 5

```
$ ls -l
Total 3
-r-xr-xr-x 1 john  1021 Sep 14 13:34  file
-rwxr--r-- 1 john  1031 Nov 30 12:03  file2
-rwxr--r-- 1 john  1031 Dec 1  14:14  file3
$ rm file
rm : override protection 555 for file?y
$
```

This example illustrates the problem that occurs when a file, (owned by the user who is deleting it) has its write-permission turned off. In such a case **rm** recognises that the user is the owner, and hence allows the owner to remove the file, but only after confirmation. An octal permission code, here **555**, is displayed (representing the current permission for the owner, group and other users). These octal permission codes are discussed later in Chapter 12 – UNIX Security, section 12.3.

The -r option

The **-r** option of the **rm** command is very powerful, and hence rather dangerous in many respects. This is because the **-r** option tells UNIX to delete all the files in a specified directory. However, the **-r** option is even more powerful because it will traverse directories that exist at lower levels, deleting their contents, and finally the directory itself. Figure 7.11 illustrates a small file-system before a typical **rm -r** command has been issued on the directory named **top**.

Example 6

```
$ rm -r top
```

This command would result in the file-system shown in Figure 7.12. This is because the command has descended through all the lower level directories of the directory **top**, thus deleting all the entries that existed in the directories concerned (including the directory itself).

Cornwall in his book, *The New Hackers Handbook* (Century Books, 1989), comments on the use of the **-r** option, and its possible use to corrupt the root file-system using a similar command found on a UNIX derivative system, namely **r -r /** (where the **r** stands for **rm** in this context and '/' is the directory to delete recursively).

Such a command would, of course, require super-user privileges. If this command were executed, vital files would be deleted rendering the whole system almost useless and the system could be brought back into operation only by restoring a backup of the entire root file-system. Mounted file-systems might be lucky and escape the ordeal, since **rmdir** cannot normally delete a file which is itself a mounted file-system i.e. a disk-storage device in the /**dev** directory. Such a command would normally result in an error similar to 'rm: mount device busy', or words to that effect.

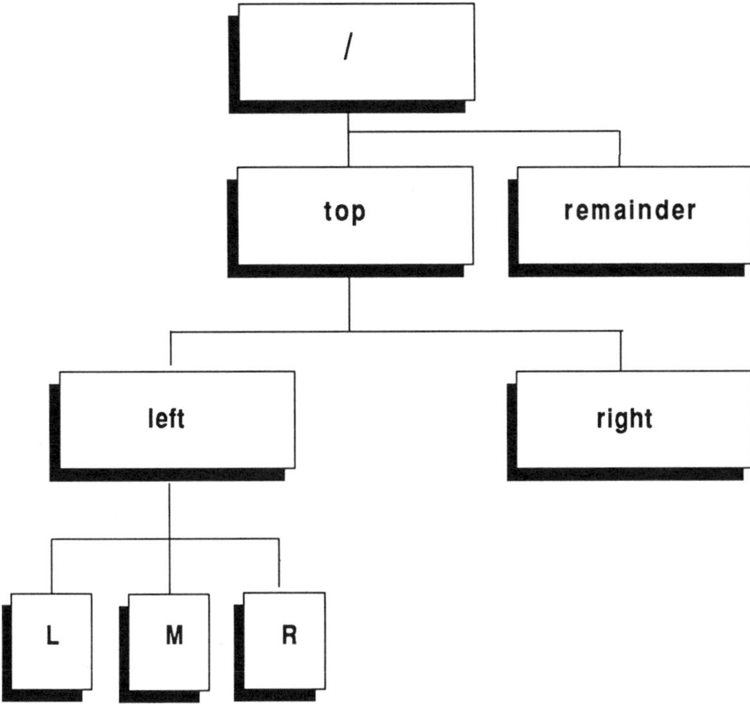

Figure 7.11 File-system before ***rm -r*** *command*

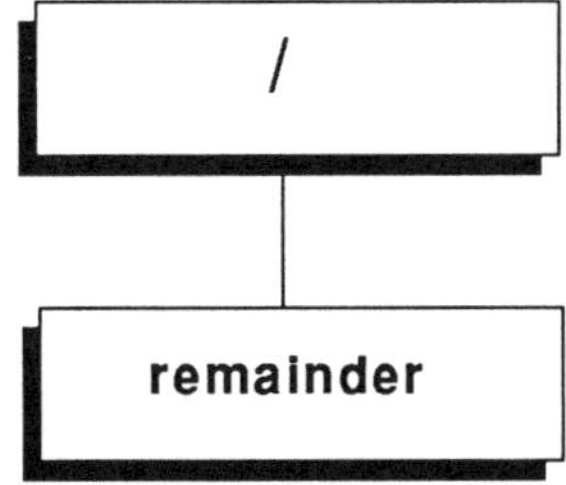

Figure 7.12 File-system after the ***rm -r*** *operation*

Example 7

```
$ pwd
/usr/john
$ ls -l
Total 1
drwx------ 1 john    591 Jun 1   11:01  dir
drwx------ 1 john    505 Jun 1   14:12  sales
drwx------ 1 john     12 Jun 3   08:17  sales2
$ rm -r /usr/john/sales
$
```

This command deletes all the files below the directory **/usr/john/sales**, including the **sales** directory itself (note the use of the fully qualified pathname). Any directories that appear on the same level as **sales** such as **dir** and **sales2** will remain intact. We can verify this by using the **ls** command:

```
$ ls
dir sales2
$
```

This tells us that **/usr/john/sales** has been removed, along with any files that were inside it. All the other files at this level can be seen to be still intact.

Common messages

rm: <*file*> **nonexistent**	The argument <*file*> cannot be found. Check the pathname or the argument name.
rm: <*file*> **not removed**	Write permission on <*file*> was not allowed. <*file*> may be a directory or ordinary file.
rm: <*dir name*> **directory**	You are trying to delete a directory using **rm** without the -r option.

7.3.11 Rmdir – remove directory

Syntax

rmdir <*directory-name-1 .. directory-name-n*>

Description

Rmdir is a UNIX utility that removes directory files. **Rmdir** works in a similar way to **rm**, except that **rmdir** removes directory files. The directory to be removed can be specified using a full or partially-qualified pathname. Another important point to note is that the directory you are attempting to remove must be empty of files.

To remove a directory, write-permission is needed on the file, or on the parent directory (in such cases where the parent directory is write-protected). If a directory is protected by the owner i.e. write-permission has been turned off, **rmdir** will return an error message; the owner can then change the permissions necessary, and continue to delete the directory. Another important fact to note is that **rmdir** will not allow you to delete either your current working directory, or the parent directory (..).

Examples

Example 1

```
$ ls -l
Total 1
drwx------ 1 john    591 Dec 4   13:01   dir1
-rwx------ 1 john    505 Dec 2   10:12   file2
-rwx------ 1 john     12 Dec 7   15:17   file3
$ cd dir1
$ ls -l
Total 1
-rwx------ 1 john    597 Dec 9   16:01   file1
-rwx------ 1 john    535 Dec 1   10:12   file2
$ cd ..
rmdir dir1 rmdir : dir1 Directory not empty
$ cd dir1
$ rm file1 file2
$ cd ..
$ rmdir dir1
$
```

This example illustrates the attempt to delete the directory file named **dir1**. We firstly examine **dir1** by moving into it using **cd**, and then by issuing an **ls -l** command. This reveals that the directory is not empty, and in fact it contains two ordinary files, here named **file1** and **file2**. Moving back to the parent directory of **dir1**, we attempt to delete it. UNIX replies to the **rmdir** command with an error message indicating that the directory is not empty.

To delete the directory we must delete all the files in **dir1**, which is also illustrated above using the **rm file1 file2** command. Once the files have been deleted, we can move to the parent of **dir1** again and issue the **rmdir** command, which this time succeeds since the **$** prompt is returned without an error message, a subtle way of telling us that all has gone well. This example is rather long winded, and this has been done on purpose to illustrate the use of the command.

Example 2

We mentioned earlier that **rmdir** can be used with pathnames; the same applies to the **rm** command. The following two commands would each carry out the same task, but without having to change directories (as shown in the example above). Assume the current working directory is **/usr/john**.

```
rm dir1/file1 dir1/file2
$ rmdir dir1
```

This example uses partially-qualified pathnames to delete the files **file1** and **file2** that reside in the dir1 directory.

Example 3

```
$ rmdir /usr/mary
rmdir : /usr/mary : permission denied
$
```

This example illustrates the attempt to delete the directory **/usr/mary**, which we do not have permission to delete. Mary could allow us to delete the directory however, if the necessary write-permission on the file was available.

Example 4

```
$ rmdir
usage: rmdir directory ...
$
```

The mistake that has occurred here is due to an error of syntax. The syntax of **rmdir** command dictates that one or more arguments must be supplied, in this case one or more directory names. In this example, **rmdir** shows a brief syntax description of itself, indicating the arguments that are required to use the command.

Common messages

rmdir: <*file*> **no such file or directory** This error simply indicates that the directory argument supplied to **rmdir** did not exist. Examine the spelling of the directory argument, and any pathnames. It may be the case that the directory name is correct but the location is not.

rmdir: <*file*> **not empty** You are trying to delete a directory which is not empty. Delete all files in the directory concerned using the **rm** command, and then continue.

rmdir: **cannot remove . or ..** You are trying to delete the current directory or the parent directory of the current directory. If the current directory is not empty, the error will still occur, since . and .. are not user directories created using **mkdir**. If you want to delete the current directory, delete all visible files using rm, and then move up a level using **cd** .., and then issue the **rmdir** command on the directory concerned.

rmdir : <*file*> **permission denied** You do not have the necessary write-permission on the parent directory of the directory trying to be deleted, or you do not have write-permission on the directory itself. Check the file permissions again, and check the owner of the directory.

7.3.12 Touch – change file modification time and date

Syntax

touch [*-options*] *<filename-1>* .. *<filename-n>*

Description

Touch is a UNIX utility that allows the user to change the time and date of a file, or group of files. The new time and date of the file is set to the current date, as set by the systems administrator when the system starts up, or by the settings stored in a battery-backed memory. Various options can be specified with the **touch** command; we will examine one of these in this section, namely the -f option.

Touch attempts to set the modification date and time of a group of arguments by simply writing back the new date and time to the file(s) concerned.

The **-f** option allows the user to force the **touch**, even if the file has write-permission turned off for the owner. This saves having to change the permission modes on the file(s) concerned, which can be time-consuming. The file being 'touched' must have the necessary write-permission, otherwise the modification dates and times of the file(s) in question cannot be modified.

Examples

Example 1

```
$ ls -l
Total 1
-rwx------ 1  john    591  Jun 4   12:01   file1
-rwx------ 1  john    505  Jun 2   12:12  file2
-rwx------ 1  john     12  Jun 7   12:17   file3
$ touch file1
$
```

This example shows the use of **touch** in its simplest form, the changing of the modification time and date for a single file. The argument in this example is the filename **file1**, which we can see from the directory listing (using **ls -l** here), is Jun 4 12:01. If we assume that the **touch** command was issued at 13:09 on July 6th, the new listing for **file1** would be:

```
$ ls -l
Total 1
-rwx------ 1  john    591  Jul 6   13:09   file1
-rwx------ 1  john    505  Jun 2   12:12   file2
-rwx------ 1  john     12  Jun 7   12:17   file3
$
```

Example 2

```
$ touch /usr/john/a_file
$
```

This example illustrates how **touch** can be used with a file name that could reside in another directory (although a fully-qualified pathname could refer to a file in the current directory). The command in this example was successful since the **$** prompt was returned without any error messages.

```
$ touch /usr
touch: permission denied
$
```

This command illustrates a typical error message that **touch** returns, when the file being modified does not have the necessary write-permission. Because **/usr** is owned by root, and the permission attributes will normally be `drwx-r--r--`, this dictates that only group or other users can read the information in **/usr**. However, the individual user directories in **/usr** (i.e. the login directories for each user) are owned by the user in question, and hence the protection attributes may not allow you to list a particular user's directory, as in the case of the directory for user **mary** whose directory protection is `drwx------`.

Common messages

touch: permission denied — As shown in the previous example, this error indicates that permission is not allowed to **touch** the file concerned. The permission that has been denied to you is most definitely write-permission, since **touch** must write back information to reflect the new modification time and date values of the file.

touch: cannot open *<file>* — In this instance **touch** cannot find the argument specified i.e. the file(s) that are to be touched. Check the pathnames that have been given, and also check the spelling of the file(s) concerned for typographical errors.

7.3.13 Tty – get terminal name

Syntax

tty [*-option*]

Description

Tty returns the name of the special device where the current user is logged in i.e. a terminal device. The terminal name returned by **tty** will be a device located in the **/dev** (devices) directory. **Tty** returns the fully-qualified pathname of the device concerned (which can be suppressed – see below). This is the directory **/dev** which resides in the root directory, followed by the device name with a terminal code prefix.

There is normally one option supplied with **tty** (although this may not be found on some systems), namely the -s option which suppresses the printing of the pathname of the device file.

Example

```
$ tty
/dev/tty14
$ tty -s
tty14
$
```

Common message

not a tty The standard input associated with the device is not recognised as a terminal.

7.3.14 Who – who is on the system

Syntax

who [*am i*] [*who-file*]

Description

Who is a UNIX utility that, when used without any qualifying arguments, displays all the users who are currently logged in to the system. It lists the the user-name; the name of the terminal being used; and the date and time that the user logged in, for each user.

However, the **who** command can also operate with arguments. Nearly all UNIX versions support an 'am i' argument which makes **who** tell the user who is logged in on the current terminal. This user-name is displayed using a fully qualified-pathname, hence the login directory is also shown. Some other UNIX versions support further options, such as a 'is <user>' argument, which allows a user on the network to be identified, where **<user>** is the user-name to be identified.

The other common argument is a 'who-file' name. Nearly all UNIX systems support these files, which contain a login history of the system concerned i.e. all the users who have logged in and out of the system. Some files are typically maintained for one day, and others are maintained since the machine was installed (or at least until the who-file was created, or whichever happened first).

Who displays the information in four columns, as shown in the examples.

Examples

Example 1

```
$ who am i
/usr/john
$
```

This command makes **who** display the user logged in at the current terminal, which might seem a waste of time, since this will be known at login time. However, its use is beneficial in some shell scripts which we will examine later.

This example uses one argument, the 'am i' argument, as can be seen in the syntax description earlier. The output from this particular command is system dependent; in some systems the terminal name, date and time will also be shown. There is an additional UNIX command called **whoami** which returns only a user-name.

Example 2

```
$ who
john tty14Jun 816:01
mary tty12Jun 814:16
root tty1 Jun 811:55
$
```

This example shows the **who** command issued without an argument. Here **who** searches, by default, a who-file called **utmp** (a temporary login and log out file). This is the default file for a **who** command without an argument.

The **utmp** file stores the login and log out information for the current day. Another file, called **wtmp**, is used to hold records about users who have logged in over longer periods (typically since the **wtmp** file was created – hence it is probably one of the largest accounting files on the system). For more information on the **utmp** and **wtmp** files, and the requirement for system monitoring, you are directed to Chapter 12, section 12.8 – Monitoring and Accounting Utilities.

7.4 Input and Output Redirection

In section 7.3 we examined many of the common UNIX utilities, and we found that there are standard input, output and error files associated with such utilities. These files are automatically opened by UNIX, and we can alter them using a technique called input/output redirection.

The standard input file for all the commands shown in the last section was in fact the keyboard. The standard output file was the terminal device where we sat while we typed in our commands e.g. **/dev/tty14**. The standard error file was also the terminal device, therefore any messages or errors returned by the various commands were also returned to our terminal screen.

It is possible to make the output of a command go to a different file that is not the screen of our terminal; or conversely derive command arguments from a file instead of from the terminal. Redirecting the input to a command is a very useful facility, since we can type in pre-defined arguments for frequently used UNIX commands.

Output redirection is also useful because we can store the output of a command for later use. We will also see how we can redirect information to other devices (remembering that UNIX devices are themselves files, which are stored in the /**dev** directory).

7.4.1 Redirecting output using '>'

We will firstly examine how to redirect the output of a command. Redirection of the standard output of a command (normally to the screen of a terminal device) can be altered using two redirection operators called '>' and '>'. The > operator is used directly after a command, and normally takes the form given below:

<UNIX command> > <file>

The **<UNIX command>** here could be any UNIX utility command that we met in the previous section such as **who**, **ls** etc..

Examples

Example 1

```
$ who > users
$
```

This command simply redirects the output of the **who** command, (which simply lists the users who are currently logged into the host system) into the file named **users**. Therefore the > operator can actually create a new file by redirecting the standard output of a command into a file. If we examined the file users by displaying the contents of this new file on the standard output, using a utility such as **cat** (concatenate files), we may see something similar in format to that shown below:

```
$ cat users
john  tty14    Jun 8  16:01
mary  tty12    Jun 8  14:16
root  tty1     Jun 8  11:55
```

This verifies that the command did send the output of the **who** command to a file which is now stored in the current directory, where it can be examined.

Example 2

We mentioned that the file created in the last example will be stored in the current directory (the . directory), and indeed this is the case. However we can redirect to another file using a partly- or fully-qualified pathname, as below:

```
$ who > /usr/john/who_files/who_1
```

The output of the **who** command in this example will be placed in the directory **/usr/john/who_files**. Redirection to a file without a preceding pathname will ensure that file is stored in the current directory. The last part of the pathname, the file **who_1**, is where the output of the **who** command will be stored. If **who_1** was a directory, and not the name of a file, an error message will occur telling you to supply a non-directory filename. If the file **who_1** already exists (as an ordinary file), then it will be overwritten with the new contents, hence all contents of the file before the command was issued will be lost.

Example 3

```
$ tty
/dev/tty20
$ who > /dev/tty20
john  tty14    Jun 8  16:01
mary  tty12    Jun 8  14:16
root  tty1     Jun 8  11:55
```

This command illustrates that the standard output is simply a device file, a 'special file' stored in the **/dev** directory. Assume that we are currently working at **/dev/tty20** (verified using the **tty** command here). In such an example the output of the who command will be displayed on our terminal screen. But what would happen if **/dev/tty20** was *not* our current terminal? In such a case, the output of the command specified would be sent to the terminal concerned, if it exists, and if the permission to write to it is allowed. Suppose we list the permissions using **ls -l /dev/tty2** and we find that the permissions are **crw-rw-rw-**, as shown below:

```
$ ls -l /dev/tty2
crw-rw-rw- 1 john 1, 0 Sep 28 02:38 tty2
```

Then the command:

```
$ who > /dev/tty2
```

will give user **john** a nasty shock, since whatever he is doing at this exact moment will be supplemented by a list of the current users, which he did not request at the time (since we sent it to him without warning). User **john** cannot do much now until the output of the command has been completely displayed.

Example 4

You may want to try something a bit more ambitious, such as the command below:

```
$ ls -l /etc > /dev/console
```

This command should wake up your systems manager, who will be greeted with a long listing of all the files in the **/etc** directory (we assume of course that the person in question has write-permission on **/dev/console** enabled for us).

Protecting your terminal

Fortunately, user **john** will be glad to know that there exists a special utility (change mode, or **chmod** command) that allows him to deny such messages being written to his terminal. We mentioned much earlier (during an explanation of the **ls** command), that a user on a UNIX system actually owns the terminal device where they initially logged on. User **john** will thus have an entry in **/dev** similar to:

```
crw-rw-rw- 1 john 1, 0 Sep 28 02:38 tty2
```

From this we can see that user **john** can read and write to his terminal. Unfortunately, so can everybody else. This is why the command **who > /dev/tty2** succeeded.

A full description of the use of the **chmod** command is given in Chapter 12, section 12.3 – File security – **chmod**. The next section examines the **mesg** command which provides a shortcut alternative to **chmod**.

7.4.2 The mesg command

Syntax

mesg [*y*] [*n*]

Description

The **mesg** command allows users to set the permissions on their terminal so that read and write access is denied to all users apart from themselves i.e. the owner of the terminal (here the user **john**). Mesg has two arguments: 'y' and 'n' (yes/no). **Mesg** used without any arguments simply returns the state of the current setting i.e. **yes** ? messages can be sent to the terminal, or **no** – messages cannot be sent to the terminal. We use the word 'messages' since **mesg** also stops incoming messages that were initiated through other UNIX communication commands (see Chapter 10 – UNIX Communication Facilities, for these commands).

All these communication facilities require the user to have write-permission on the terminal (special file) concerned, (except for the super-user).

Examples

Example 1

```
$ mesg n
$ tty
/dev/tty20
$ ls -l /dev/tty20
crw------- 1 john 1, 0 Sep 28 02:38 tty2
$
```

Example 1 illustrates the permissions that are set on the terminal device **/dev/tty20** when the command **mesg n** (turn messages off) command is issued.

Example 2

```
$ mesg y
$ tty
/dev/tty20
$ ls -l /dev/tty20
crw-rw-rw- 1 john 1, 0 Sep 28 02:38 tty2
$
```

This shows the permission settings associated with the terminal device **/dev/tty20** when messages are enabled. We can see that users in the same group as **john** can write to the terminal, as can any other users of the system. When a user initially logs in, messages can be written to that user's terminal via a default file protection similar to **-rw-rw-rw**.

7.4.3 Redirecting output using '>'

Output that is redirected to a file using the '>' redirection operator will overwrite that file if it already exists in the directory specified. The '>>' redirection operator is similar to the '>' operator except that **>>** appends data to a file.

Examples

Example 1

```
$ who > a_file
$ who >> a_file
$
```

These two commands redirect the output of the **who** command to a file named **a_file**. The first command initially creates the file **a_file** which will hold the standard output of the who command. The second command achieves the same outcome as the first, but the output is appended to the file **a_file**. The file **a_file** should contain the following:

```
$ cat a_file
john  tty14    Jun 8  16:01
mary  tty12    Jun 8  14:16
root  tty1     Jun 8  11:55
john  tty14    Jun 8  16:01
mary  tty12    Jun 8  14:16
root  tty1     Jun 8  11:55
```

Example 2

In the previous example we mentioned that the **>>** operator will append data to an existing file, but it can also create the file if it does not already exist. If we assume that the file named 'a_listing' did not exist in the current directory, the example below shows how we can use > to create this file.

```
$ who > a_listing
```

This command creates the file **a_listing** in the current directory. This is because UNIX has appended the standard output of the **who** command into a new file. This action does not rule out the need for the **>** command, since there will be many instances when we will want to overwrite the contents of an existing file.

Example 3

```
$ who >> /who_file
who_file : cannot create
$
```

This command will fail if we do not have super user privileges because we have told UNIX to redirect the output of the **who** command into the root directory, to a file named 'who_file'. Write-permission on the root directory is denied to normal users, so the error message 'cannot create' is the result. This error message will always occur if we try to redirect the output of any UNIX command to a user's directory where the write-permission is denied, for security reasons.

You may want to try redirecting output from some of the other UNIX commands examined earlier. Why don't you create a directory in your account using **mkdir** and play about. Alternatively you could redirect some output to the /**tmp** directory, since all users normally have write-permission to this directory. Its contents will usually be deleted the next time the system is booted.

Example 4

```
$ cat file1 file2 > file3
```

This command concatenates the two files **file1** and **file2**, so that they are they are written to the file called **file3**. The file called **file3** now contains the two files **file1** and **file2** (the original contents of **file3** being overwritten, unless the >> operator is used).

7.4.4 Redirecting the standard input using '<'

Redirecting the standard input of a command can be quite useful. If we continue with the **who** command, we can illustrate this. **Who** displays a list of the current users who are logged in to the system. We also know that **who** can take input from a **who-file**. **Who-files** are maintained by UNIX for monitoring purposes. The **wtmp** file for example, holds the login and logout information going back to the time when the **wtmp** file was first created. On System V UNIX, **wtmp** can be found in the /**etc** directory, whereas in Berkeley UNIX it can be found in the /**usr/adm** directory. We will use the System V naming convention in these examples.

Examples

Example 1

The command:

```
$ who /etc/wtmp
```

will produce output similar to that given below:

```
root  console Jan 15 12:04
paul  console Jan 17 12:07
john  tty20   Jan 17 14:01
.     .       .      .
.     .       .      .
```

The listing will probably continue for a few quite some time, so if you have typed this command, try pressing **<ctrl-c>** to interrupt the output, or **<ctrl-s>** followed by **<ctrl-q>** to pause and restart the output. In the example we have told **who** to take its input from a file named **/etc/wtmp**. This could be considered a type of input redirection, but where is the '<' operator? In this case, it is implied. The **who** command assumes that the input is arriving from a file.

Example 2

```
$ who < /etc/wtmp
```

This command achieves the same result as **who /etc/wtmp**. This is because we have told **who** to take its input from the file **/etc/wtmp**. The **<** is unnecessary in this case.

As a general rule of thumb, commands which accept data on the standard input until a **<ctrl-d>** (end of file) signal is generated, can have their input redirected using the '<' operator. One such command, called **mail** is a large UNIX utility that allows users to send mail messages to each other over a network. This utility is described in detail in Chapter 10, but is mentioned here because it demonstrates input redirection.

Mail normally takes arguments in the form of the user-names of the people that exist on the network. Once the names of the users have been specified, and the necessary options supplied, mail reads from the standard input to allow you to enter a textual message, which will be sent over the network. The message is terminated by a **<ctrl-d>** signal (the end-of-file signal). This tells **mail** that the message has ended, and it then proceeds to try to forward it to the person(s) concerned.

Example 3

The rule of thumb that we mentioned earlier, dictated that utilities which accepted data from the standard input (i.e. from a keyboard device), can have their input redirected using the **<** operator. This example demonstrates this concept:

```
$ mail john < data
```

This command illustrates how UNIX **mail** facility can be invoked with its standard input arriving from a file, here named **data**. The file 'data' could be a textual message that we typed in earlier. This command would be much faster than having to type in the message beforehand. Note that the information being redirected in this sort of operation is assumed to be a file.

Example 4

```
$ cat < file1 file2
```

This **cat** command allows the contents of a file, or files, to be displayed. Without any arguments **cat** simply reads from the standard input until a **<ctrl-d>** signal is generated.

This allows us to redirect the input to **cat**, and this is achieved here. The example tells **cat** to concatenate the files named **file1** and **file2**, which are assumed to be in the current directory (since no pathnames prefix the filenames). This command is slightly wrong though, because the syntax of the **cat** command indicates that multiple arguments are allowed. In this case the **<** is implied, although it demonstrates just how versatile the shell is.

7.4.5 Redirecting the standard error

The standard error file is normally associated with the user's terminal, so that any error messages that the shell may display can be seen on the terminal's VDU screen. However, we can redirect the standard error file to other locations – to a file for example. The standard files to which we keep referring each have a file-descriptor number which allows us to specify which standard file we are referring to. The standard error file has the descriptor number **2**, the standard input and output files have the descriptor numbers **0** and **1** respectively.

The time command

Some UNIX utilities produce output on the standard error, even when they work successfully. The **time** command is an example of this. This command returns the length of time taken to execute a particular command. Some examples will illustrate the use of **time** with error redirection, (the display on your terminal may be slightly different from the one shown here):

Examples

Example 1

```
$ time cat file1
793  5672 27623 file1

real 1.8
user 0.8
sys  0.7
```

Thls example illustrates the output of the **time** utility on the UNIX command 'cat file1', assuming that the file **file1** actually exists.

Example 2

```
$ time cat file1 > data_file

real 2.8
user 0.8
sys  0.7
```

Here we redirect the standard output of the **time** command to a file, named **data_file**. In such a case, **time** still displays some data, because the standard error is associated with the terminal, which has not been redirected. All that is lacking is the first part of the command (the figures 793, 5672 and 27623 and the filename **file1**). This is because the first part of the command is sent to the standard output, which we have redirected using the '>' operator.

Example 3

To stop the output of the **time** command being displayed on the standard output and error files (by default, the user's terminal), we have to specify the file descriptors for the standard files we want redirected. This is shown below:

```
$ time cat file1 > data_file 2>error_file
```

This examples shows how all output is suppressed. This is done using the notation below:

descriptor-number>output-file

The descriptor number in this case is **2** (the standard error file), and the output file is named **error_file**. It is important to remember that the descriptor number always appears before the redirection operator, and the filename immediately follows this. There must be no spaces in this notation. If we now typed out the contents of **error_file** (for this example) we would see that the contents are similar to those given below:

```
$ cat error_file

real 1.8
user 0.8
sys  0.7
```

This example verifies that only the contents of the standard error file were put in the file **error_file**. This was made possible by using the **2>error_file** notation.

Example 4

```
$ time cat file1 > data_file 2>&1
```

This example illustrates how we can merge the standard error and standard output files for the command specified (**cat file1 > data_file**) and place the result in file **data_file**.

The ampersand (&) used in the example is a convention that should be noted and understood. Used in this context the ampersand tells the shell to mix, or simply combine, two file streams. If we typed out the contents of **data_file** we would see the complete output of the **time** command, as in the final example below:

```
$ cat data_file
793 5672 27623 file1

real 1.8
user 0.8
sys  0.7
```

This example shows that both the standard error and standard output portions of the file are all contained in the same file, which could not be achieved if we simply used the > operator on its own since this redirects only the standard output – the time command produces output on two streams, the standard output and the standard error streams.

Combining operators

We have not yet mentioned the combination of the redirection operators, although this is quite possible. Later chapters will explain how to implement our own programs which will be able to read data from a file on the standard input, and write the results to a file as shown in the command below

```
$ cat < data_file > new_data
```

In this command the **cat** utility reads in data from the file called **data_file**. This data is processed and the results are written to a file called new_data. This command can be included in an executable shell-script file which has been programmed previously. This is similar to the concept of 'pipelining' which is discussed in the next section.

7.5 Pipelines and Filters

Pipelining is another facility of the shell which increases UNIX's flexibility. A pipeline (or pipe as it is more commonly known), consists of one or more UNIX commands joined together to form a product that is tailored to the needs of the user. In a pipeline, the standard output of one command is used as the standard input to another. Figure 7.13 illustrates this concept. It allows the user to construct totally new UNIX utilities using existing ones.

The pipelining facility is accessed through a special character: '|', which is known as the pipeline character. In general, a pipeline will take the form:

<command> | <filter command>

The **<filter command>** specified here is simply another UNIX command, which is used to transform the data sent to it in the standard input stream. Filters are examined in the next section, and some examples will demonstrate their combined use. Filters are UNIX utilities that are designed to accept data from a single input file, process this data, and present the results in a single output file.

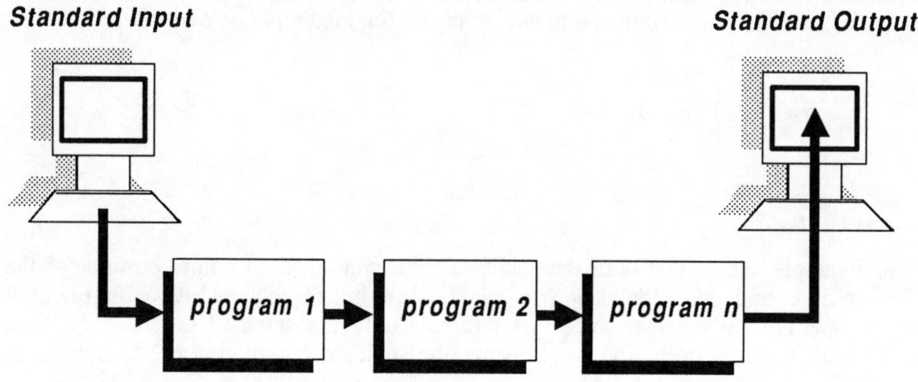

Figure 7.13 A UNIX pipeline

7.5.1 UNIX Filter Commands

The following sections examine the most common UNIX filters.

7.5.2 Sort – sort contents of a stream or file

Sort is one of the most useful UNIX filters. It simply rearranges data arriving on the standard input stream, and sends the results to the standard output stream, a VDU screen, for example.

Sort can be used with many options and we will cover the majority of the standard ones in this section. By default, without any options or arguments, the **sort** command arranges data alphabetically. If we were to type **sort** on its own at the shell prompt, it would simply read from the standard input stream, whereupon it would either expect an interrupt signal: **<ctrl-c>** or an end-of-file signal: **<ctrl-d>**. If **<ctrl-c>** were detected, the utility would be interrupted, and you would be returned to the shell prompt. A **<ctrl-d>** makes **sort** process the data given to it on the standard input stream.

Examples

Example 1

```
$ sort
january
march
february
april
december
june
<ctrl-d>
april
december
february
january
june
march
$
```

Sort wil reply with the names of the months in alphabetical order. We are working with the standard input stream here, and the **<ctrl-d>** allows **sort** to process the input.

Example 2

```
$ sort < data_file
```

This command makes **sort** read its standard input from a file, here called **data_file**. This file could contain any sort of data, although you should note that the sort utility works best with plain ASCII files. If we were to examine the contents of **data_file**, using the **cat** utility, we would find the following data:

```
$ cat data_file
John Smith   00001  Programmer
Fred Bloggs  00002  Analyst/Programmer
Mary Brown   00003  Programmer
John Smith   00001  Programmer
$
```

The data in this case is simply a list of employees, their occupations, and employee-numbers. Redirecting this file into the **sort** utility would produce:

```
$ sort < data_file
Fred Bloggs  00002  Analyst/Programmer
John Smith   00001  Programmer
John Smith   00001  Programmer
Mary Brown   00003  Programmer
$
```

Sort options

We mentioned earlier that **sort** provides the user with many different options. Some of the most commonly used ones are explained in this section, with examples.

Example 3

The **-u** option makes **sort** discard any duplicates. Since the name 'John Smith' has been duplicated in **data_file**, the command:

```
$ sort -u < data_file
```

will produce the following output:

```
Fred Bloggs  00002  Analyst/Programmer
John Smith   00001  Programmer
Mary Brown   00003  Programmer
$
```

Example 4

The **-r** option reverses the order of the **sort** operation and discards any duplicates, hence the command:

```
$ sort -r < data_file
```

will produce the following 'reversed' output:

```
Mary Brown   00003  Programmer
John Smith   00001  Programmer
Fred Bloggs  00002  Analyst/Programmer
$
```

Example 5

Note that using **sort** in this way, does not *permanently* alter the file **data_file**. To do this we would have to redirect the standard output back to the same file:

```
$ sort < data_file > data_file
```

This sorts the data in the file **data_file** and then writes the standard output back to the file (overwriting it in this case). If the file **data_file** was rearranged due to the sorting process, then a new order will have been created. The old order will have been be lost since it will have been overwritten.

Alternatively, we could write the sorted data to a different file: **data_file1**, for example, using the following command:

```
$ sort < data_file > data_file1
```

If **data_file1** was already in existence, then it would be overwritten with the new data; if not, then > would create a new output file, called **data_file1**.

Example 6

To append the sorted data to the same file we would use the following command:

```
$ sort < data_file > data_file
```

This command allows us to append the sorted version of the file to **data_file**, so that this file will then contain both the unsorted and sorted versions of the data. **>** can also append data to a different file, which will be created if it does not already exist, as demonstrated for **>** in the previous example.

Sorting fields of data

The **+f** option allows the user to sort on specified fields within the data, where **f** is the required field number. If we examine the original contents of the file **data_file**, which are shown below, we can see that each column of information is an individual field in the file.

```
John Smith   00001  Programmer
Fred Bloggs  00002  Analyst/Programmer
Mary Brown   00003  Programmer
John Smith   00001  Programmer
```

A *row* of data applies to one person in this context i.e. an employee record. The concepts of files, records, and fields were originally derived from relational databases, where the term ‘record’ refers to a single entity (or row) within the database; for example, an employee record in an employee database. The term ‘field’ is used for smaller components of a record (the columns), such as the employee’s address or telephone number. Thus, in its simplest form, a relational database can be described as a number of rows and columns, where each row is a record, and each column a particular field of each record. A true relational database file structure will, of course, be more complex in reality, but for our purposes we will imagine the file **data_file** to be a simple database, as is illustrated in Figure 7.14.

Now that we know how to number our individual data fields (noting that fields start from **0** and not **1**), we can sort any file of data using the sort **+f** notation. Some examples will illustrate this:

Example 7

```
$ sort +1 < data_file
```

This command sorts the file **data_file** on the second field i.e. the person’s surname in this context. The results will shown on the standard output as below:

```
Fred Bloggs  00002  Analyst/Programmer
Mary Brown   00003  Programmer
John Smith   00001  Programmer
John Smith   00001  Programmer
```

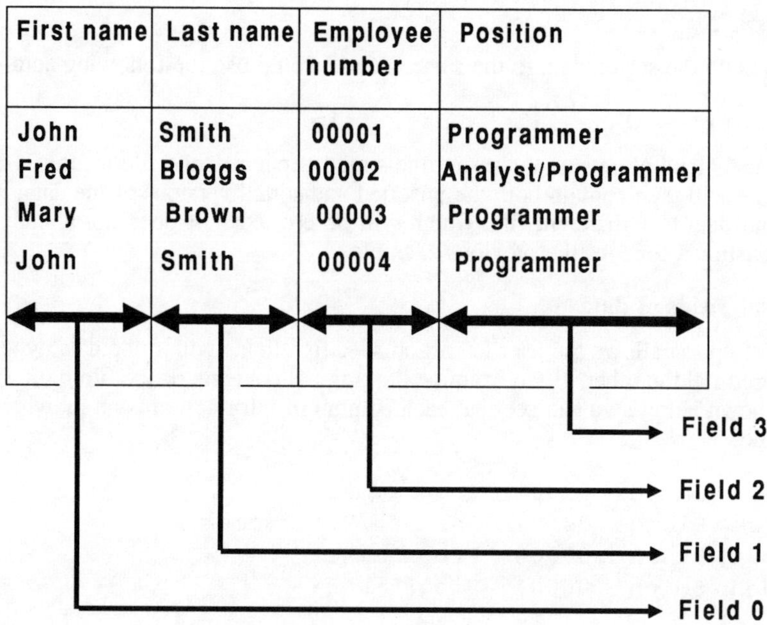

Figure 7.14 Field structure of a typical data file

Example 8

```
$ sort +2n < data_file
```

This command sorts the file **data_file** using the third field of information, hence the +2 notation. The **n** option tells **sort** to arrange the output by numeric value, since the column we are sorting is numeric.

```
John Smith  00001  Programmer
John Smith  00001  Programmer
Fred Bloggs 00002  Analyst/Programmer
Mary Brown  00003  Programmer
```

Example 9

```
$ ls | sort -f > a_file
```

This command uses the pipeline and redirection concepts discussed at the beginning of this section. In this example the standard output of the **ls** command is passed to the **sort** utility, hence the standard output of **ls** is transformed into a sorted listing.

The use of the **-f** option prevents the case of the files being a distinguishing factor i.e. upper and lower case letters are not distinguished from each other.

Finally, the contents of the standard output are redirected into a file named **a_file**.

This file will be overwritten if it already exists (remembering that a file without an initial pathname is assumed to reside in the current working directory), or created if it is a new file.

Example 10

```
$ ls -s | sort -n
```

The standard output from the **ls -s** command in this example is given to the **sort** command as its standard input. The **-s** option of the **ls** command lists the sizes of each file, in bytes. The **-n** option of the **sort** command is used to order numeric values, therefore this command will list all the files starting with the smallest, up to the largest (because, by default, sort arranges data in ascending order).

Example 11

```
$ ls -s | sort -nr
```

This command has the opposite result to the previous example – the **-r** option causes the files to be arranged in descending order.

Example 12

```
$ who | sort + 4n >> who_users
```

This command takes the standard input from the **sort** command and makes it the standard output of the **who** command. The **who** command lists the current users of the system in four columns, as follows: column 1 is the user-name; column 2 is the terminal number; and columns 3 and 4 are the date and time respectively, when the user logged in to the system.

Figure 7.15 illustrates Example 12 diagrammatically. Note that the commands 'who | sort + 4n' could be seen as being treated as one command. The output is never actually seen on the screen, since the standard output is redirected into a file (**who_users**) using the **>>** operator. Removing the **>>** operator and the filename, would send the output to the default standard output destination, the VDU screen.

The output of a typical **who** command is shown here:

```
john  tty14   Jun 8  16:01
mary  tty12   Jun 8  14:16
root  tty1    Jun 8  11:55
$
```

Since the fourth column is numeric, we have specified the **-n** option to the **sort** command in this example. The resulting output is appended to the file called **who_users**. If this file does not exist, it will be created (because > can also create a new file, if the specified file does not exist). If we assumed the **who** listing displayed the details shown above, the final output of the command in example below should reside in the file **who_users**. We can examine this file using the **cat** utility:

```
$ cat who_users
root  tty1    Jun 8  11:55
mary  tty12   Jun 8  14:16
john  tty14   Jun 8  16:01
$
```

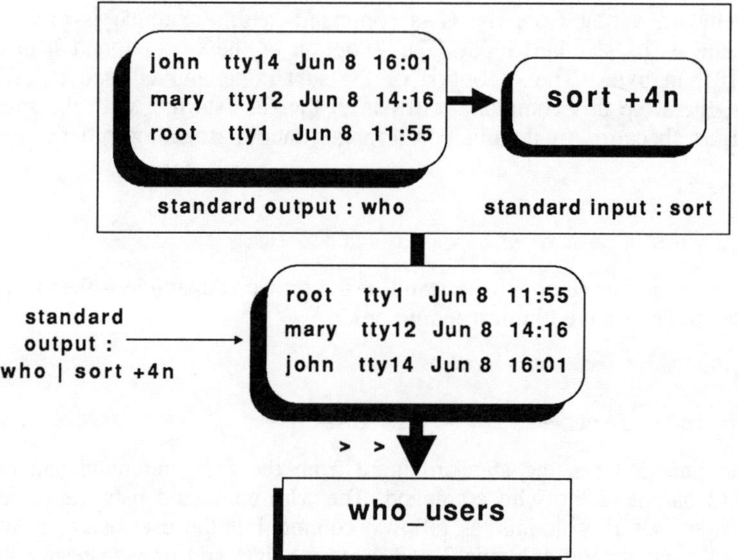

Figure 7.15 ***who | sort +3n >> who_users***

This output also verifies that the file **who_users** was either empty or did not initially exist. This is because **>>** was specified in the command, and therefore we are *appending* data to the file leaving any existing data intact. No existing data was found in the file in this instance.

7.5.3 Wc – word line and character count

Wc is another UNIX command which can act both as an autonomous command and as a filter. When acting as a filter, **wc** is used in a pipeline i.e. the standard output stream of a command or a file is passed to it. The **wc** utility has three main options: namely **-l** – count *lines* in an input stream; **-w** – count *words* in an input stream, and **-c** which counts *characters* in an input stream. Without any options **wc** produces the number of lines, words, and characters for an input stream (the default).

Wc also takes arguments on the command line as filenames. These can either be in the current working directory, or in another directory in the file-system. Files are accessed using full or partially-qualified pathname notation.

Multiple arguments have their respective names printed alongside them, with a final total. If no arguments are passed to a **wc**, it simply reads from the standard input stream until either an interrupt signal is generated, i.e. a **<ctrl-c>** signal, which returns the user to the $ prompt; or until a end-of-file signal is generated, i.e. a **<ctrl-d>** signal.

A **<ctrl-d>** signal makes **wc** process the standard input stream, i.e. all the data that was typed in after **wc** was invoked, up to the point where **<ctrl-d>** was finally pressed.

Examples

Example 1

```
$ wc data_file
```

This command makes **wc** process the file named **data_file** which is assumed to exist in the current directory. It is analogous to **wc < data_file** except that the < is implied with this type of command. Imagine that the file **data_file** contains the data:

```
UNIX was developed by Bell Laboratories in the late 1960s.
Ken Thompson, with support from people such as Joe Ossana,
Doug McIlroy, Rudd Canaday and Dennis Ritchie wrote a
small time-sharing system, which was then moved to a
PDP-11 computer in 1970.
```

In this context, **wc** would return the output:

```
5     42        254
```

The number 5 represents the number of lines, 42 the number of words, and 254 the number of characters. This is the format for the **wc** utility without any options. A line is simply a group of characters delimited by a special control character commonly called a **<hard-return>**. This is simply the press of the **<return>** key representing the creation of a new line. The name **<newline>** may be used in place of **<hard return>** in some instances.

A *character* is a visible alphanumeric or other character, including punctuation symbols, or a space. A *word* is defined as a string of characters that does not include a space, a **<tab>** or a **<hard return>/<newline>** control character. A **<tab>** is simply a control character that generates a series of blanks, mostly used for indentation purposes e.g. on a word-processing system. The majority, if not all, keyboards include a **<tab>** key.

Example 2

```
$ wc -c data_file
254
$
```

This command invokes **wc** with the **-c** option, which tells **wc** to supply only the number of characters in the file (or stream) concerned.

Example 3

```
$ wc -wlc data_file
5     42       254
$
```

This command has the same result as the first example. This is because we are specifying a count of lines, words, and characters – the default operation of **wc** with no options. We could equally well type **wc data_file** to achieve the same result.

Example 4

```
$ cp data_file data_file2
$ wc data_file data_file2
5     42       254    data_file
5     42       254    data_file2
10    84       508    total
$
```

Here, we are making a copy of **data_file** using the **cp** (copy files) command. This is to demonstrate the use of **wc** on a group of files. **Cp** takes the name of the existing file as an argument, and requires a new name for the copy of the file. In this example, **data_file**2 has been specified as the name for the copy of **data_file**.

Now that a copy has been made, we can invoke **wc** on the two files by specifying their names as arguments on the command line (separated by spaces). Wc then displays the line, word and character counts for each file, and prints the name of the file by the side of each line of statistics, as is shown above. A total has also been supplied as the last line of output, which is simply a summation of the statistics for each filename argument supplied to **wc**.

Example 5

```
$ who | wc -l
```

This command is using a pipeline to make **wc** use the standard output of **who** as its standard input. The **-l** option tells us the number of users logged into the system.

```
$ who | wc -l
3
$
```

Example 6

```
$ who
root  tty1     Jun 8  11:55
mary  tty12    Jun 8  14:16
john  tty14    Jun 8 16:01
$ who | wc -w
12
$
```

This example makes **wc** count the words in the standard output stream from the **who** command. The result is 12 since there are 3 users logged in (as seen from the who listing above), and there are 4 fields in each who listing. Words and fields in this context are very similar, except that we use the word *field* to refer to one entity e.g. one user. A **who** record for one user consists of 4 fields.

The **wc** utility does not distinguish between fields and words, but treats them in a similar way using the basic criteria that we put forward earlier when we defined a word, a character, and a line.

Example 7

```
$ wc
january
february
march
april
<ctrl-d>
4 4 25
$
```

This example invokes **wc** without any arguments. In such a situation **wc** simply reads from the standard input, and waits for an end-of-file signal **<ctrl-d>**, whereupon it processes the data supplied to it on the standard input stream. The first four months of the year have been typed in. The months take up 4 lines, and comprise 4 words and 25 characters.

7.5.4 Tail – print lines from the end of a file

Tail is a UNIX utility that allows the user to examine the *contents* of a file or stream. It can be used either autonomously, or in a filter via a pipeline. When used on its own or with any argument, (apart from the **+n** option, described in the next paragraph) **tail** always prints lines from the end of a file or input stream (hence the name **tail**). By default, it prints the last 10 lines of a file or input stream.

However, the lines to be printed can be specified using a similar notation to the one used with **sort** to identify specific fields. This is the **+n** notation, where **n** in this context represents the line *number* where printing is to start. Conversely, **-n** can be used to indicate the number of lines from the *end* of a file or input stream to be printed (the default being -10).

Some examples illustrate the use of **tail**:

Examples

Example 1

```
$ tail -2 data_file
```

This command makes **tail** print the last two lines of the file **data_file** which was introduced earlier:

```
Dennis Ritchie wrote a small time-sharing system, which
was then moved to a PDP-11 computer in 1970.
```

Example 2

```
$ tail +1 data_file
```

This command prints out the file **data_file** from line 1 (the starting line of the file). The whole of this short file is therefore printed out on the standard output:

```
UNIX was developed by Bell Laboratories in the late 1960s.
Ken Thompson, with support from people such as Joe Ossana,
Doug McIlroy, Rudd Canaday and Dennis Ritchie wrote a
small time-sharing system, which was then moved to a
PDP-11 computer in 1970.
```

Example 3

```
$ who | tail -1
```

This command prints out the last person in the list of users supplied by the who command using a pipeline. Assume the current **who** listing was:

```
root  tty1    Jun 8  11:55
mary  tty12   Jun 8  14:16
john  tty14   Jun 8  16:01
$
```

If the **who** command displayed the listing above, the command in the third example would display the last user, as shown here:

```
$ who | tail -1
john  tty14   Jun 8  16:01
$
```

The **who** command actually sorts its output, not in user name order, but by terminal number order i.e. **tty1**, **tty5**, **tty8** etc.

Example 4

```
$ who | tail +1
```

This command is the same as a simple who command without any arguments or options i.e. the default operation. This is because **who** prints all users from line 1 by default.

7.5.5 The more command

More, although described as a filter to be used in conjunction with another shell utility, is also an autonomous command. Basically its purpose is to allow the casual viewing of long files by displaying only a page or a line at a time. Its operation is similar to that of the **cat** command, since **more** concatenates the contents of one or more files to the standard output (although such output can be redirected). The syntax of the command is:

more *[options] [+line] [file ...]*

The [**file ...**] part is optional because if it is run without any options or filename arguments, **more** simply reads from the standard input, just like **cat**. The **-s** option compresses multiple blank lines into one blank line, thus maximising the information that is present on the screen. Another option, **-n**, where **n** is replaced with a number, allows the user to specify an integer representing the number of lines on a typical screen (see examples). The **-n** option overrides the normal default setting, which may be taken from the file **/etc/termcap** (terminal capabilities file) – about 24 lines for many VDU screens (22 is a common default).

The [**+line**] option allows the user to specify a line number from which a file or files are to be displayed. After every full screen of text displayed using **more**, the prompt '`--More--`' will appear at the bottom of the screen.

Pressing the *Return* key makes **more** display the next line of the file (and so on), while pressing the *space-bar* results in another screenful of text. When the the *interrupt key* (normally **<Ctrl-C>**) is pressed at this prompt, the program will exit (the DEL key is used on some systems to cause an interrupt).

Examples

Example 1

```
$ more file1 file2
```

This command makes **more** display the contents of the files named **file1** and **file2** in succession. When **more** reads from a file it displays the amount of the file that has already been read as a percentage, usually next to the '`--More--`' prompt (for example, '`--More--(24%)`' indicates that nearly a quarter of the file has been displayed up to the current point).

Example 2

```
$ cat file1 | more
```

This command uses **more** as a filter in a pipeline. The **cat** command is used to display the contents of the file named **file1** and the output from **cat** (the concatenated file) is then sent to **more** whereupon it proceeds to display a screenful of text from the file. The percentage display is not shown when **more** reads from a pipeline. Remember also that **more** is a substitute for the **cat** command, since both output data from a file. Therefore using **more** as a filter from the **cat** command is self-defeating.

Example 3

```
$ more +40 file1
```

This **more** command uses the [+**line**] option which allows a file to be displayed starting from a given line number, in this example, line 40. A screenful of text will appear from this line onwards.

Example 4

```
$ more -50 file1
```

This command uses the **-n** option. This changes the number of lines which can be displayed on the screen. The '`--More--`' prompt will not appear until fifty lines have been printed from the file.

7.5.6 Grep – pattern matching utility

Grep (global regular expression print) is a utility that allows searches for a pattern of text in a file or input stream. In UNIX, these patterns are referred to as regular expressions, strings, or patterns. These patterns are similar to the regular expressions found in the **ed** editor (see Section 9.4.10 for more information on the **ed** editor). **Grep** searches for these patterns on what is termed a global basis i.e. throughout an entire file or input stream. It then prints the line(s) containing the pattern that was matched.

The usual format for the **grep** utility to find an expression or pattern in one or more files is:

grep <pattern> <filename-1> .. <filename-n>

It can also be used as a filter using pipelines; here the format normally is:

<UNIX commands> | grep <pattern>

The **grep** utility can be used with many options, a few of which are examined shortly. These include:

- ❑ the **-v** option which prints all lines that do *not* match the specified pattern, i.e. reverses **grep**'s default operation
- ❑ the **-c** option which makes **grep** print the number of matches it finds
- ❑ the **-i** option which ignores the case of the pattern criteria.

There is also a small family of **grep** utilities, which include **fgrep** and **egrep**; these are similar to **grep** except that they work in slightly different ways. All this will be explained in due course.

Some examples now illustrate the use of **grep**:

Examples

Example 1

```
$ who
root  tty1    Jun 8  11:55
mary  tty12   Jun 8  14:16
john  tty14   Jun 8  16:01
$ who | grep john
john  tty14   Jun 8  16:01
$
```

The last command in this example pipes the standard output of the who command into the **grep** command as its standard input. The one argument given to **grep** in the example above is the pattern itself; therefore this command will return, by default on the standard output, a line (or lines) from the **who** command that contains the name **john**, as shown.

Example 2

The output from **grep** in the previous example also implies that user **john** is only logged in once, since only one line has been returned by **grep** (remembering that **who** allocates one line for each user who is logged in on at a terminal).

```
$ who | grep fred
$
```

In this example **grep** has not returned any matches to our pattern argument. This is because user **fred** is not currently logged in. Note that **grep** does not tell the user a match has not been found. Normally, the only indication that **grep** did not find a match is the immediate return of the shell prompt, here the **$** (although some versions do display a message, such as 'No Match').

Example 3

```
$ grep PDP data_file
which was then moved to a PDP-11 computer in 1970.
$
```

This command makes **grep** search the file **data_file** for any matches of the word ''PDP'. If we take a look at the contents of the file **data_file**, as shown below, you will note that this word only occurs once, hence **grep** only prints the one line that contains this particular word.

```
UNIX was developed by Bell Laboratories in the late 1960s.
Ken Thompson, with support from people such as Joe Ossana,
Doug McIlroy, Rudd Canaday and Dennis Ritchie wrote a
small time-sharing system, which was then moved to a
PDP-11 computer in 1970.
```

Example 4

```
$ grep was data_file
UNIX was developed by Bell Laboratories in the late
which was then moved to a PDP-11 computer in 1970.
$
```

This command is similar to Example 3, except that we have supplied a different pattern argument – the word 'was'. **Grep** finds two occurrences of this word in the file **data_file** and hence it prints both the lines that contain the word 'was'.

Example 5

```
$ who | grep -v john
root tty1 Jun 8 11:55
mary tty12 Jun 8 14:16
$
```

This command makes **grep** match all lines in output from the **who** command that do *not* contain the word **john**. If we assume that user **john** is logged in, then the output would appear as displayed. However, if **john** was not logged in, the command would fail because **john** would not exist as a pattern; the user will just be returned to the **$** prompt.

Example 6

```
$ grep the file1 file2 file3
```

This command makes **grep** search for the word **the** in the files named **file1**, **file2** and **file3** which are assumed to exist in the current directory. We can, of course, use the pathname notation for a file that exists in another directory, as shown in the next example.

Example 7

```
$ grep john /etc/passwd
```

This command makes **grep** search for the user named **john** in the file **/etc/passwd** which is the UNIX password file. If successful, **grep** may return something similar to:

```
john:Y3ld/hdc2JVl6:11:20:john:/usr/john:/bin/sh
```

The format of the password file is examined in Chapter 11, however, here is an explanation of the structure of the line given above. Each line in the **/etc/passwd** file contains 7 fields, which are separated by colons (:). The first field contains **john**'s name; the second, **john**'s encrypted password; the third and fourth fields hold the numerical codes for the user and group identification for user **john**; the sixth is the full pathname to **john**'s home directory; and the final field is another full pathname, but to the shell that **john** has been allocated.

Example 8

```
$ grep -i john /etc/passwd
```

This **grep** command is using the **-i** option, which tells **grep** to ignore the case of the pattern. **Grep** may therefore match the following patterns from **/etc/passwd**:

```
john:Y3ld/hdc2JVl6:11:20:john:/usr/john:/bin/sh
John:3dz81Lt.Da4X:16:20:John:/usr/John:/bin/sh
```

These two users (**john** and **John**) each have their own account on the host UNIX system. Since the login program mentioned much earlier is a case-sensitive system, it will discriminate between the entry of these user-names.

Example 9

```
$ grep -ni John /etc/passwd
56:john:Y3ld/hdc2JVl6:11:20:john:/usr/john:/bin/sh
60:John:3dz81Lt.Da4X:16:20:John:/usr/John:/bin/sh
$
```

The option **-n** in this command tells **grep** supply the line numbers where the pattern, the user-name **John**, was matched (notice that case distinction will not be made, since **-i** has been used also). In this example **grep** has returned the line numbers 56 and 60 for users **john** and **John** respectively.

Example 10

```
$ grep -ci John /etc/passwd
2
$
```

The **-c** option used here with **grep** makes it display the number of matches that were found, here 2.

Example 11

```
$ ls -l | grep 13:01
```

This command tells **grep** to search the standard output of the ls command (which, if we remember, supplies a long listing of all the files in the current directory). The pattern we have specified for **grep** to search for is 13:01 which we can recognise as being a creation/modification time (in 24 hour format). This time is provided by the ls option **-l**.

Example 12

```
$ cat data_file | grep -i was
```

This command uses **cat** to type the contents of the file named **data_file** (which we introduced earlier). The standard output of **cat** (the contents of the file **data_file**) is never seen on the screen, since it is immediately piped into **grep** to be used as its standard input. The **grep** command in this example includes the **-i** option, therefore the case of the pattern (the word **was**) will be ignored. The following output will be returned:

```
UNIX was developed by Bell Laboratories in the late which
was then moved to a PDP-11 computer in 1970.
```

The power of **grep**'s pattern matching abilities have not been fully explored in this section. The use of metacharacters (to be explained in the next section) enhances the search patterns supplied to **grep** thus allowing the user to search for more specific patterns in files and input streams.

7.5.7 Grep metacharacters

Metacharacters can be used with the **grep** utility to increase its effectiveness. They have a special meaning to the shell, and are interpreted and processed in a different way to the normal alphanumeric characters that we have used as patterns in our earlier examples.

Usually metacharacters are used to match one or more types of character from a file or input stream (depending on whether **grep** is invoked on a file, or used within a pipeline). The table below lists the metacharacters that can be used with the **grep** utility.

Table 7.1 Metacharacter Meaning

Character	Matches
.	Matches any single character
\	Quote a special character to remove its special meaning to shell
[...] [.-.] [.-..-.]	Matches any one single character within the brackets (see examples)
[^...] [^.-.] [^.-..-.]	Matches any character that is not enclosed in the brackets
*	Matches any group of characters
^	Matches the beginning of a line
$	Matches the end of a line

Examples

The metacharacters introduced in the table are used with **grep** within the **<pattern>** string. The examples which follow illustrate the use of **grep** and these metacharacters.

Example 1

```
$ who | grep 'tty[789]'
```

This **grep** command uses the standard output of the **who** command. The metacharacter used here is the bracketed notation, which matches any one character within the brackets. Hence, this command will match any terminal name that is either 'tty7', 'tty8' or 'tty9'.

Example 2

```
who | grep -i 'j*'
```

This command also uses the standard output of the **who** command, which is piped into **grep** as its standard input. We are using the **-i** option with **grep** to tell it to ignore the case of the pattern that follows. The pattern in this example is **j***. The * metacharacter matches any (or no) characters and because it is preceded by the letter 'j', the pattern argument will match anything that starts with 'j' or 'J' (remembering the **-i** option has been included). This pattern will also match the single letters 'j' or 'J' (because * can also represent zero characters). The pattern is enclosed in quotes, so the * is ignored by the shell and used by **grep**. The chances of a user being called 'j' or 'J' are unlikely, although possible. If we typed **who** and received the following list:

```
$ who
john  tty14   Feb 8  14:01
jim   tty12   Feb 8  11:16
root  tty1    Feb 8  13:55
$
```

we could expect

```
$ who | grep -i 'j*'
```

to display the output shown below:

```
john  tty14   Feb 8  14:01
jim   tty12   Feb 8  11:16
```

Example 3

```
$ who | grep -i 'j..n'
```

This command would search for any user-name beginning with the letter 'j', followed by *two* characters, and a final the letter 'n' ('john' or 'John', for example). This is distinctly different to **grep -i j*n** which would also include 'jn', 'jan', 'jon', or 'jason' in the match.

Example 4

```
$ ls | grep 'file*'
```

This command matches all files that have the name 'file' followed by any (including no) characters. Examples of patterns that will match include 'file1', 'file', 'filea', and 'fileb'. The case of the pattern will be taken into consideration in this command, since the **-i** option is absent (so 'FILE' or 'FILE1' would not be matched).

Example 5

```
$ cat /etc/passwd | grep -n '^fred'
78:fred::11:20:john:/usr/john:/bin/sh
$
```

This command uses the ^ metacharacter to find the pattern **fred** which we have indicated will start at the beginning of a line. The **-n** option stipulates that we want the line number of any matches. Remembering the format of **/etc/passwd**, we know that a user-name starts every new line of information. In the example **grep** has displayed the line number as 78. We can also see that **fred** does not seem to have a password (hence the empty password field). **Fred** should use the **passwd** utility to rectify this fact.

Example 6

```
$ grep :: /etc/passwd
```

This simple command should give us a list of all the people who have an empty field in the password file. The double colons (**::**) represent the empty field in this case.

Example 7

```
$ ls | grep -v sales
```

This command lists all the files that do *not* contain the word **sales**. The **-v** option inverts the normal **grep** operation.

7.5.8 Fgrep and Egrep

These two utilities operate in a similar way to **grep**, but each has its own particular usage, and there are there are small differences in the way that each works, which will be made clear in this section. Both **egrep** and **fgrep** (like **grep**) search for specific pattern (known as the expression, or search string) in either the standard input stream, (the default operation, without argument) or a series of input files on supplied the command-line.

As with **grep** the search pattern is specified by the user, and the results (the lines that contain the search pattern) are then displayed on the screen for viewing.

Grep can use a whole series of metacharacters, as shown in the Table 7.1 in section 7.5.7. **Egrep** can also use patterns that contain metacharacters which are shown in Table 7.2 below. You may notice that some of the **egrep** metacharacters are similar to those which can be used with **grep** (in most Unix implementations, **grep** can also use **egrep** regular expressions).

The **fgrep** utility can normally only search for fixed strings i.e. character strings *without* embedded metacharacters e.g. 'john', or 'CI403', etc. However, some implementations of the **fgrep** utility do allow it to be used with a few metacharacters – check your version to make sure.

Table 7.2 Egrep regular expression metacharacters

Character	Matches
^	Matches the beginning of a line
$	Matches the end of a line
.	Matches any single character
[a-z]	Matches range of single characters (here a to z, but this can be changed to a shorter range e.g. [a-d], or a numeric equivalent e.g. [0-9], etc)
*	Matches zero or more occurrences of a string
Additional 'extended' metacharacters include:	
+	If placed after the regular expression, this will make egrep match one or more occurrences of the regular expression
?	If placed after the regular expression, this will make egrep match zero or more occurrences of the regular expression
|	Can be used to separate two regular expressions (either expression string will be matched)
( )	Parentheses (brackets) can be used to group expressions together

The **egrep** ('extended' **grep**) utility is extended in two major ways:

1 – it admits *alternates* (described below), and

2 – it enables regular expressions to be bracketed (or grouped) using the '(' and ')' symbols (also know as 'factoring').

Alternates are groups of alternative patterns that must be searched by **egrep**. They are initiated by use of the '|' (pipe) character (although we are not constructing a pipeline in this instance). This character is also known as an **or** operator i.e. 'match this pattern *or* that pattern'.

Other metacharacters that can be used by **egrep** (and **fgrep** in certain installations) include the **?** and **+** metacharacters. These are both used as wildcards in conjunction with a pattern in the following way:

a?, for example, matches one or no occurrences (only) of the letter 'a', while **a+**, for example, matches one or more occurrences of the letter 'a'.

Examples

Example 1

```
$ fgrep jim /etc/passwd
jim:uxBaL7YY33xnY:99:20:REMOVE90:/home/STUDENTS/jim:/bin/csh
$
```

This **fgrep** command has retrieved the **/etc/passwd** entry for the user **jim**.

Example 2

If we wanted to find out whether or there were two (or more) users with exactly the same username, **jim**, we would use the command below:

```
$ fgrep jim+ /etc/passwd
jim:uxBaL7YY33xnY:99:20:REMOVE90:/home/STUDENTS/jim:/bin/csh
jim:Cfd4SZZxYPqTX:201:20:REMOVE90:/home/STUDENTS/jimB:/bin/csh
$
```

Here, the + metacharacter has been used with **fgrep**. It specifies that we want to search for one or more copies of the expression 'jim'. This command has retrieved two 'jim' entries (which is ambiguous and, in fact invalid, since the **/etc/passwd** file must contain unique usernames).

Example 3

```
$ egrep st(ew u)art /etc/passwd
stewart:RxBaL7DD11xnR:94:20:REMOVE90:/usr/stewart:/bin/csh
stuart:CsR4SXXxYPqTX:208:20:REMOVE90:/usr/stuart:/bin/csh
$
```

This command makes **egrep** match the similar, but alternatively spelt, names 'stewart' or 'stuart'. We are making the 'ew' and 'u' strings within the name optional. This is done using the bracketed notation (also known as the 'factored' notation). **Egrep** has returned both instances of the pattern in this example.

Example 4

```
$ egrep to(day|morrow) days
$
```

Here **egrep** is scanning the file named **days** (which is assumed to reside in the current directory, since there is no pathname prefix) for the pattern 'today' or 'tomorrow'. The bracketed notation allows the pattern to be broken up internally, thus allowing further pattern combinations to be searched.

The '|' symbol has been used in the example, and it is specifying that *either* the first part of the pattern *or* the second is to be matched. The '|' notation can normally only be used with the **egrep** utility. No match of the pattern(s) were found in the example, hence only the Unix **$** prompt is returned.

Example 5

```
$ egrep john|fred /etc/passwd
john:XXcVG33EEwqT:41:20:REMOVE90:/usr/john:/bin/csh
fred:JiOpZaRRx41:61:20:REMOVE90:/usr/fred:/bin/csh
$
```

This command matches the patterns 'john' or 'fred' who in this example are assumed to be usernames, as stored in the **/etc/passwd** file, as is verified in the output.

Example 6

```
$ egrep ^Unix my_file
Unix metacharacters are cumbersome, yet powerful!
$
```

This example illustrates the use of the ^ metacharacter to search for the word 'Unix' that appears at the start of a line. The file 'my_file' (a plain ASCII file, which could have been created using a Unix text editor) has been named as the file to be searched in this instance. The line 'Unix metacharacters are cumbersome, yet powerful!' has been matched in this instance.

Metacharacter protection

Note that some patterns may need to be enclosed in single quotes ('). This notation simply protects the metacharacters in pattern expressions supplied to the **grep** family of utilities from being interpreted by the shell. The shell also recognises metacharacters, although it interprets them slightly differently – normally applying them to filenames rather than to string patterns in most cases (see Chapter 8.2 for more details on shell metacharacters).

7.6 Complex patterns and Quoting

This small section deals with some more complicated searching capabilities using metacharacters with the many shell utilities. It also deals with other metacharacters that can be used with the **grep** commands and examines methods of disabling the shell metacharacters, using UNIX quoting conventions.

7.6.1 Quoting conventions

The shell interprets metacharacters in a very different manner to that used for conventional characters. We have constantly mentioned that metacharacters have a special meaning to the utilities that make use of them. One use of quoting is to take away this special meaning (such as their use with pattern arguments supplied to **grep**), but the main use is to quote pattern expressions that may be interpreted differently by the shell.

We must not forget that the shell, our working environment, is also a utility (a program like **grep** but much larger). The shell interprets metacharacters just like the **grep** family, although different metacharacter notations are used with the shell, and problems can occur if care is not taken.

When using **grep** commands, the single quote character (') can be used to prevent a metacharacter from being interpreted by the shell (although the back slash character (\) is more commonly used here); and to combine multiple arguments into a single argument. More commonly it used to enclose patterns that are used with the **grep** utility because these regular expressions overlap some shell metacharacters. The metacharacter tables at the end of section 7.5.4 reveal such differences.

The period (.) is a metacharacter in **grep**, but not under the shell. This is because the period is commonly used in filenames as a filename extension. For example, C source-code files are commonly of the format **<filename>.c**, where **<$filename>** is a group of up to fourteen characters (System V specific), and **.c** is an extension telling the user what the contents of the file are (a C source-code program). Thus the use of the period as a metacharacter would make it very difficult for the user to refer to files easily.

A double quote (′′) can be used to protect single quotes, but be warned, the shell will look inside of any quoted string to detect certain metacharacters, so only use double quotes if you intend the string to be processed internally. A command named **echo** is commonly used in shell scripts to display a line of text on the screen. It has one option, namely **-n** which does not force a carriage-return signal (which is the default – see the later examples for more uses of the **echo** command, and also Chapter 13 on shell programming). The **echo** command can be used directly from the shell prompt like all UNIX utilities, for example:

```
$ echo UNIX's quoting mechanisms are clumsy!
```

We can see that this message has a single quote after the word 'UNIX'. This may cause problems to the shell, and even more so, if used with a utility such as **grep**. To be more accurate we could double quote the whole sentence to avoid potential ambiguity, as shown in the appropriate command below:

```
$ echo "UNIX's quoting mechanisms are clumsy!"
```

If you are already proficient with such quoting methods, you are directed to the further topics of double quoting, command substitution, and grave accent quoting which is covered in more detail in Chapter 13 – Shell Programming.

Examples

Example 1

```
$ cat data_file | grep 'john smith'
```

This command makes **grep** interpret the two words which follow it as one pattern. If the single quotes were left out, **grep** would treat the names **john** and **smith** as two individual arguments. This example also demonstrates a major use of the single quote character to form a single argument where a pattern expression contains spaces.

Example 2

```
ls d*e
data_file
$
```

This command makes **ls** tell us if a file beginning with 'd' and ending with 'e' exists.

The file does exist because **ls** lists the file called **data_file**. The * metacharacter has been directly interpreted here, by the shell only.

Example 3

```
$ ls 'd*e'
d*e not found
$
```

In this example we have quoted the argument **d*e**, with the result that the special meaning of * as a metacharacter is lost, and the **ls** command simply tries to find a file called 'd*e' in the current directory. In fact, the **ls** command is being specifically told to interpret the argument literally. The literal interpretation of such arguments is the most common use of the ` and `` quotes (although they are not used for exactly the same purposes). Also note that the command **ls *** is the same as **ls** typed on its own, since by default **ls** lists all the visible files in the current directory. The * metacharacter is also interpreted in the same way by the shell as it is by **grep** (and also **egrep** – the extended version of grep).

We can see how one metacharacter can be used for two purposes: the single quote metacharacter can be used to remove the special meaning from another metacharacter; alternatively, it can allow the formation of a single **grep** argument.

Example 4

```
$ ls d\*e
```

This command uses the \ metacharacter, which tells the shell to ignore the character that immediately follows it, which in this case is a * metacharacter. This command is similar to the one demonstrated in Example 3, except that we have left out the single quotes.

Example 5

```
$ echo X times Y will be denoted as X'*'Y
```

This command quotes the * metacharacter, hence the output from the command will be:

```
X times Y will be denoted as X*Y
```

The quotes have been used so that the shell does not interpret the * as a metacharacter, thus not printing the all filenames in the current directory (*note* **ls *** will list all the filenames).

Example 6

```
$ echo 'UNIX is a great [RETURN]
> operating system' [RETURN]
UNIX is a great operating system
$
```

This command shows the effect when we start an **echo** command using the single quote notation. Since we have not ended the message with another single quote on a single line, the shell displays the > prompt which means that more input needs to be supplied. The > (or 'secondary' prompt) is the default prompt in this case and can be changed, as explained in Chapter 8, section 8.3.1. The other input that is needed in this case, is the termination of the line with a single quote.

Example 7

```
$ echo UNIX    is    great
UNIX is great
$
```

This command shows the effect when we insert multiple spaces into a line using the **echo** command. The shell discards all but one space between the individual words when processing such a command.

Example 8

We have to use quotes to make **echo** print the spaces, as illustrated below:

```
$ echo 'UNIX    is    great'
UNIX    is    great
```

This line is quoted, so the shell will display all the spaces in the echoed line. The **echo** command must be used with quotes whenever multiple spaces are required in the display, if centring a line, for example. Double quotes can also be used.

Echo can also be used to display multiple lines (by entering the **echo** command followed by a single quote, followed by the multiple lines, delimited by an ending quote), although to gain this effect **echo** must be entered in a shell script and not from the shell prompt (such commands are treated differently at the interactive level).

Example 9

```
$ echo -n 'The prompt will appear here -->'
The prompt will appear here -->$
$
```

We have used the **-n** option of the **echo** command here. This specifies that **echo** should not generate a carriage return. The end result here is that the shell prompt (**$**) will be displayed on the same line. We generate our own carriage returns by pressing **[RETURN]**, and the default action by **echo** will also do this. Only the **-n** option specifies the contrary.

Example 10

There have been problems with the **echo** statement, specifically about how **echo** responds when no arguments are supplied. The convention used by current UNIX systems, and which we will adopt, is simply to display a blank line. This example illustrates an **echo** command used without an argument.

```
$ echo
$
```

If you have an ancient version of UNIX that does not display a blank line when using **echo** in this way, and you need to generate one, you can use **echo** followed by a few spaces enclosed within quotes. You need not enter a whole line of spaces, the effect on the screen will still be the same (MS-DOS users may like to note the outcome on their machines).

Example 11

If you are using System V UNIX, the **-n** option is available. The **-n** option is provided from the 7th edition of UNIX onwards. System V UNIX introduced a new way of disabling the carriage return (**<newline>** signal) in an **echo** statement by using conventions that are common to the C language. The C language uses a slash (\) followed by a single character which indicates the control character to be used. Chapter 13 – Shell Programming – examines **echo** in use within shell scripts.

A '\c' character suppresses the **<newline>** (carriage return) code under System V, as the example here illustrates:

```
$ echo 'The prompt will appear here -->\c'
The prompt will appear here -->$
```

This is the same as the

```
echo -n 'The prompt will appear here -->'
```

version. Also note the **-n** option and the **\c** notation are both valid under System V.

Example 12

```
$ echo -n -n
-n$
```

This strange command illustrates that **echo** only interprets the first **-n** option. The second **-n** option is assumed to be an argument to the **echo** command i.e. a piece of text to be displayed on the standard output. It may be worthwhile quoting the second **-n** to avoid confusion e.g. '-n'.

Complex patterns

Now that we have a moderate understanding of the many quoting mechanisms, we can proceed to demonstrate some of the more complex pattern matching possibilities of the **grep** command. Some further examples illustrate some of the more complex metacharacter notations.

Example 13

```
$ ls -l | grep '^d'
```

This command lists all the files that are also directories. If you remember, the **ls -l** command displays a long listing on each file in the directory (excluding 'dot files' i.e. **.profile** etc.) The first character in any **ls -l** listing displays the type of file concerned e.g. 'd' for directory file; '-' for an ordinary file; 'c' for character special files and lastly 's' for special files.

When the ^ metacharacter is used as a pattern with **grep**, this indicates that the search begins at the start of the new line i.e. at the first character. The letter 'd' indicates the types of file we are searching for (here a directory file). The pattern has again been quoted, although we could probably ommit the quotes here because there are no conflicts between the shell metacharacters and the **grep** regular expressions.

Example 14

```
$ ls -l | grep '^...x......'
```

This command lists the files for which the owner has execute permission. Each period (.) **grep** metacharacter used here represents a single character, and the first ten characters of the **ls -l** listing include the type of file and permission settings. This command is a bit long-winded; we could use a shorter pattern using the * metacharacter, as shown below:

```
$ ls -l | grep '^...x*'
```

This command still matches the files with execute permission that are owned by the user. The * metacharacter is used to match any character(s) following the **x**, since we are not concerned with them. In fact we could use an even shorter version, such as **ls -l | grep '^...x'**, because we are not concerned with the other user permissions. The pattern has again been quoted, so the shell does not interpret the * metacharacter (which is also used by **grep**). We can reverse the search using the **-v** option of **grep**, so that we list all the non-executable files that are owned by the user, as shown below:

```
$ ls -l | grep -v '^...x'
```

The **-v** option inverts the expression, therefore matching patterns opposite to the default operation.

Example 15

```
$ who | grep 'tty[345]'
fred  tty4    Feb 8  14:01
mary  tty3    Feb 8  11:16
```

We met a similar command earlier. This command uses the **[...]** regular expression, which makes **grep** match one character within the [and] brackets. Therefore this command would match either **tty3**, **tty4** or **tty5**. Note that the three characters within the brackets are optional. The output from this command is simply a list of line(s) that contains the matched pattern, shown here as a list from the **who** command which was used as the standard input to **grep**.

Example 16

```
$ who | grep 'tty[^345]'
mark  tty6    Feb 8  14:34
susan tty7    Feb 8  14:01
```

This command uses the [^...] regular expression, which tells **grep** *not* to match any of the characters enclosed within the [and] brackets. Note the use of the ^ here, which does *not* mean the start of a new line. In this context it simply inverts the search criteria. We can expect the output to be a list of users who are not using a terminal with codes **tty3**, **tty4**, or **tty5**, as has been shown in the hypothetical example above. As indicated, the pattern should be quoted in this case.

Example 17

```
$ who | grep 'tty[a-c]'
bob   ttya    Feb 10 11:17
paul  ttyb    Feb 10 12:09
```

This command is again using the [...] regular expression, but the optional hyphen (-) has been included. This tells **grep** to match a series of characters, here characters within the range 'a' to 'c' (the **[a-c]** notation). The other part of the pattern (outside the bracket notation) is the word tty. We can therefore expect this command to list users who are using the terminals **ttya**, **ttyb** or **ttyc**. This expression will not match upper-case letters; to do this we need another expression, as shown below:

```
$ who | grep 'tty[a-cA-C]'
```

This command matches the users who are using the terminals **ttya**, **ttyb**, **ttyc**, **ttyA**, **ttyB** or **ttyC**. As we have mentioned previously, UNIX is a case-sensitive system, so we have to be accurate about such expressions when referring to them in searches of this nature. Also note the format for the **[.-..-.]** expression, and remember that no spaces are allowed within the brackets.

Example 18

```
$ who | grep 'tty[^a-cA-C]'
```

This simply inverts the pattern that **grep** will use. We can expect the output from this command to be a list of all the users who are *not* using the terminals **ttya**, **ttyb**, **ttyc**, **ttyA**, **ttyB** or **ttyC**. All other terminals will be matched and displayed on the standard output.

Example 19

```
$ grep 'and$' data_file
```

This command makes **grep** search the *end* of a line using the **$** expression. The **$** appears directly after the pattern that is to be matched in such a case. The pattern has also been quoted to stop the shell interpreting the **$**, as this is also part of a shell metacharacter as we will discover in Chapter 8. We can expect the output to be a list of lines that each have the word 'and' at the end of the line:

```
as Joe Ossana, Doug McIlroy, Rudd Canaday and
```

The file **data_file** was introduced in section 7.5.2 in Example 1, and contains a few lines of text for use with our **grep** examples.

Example 20

```
$ grep '^' data_file
```

This command uses the **grep** metacharacter ^, which matches the start of a line. Applied to the file **data_file**, this command will simply return all the lines in the file:

```
UNIX was developed by Bell Laboratories in the late
1960s. Ken Thompson, with support from people such as
Joe Ossana, Doug McIlroy, Rudd Canaday and Dennis
Ritchie wrote a small time-sharing system, which was
then moved to a PDP-11 computer in 1970.
```

To find the single occurrences of the ^ symbol in a file we would need to quote the ^ metacharacter (to take away its special properties), as shown in the next example:

```
$ grep '\^' data_file
```

The \ quote has been used here to remove the significance of the ^ metacharacter. The command will then return the lines that include a ^ character. This example uses the file **data_file** again, which we know is free from embedded ^ symbols, so the shell simply returns its prompt ($) indicating its failure to match the pattern.

Example 21

```
$ grep '^.' data_file
```

This command matches all lines that have at least one character in them, hence blank lines are not matched in this command. The pattern is quoted in this command, because the shell may interpret the **.** (period) character as a directory i.e. the current directory. We noted earlier that the shell does not use '.' as a metacharacter, but it will interpret it as another name for the current directory. The file **..** will also cause similar problems when used as a pattern with **grep**. Note that filename matching characters (such as '.') only match filenames beginning with a period if they are explicitly supplied in a pattern expression.

Example 22

```
$ ls | grep '[abcd]'
```

This command makes **grep** search the standard output of a **ls** command. The argument is quoted, so that each of the letters in the square brackets is matched against a filename i.e. a filename that contains the letters 'a', 'b', 'c' or 'd'. Typical output from such a command could be the filenames **d_file**, **a_file**, etc (assuming these files exist in the current directory).

Example 23

```
$ ls | grep [abcd]
```

This command is similar to the previous one except that the regular expression is not quoted. We noted earlier that patterns that are not quoted may be interpreted by the shell as a filename, for example. The shell recognises the [...] expression (since there are no quotes) so the effect of this command will produce a list of filenames(s) that consist of a single letter, – 'a', 'b', 'c' or 'd' (since they are specifically mentioned in the pattern argument).

7.7 Summary of commands

The following commands were introduced in this chapter. We start with the general file utilities such as **cp** and **ls**, etc. that were introduced first. Later commands refer to the filter utilities, such as **grep**. The key below categorises all the commands and metacharacters that have been explained in this chapter.

Files

<file ...> - a group of files (full/partial pathname)
<file> - an ordinary file (full/partial pathname)
<directory> - a directory file (full/partial pathname)

Special Characters

/ - directory (level) separator
.. - parent directory
. - current working directory
< - redirect standard input
> - redirect standard output (overwrite file)

Table 7.3 General file utilities

Command	Action
cd	Move to login directory
cd ..	Move to parent directory
cd /	Move to root directory
cd .	Move nowhere (current directory)
cd <directory>	Move to directory called **<directory>**
cat	Concatenate standard input
cat <file>	Concatenate file named **<file>**
cat < <file>	Concatenate file named **<file>** – The < is implied when using **cat**
cat <file ...>	Concatenate a group of files

General file utilities (continued)

Command	Action
cat <file ...> > file	Concatenate a group of files and store mass contents in one file
file <file>	Verify contents of file named **<file>**
file <file ...>	Verify contents of a group of files
cp <file1> <file2>	Copy file named **<file1>** to file named **<file2> <file2>** is a copy of **<file1>**
cp <file> <directory>	Copy a file into directory named **<directory>**
cp <file ...> <directory>	Copy a group of files in the directory called **<directory>**
cp <file> /dev/lp	Copy a file to a printer device thus printing the file
cp <file> ..	Copy a file to the parent directory
cp <file> /	Copy a file to the root directory
cp <file ...> ..	Copy a group of files to parent directory
cp <file ...> /	Copy a group of files to the root directory
cp <file> .	Copy a file in another directory to current directory (using pathname). If **<file>** is in current directory an error will occur
ls	List files in current directory
ls <directory>	List files in another directory (using full/partial pathnames)
ls <file>	Verify **<file>** exists
ls -l <directory>	Long listing of file(s) in another directory (using pathnames)
ls -l <file>	Long listing of the file **<file>**
ls -a	List all entries in current directory. Ordinary listing
ls -la <directory>	List all entries in **<directory>** including hidden files. A Long listing is given
ls -la	List all entries in the current directory including '.' and '..'
ls -A	List only 'dot' files in current directory i.e. ? ., .., etc.
ls -A <directory>	List all 'dot' files in another directory named **<directory>**
mkdir <directory>	Make a directory called <directory> that is subordinate to the current working directory, unless a different pathname is specified in front of the filename **<directory>**
mkdir <directory ...>	Makes a group of directories that are all subordinate to the current working directory, unless a different pathname is specified in front of the filename **<directory>**
mv <file1> <file2>	Move file called **<file1>** to file called **<file2>**. **<file1>** is lost
mv <file> <directory>	Move a file called **<file>** into a directory called **<directory>**
mv <file ...> <directory>	Move a group of files into a directory called **<directory>**
pwd	Print the current working directory
passwd	Change password for the user who is issuing the command
passwd <name>	Change password for the user named **<user>**. Must be super-user

General file utilities (continued)

Command	Action
rm <file>	Remove the file named **<file>**. **<file>** may exist in current directory, or may exist in an other directory
rm -r <directory>	Remove all files in directory named **<directory>**. **<directory>** is also removed
rm -i <file ...>	Prompt for removal i.e. where user or owner write-permission is disabled, when owner issues the command
rm <file ...>	Remove a group of files
rm <directory ...>	Remove a group of directories, and the files within them
touch <file>	Change time/date stamp on **<file>**. **<file>** may be in current working directory or in another directory
touch <directory>	Change time/date stamp on the directory file called **<directory>**
touch -f <file>	Force time/date stamp on **<file>** in case where user/owner write-permission is disabled for the owner issuing the command
tty	Display terminal identity
who	Show list of current users who are logged in
who [who-file]	Make **who** process a 'who-file'. An example is **/etc/adm/wtmp** (BSD)
who [am i]	Make **who** tell you your login name
who > <file>	Create a file called **<file>** that contains a list of the current users. **<file>** is overwritten if it already exists
mesg	Show if messages can be received or sent
mesg n	Disable outgoing and incoming messages
mesg y	Enable outgoing and incoming messages
mail <user> < <file>	Send mail to user named **<user>** and take input from a file called **<file>**
time <command>	Time the execution of a UNIX command named **<command>**
time <command> 2><file>	Time the execution of a UNIX command named **<command>** and store the standard error file contents in the file named **<file>**
time <command> ><file> 2>&1	Same as above, but merge standard output and error files, and store in a file named **<file>**
sort <file>	Sort the file **<file>** in ascending ASCII order
sort <file ...>	Sort a group of files in ascending ASCII order
sort -u <file>	Sort a file in ascending ASCII order and discard the case of the input. May be used on multiple files also
sort -ru <file>	Same as above, but reverse the order of the sort

sort +f <file>	Sort a file called **<file>** on basis of field number 'f', where **<file>** contains columns of data, separated by spaces. May be used on multiple files i.e. **<file ...>**
wc <file>	Count lines, words and characters in a file named **<file>**
wc <file ...>	Same as above, but totals also given in output, along with file names
wc -c <file>	Count number of characters in a file named **<file>**. No totals unless multiple file name arguments used
wc -l <file>	Same as above, except that only lines are counted
wc -w <file>	Same as above, except that only words are counted
tail <file>	Show last 10 lines of the file named **<file>**
tail -<n> <file>	Show the last **<n>** lines of the file named **<file>**
tail +<n> <file>	Show lines from a file starting from line number **<n>**

Table 7.4 Commands using metacharacters

<table>
<tr><th>Command/Expression</th><th>Action</th></tr>
<tr><td>**who | tail -1**</td><td>List last user in a **who** listing</td></tr>
<tr><td>**who | tail -<n>**</td><td>List last **<n>** lines of **who** listing</td></tr>
<tr><td>**who | tail +1**</td><td>List all users (from line 1)</td></tr>
<tr><td>**who | tail +<n>**</td><td>Show who listing from line **<n>**</td></tr>
<tr><td>**who | grep <user>**</td><td>Is **<user>** logged in?</td></tr>
<tr><td>**who | grep -v <user>**</td><td>Show all users apart from **<user>**</td></tr>
<tr><td>**who | grep 'tty[789]'**</td><td>List all people using **tty7**, **tty8** or **tty9**</td></tr>
<tr><td>**who | grep 'tty[^789]'**</td><td>List all users other than the ones using **tty7**, **tty8** or **tty9**</td></tr>
<tr><td>**who | grep -v 'tty[789]'**</td><td>Same as above</td></tr>
<tr><td>**who | grep -i 'J*'**</td><td>Find a user whose name begins with 'J' or 'j'. Ignore case</td></tr>
<tr><td>**grep <data> <file>**</td><td>Find pattern **<data>** in file named **<file>**. Match all lines</td></tr>
<tr><td>**grep <data> <file ...>**</td><td>Find pattern **<data>** that may reside in a group of files. Match all lines with the pattern</td></tr>
<tr><td>**grep -v <data> <file>**</td><td>Match all lines that do not contain the pattern **<data>**. Search inverted</td></tr>
<tr><td>**grep -i <user> <file>**</td><td>If file is **/etc/passwd**, does **<user>** exist on system? Ignore case. Match all lines in **<file>**</td></tr>
<tr><td>**grep -c <data> <file>**</td><td>Count the number of matches of **<data>** in the file **<file>**</td></tr>
<tr><td>**grep -ci <data> <file>**</td><td>Count the number of matches of **<data>** in the file **<file>** and ignore the case of **<data>**</td></tr>
<tr><td>**ls d*e**</td><td>List all files that begin with the letter 'd', and end with the letter 'e'. The * matches 0 or more occurrences</td></tr>
<tr><td>**ls 'd*e'**</td><td>List the file named 'd*e'. Make the shell ignore the '*' metacharacter using single quotes</td></tr>
</table>

Commands using metacharacters (continued)

Command/Expression	Action
ls | grep [abcd]	List files that are named using the single letter 'a', 'b', 'c', or 'd'. The shell will interpret this command
ls | grep '[abcd]'	List all files that contain a letter 'a', 'b', 'c' or 'd' within them. **Grep** will interpret this command, not the shell (because of single quotes)
ls '^'	List all files. The '^' simply matches all new lines
ls | grep 'd$'	List all files that end with the letter 'd'. The **$** matches the end of a line in this instance
ls -l | grep '^d'	List all directory files. The **'^d'** matches the letter 'd' (for directory) which is the first character in a **ls -l** listing. The ^ makes sure the start of the line is searched
ls -l | grep '^...x'	List all executable files. Dots match single characters in the **ls -l** listing
ls -l | grep '^drwx'	List all directory files on which the owner has all permissions
ls -l | grep -v '^d'	List all non directory files. The search is inverted using **-v**
ls -l | grep 'file[A-C]'	List all files that are either called 'fileA', 'fileB', or 'fileC'

7.8 Questions for Chapter 7

1. What is a metacharacter?
2. Name two uses of the single quote (') notation.
3. Why are single quotes used in patterns supplied to utilities such as **grep**?
4. What is the difference between **grep** and **fgrep**?
5. Explain what the standard input, output and error files are.
6. Explain what a pipeline is. How does it relate to the standard files in the last question?
7. Write a **grep** command to find the users who are not using the terminals **tty2**, **tty3**, or **tty4**. Hint: A pipeline will be needed, as will two UNIX utilities.
8. What action does the **touch** command perform?
9. A typical **who** command displays data in the following format:

   ```
   root tty1 Jun 8 11:55
   mary tty12 Jun 8 14:16
   ```

   How can we sort the fourth column of data in this listing using the **sort** command? Hint: use the + notation in conjunction with a pipeline connected to the **who** command.

10. How can the **ls** command list hidden files? What actually constitutes a hidden file under UNIX?

11. Explain the function of the **tail** command. How many lines does the tail command 'display' by default?

12. What is the difference between the two commands below?

```
(a) who | tail +1

(b) who
```

Explain any conclusions that you arrive at.

13. What does the **-i** option of **grep** perform?

14. The common UNIX prompt is the **$**. The secondary prompt is the **>**. What does it prompt the user for? Give an example of how we could invoke the **>** prompt.

15. The files **file1** and **file2** exist in your current working directory (**/usr/john**). How could these two files be copied into the directory **/usr/john/sales**?

16. Explain why the **-r** option of **rm** is dangerous.

17. Explain the **mkdir** and **rmdir** commands.

18. Draw the tree structure of the file-system created by the following commands (assume you are in the directory **/usr/john** – which is your login or 'home' directory):

```
$ mkdir left
$ mkdir middle
$ mkdir right
$ cd left
$ mkdir left middle right
$ cd ../middle
$ mkdir dir dir1 /usr/john/right/dir3
```

19. With reference to the last example, why is it not possible to issue the command **rmdir /usr/john/right**?

20. Give any three circumstances when a directory file cannot be removed using the **rmdir** command (not including any factors involving file permission settings).

Shell Metacharacters and Variables

8.1 Introduction

In this chapter we will examine the metacharacter conventions used by the shell, and some new conventions, such as grave-accent quoting also known as command substitution. We will examine Shell variables in detail to strengthen our understanding for Chapter 13 on Shell Programming. We will also deal with background processing, and the concept of a UNIX process.

8.2 Shell Metacharacters

We looked at metacharacters in the previous chapter but the subject does not end there. The shell interprets very many metacharacters, a few of which are the same as the ones used in tools such as **grep**.

Table 8.1 shows metacharacters which apply to the shell and have yet to be introduced. A separate section will be devoted to each such metacharacter, including examples of their use in conjunction with other shell commands. Most of the metacharacters in the shell match themselves against filenames, therefore it is possible to combine shell commands with shell metacharacters to speed up common tasks.

Table 8.1 Metacharacters applicable only to the shell

Metacharacter	Meaning
?	Match any single character in filename(s)
(...)	Run commands ... in a sub-shell
<command>&	Run **<command>** in background
$0, $1 $n	Replaced by arguments on command line
$<var>	Value of shell variable **<var>**
<c1>;<c2>	Run command **<c2>** directly after **<c1>**
'...'	Run commands inside ' quotes. Output replaces the ... part
<var>=<v>	Assign a value called **<v>** to the shell variable **<var>**
<c1>||<c2>	Run command **<c1>**; if unsuccessful run **<c2>**
<c1>&&<c2>	Run command **<c1>**; if successful run **<c2>**
#	Ignore all characters after **#** sign

8.2.1 The ? and * metacharacters

These metacharacters operate as wildcards: **?** replacing a single character and ***** any number of characters (including no characters). So the **?** metacharacter has the same function as the period (.) metacharacter used with the **grep** tool introduced earlier, which can cause problems because the shell uses a period to represent the current working directory.

Examples

Example 1

```
$ ls
file1 file2 file3 file4 dir1 dir2
$ ls file?
file1 file2 file3 file4
$
```

This command requests that all filenames that start with 'file' and end in any single character. The shell matches the ? against the single characters '1', '2', '3', and '4' of the filenames **file1, file2, file3** and **file4.**

Example 2

```
$ ls ????
dir1 dir2
$
```

The command in the example requests that the shell display filenames that consist of four characters. The only filenames that match this criterion are the files named **dir1** and **dir2.**

Example 3

```
$ ls *
file1 file2 file3 file4 dir1 dir2
$
```

This example illustrates the effect of the * wildcard when used as an argument with the **ls** command. **Ls** can take individual filenames as arguments, echoing them back to the user if they exist.

Note that if a directory file is given as an argument, and it exists, its contents will be displayed to the user. Since a * matches zero or more characters in a filename, the * matches all the files in the current directory, and hence the command simply emulates the default **ls** command which, used by itself, lists all files in the current directory.

Example 4

```
$ rm *
$
```

This command deletes all the ordinary files in the current directory, but not the directory files. The **-r** option is needed to achieve this, i.e. a **rm -r *** command. When used in this way, **rm** will descend any lower directories, deleting the files within them, followed by the directory itself. Only the owner of the files to be deleted (or the superuser) can issue this command. If the write-permission for the owner is rescinded **rm** will prompt the user for deletion, overriding the current permission settings. If a user who is not the owner attempts to delete files with **rm**, the result will be an error message stipulating that the file(s) cannot be removed.

Example 5

```
$ echo *
file1 file2 file3 file4 dir1 dir2
```

This **echo** command simply prints its arguments out on the standard output (unless redirected using >> or >>). Arguments to **echo** are normally messages in the form of some title, or instructions for the user. Here the argument is the asterisk metacharacter and so **echo** will match the * against all the files in the current directory, and print them out. Used in this way, the **echo** command achieves the same result as **ls**, or **ls ***.

Example 6

```
$ ls '?'
?
$
```

This command shows the use of the single quote notation to list a filename that is actually the name of a shell metacharacter (which is rather an absurd name for a file, although quite valid). The shell returns the name **?** verifying its existence in the current working directory. To access this file we have to make the shell ignore the **?** character's special properties so we enclose the filename in single quotes. We could also use the \ symbol to take away the special properties of a metacharacter.

Example 7

```
$ mv * /usr/dirl/sales
```

This command moves all the files in the current directory into the directory **/usr/dir1/sales** (we need write permission on this directory to do so). The **mv** command will also move a complete directory with this command, therefore if any sub-directories exist within the current directory, they (and their contents) will be moved to the destination directory.

Example 8

```
$ who *
$
```

This command will not work, since the **who** command only takes filename arguments in the case where the file is a who-file such as **/usr/adm/wtmp** (Berkeley Systems Distribution specific). In this example **who** is being told to open every file in the current directory, and therefore an error message similar to:

```
who : cannot open wtmp
```

may occur.

Example 9

```
$ cp /usr/src/bin/*.c .
```

This command copies all the C source-code files (i.e. ***.c**) from **/usr/src/bin** into the user's current directory (.). When using this command you must ensure that you are logged into the directory that the files are to be copied to, and you should be aware that any files already in this directory which have the same name as those being copied, will be overwritten (some versions of UNIX may display an error message to advise you of this fact). Alternatively, the user could move into the **/usr/src/bin** directory (the source files for most of the common UNIX utilities) using the **cd** command, and type **cp *.c <full pathname of directory>**, for example:

```
$ cp *.c /usr/john
```

This command copies all files with a **.c** extension to the directory **/usr/john** directory (e.g. **file.c, file2.c** etc.)

8.2.2 The ; metacharacter

The ; metacharacter allows the user to join UNIX commands together, to be executed one after the other. As many ; symbols can be used as required. The general format is:

<command 1> ; <command 2> ... <command n>

Some examples will illustrate the use of the ; metacharacter in conjunction with some of the common shell utilities we have already met.

Examples

Example 1

```
$ ls -l ; who
drwx------ 1  john      591  Dec 4   13:01   dir1
-rwx------ 1  john      505  Dec 2   10:12   file2
-rwx------ 1  john       12  Dec 7   15:17   file3
root tty1  Jun 8  11:55
mary tty12 Jun 8  14:16
john tty16 Jun 8  11:06
$
```

This example shows the **ls** and **who** commands being run, one after the other, with the output displayed on the screen (the standard output).

Example 2

```
$ ls -l ; who > users
drwx------ 1  john      591  Dec 4   13:01   dir1
-rwx------ 1  john      505  Dec 2   10:12   file2
-rwx------ 1  john       12  Dec 7   15:17   file3
$
```

This command demonstrates the same command as in Example 1, except that the standard output of the **who** command is being redirected to a file named 'users'. The shell responds to the command by executing the **ls** command, displaying the result on the screen, and then executing the **who** command, sending the output to the **users** file, so that it not seen on the screen.

Example 3

```
$ who ; ls -l | wc
root tty1  Jun 8  11:55
mary tty12 Jun 8  14:16
john tty16 Jun 8  11:06
3    24    146
$
```

In this command the **who** command is executed, and its output displayed on the standard output stream. The output from the **ls** command, however, is piped into the **wc** utility, and only the standard output from **wc** is seen (here a count of the lines, words, and characters from the **ls** command that was sent to **wc** as its standard input). Another group of metacharacters, (and), can be used with the ; metacharacter to form one command in a sub-shell (see next section).

8.2.3 The (and) metacharacters

The (and) metacharacters are normally used in conjunction with the semi-colon metacharacter (;). They are used to execute commands in a sub-shell.

When commands are executed one after the other using ;, but without the use of the bracket notation, each has a separate stream associated with it. This was demonstrated when one command could be sent to the standard output stream (i.e. displayed on the screen), while another was redirected to a file. When commands are encapsulated in brackets they are treated as one stream, thus a stream of individual commands is merged with another to form a single stream. This can be demonstrated with some examples.

Examples

Example 1

```
$ (ls -l ; who) | wc
6    36    233
$
```

This command uses the bracket notation to run an **ls -l** command followed by a **who** command. Only one output stream is formed and this is passed to the **wc** utility. **Wc** counts the lines, words and characters of the whole stream (the output from two commands) and displays it (by default) on the standard output, as shown in the example. Because the output from the **ls** and **who** commands is merged, no other output is seen on the screen (compare Example 3 in the previous section) and the data received by **wc** appear to originate from a single source.

Example 2

```
$ (ls -l) | wc
3    24    146
$
```

This example shows one command enclosed in the brackets (the **ls -l** command). Its standard output is passed to **wc** which displays its results on the standard output. This command would have produced exactly the same result without the brackets, since only one stream was generated by the **ls** command. However, it is a valid command.

The tee command

Tee is a UNIX utility that is worth mentioning at this point. It simply saves the results of intermediate output in a specified file. In the first example shown above, we saw a command that merged two output streams, so that the streams themselves were never seen individually. However, if we used **tee** in a pipeline before the contents were passed to the **wc** utility, we would be able see the two separate streams, when we examine the specified file.

Example

```
$ (ls -l ; who) | tee save_output | wc
6    36    233
$
```

This example uses **tee** to save the results of the standard output of the **(ls -l ; who)** commands in a file called save_output. The name of file that will eventually hold the output always immediately follows the command name in such a case (i.e. **tee**

<filename>). We can now examine the contents of the file **save_output** using the **cat** utility, as shown below:

```
$ cat save_output
drwx------ 1  john      591  Dec 4   13:01   dir1
-rwx------ 1  john      505  Dec 2   10:12 file2
-rwx------ 1  john       12  Dec 7   15:17   file3
root tty1  Jun 8  11:55
mary tty12 Jun 8  14:16
john tty16 Jun 8  11:06
$
```

8.2.4 The & metacharacter

The **&** metacharacter is synonymous with background processing, and it is typed immediately after the command that is to be processed in this way. By the 'background' we mean that the command is processed away from the interactive level so that the user can continue to type other UNIX commands in the foreground, in response to the **$** prompt. When the background task is completed command displays any results, and then terminates.

Each task processed in the background is given a unique process-id number, so that it may be referred to should the need arise, e.g. to kill it if process must be stopped. There are similarities between the **&** and **;** metacharacters, the main difference being that the semi-colon is used as a separator and that these commands are executed immediately, whereas the ampersand notation implies a longer period for completion.

The type of command that should be executed as a background process should normally be quite time-consuming. There is no point in making an 'ls' command a background process, since it completes its task within a few seconds. A typical background command would be to search an accounting file for a pattern of data, for example, a username. Some accounting files are huge e.g. **/usr/adm/wtmp**, and are thus ideal for inclusion in a background task, whatever it may be.

Example

The example below demonstrates a time-consuming command. Note that if you are using System V UNIX, the **wtmp** (login/logout accounting) file resides in **/etc/wtmp**.

```
$ grep john /usr/adm/wtmp > log_file &
5731
$
```

This command makes **grep** run as a background process, searching for user **john**, and his login/logout entries i.e. times, dates, and terminal code etc. When the job is completed, any pattern matches should be stored in the file **log_file**. The process number assigned to the background task is 5731 and it is used to identify the process if the user need to terminate the task, for example.

When the process is complete, the current directory should contain a file called **log_file**, which contains lines from the accounting file **wtmp** with **john**'s name mentioned in them. The file could now be examined using **cat**, after using **ls** first to check if the file **log_file** exists. Commands to monitor other user processes on a UNIX system are discussed in Chapter 12 – UNIX Security section 12.8. Detailed examination of these commands is beyond the scope of this chapter.

8.2.5 The || metacharacter

The || metacharacter (which is simply two pipe symbols joined together) allows the user to set up two commands, but the latter is only executed if the first one is unsuccessful. Failure of a command could be something simple like a **grep** command that did not find a matching pattern, or a misspelt command. The normal form for using the || metacharacter is:

<command1> || <command2>

In this context <command1> and <command2> are simply normal UNIX utilities commands such as **grep**. We could bracket the whole command line as shown below:

(<command1> || <command2>)

In this case, the commands would be executed as one stream using the bracket metacharacters (see the earlier section 8.2.3 for more details on this convention). This could then be piped into a filter such as **wc** etc.

Because the || metacharacter only executes <command2> if <$command1> is unsuccessful it is necessary to find out which command concluded successfully. This can be detected by examining the *exit code*, (also known as 'return code' or 'exit status') which is supplied when the command terminates.

Exit codes

All UNIX utilities, such as **grep**, return an exit status code which is an integer value. A zero exit status code means success (also known as true). Any other value means failure, the actual value indicating the reason why the command failed. For example, **grep** returns the value 2 when a nonexistent file is specified, or if there was an error in the regular expression supplied by the user.

An exit code is supplied as a variable (discussed later), whose value can be examined by the user after a command has been executed. The exit code value will change continuously as new commands are typed in. This variable is examined later in this chapter. All these error codes are useful when we are using shell utilities in a programming sense i.e. in a shell script, since we can capture the exit codes and inform the user of the error that has occurred. Of course, this is not always very precise, for example, **grep**, as mentioned above, returns one code indicating two possible conditions: an error with a nonexistent filename or in a regular expression (code 2). Either of these errors could have occurred, and hence the cause is not precisely determined. Only additional code, and the proper use of the shell programming language can lead to code that determines the cause of such errors.

We examine exit codes in Chapter 13 on Shell Programming, but for now, you should understand the concept of an error code being detected by a shell utility.

Using the || metacharacter

To use the || metacharacter we need a minimum of two shell utilities, one which precedes the || and one that follows after it. Some examples will illustrate this.

Examples

Example 1

```
$ who | grep john || echo john is not logged in
john is not logged in
```

This example uses **who** and **grep** to indicate that user **john** is not logged in. The first command is the **who | grep john** command (although there are two commands ? it is really treated as one command because of the pipeline) and in this example we want this first command to fail. The second command (on the same line) is an **echo** command that displays a simple message on the standard output (the terminal screen) telling us that user **john** is not logged in.

In the example the message argument supplied to **echo** has been displayed, thus indicating that the first command failed. It failed because **john** was not logged in (the condition that we wanted). If user **john** had been logged in, the first command would have succeeded, and the command after the || metacharacter would not have been executed.

Example 2

```
$ ls | grep data || echo File data does not exist
File data does not exist
```

This example is similar to the first one except that we are searching for a file named 'data'. If the file does not exist in the current directory the **grep** command returns a failure code and the || metacharacter is invoked thus executing the second command which uses **echo** to tell the user that the file did not exist.

Example 3

```
$ grwp || echo Command failed
Command failed
```

This command worked successfully since the command **grwp** does not exist as a standard UNIX utility. The command thus failed, and the command to the right of the || was invoked.

Example 4

```
$ who > who_file || echo who failed
$
```

Here the **who** command to the left of the || was executed and the output directed to **who_file**, so the second command to the right of the || was not invoked. This is confirmed by returning of the shell prompt ($). Had the first command failed, the message 'who failed' would have been displayed before the shell prompt was returned.

8.2.6 The && metacharacter

The **&&** metacharacter works in the opposite way to the || metacharacter. Here the second command is executed only if the first one is *successful*. Note that the output of the first command is shown on the screen (if not redirected to a file). The structure of the command line is similar to that for ||:

<command1>&&<command2>

You must not confuse the && with the & background process metacharacter, described in section 8.2.4 above. Here are some examples using **&&**:

Examples

Example 1

```
$ who | grep john && echo john is logged in
john tty16 Jun 8  11:06
john is logged in
```

This command requires **grep** to find user **john** in order to invoke the **echo** command. The **who** command is needed to send a list of users on the standard output as the standard input to the **grep** command (the output from this command is also shown). Note that the success of the last command to the left of the **&&** metacharacter determines that the second command should be executed.

Example 2

The previous example displays the message supplied as an argument to **echo**, therefore we can safely conclude that user john is currently logged in.

```
$ who | grep john && mail john < message
```

This command checks whether **john** is logged in, and if he is, then some mail is sent to him. Mail is stored and forwarded to users if they are not logged in (they are notified at login time of any new mail), but some systems have commands to notify users of any incoming mail during the login session (examined in Chapter 10 on UNIX Communication Facilities).

8.2.7 The # metacharacter

The # (hash) metacharacter that tells the shell to ignore all text on the rest of the line (following the # sign). For this reason it is very popular to use it for adding comments to shell-scripts, a convention that we will use in Chapter 13 on Shell Programming.

We can use also the # character interactively, as is shown in the later examples. This metacharacter was not originally made part of the 7th edition of the UNIX system, although it is now available on the majority of UNIX and UNIX-like systems.

Examples

Example 1

```
$ # this is a comment and will be ignored
$
```

This shows that the shell has indeed ignored the entire line. This is because the line starts with the # metacharacter. In such a case the shell ignores all characters to the right of the hash.

Example 2

```
$ who | wc -l # count users on system
6
```

This example shows a # on an actual command line. The shell executes the command (here a **who** command piped into the **wc** filter). The shell carries out the command specified, since the # metacharacter appears to the right of the command in question.

This sort of comment is mainly used in shell scripts to explain various commands to the user(s) who may be using your script. Commenting the command line is a pointless task, although possible, as demonstrated above. We will meet the # metacharacter again later in Chapter 13 on Shell Programming, when we will use it to add comments to our shell-scripts.

8.2.8 The ‘ metacharacter

The back quote (‵ - also known as the *grave-accent*) is synonymous with a concept known as command substitution. As the name suggests, UNIX commands are substituted into the command line using the grave-accent (which encloses the UNIX command to be performed).

Command substitution

In command substitution, program output is used as an argument in the command line. Most UNIX commands can be used for command substitution, although one stands out, namely the **echo** command.

Examples

Example 1

```
$ echo "There are `who | wc -l` users logged in."
There are 3 users logged in.
```

This command substitutes the command **who | wc -l** (which counts the number of users on the system) into a sentence which is displayed on the screen using **echo**. The output from the **who | wc -l** in this case is 3 (indicating three users are logged in) and this is substituted into the line displayed using **echo**.

This example is ideal for command substitution using **echo**, since only one line of text is returned from the substituted command (a line from a **who** listing). Notice the use of the double quotes (") which are necessary because the substitution takes place in the middle of a sentence. To be on the safe side, always enclose the sentence to be displayed in double quotes.

Example 2

The **date** command, which returns the current date and time is ideal for use in command substitution because it returns only one line of output. If we typed **date** on its own at the shell prompt we would see a display similar to that shown below:

```
$ date
Tue May 15 13:09:45 GMT 1990
$
```

Alternatively, **date** can be incorporated into an **echo** command as an argument as shown in the example:

```
$ echo "The date and time is :`date`"
The date and time is :Tue May 15 13:09:50 GMT
$
```

As soon as the shell comes across the grave-accent (`) it expects an executable UNIX command to follow. It then attempts to execute the command. If the command is invalid, i.e. is misspelt or does not exist, an error message will appear in the substitution instead of the expected output.

You need to leave a space immediately before a grave accent, unless you wish the substituted output to appear joined to the preceding text that is to be displayed. An alternative is to use a single colon (:), as shown in this example.

Example 3

```
$ echo "The current directory is `pwd`"
The current directory is /usr/john
$
```

In this command we are using the output of **pwd** (print working directory) as an argument to the **echo** command by including **pwd** in the command line enclosed in grave-accents. This is an ideal command to use in this way, because it returns only a few characters on a single line of output.

Example 4

```
$ echo "Your terminal is `tty`"
Your terminal is /dev/tty20
$
```

This command uses another small UNIX utility, **tty**, which returns the name of the current terminal that is being used (a device that exists in the **/dev** directory).

Example 5

```
$ echo"You are logged in as `who am i`"
You are logged in as /usr/john
$
```

This substitutes the **who am i** command into a sentence which is displayed using **echo**. The argument passed to **who** is the **[am i]** option, which makes who tell you the name of the current user (a full pathname of that user's directory). The result is a command that prints the name of the current user, but in a more friendly fashion than 'who am i' on its own. Who said UNIX wasn't user friendly?

Example 6

Slightly more complex commands can be enclosed in grave-accents, such as arguments to the **mail** command that we met earlier.

```
$ mail `cat` < a_message
john
fred
mary
<ctrl-d>
$
```

This command needs a little explaining. The command here is basically invoking the mail system and the message to be sent is stored in a file called 'a_message' which is redirected as the standard input to **mail**. The only unusual thing is the actual username argument(s) to whom the mail is to be sent.

In this command we have used grave-accents to substitute the **cat** command in place of the username(s) to which the mail message will be sent. Because **cat** used without any arguments simply reads from the standard input stream i.e. the keyboard, the user can simply type in the names of the user(s) to which the message is to be sent, terminating the input with a **<ctrl-d>** signal (the end of file signal).

Once a **<ctrl-d>** is encountered, **cat** will stop reading the standard input i.e. the stream will be closed, and the whole input will be substituted as an argument to the **mail** utility. This shows how more complex commands can be used in conjunction with command substitution; we could have typed the shorter command: **mail john fred mary <a _message** to achieve the same result.

Example 7

In this example we need the names of the users to which mail is to be sent, which are held in a file called 'users'. This file could be created in the following way:

```
$ echo john fred mary > users
```

The output from the **echo** command (the supplied usernames) is redirected to the file called 'users'. This will now be used in our next example:

```
$ mail `cat users` < a_message
```

This command makes **mail** send the message contained in the file 'a_message' to the users in the (previously created) file called 'users'. When **mail** is executed, it expects to find a user, or a list of users, to whom the message will be sent. Instead it finds the two ' metacharacters so it examines the enclosed text. Here mail finds the command **cat users** (i.e. **cat** with the filename argument 'users'). This command is performed by the shell (although not seen by the user), and the resulting output from **cat** (a list of usernames) is substituted as an argument to **mail**.

The format of the file 'users' is not important, provided each username is separated by one or more spaces. Carriage-returns (or blank lines) are not important either, they are simply ignored until the next character string is encountered.

8.3 Shell variables

A shell variable (or parameter as it is also known) is an identifying character string that can contain a range of alphanumeric data. Variables are used extensively in the shell, and they allow the user to substitute arguments to shell commands. They fall into two categories: standard shell variables, some of which are set up by the shell when you log in (the **login** program is normally responsible for this); and user-defined variables which can be created by the user as required.

Every variable must have a name, which begins with $ (dollar) e.g. $name. This section describes the standard shell variables of the Bourne Shell, and explains the various UNIX utilities that can be used to create and manipulate these variables. The next section (8.4) explains how to create user-defined variables.

8.3.1 The standard Bourne Shell variables

A number of standard variables are recognised by the shell, although the actual variables being interpreted at any time depend on the type of shell currently in use. Those variables that are recognised by **/bin/sh**, the 'Bourne' Shell (named after Steven Bourne in 1975) are shown in Table 8.2.

Table 8.2 Bourne shell standard variables

Variable Name	Meaning
$HOME	A variable containing the full pathname of your home directory i.e. your 'login' directory
$SHELL	A variable containing the name of your login shell i.e. the Bourne Shell (**/bin/sh**)
$TERM	A variable containing the name of your terminal (or emulation) i.e. vt100
$USER	A variable containing your user name e.g. **fred**
$PATH	A variable that contains the full pathnames of the directories that are searched for UNIX commands i.e. **ls, who** etc. Directory pathnames are separated by colons
$?	A variable that contains the exit status of a command (numeric)
$#	A variable that holds the number of arguments that a shell utility was invoked with
$-	The number of options in a command
$$	The process identification number of a shell command (and the login shell itself)
$PS1	A variable holding the primary prompt string i.e. $
$PS2	A variable holding the secondary prompt string i.e. >.

$HOME

The **$HOME** variable contains the login directory (known as the home directory) value. It includes a fully qualified pathname of the directory concerned such as **/usr/john**. **$HOME** can be incorporated into any shell command that needs a pathname as an argument e.g. **cp** and **rm**. The existence of the **$HOME** variable saves repeated typing of the pathname (e.g. **/usr/john**).

Examples

Example 1

```
$ cp /usr/fred/letters/letter1 $HOME
```

This command copies the file **letter1**, which resides in the directory **/usr/fred/letters**, into the home directory of the user who is issuing the command. This command is directly equivalent to:

```
$ cp /usr/fred/letters/letter1 /usr/john
```

The **$HOME** variable is more useful when your login directory pathname is larger in size e.g. **/usr/users/dept4/john** is a long pathname to type in repeatedly. Another way to copy the file **letter1** would be to use the '.' directory name, where '.' is **/usr/john** as shown below:

```
$ cp /usr/fred/letters/letter1 .
```

In this command the value of '.' is assumed to be **/usr/john** (the current working directory). This assumption though, may be incorrect, in which case the file would have been copied into the wrong directory. A 'permission denied' message might also appear halting the process. Using **$HOME** would ensure that the file was copied into the **/usr/john** directory, without having to use another command, such **cd**, to make sure the value of **.** was our home directory.

Example 2

```
$ rm $HOME/letter1
```

This command removes the file **letter1**, which resides in the current directory. This command also assumes that the file exists in the user's home directory, since **$HOME** has been specified. The value of **$HOME** is substituted into the pathname, and hence the command becomes:

```
$ rm /usr/john/letter1
```

The command in this example is a bit long-winded, although completely valid. If our current working directory were **/usr/john** we could have simply specified the name of the file to be deleted without a needing fully-qualified pathname i.e. the command **rm letter1**, would achieve the same result.

Example 3

```
$ cd /bin
$ pwd
/bin
$ cd $HOME
$ pwd
$ /usr/john
```

Here, **$HOME** has been used with the **cd** command to change to our home directory. This is directly equivalent to using **cd** on its own. Using the **pwd** (print working directory) utility verifies where we are in the file-system.

Example 4

```
$ echo $HOME
/usr/john
```

This command uses the **echo** command to display the contents of the **$HOME** variable. The **echo** utility can be used with all of the shell variables in this way.

$SHELL

The **$SHELL** variable holds the fully-qualified pathname of our login shell. The name our shell is held in the **/etc/passwd** file as the last field value. You can see your own login shell by typing the command below:

```
$ echo $SHELL
/bin/sh
```

This verifies that your login shell is the Bourne Shell. Another popular shell is **/bin/csh** – the C-shell. The **$SHELL** variable is not really that useful. It is used by many UNIX utilities to simply display the login shell that a given user is allocated. Some systems do not even have a **$SHELL** variable, so check yours now to make sure. Use the command in the example above to do this.

$TERM

The **$TERM** variable stores the name of the terminal you are currently using. The file **/etc/termcap** (terminal capabilities file), an ASCII text file which defines the control codes and escape sequences for a wide range of terminal devices. These control codes define how a terminal should interpret the various control character sequences it receives, for example, cursor key movement values. The name held in **/etc/termcap** should reflect your **$TERM** variable. Try the command below to obtain a line of information about your terminal which is held in the in the **termcap** file.

```
$ grep $TERM /etc/termcap
```

You should now see a line of text that may seem totally meaningless, although it is of considerable significance to UNIX. The ^ (caret or hat) symbols that you may see on the screen represent the <control> key, hence the characters that appear following the ^ symbol are control characters. The **/etc/termcap** file is usually well commented, so have a good read, but I don't recommend that you print it, since it is normally very large. You can use **more** to display the whole file screen-by-screen.

You may see the control codes for the 'common keys' such as **[DEL]** – the delete key; **[RETURN]** – the enter/return key and many others. Make a note of the control code that appears after the name of the key and then try it on your terminal. For example, you may see the carriage return (cr) defined as **^M**, so press **<control>** and the letter 'M', and you should emulate the **[RETURN]** key.

Because UNIX can support a wide range of terminals, the system must be told about the capabilities of a particular manufacturer's terminal device e.g. if it can handle the underlining of characters etc. The VT range of terminals (Video Terminals) supports a wide range of screen display capabilities. Control codes are normally embedded in the text of a file so that special effects for the presentation of text can be utilised.

Because some devices may emulate others e.g. a personal computer (smart terminal) running a VT100 emulation, the codes that are interpreted through the screen by the terminal must be clearly defined. The **/etc/termcap** file provides this facility. Some UNIX utilities are very dependent on the value of **$TERM**, so if you ever have any problems with a terminal which complains with messages similar to 'unknown terminal type', you it is worth trying a different **$TERM** value – VT100 (a common emulation), for example, or another value from the **/etc/termcap** file that relates to the make of your terminal.

A typical **/etc/termcap** entry for an IBM PC machine emulating a VT100 terminal on our system is shown here:

```
# IBM PC connected to Ethernet (Sun). Emulating VT100
#
Ib|IBM-PC|vt100:\
        :ce=\E[B:\
        :cl=\E[2J\E[H:\
        :co#80:\
        :cr=^M:\
        :dc=^H:\
        :dl=\EM:\
        :do=\E[%B:\
        :ho=\E[H:\
        :li#23:\
        :nl=^J:\
        :kd=^[[B:\
        :kh=^[[H:\
        :kl=^[[D:\
        :kr=^[[C:\
        :ku=^[[A:\
        :so=\E[7m:\
        :si=\E[0m:
```

The entry above may seem confusing, but basically the concept is quite simple. Each line in **/etc/termcap** defines a code that will be interpreted by the terminal device in question.

Every line starts with the name of the code to be defined, for example 'cr' is the carriage return signal (**<control>-M**), 'dc' is the delete character signal (**<control>-H**) and so on. 'cl' is the clear the screen signal, and it uses a special code sequence, known as an escape code sequence (E[). The E[prefix on many codes are mostly relevant to screen-based functions.

The **E[** actually represents the **<escape>** key. This is used to start sequences that affect the screen display i.e. cursor movement etc. Some other operating systems e.g. MS-DOS use the square bracket on its own. The **E[2J\E[H** code is a common escape sequence to clear the terminal screen. In MS-DOS the code is simply **[2J** (note that the E is not used). Other codes that may seem familiar are the entries **:co#80:** and **:li#23:** which define the number of columns and rows on the terminal's VDU screen i.e. 80 columns (co) and 23 lines (li), which are common settings for most personal computers (PCs).

The **/etc/termcap** (terminal capabilities file) is discussed further in Chapters 9 and 11.

$USER

The **$USER** variable may exist on your system. It contains your login username. To see if it exists, use the command in the example below:

```
$ echo $USER
john
$
```

This command uses **echo** to display the contents of the **$USER** variable on the standard output.

```
$ mail $USER < message
```

This command can be used to mail a message to yourself. The file **message** is a text file that contains the message to be sent. It is redirected as the standard input to the **mail** utility. If you log out, using **<ctrl-d>** (or exit on some systems) and then log back in, you should see the message **You have mail**. In the example, the value of **$USER** is simply substituted as a username argument to the **mail** utility.

$PATH

The **$PATH** variable is probably one of the most important variables in the UNIX system. **$PATH,** as the name suggests, contains a pathname (a fully-qualified pathname) that relates to one or more directories in the file-system that contain the UNIX utilities that you will eventually use.

Examples of commands that you use frequently include **ls** and **who** etc. These commands are themselves executable programs (written in the high level language C). Every user on the system will have a **$PATH** variable that is set to one or more directories, for example **/bin** (the binary executables directory).

If **$PATH** has not been set, UNIX automatically searches (by default) the user's home directory, the **/bin** directory and the **/usr/bin** directory, which stores the common UNIX utilities mentioned above.

Examples

Example 1

To see a typical path setting, you can display the current setting that has been allocated to you by the login program using **$PATH** in the following command:

```
$ echo $PATH
$HOME:/usr/bin:/bin
```

The response to the command has revealed that the current path has been set to search three directories in the file-system: the shell variable **$HOME** (the pathname of the user's home directory); **/usr/bin**; and **/bin**. The value held by the variable **$HOME** is substituted into the pathname when a command is invoked from the command line.

If you receive an error message, such as 'no such file or command', when invoking a standard UNIX command, you should check the value of **$PATH** which may be set incorrectly. Failing this, the command may not actually exist in the expected directory. In this case use **cd** to change to a different system directory such as **/etc** to look for the command(s) in question.

This example also shows how separate directories are specified in the **$PATH** variable. A single colon (**:**) is used to separate directory names. The **$PATH** variable is normally only set to examine the most common directories, such as **/bin**, because commands held elsewhere are not considered to be needed by normal users. Often such commands may only be used by administrative users, such as the superuser, or by privileged users who have superuser powers. There is no reason why you should not set your **$PATH** variable to scan other system directories (discussed later), although permission may be denied when you try to use certain commands.

Example 2

Another way to make UNIX search the home directory is to specify a null search path, by starting it (the search path) with a single colon (:), as shown below (this saves using the **$HOME** variable):

```
$ echo $PATH
:/usr/bin:/bin
$
```

This colon, at the start of the pathname, tells UNIX to search the home directory of the user first, and then the each of directories **/usr/bin** and **/bin** (the standard system directories) in turn. The order in which the directories are to be searched is quite important; the search starts from the left-hand end of the list i.e. each directory specified in the **$PATH** is searched sequentially for the required command. Some systems precede the first : with a period (.) to specify the home directory.

The facility to specify the order in which directories are to be searched, when a UNIX command is issued, allows the user to change the working environment when required.

Switching environments

Some Berkeley UNIX systems include commands, such as **sv**, which allows the user to switch to a UNIX System V environment. This is done by simply altering the value of **$PATH**. A combination of both System V and Berkeley commands are present in some UNIX systems have . Here the default value of **$PATH** can be set according to the main version of UNIX being used i.e. Berkeley UNIX or System V etc.

In Berkeley UNIX, the default search path will normally be set to search a directory path setting such as **:/usr/ucb;/bin:usr/bin** (**ucb** stands for University of California Berkeley in this context) which contains the Berkeley UNIX utilities. Other directories, such as **/bin** and **/usr/bin**, contain UNIX utilities (**ls** and **cat**, for example) which are common to all UNIX systems.

In a System V environment, the **$PATH** is usually set to a string such as **:/usr/5bin:/bin:/usr/bin**, where **/usr/5bin** is the name of the standard directory on most Berkeley systems which holds many of the UNIX System V utilities. It is important to notice order of the pathnames in the **$PATH** variable, since this specified which directories will be searched first.

Note that System V version 4.0 combines commands from System V UNIX, SunOS (Berkeley orientated), and Xenix (System V). This means that differentiating between the origins of the various UNIX commands should no longer be a problem, although you are advised check your path settings to make absolutely sure.

$?

The $? variable contains the exit code or status value (described in section 8.2.5). When a UNIX utility is executed, it has either a successful or unsuccessful conclusion. When a command is successful, the value of $? is changed to zero; however, if it executes unsuccessfully the value of $? is changed to a non-zero value. This latter value will usually vary according to the utility being used. Be aware that some Berkeley UNIX systems do not use $? but supply an alternative variable, sometimes named 'status' which should be used. All the examples given here use $?.

Examples

Example 1

```
$ grep '^mike' /etc/passwd
$ echo $?
1
```

Here we have invoked **grep** to search the **/etc/passwd** for the user named 'mike'. **Grep** has returned no matches and the command has failed. The **echo** command has been used to display the contents of the **$?** variable in this example. The value displayed is 1 which verifies that the command failed in this case. The value 1 conveys a little information in the case of **grep** -it means that a match was not found. A return status value of 2 from **grep** would have signified an error in the regular expression (an invalid or mistyped command, for example).

Example 2

```
$ who | grep john
john tty14 Jun 8 16:01
$ echo $?
0
```

The first command uses **who** to output a list of users to **grep** on the standard input stream. **Grep** has been asked to find the pattern 'john' (in fact a username) and a line containing the name 'john' is displayed once the pattern has been found. The final command uses **echo** to display the value of the return status, and we can see this is zero, which indicates success i.e. the command **who | grep john** ran successfully.

$#

The **$#** variable holds a value that represents the number of *filename* arguments supplied to a command.

Examples

Example 1

```
$ lpr file1 file2 file3
$ echo $#
3
```

The first command in this example uses the **lpr** command to print the three files: **file1**, **file2** and **file3**. The second command uses **echo** to display the value of $#, which as we can see is 3, indicating three filename arguments here.

Example 2

```
$ pwd
/usr/john
$ echo $#
0
```

This shows the value held by the $# variable when a UNIX utility is invoked with no arguments. The **pwd** command requires no arguments, hence $# is simply zero.

$-

The **$-** variable contains a numeric value representing the number of *options* supplied with a command. It is similar to the $# variable just discussed.

Examples

Example 1

```
$ ls -l
Total 1
drwx------ 1 john 591 Dec 4 13:01 dir1
-rwx------ 1 john 505 Dec 2 10:12 file2
$ echo $-
1
```

In this example we have issued a **ls -l** command. This contains only one option (**-l**), and hence **$-** contains the value 1, as verified in the **echo** command in the example.

Example 2

```
$ ls -lA
Total 1
drwx------ 1 john 45 Dec 6 11:09 .login
$ echo $-
2
```

This command has two options (**l** and **A**), hence **$-** is 2. This has been verified above using **echo** with the **$-** variable.

$$

The **$$** variable holds the process identification number that is assigned to our shell when we log in. In this context, something as simple as an program in execution can be considered as a process.

The Bourne Shell (also known as the 'default' shell) is also a program (**/bin/sh**) that is running continuously, until terminated when we log out using **<ctrl-d>** etc. Every user on the system will have a unique shell process identification number; this allows the shell to be recognised so that it can terminated by another process, if required.

As mentioned, a shell is terminated by the user logging out; however, if the terminal being used to communicate with UNIX should hang, then the user will be unable to log out using the normal **<ctrl-d>** signal. In this case, because the user will still be logged in on their original terminal, it will be necessary to login at a different one to terminate the shell that is still running on the machine that hung.

Users can only terminate processes that they own (for obvious reasons) although the superuser, e.g. **root**, can terminate any process on the system. Terminating a process is achieved via the use of the command **kill**, and it can be specifically used with the **$$** command, as shown below:

```
$ kill -9 $$
login:
```

This command demonstrates how a **kill** command can be used to terminate the current shell, which has the same effect as logging out. The **kill** command has many options, which specify which type of process to kill. For example, a user may wish to terminate a background process but not the shell itself. In some cases the option **-3** can be used for this.

The **-9** option, which has been used in the example above, is known as a *sure kill*, and it allows the process no time to sort out its affairs; it is simply terminated immediately in a rather undignified way. **Kill** would be used with this option when a machine has hung, in the manner previously described.

In order to kill any process, excluding the current shell, it is necessary to know the process-id number. Fortunately UNIX supplies a command called **ps** (the processor status command), which can be used to display a list of all the processes invoked by the current user, or even those that are running on a system-wide basis. This is achieved through the use of the many options that **ps** supplies ('ps -aux' may be useful). The **ps** command is examined in more detail in Chapter 12 on UNIX Security. By definition, **ps** is a monitoring command, and therefore it used very effectively by the administrative user.

The **$$** variable can also be used to create unique filenames. UNIX creates files in the temporary directory **/tmp** (to which all users have write permission), when files are waiting to be printed on a line-printer, for example. Rather than keeping these files in memory, UNIX stores them in a directory file and refers back to them only when it is their turn to be printed (a typical 'queue' scenario). For this to work, every file in the temporary directory must have a unique name, otherwise files with the same name will be overwritten.

To obtain a unique filename, the **$$** variable can be used as a type of extension to a filename. This ensures that the file in question is unique from all other users' files (since they will have different process-id numbers). To create file for purposes of an example, we can use the > redirection operator with the **echo** command, as below:

```
$ echo $$
5631
$ echo This is some dummy data > file$$
$ ls file*
file5631
```

This example illustrates how **$$** has been used as part of a filename. The first command here (**echo $$**) shows the current process-id number assigned to our login shell. The second command simply creates a file called **file5631** by using **echo** to put some dummy data into the file using output redirection. The shell interprets the **$$** and the contents of this variable are appended to the characters already specified as the first part of the filename (here called **file**). The third command (**ls file***) verifies that the file was created.

$PS1 and $PS2

The **$PS1** variable (prompt string 1) holds the character string that is associated with the primary shell prompt which is used at the interactive level to allow the shell to tell us that it is ready to process another command.

In this book we have used the **$** prompt; however, we could include a much longer series of characters in the prompt, if we wished (see section 8.4.1). To verify that the prompt is the **$**, we can use the **echo** command to display the contents of **$PS1**:

```
$ echo $PS1
$
$
```

The other prompt that is used in UNIX is the secondary prompt, also known as **$PS2** (prompt string 2). The **>** prompt is used to represent the secondary prompt in this book. It is displayed when the shell requires more input; for example, when we quote an expression, but do not provide a final quote before a new line is forced, as illustrated on the next page:

```
$ echo 'This made the shell
> display the secondary prompt'
This made the shell display the secondary prompt
$
```

As with **$PS1**, we can display the value of **$PS2** at any time using **echo**, as shown here:

```
$ echo $PS2
>
$
```

8.3.2 Positional parameters

Positional parameters are shell variables that correspond to individual filename and option arguments in the command line. They are more useful during programming, but their use can be demonstrated if we introduce a new command called **set**.

The **set** command is employed when manipulating shell variables, and it performs many actions. When used without any arguments, it simply prints a list of all the currently defined variables, including both the standard variables, such as **$PS1**, **$PS2**, **$PATH** etc.; and any user-defined variables that may have been created.

The arguments that can be used with **set** are themselves valid UNIX commands which must be enclosed in grave-accents (`), but *not* single quotes. Once such an argument has been supplied and the command executed, the shell assigns a unique value to each individual string produced by the output from the command used as an argument. These values are themselves variables, and they are stored in the variable identifiers **$0, $1, $2 ... $n**.

Examples

Example 1

```
$ set `date`
```

This command makes the shell assign variables to each output string produced by the **date** command. This command displays six individual strings of information (separated by spaces), each of which consists of a group of one or more characters. Each string of information is stored in a variable ranging from $0 to $5. These six pieces of information are:

- ❑ The name of the day (Mon, Tue, Wed ... Sun).
- ❑ The month (Jan, Feb, Mar, Apr ... Dec).
- ❑ The day number (i.e. 1, 2 .. 31).
- ❑ The time (i.e. 08:01:09 ? 24 hour format, including seconds).
- ❑ The time Zone code (e.g. GMT).
- ❑ The year (e.g. 1990).

This can be seen diagrammatically in Figure 8.1 on the next page.

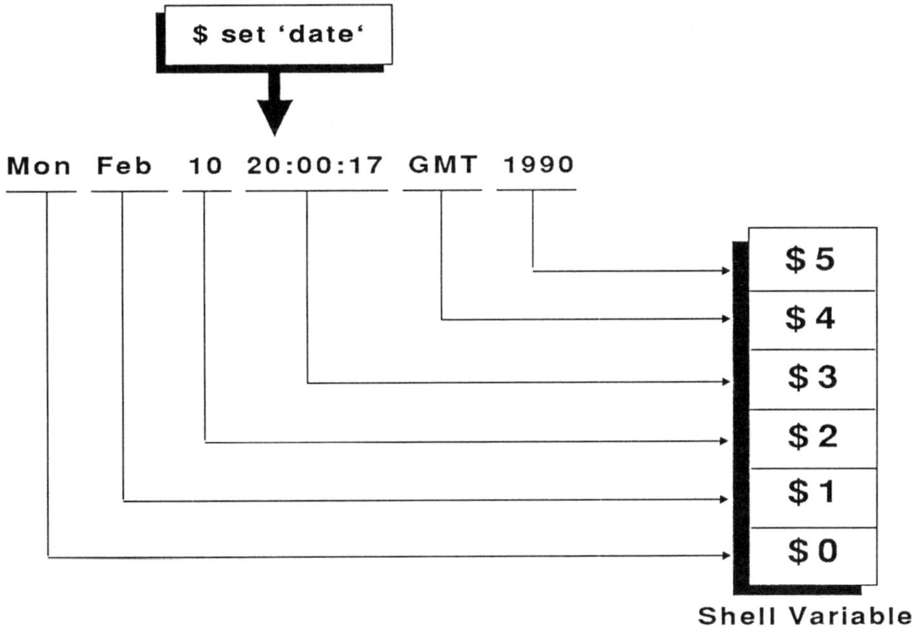

Figure 8.1 Parameter substitution with the date command

Now that the set 'date' command has been executed, we can examine the contents of the resulting variables using **echo**.

```
$ echo $0
Mon
$ echo $1
Feb
$ echo $2
10
$ echo $3
20:00:17
$ echo $4
GMT
$ echo $5
1990
```

The **set** command can be used with any UNIX command that displays its results on the standard output. A problem may occur when using it with commands such as **who** and other commands that tend to display a considerable amount of information. Because the shell variables discussed in this section range from **$0** to **$9** only, any data that appear after **$9** cannot be accessed without employing a command called **shift.** This command (which is built into the shell) is used to move an entire argument list (the variables **$0** .. **$9**) one place to the left, so that **$1** becomes **$0**, **$2** becomes **$1** and so on. The shifting process allows the user to access other data that may have appeared behind the **$9** variable before the shift operation was carried out. The value of **$0** now contains the previous value of **$1**, so its own previous value that was shifted left, is lost forever. Figure 8.2 illustrates the concept of the **shift** command.

In Figure 8.2 the letters **A** to **T** have been used as example arguments in the unshifted argument list. When the **shift** command is invoked, all variables are shifted left one place. This is shown in the lower diagram in Figure 8.2, where the variable **$0** holds the letter **B** (which initially held letter **A**). We can also see that a new letter, **U**, has been introduced at the end of the list.

Figure 8.2 assumes that actual values exist to be shifted. If they do not, we are simply shifting null values – a pointless exercise. To try a shift operation by yourself, try a command such as **set 'set'** which sets up a list of variables that exceed the **$9** value.

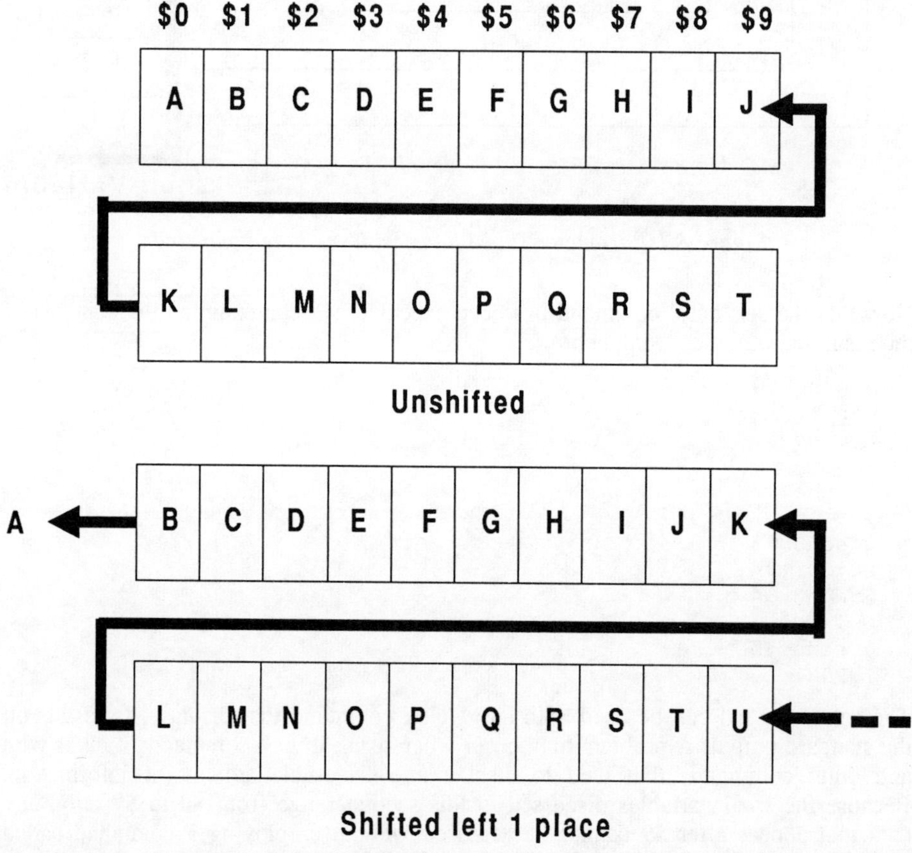

Figure 8.2 An unshifted/shifted argument list

Example 2

We mentioned earlier that **set** used without any arguments simply results in a list of all the currently defined variables. Here is an example:

```
$ set
HOME=/usr/john
IFS=
PATH=:/usr/ucb:/usr/bin:/bin
PS1=$
PS2=>
USER=john
$
```

Note that only the standard shell variables and user-defined variables are defined when we use **set** without any arguments. The **set** and **shift** commands are discussed again in Chapters 10 and 13.

8.4 Creating shell variables

This section introduces the various techniques that allow the user to create and manipulate shell variables. All of the standard shell variables can be manipulated, including any user-defined variables that the user may wish to create.

8.4.1 User-defined variables

Creating a variable is a simple exercise, achieved by assigning a value to a variable identifier. We have met several variable identifiers already, such as PS1, PS2, and PATH etc. To create a user-defined variable i.e. a variable name that is not the same as any standard shell variable, we use a command of the form:

<variable-name>=<value>

Examples

Some examples will illustrate the creation of some user-defined variables:

Example 1

```
$ dir=/usr/john/sales
```

This command creates a variable called **dir** which is assigned the value **/usr/john/sales**, a pathname in this instance. This variable can now be incorporated into a command such as **cd**, which uses a pathname as an argument:

```
$ cd $dir
```

This command changes directory to make the value of the variable dir, i.e. the directory /usr/john/sales, the current working directory. Note the **$** sign on front of the variable. This is essential when referring to any shell variable in UNIX.

Example 2

Shell variables can be of any data-type i.e. numeric, character, or alphanumeric. This fact makes variable creation very flexible. A numeric variable is created in the same way as shown in the first example above.

```
$ x=0
$ echo $x
0
```

This example illustrates the creation of the shell variable 'x'. This variable contains the numeric value 0. Since this is a numeric data-type, it can be used in any command that requires a numeric value as an argument, such as the **sort** command used in the following way:

```
$ who | sort +$x > sorted_who
```

This command pipes the standard output of the **who** command (a list of users) into the **sort** filter (as its standard input). The column notation has been specified in this **sort** command, and the contents of the shell variable **$x** has been specified as a numeric argument. Column **$x** will be sorted (here the username). We can examine the file 'sorted_who' using the **cat** command, as shown below. We can note that the list has been sorted, and on the basis of the first column as we specified in the original command.

```
$ cat sorted_who
john tty16 Jun 8  11:06
mary tty12 Jun 8  14:16
root tty1  Jun 8  11:55
```

Incorporating variables into text

Shell variables can be incorporated into any text displayed using the **echo** command. This is done by explicitly placing the shell variable within the text to be displayed.

The **echo** command will not print multiple spaces unless the text string is quoted, but there are problems quoting **echo** statements. This is because the single quote (') will remove the special meaning from any shell metacharacter. Since the **$** sign is a metacharacter (when used as a variable identifier), its value will not be displayed when it is included in a string enclosed within single quotes:

Example 3

```
$ echo $PS1
$
$ echo 'The value of PS1 is $PS1'
The value of PS1 is $PS1
```

This example demonstrates the result when we use single quotes to enclose a textl string with the **echo** command. In this example **echo** has printed the string literally. There has been no interpretation of any metacharacters within the string itself.

To make the shell interpret shell variables within an **echo** statement, we should really use double quotes, or no quotes at all. However, if multiple spaces are required, you should use double quotes. This is because the double quote allows the shell to interpret any metacharacters that may exist.

Example 4

```
$ echo The value of PS1 is $PS1
The value of PS1 is $
$
```

This example shows the use of **echo** without any quotes of any kind. However, if multiple spaces were required e.g. to centre a piece of text, double quotes must be used, as shown in the next example:

Example 5

```
$ echo The      value      of      PS1      is $PS1
The value of PS1 is $
$
```

This example shows the effect of multiple spaces in an **echo** statement which has not been quoted. The shell simply ignores them and prints the argument string from the first column onwards.

```
$ echo "The value of PS1 is $PS1"
The value of PS1 is $
$
```

Here we see the effect of an **echo** statement with multiple spaces encapsulated in a quoted string. The spaces in this command are printed as they appear (simply because of the quotes). The standard shell variable **$PS1** is also interpreted correctly, since the shell can interpret the **$** metacharacter when the argument string is enclosed in double quotes.

The point to remember is that when combining multiple spaces and embedded shell variables in a textual string, always use double quotes ("); but either single or double quotes can be used if no shell variables are to be included in the string. As a general rule of thumb, always use double quotes when you wish the shell to interpret the metacharacters `...`, or **$** occurring in an argument string.

Command substitution and shell variables

Command substitution can also be used within an **echo** statement when creating shell variables.:

Example 6

```
$ current_dir=`pwd`
$ echo $current_dir
/usr/john
```

Here a standard UNIX command (**pwd**) is assigned to a shell variable. Note that the *output* of the command is substituted into the variable and not the name of the command. The **pwd** command (print working directory) displays the current working directory on the standard output. We have used the output of the **pwd** command as the contents to be stored in the shell variable 'current_dir'. Using **echo** to print the contents this variable is tantamount to simply executing the command which was initially assigned to the variable (the pwd command)!

Example 7

Command substitution can also be used within string arguments passed to the **echo** command:

```
$ echo "We are inside the `pwd` directory"
We are inside the /usr/john directory
```

This shows how the **`...`** convention can be used within a string displayed by the **echo** command. The double quotes ensure that the ` metacharacters (grave-accents) are interpreted by the shell. If single quotes had been used, **`pwd`** would have been printed literally i.e. as it appears. Double quotes have been used to encapsulate the string argument in this **echo** command really only for the purposes of accuracy. The double quotes could have been omitted here, and the **`pwd`** would have been interpreted correctly; however, the common convention is to quote such strings that have quoted expressions within them.

Example 8

Don't forget that a list of all the user-defined variables (as well as the standard shell variables) can be seen using the **set** command without any arguments:

```
$ set
HOME=/usr/john
IFS=
PATH=:/usr/ucb:/usr/bin:/bin
PS1=$
PS2=>
USER=john
$ PATH=$PATH:/usr/john/bin:/bin
$ USER2=fred
$ set
HOME=/usr/john
IFS=
PATH=:/usr/ucb:/usr/bin:/bin:/usr/john/bin:/bin
PS1=$
PS2=>
USER=john
USER2=fred
$
```

Here we used **set** to display the existing shell variables; then we defined two variables (**$PATH** and **USER2**), and finally used **set** again to list *all* the variables currently available. Note that **$PATH** now includes the old **$PATH** variable value (**:/usr/ucb:/usr/bin:bin**) in full. Including the **$PATH** variable in the **PATH=** command is a useful short cut to save typing the existing pathname definitions. If we needed to set an entirely new **$PATH** setting, we would, of course, make no reference to the old **$PATH**.

Creating a new shell environment

When a shell variable is created, its value can only be accessed in the current shell.

As we have mentioned, the shell is itself a program, called **sh**, the Bourne Shell, which commonly resides in the directory **/bin**. Since the shell is an executable program, we can execute a new shell (a sub-shell) from within the current shell by typing the command **sh** at the UNIX prompt (the Bourne-Shell). This creates a new working environment, using the default values for the standard shell variables, (e.g. $ for PS1 and > for PS2) so any user-defined shell variables created for the previous shell are no longer available. When the new shell is terminated, normally using the **<ctrl-d>** keystroke, the values of the previous shell variables are restored – although exported variables are a notable exception. See Figure 8.3.

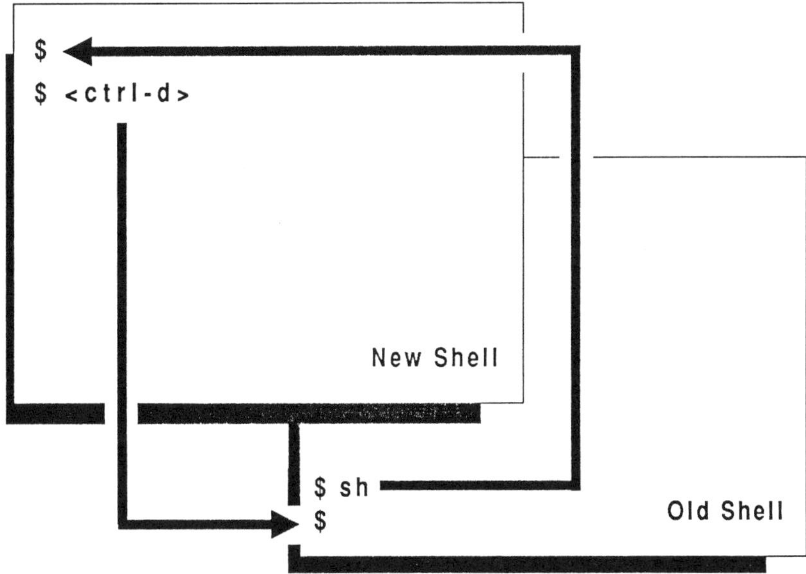

Figure 8.3 Creation and termination of a new shell

The following examples illustrate the effect of a new shell on some newly-defined variables.

Example 9

```
$ echo $PS1
$ PS1=Yes?
Yes?
Yes? sh
$<ctrl-d>
Yes?
```

This shows how the **$PS1** variable (the primary prompt) can be redefined. Once the new shell is created, the previous value of **$PS1** is lost until we exit the new shell.

Example 10

```
$ newpath=:/usr/bin:/usr/john/bin
$ sh
$ echo $newpath
variable undefined
$<ctrl-d>
$ echo $newpath
:/usr/bin:usr/john/bin
```

Here we see how the creation of a new shell can make any previously-defined shell variables disappear. In this example, the shell variable 'newpath' is created and then a new shell is invoked. The user has tried to display the value of the variable 'newpath' using the **echo** command, only to be shown the error message 'variable undefined'. Once the new shell is terminated, the user issues the previous command to find that the variable can be accessed again.

Exporting shell variables

The last two examples illustrate the problem that arise concerning the existing shell variables when a sub-shell is created. However, this can be overcome using the UNIX command named **export**, which is used directly with an existing shell variable. As the name suggests, **export** allows the value of a shell variable to be accessed from outside the environment in which it was originally created. Its use is shown in the next example:

Example 11

```
$ PS1=Yes?
Yes? export PS1
Yes? sh
Yes?
```

In the example the **$PS1** (primary prompt) has been changed to the string **Yes?**. It illustrates how the variable **$PS1** can be exported (note that the **$** sign is not seen, because **$PS1** does not revert back to its default value). The exported variable **$PS1**, now known as a global variable, is available to be used by any new sub-shells which may subsequently be created. We can see that the new shell is using the previous definition of **$PS1** since the prompt has remained unaltered in the new sub-shell.

Example 12

```
$ export dir1 dir2
```

This example demonstrates how multiple variables can be exported by listing them individually on the command line, each one being separated by a space.

You will find that the standard shell variables (such as **$PATH**, **$HOME** etc.) do not have to be explicitly exported when you create a new shell, since the default values assigned to these variables are automatically exported when a new shell is created. However, if any changes have been made to the values of the variables **$PATH**, **$HOME** and **$TERM**, these should be exported to maintain a consistent environment throughout your UNIX session (although they can be redefined when required).

Your system may include the hidden file **.profile**, and this can contain instructions to export the required variables (**$PATH**, **$TERM** and **$HOME**). Alternatively,the systems administrator may alter the source code of the login shell, **/bin/sh**, so that it calls a system-wide **.profile** file that is executed by all users (the **login** program normally being responsible for the creation of these variables). This will then carry out the process of exporting the variables **$TERM** and **$PATH**. So, one way or another, you may find that your current values for the standard shell variables will be exported automatically for you, and available for any sub-shells you may create.

Example 13

If the user wishes to see a list of all the currently exported variables, the **export** command can be issued without any arguments, as shown in the example below:

```
$ export
HOME
PATH
PS1
PS2
```

The output from this command confirms that the standard variables **$HOME**, **$PATH**, **$PS1** and **$PS2** are all exported (global) variables, although **$PATH** and **$TERM** are most commonly set. Any variables that can be seen using the **set** command (used without any arguments) and which do not appear in the list of variables supplied by the **export** command are considered to be local variables i.e. they are local to the shell in which they were initially created.

Temporary variables

A shell variable which is *temporary* can also be created. Once the command has been executed, the value of the variable will be lost. A temporary variable is created and applied to a command using the following notation:

<variable>=<value> <command>

Some examples will illustrate the creation and use of a temporary variable:

Example 14

```
$ PATH=/usr/5bin echo 'prompt appears here :'\c
prompt appears here :$
```

The **echo** command in this example uses the System V convention **\c**, which is the same as the **-n** option (suppress carriage-return code) that is found on UNIX systems later than version 7. The standard variable **$PATH** will remain only while the command executes. The pathname defined in the variable **$PATH** in this example has been temporarily redefined to **/usr/5bin** which is the directory for executable files that are System V orientated. The command could have been shortened by simply quoting the full pathname of the **echo** command:

```
$ /usr/5bin echo 'prompt appears here :'\c
prompt appears here :$
```

This achieves the same outcome, except that the value of the standard variable **$PATH** has not been temporarily redefined. The version of **echo**, or any other UNIX command executed by the user, is normally determined by the pathname stored in **$PATH**. However, this pathname can be overridden by typing in the pathname of the particular command to be executed (which in this example is the **/usr/5bin/echo** command) although this is a rather long-winded solution.

Example 15

```
$ TERM=uni /UII/uniplex
```

This command temporarily redefines the **$TERM** variable. This variable contains a code describing the type of terminal that is being used. It is common for systems administrators to add their own entries to the **/etc/termcap** file (see section 8.3.1) so that different manufacturers terminals interpret the correct escape sequences and control codes etc.

The keyword 'uni' is purely hypothetical, and in this example refers to an entry in the **/etc/termcap** file that sets up a VT100 emulation on an IBM PC to interpret the necessary codes and escape sequences for the Uniplex package. Uniplex is an integrated office system that incorporates word-processing, electronic-mail and spreadsheet facilities etc. The new value assigned to the **$TERM** variable will revert back to the previous setting when Uniplex terminates. We will discuss these variables further in Chapter 13 where they will be used in various shell-scripts.

8.5 Summary of commands

Table 8.3 Commands using metacharacters and variables

Command	Action
ls ????	List files with 4 characters in name.
ls *	List all files.
rm *	Remove all files (beware)
echo *	List all files (same as **ls** or **ls ***).
ls '?'	List the file called ?.
mv * <directory>	Move all files into directory named **<directory>**.
cp * <directory>	Copy all files into directory named **<directory>**.
cp *.c <directory>	Copy files with a **.c** extension into the directory named **<directory>**.
ls -l ; who	Give long listing of files and then list all users logged in.
(ls -l;who) | wc	Run the **ls** and **who** commands and merge both standard output streams. The one stream is then passed to the **wc** filter as its standard input.

continued . . .

Table 8.3 Commands using metacharacters and variables (continued)

<table>
<tr><th>Command</th><th>Action</th></tr>
<tr><td>(ls -l;who)|tee <f>| wc</td><td>Run the ls and who commands, merging both standard output streams into one. The intermediate output from the commands is saved in the file named <f> before the output stream is sent to the wc filter.</td></tr>
<tr><td>ls -l /etc|grep '^d' &</td><td>Display all directory files, and run the command as a background process.</td></tr>
<tr><td>cat <file> | lpr &</td><td>Display the contents of the file named <file> and pipe this into the line printer command thus printing the file from the standard input stream. The command is made into a background process.</td></tr>
<tr><td>ls | grep '^d' || ls</td><td>Find all directory files. If none are found list all files.</td></tr>
<tr><td>ls | grep -v '^d' && ls</td><td>Find all non-directory files and there are some list them, and then list all files afterwards.</td></tr>
<tr><td>echo "Date is 'date'."</td><td>Substitute the standard output of the date command into an argument string displayed using echo.</td></tr>
<tr><td>mail 'cat' < data</td><td>Send a mail message to all users that are read in during the standard input of the cat command. The message being sent resides in the file data.</td></tr>
<tr><td>mail 'cat file' < data</td><td>Send mail to the list of users that reside in the file named data.</td></tr>
<tr><td>cd $HOME</td><td>Change the current working directory to the user's login (home) directory). Same as cd on its own.</td></tr>
<tr><td>cp * $HOME</td><td>Copy all files in the current directory to the user's home directory.</td></tr>
<tr><td>rm $HOME/a_file</td><td>Delete the file named a_file that resides in the user's home directory.</td></tr>
<tr><td>mail $USER < message</td><td>Send some mail to yourself (assuming that $USER holds the current username). File 'message' contains mail.</td></tr>
<tr><td>kill -9 8962</td><td>Kill the process identified by the process-id number 8962. The signal sent to the process is the sure kill (SIGKILL) signal.</td></tr>
<tr><td>kill -3 8963</td><td>Kill the background process identified by the process-id 8963.</td></tr>
<tr><td>kill -9 $$</b></td><td>Log out. Kill the current shell process (<b>$$ is the process-id for the user's shell).</td></tr>
<tr><td>set 'date'</td><td>Store the output of the date command in the positional parameters $0 ..</td></tr>
<tr><td>shift</td><td>Shift the argument list left one place i.e. $2 -> $1, $3 -> $2 etc.</td></tr>
</table>

Continued . . .

Table 8.3 Commands using metacharacters and variables (continued)

Command	Action
x=100	Create a numeric variable called **x** that holds the value 100. The variable is local to the shell.
y=hello	Create a character variable named **y** that contains the string 'hello'. The variable is local to the shell.
PS1=Yes?	Redefine the primary prompt to be the character string **'Yes?'**.
echo $y	Display the contents of the variable **$y** i.e. the string 'hello'.
export x	Make the **x** variable global i.e. make it accessible to any new shells that are created with **/bin/sh**.
PATH=/usr/5bin echo	Use the System V version of echo (assuming **/usr/5bin** exists). The **$PATH** variable is temporarily redefined for the duration of the command.

8.6 Questions

1. What is the purpose of the **export** command?

2. Explain the contents of the **$PATH** variable.

3. The current shell process-id is contained in which shell variable?

4. What would be the effect of the command: **$ PATH=**

5. What would be the outcome is the user now typed the command **who** (in context to question 4)?

6. Show how the format for the command line when a temporary variable is used in conjunction with a UNIX command.

7. Explain what the following commands achieve:

   (1) `who | grep fred && who`

   (2) `who | grep fred || who`

8. What is the command **cd $HOME** equivalent to?

9. Explain what the **/etc/termcap** file is.

10. What System V notation is equivalent to the **-n** option of the **echo** command?

9

UNIX Editors

9.1 Introduction

This chapter describes the use of the UNIX file editor **ex** which is at the top of a hierarchy of UNIX file editors, that include **vi** and **edit**. The **ex** editor is a more sophisticated version of the **ed** editor (in fact, it is a superset of **ed**), and both are very similar. Once you have learned to use **ex** you should be able to use **ed** without any difficulties. **Ed**, and other editors such as **edit** and **vi** are discussed later.

In this chapter, you will learn how to create and manipulate text files. These can contain relatively simple data for use with a tool such as **grep**, or more complex data, such as an executable shell-script.

Ex, like **ed**, is powerful in its ability to handle regular expressions, allowing the user to search a file for a particular occurrence of a group of characters in much the same way as **grep**. These pattern expressions will be explained in this chapter.

9.2 Using the ex editor

Ex was originally developed as a part of the Berkeley tool set, as were the similar tools **edit**, and **e**. The fundamental syntax of the **ex** command is shown below:

```
ex [-] [-v] [+ command] [-r] [file ...]
```

As can be seen, **ex** can be invoked with or without a filename. If a filename is specified, **ex** (like ed) loads a *copy* of the file into its buffer area, which it works with while you are editing, and then copies the edited file back to disk when you have finished.

Ex is a line editor (unless used with the -v option – see 2 below). For this reason alone its popularity has suffered (much like **ed**, which is also a line-based editor). **Ex** allows the user to issue commands from its interactive mode, whereupon lines can be amended, deleted, or augmented. In edit mode, text can be added at will, line by line.

Multiple arguments can also be used with **ex**; here **ex** will edit each file in turn, as explicitly mentioned on the command line. The four main options used with **ex** when it is executed from the interactive level are briefly described here, as they appeared in the earlier syntax description.

1. [-]

The optional hyphen (-) tells **ex** to suppress all the interactive feedback that is supplied to the user. This is mainly used when **ex** is invoked from a shell-script.

2. [-v]

The **-v** option tells **ex** to invoke the **vi** editor (visual screen editor). The use of the **-v** option is useful for switching from line to screen editing mode.

3. [-r]

The **-r** option makes **ex** load the last version of the file that was saved. This is a useful option to use if the editor, or indeed the entire system, crashed without warning. If a file is not supplied using the **-r** option, a list of files that were previously saved is displayed.

4. [+ command]

The + command option allows the user to specify a command to be executed on entry into the editor environment. The command to be executed can be any valid editor command. An example is **ex +10** which invokes **ex** with the line number set at 10.

9.2.1 Simple commands

Commands are supplied to **ex** by typing them next to the interactive prompt, which is normally a colon (:). The most fundamental commands that are used with **ex** are single letters. These are shown in Table 9.1.

Table 9.1 Basic editing commands used with ex

Command	Action in interactive mode
a	Append data after a specified line. Typing a on its own will make **ex** enter edit mode, allowing the user to type in text. A period (.) is typed in the first column (in edit mode) to end.
p	Print the current line.
d	Delete a line.
w	Write the current file to disk (overwrite the file with the contents of the buffer).
i	Insert text at current point.
x	Write file and exit **ex** to the shell level.

9.2.2 Creating a simple file

This example shows how a simple text file can be created:

```
$ ex memo
"memo" [New file]
:a
John, meet me at room 310 at 2.15 pm so we can have a chat.
Jim
.
:x
"memo" 4 lines, 65 characters
$
```

Firstly **ex** is invoked from the shell level (**ex memo**). The message **memo [New file]** tells us that the file **memo** is a new file, i.e. it is newly created and does not already exist in the current directory. **Ex** then places us in its interactive mode (note the ':' prompt).

The first command typed next to the **:** prompt is 'a', the append text command. Since no lines exist in this new file, we simply start to append text from line one. After the **a** command is typed, **ex** enters edit mode (note the absence of any prompt). Some text is then typed in, and then the period . in the first column signifies the termination of the editor mode back to the interactive level. If you dislike the period to end the append mode, you can use a more forceful keystroke such as **<ctrl-c>**, which returns you to edit mode.

From the interactive level we have issued the **x** command (write the file and exit). The file is then saved, and we are returned to the shell level (note the **$** prompt). The file memo now exists in the current directory. We can verify this by issuing an **ls** command, as follows:

```
$ ls -l memo
-rwx------ 1 john 65 Feb 8 13:17 memo
```

This text file can now be searched by tools such as **grep**, and since the file that was created is a memo to John, we could mail it to him immediately:

```
$ mail john < memo
```

9.2.3 Other interactive commands

The remainder of this section deals with the miscellaneous commands that can be used with **ex** at the interactive level.

9.2.4 Printing lines – the p command

The **p** option is used to print lines from a text file i.e.display them on the screen of the terminal. When used without any qualification, it selects the current line for display; example 1 illustrates this use of the 'p' command.

Examples

Example 1

```
$ ex memo
"memo" 4 lines, 65 characters
:p
John, meet me at room 310 at 2.15 pm so we can have a
:
```

In this example we have made **ex** print the first line of the file memo. After loading the file, **ex** automatically places us at the first line in the file, hence this becomes the current line if **p** is the first command typed. This is how most similar commands work i.e. the current line is processed by the command. Notice that **ex** has shown us the name of the file (memo), and its size (given in bytes or characters).

Example 2

P can also be directed to other lines in the file and used to print several lines of text. This is done by specifying the range of lines to view, separating the start and end line values by a single comma (,), in front of the p command, to tell **ex** that we want it to print these lines. This is shown in the next example:

```
:1,2p
John, meet me at room 310 at 2.15 pm so we can have a chat.
:
```

Here, we have specified that **ex** should print only lines one and two (1,2p). After this has been done **ex** returns us to the interactive level i.e. to the : prompt.

Example 3

The command **nu** (also known as #) allows lines of text to be displayed along with their corresponding line numbers. Since lines are numbered consecutively i.e. 1,2,3 .., a line can be explicitly mentioned on the command line, as shown here:

```
:1
John, meet me at room 310 at 2.15 pm so we can have a
```

9.2.5 Inserting text – the i command

Apart from appending text to the end of a file, there will always be a time when text has to be inserted between existing lines of text. This is achieved using the **i** (insert) command, which can be can be used either on its own, or qualified by a specified line number. When used unqualified, the new text is inserted before the current line, as shown in Example 1 below. A single period is used to exit insert mode.

Examples

Example 1

```
:i
This is how a line is inserted
```

Example 2

Inserting text at a specific line number, is done using the command in the following way:

```
:i10
We are inserting just before line 10
```

9.2.6 Deleting text – the d command

Lines can be deleted from a file using the **d** (delete) command. It is used in a similar way to the other commands we have already met (such as **i** and **a**). To delete one particular line we explicitly specify it on the command line. Ranges of lines can also be deleted. When used without a line number the **d** command deletes the currently selected line. These features are illustrated in the following examples.

Examples

Example 1

```
:1-8p

A very brief history of UNIX

----------------------------

UNIX was developed by Bell Laboratories in the late 1960's. Ken
Thompson, with support from people such as Joe Ossana, Doug
McIlroy, Rudd Canaday and Dennis Ritchie wrote a small time-
sharing system, which was then moved to a PDP-11 computer in 1970.
 :1-2d
 :1-8p

UNIX was developed by Bell Laboratories in the late 1960's. Ken
Thompson, with support from people such as Joe Ossana, Doug
McIlroy, Rudd Canaday and Dennis Ritchie wrote a small time-
sharing system, which was then moved to a PDP-11 computer in 1970.
 :
```

This example shows how a range of lines can be deleted. The first eight lines of text in the file are displayed first, using **p**, and then the first two lines are deleted. When the first eight lines are displayed again, we can see that only five lines of text remain in the file.

Because **ex** (and **ed**) manipulates a *copy* of the file being edited (in a buffer area), any deletions made are not permanent until the file is saved i.e. leaving the editor using the **x** command, or by using the **w** (write) command (discussed in the next section – 9.4.4). It also means, if you are working on an existing file, that you can use the **q** (quit) command to abort any changes that have been made. However, if the file you are working with is newly created, then any deletions are permanent because no earlier version of the file exists for you to refer back to.

Example 2

```
$ ex memo
"memo" 4 lines, 65 characters
:p
John, meet me at room 310 at 2.15 pm so we can
:d
:
```

This example illustrates how the **d** (delete) command can be used in its implied mode. In the example we have edited an existing file called **memo**. When the file has been read into the buffer area, the current line number address is automatically set to 1 (the default setting). If we now type **d** on its own and press the **[RETURN]** key, **ex** deletes the current line (although it isn't specified). Also note that the **p** command works in a similar fashion here.

9.2.7 Saving text – the w command

Text can be saved from the buffer and written to disk, without leaving the **ex** editor, using the **w** command. This is shown in the next example:

```
:a
John, meet me at room 310 at 2.15 pm so we can
have a chat.
Jim
.
:w
"memo" 4 lines, 65 characters
:
```

Once the **w** command has been issued, the name of the file and its size (in lines and characters) are shown, and we are returned to the colon prompt (:), ready for the next **ex** command.

9.2.8 Moving text – the m command

Individual lines, or groups of lines, can be moved to a different location within the same file using of the **m** (move) command. This command needs skillful handling, the format being:

<start-range>,<end-range>m<destination-line>

The **<start-range>** and **<end-range>** are both numeric values representing the line numbers of the limits of the range of lines to be moved. The range is specified using the comma (,) symbol separating the **<start- range>** and **<end-range>** line numbers and it precedes move command (**m**) itself. The **<destination-line>**, which follows the command, is the number of the line that the moved lines are to follow.

Examples

Example 1

```
:1,7m10
```

This move command will move the range of lines (lines 1 to 7 in this case) to the destination line, line 10. Remember that any lines that are moved are placed after the **<destination-line>** value, so in this case the lines that have been moved will appear from line 11 onwards.

Example 2

Valid line numbers normally occur in the range 1 .. n. However, to move a group of lines to the beginning of the file, we will need to specify 0 as a **<destination-line>** value. The example below illustrates a valid zero value for the destination line. In this command lines 1 to 7 are moved to line 1:

```
:1,7m0
```

9.2.9 Substituting text – the s command

The **s** (substitute) command is used to search for and substitute occurrences of specified text in the current file. There are many formats for this command, the most common of which are:

(a) s/<word-to-replace>/<new-word>/

When this command is used on its own, it changes the first occurrence only of **<word-to-replace>** into the new word **<new-word>** in the current line. No other occurrences of **<word-to-replace>** are replaced (even if on the same line).

(b) If it is used in conjunction with the **p** command (print the current line), in the following way:

s/<word-to-replace>/<new-word>/p

it achieves the same result, except that the new line is reprinted on the screen following the substitution.

(c) s/<word-to-replace>/<new-word>/g

This format uses the **g** (global) command variant. This causes substitution of all matches of **<word-to-replace>** which occur on the current line. (This is an extension of format (a) above).

(d) s/<word-to-replace>/<new-word>/gp

This command makes all the substitutions of **<word-to-replace>** on the current line, and then reprints the new line. Some example commands are on the next page:

Examples

Example 1

```
:1p
UNIX was developed by Bell Laboratories in the late
:s/Laboratories/Labs/
```

This command substitutes the word **Labs** for **Laboratories** on the current line. There is only one occurrence of the word therefore the **g** (global) option is not needed here.

Example 2

```
:1p
UNIX was developed by Bell Laboratories in the late
:s/Laboratories/Labs/p
UNIX was developed by Bell Labs in the late
:
```

This example is similar to the previous one, but we have asked for the line to be printed once the substitution has taken place.

9.2.10 Addressing characters

Addressing characters are simply characters that refer to a certain set of lines in the current buffer. They are useful when a specifying commands that have to act on a range of lines. The most common addressing characters are shown in Table 9.2.

Table 9.2 Addressing characters used with ex

Character	Meaning
$	The last line in the buffer.
n	The nth line in the buffer i.e. line 1, 2, or 3 etc. The letter is substituted for the line in question.
%	The entire buffer i.e. the range 1,$ (line 1 to the last line in the buffer).
+n or -n	Offsets relative to the current line. The – sign refers to a line previous to the current, the + refers to a line after the current. Normally used to print a range of lines that lie around the current.

Examples

This section describes how the addressing characters described above can be incorporated with other common interactive **ex** commands.

Example 1

```
:.,$d
```

This command deletes (note the **d**) all lines from the current line onwards, in the buffer. The '.' (period) matches the currently selected line, and the **$** matches the last line in the buffer. A range is necessary for this command (note the comma sign inbetween the '.' and '$').

Example 2

```
:1,$d
```

This command deletes *all* the lines in the current buffer. A range has again been specified, which starts from line 1 through to the last line in the buffer (note the **$** symbol).

Example 3

```
:$d
```

This simple command deletes the last line in the buffer. A range is not required for this command, the single line to delete being specified by the **$** sign (the addressing character that represents the last line in the buffer).

Example 4

```
:1,$s/Unix/UNIX/p
```

This command demonstrates how addressing ranges and substitution commands can be combined. The command is using two **ex** commands:

s (substitute text), and

p (print current line)

The substitution of the word 'Unix' (with the word 'UNIX' in upper case) is carried out for the first occurrence of the word 'Unix' in every line in the buffer (note the address range **1,$**). Any other occurrences of the word 'Unix' on the same line are ignored.

The **p** command that has been specified following the substitution ensures that all lines containing the substituted word are displayed.

Example 5

```
:1,$s/Unix/UNIX/g
```

This command ensures that *all* occurrences of the word 'Unix' are replaced by the upper case version 'UNIX'. This is because the **g** (global) command has been used, which ensures that the substitution is carried out for every occurrence of the specified word that appears on the selected single line. Because the range specified is **1,$**, the substitution can take place in every line in the file.

The **p** (print) command has not been used in this example, therefore all lines that have substituted words within them are not displayed to the user.

Reversing a substitution

An incorrect substitution can be a nuisance since the substitution may range over the entire file in the buffer. However, **ex** provides the **u** command which undoes the effect of the last used substitution The example below illustrates this used in conjunction with the current line (**.** address):

```
:.s/Unix/UNIX/gp
UNIX was developed by Bell Laboratories in the late
:u
:Unix was developed by Bell Laboratories in the late
:
```

9.2.11 Searching lines for text

Searching lines for text is done using regular expressions. These are similar to the regular expressions used by **grep** (some are identical). The most fundamental regular expressions used with **ex** are shown in Table 9.3:

Table 9.3 Regular Expressions used with ex

Character(s)	Action
^	Match a pattern that occurs at the beginning of a line (same as **grep**).
$	Match a pattern that occurs at the end of a line (same as **grep**).
.	Match any character (same as **grep**).
[...]	Match any single character between [and]. Same as **grep**.
[^...]	Matches characters not present within the [and] brackets. Same as **grep**.
/<	Match start of a word.
/>	Match end of a word.

The / command

The / symbol is used to find the next occurrence of a particular pattern which is typed following the symbol. The pattern may include regular expressions, if required. An optional second / symbol, following the pattern, (enclosed within [and] brackets to denote an optional part of the command) allows further **ex** commands to be specified. The format for a simple search is:

/<pattern>[/<command>]

The **<pattern>** is a string of text (that may or may not a contain a regular expression), and the optional **<command>** is used to execute an **ex** command on the lines(s) that contain the matching patterns. The 'p' option can be specified to print, or the **d** command can be used to delete, the lines found lines containing the matching patterns. Note that a pattern may be matched within an existing word e.g. '/store' matches 'restore', 'stores', etc.

Examples

Example 1

```
:/Unix/p
```

This illustrates how the next occurrence of the word 'Unix' can be displayed.

Example 2

```
:/Unix/d
```

This finds the next occurrence of 'Unix', and then deletes the line in which it occurs.

9.2.12 Global commands

Global searches allow the user to apply **ex** commands to a set of lines (or all the lines) in the current buffer (notice the difference between this command and the operation provided by the /<pattern> command). The format for a global search over all lines in the buffer is:

g/<pattern>[/<command>]

The **<command>** is optional (as denoted by the square brackets). Global searches are initiated using **g** at the beginning of the command. When used in this way all lines in the buffer are searched without specifying an address (such as **1,$**). We met the **g** command earlier, when it was placed at the end of a substitution command to replace all occurrences of the required pattern.

Example searches

To carry out a search, first the **g** command is specified, followed by the back-slash (/) symbol. The regular expression is terminated with another / sign, which may be followed by a command to act on the matched line(s).

Example 1

```
:g/Unix/p
```

This example searches all lines for the word 'Unix' (case sensitive). The **p** command causes **ex** to display the lines that the word was found in.

Example 2

```
:g/Unix/d
```

This command deletes all lines containing the word 'Unix' because the **d** command has been specified at the end of the regular expression.

Example 3

```
:g/Unix/s/Unix/UNIX/p
```

This command causes **ex** to search all the lines (globally) in the buffer that contain the word 'Unix'. If any matches are found, they are substituted (note the 's' option) with the word 'UNIX' (in upper-case). The lines that have words matched within them are also printed (using the 'p' option).

Example 4

```
:g/[uU]nix/UNIX/p
```

This command uses the [...] regular expression to match the words 'Unix' or 'UNIX' (note the case of the 'U'). You may remember that the [...] regular expression matches any single character enclosed in the square brackets. The **p** command ensures that any matched lines are displayed on the screen.

Example 5

```
:g/^Unix/UNIX
```

This command matches all lines that begin with the word 'Unix'. Using the ^ symbol (caret or hat) indicates that only the start of a line is to be matched.

Global ranges

Ranges can also be specified with the **g** (global command). Ranges are specified on the command line using the following format:

<start-line>,<end-line>g/<pattern>[/<command>]

The **<start-line>** and **<end-line>** values are simply the line number values that define a range of lines to be scanned. The letter 'g' represents the global command variant, and **<pattern>** is the text to be sought. The **<pattern>** can also contain regular expressions. Note also, that the /**<command>** is optional here.

Global range examples

Example 1

```
:1,10g/Unix/p
```

This command searches lines 1 through to 10, to try to find the word 'Unix'. If the pattern is matched then that line is displayed on the screen (invoked by the **p** command).

```
$ who > who_file
$ ex who_file
"who_file" 3 lines, 63 characters
:1-3p
root  tty1   Jun 9   09:55
mary  tty2   Jun 9   11:16
john  tty8   Jun 9   12:06
:g/tty[12]/p
root  tty1   Jun 9   9:55
mary  tty2   Jun 9   11:16
:
```

This longer example shows the creation of a file (a **who** command listing using output redirection to create the file). The search command in the example is global, and a regular expression, 'tty[12]', using the **[...]** notation has been used to match the patterns 'tty1' or 'tty2'. The **p** (print) command then prints all the lines matching the search pattern onto the screen.

Example 2

```
:/Unix$
```

The regular expression in this example uses the **$** symbol to make **ex** match the first occurrence of the word 'Unix', but only if it appears at the end of a line.

Example 3

```
:/^Unix$
```

Here the regular expression will match the pattern (the word 'Unix') occurring alone on a line. This is because the **^** specifies that the pattern must start at the beginning of the line, and the **$** that it must be matched at the end of a line.

Remembering search patterns

When searching for a pattern in a group of one or more lines, a repeated search pattern can be abbreviated to //. This is because the last search argument is remembered. For example:

```
:/Unix/s/Unix/UNIX/p
:/Unix/s//UNIX/p
```

The first command in this example is starting a search for the word 'Unix'. Once the first occurrence has been found, it is substituted with the new version 'UNIX' (in upper-case). Note also the format of the substitution command, which in this example appears after the search pattern.

The second command in the example shows the same command in operation, except the // notation has been used in place of the sequence **/Unix/**. This is because **ex** makes a note of the last search pattern. The // notation could therefore be considered a shorthand notation for the last search pattern.

Searching backwards

It is also possible to search backwards for a pattern. This is done by enclosing the search pattern in question marks i.e. **?<pattern>?**, instead of the // notation used for the normal forward search. This is shown in the examples which follow:

Examples

Example 1

```
:?Unix?
```

This command searches the previous lines in the buffer for the word 'Unix'.

Example 2

```
:??
```

This searches the previous lines in the buffer for the pattern entered in the previous command e.g. if we specified **?Unix?** as a search pattern, **??** would be a shorthand notation for the same command.

9.2.13 Further addressing techniques

Other shorthand notations which can be used to address individual lines in the buffer are shown in Table 9.4 below. They can be used in conjunction with all the commands described in previous sections.

Table 9.4 Shorthand address notations

Character	Action
-	The last line (same as .-1).
+	The next line (same as .+1).
+n	The line n after the current line. (Same as .+n and .n).
++	The line after the next (same as +2).
--	The line after the last (same as .-2).
.n	The line n after the current line.

The \< and \> addressing techniques

The \< and \> notations are used with a regular expression to match a pattern found at the start or the end of a word, respectively. The \< notation must be placed at the beginning of the search pattern (i.e. /\<**pattern**) while the \> notation always ends the pattern (/**pattern**\>). Notice that each expression must be preceded by the / character, to initiate the search. A few examples demonstrate the use of these addressing techniques:

Examples

Example 1

```
:/\<ran
```

This command will match **ran** but only at the start of a word, thus it will will match 'range' but not 'arrange' (because the pattern 'ran' occurs in the middle of the word).

Example 2

```
:/ran\>
```

This command initiate a search for a pattern, where the character string 'ran' occurs at the end of a word, for example 'overran'.

Example 3

To find an entire word, that is, a separate word within a line we would use a combination of both notations.

```
:/\<ran\>
```

This command matches only the word 'ran' and not any other words that may contain this pattern embedded within them.

9.2.14 Running shell commands

The user can invoke a shell command from within **ex** by preceding the command with an exclamation mark or shriek (**!**).

Examples

Example 1

```
:! who
root  tty1   Jun 9   09:55
mary  tty2   Jun 9   11:16
john  tty8   Jun 9   12:06
:
```

This example shows how the **/bin/who** command can be executed from within the **ex** editor.

Example 2

A working shell environment can also be created, allowing the user to enter shell commands at the interactive level. This is done by executing a new shell i.e. **/bin/sh**, the Bourne shell (or **/bin/csh**, for the C-shell) from within the editor, as shown in this example:

```
:! /bin/sh
$ ls -l Total 1
drwx------ 1  john      591  Dec 413:01dir1
-rwx------ 1  john      505  Dec 210:12file2
$ <ctrl-d>
:
```

Figure 9.1 shows how the editor waits in the background (although it is not a background process) until the user terminates the shell process, and is returned to the editor's interactive mode. The **!** command must be used to invoke the shell, since the shell is itself an executable file, similsr to **/bin/ls** and **/bin/who**.

Example 3

The **!!** command operates in a similar way to the **//** and **??** notation described previously, and repeats the last shell command executed, as is illustrated below with the **/bin/who** command:

```
:! who
root   tty1   Jun 9   09:55
mary   tty2   Jun 9   11:16
john   tty8   Jun 9   12:06
:!!
root   tty1   Jun 9   09:55
mary   tty2   Jun 9   11:16
john   tty8   Jun 9   12:06
:
```

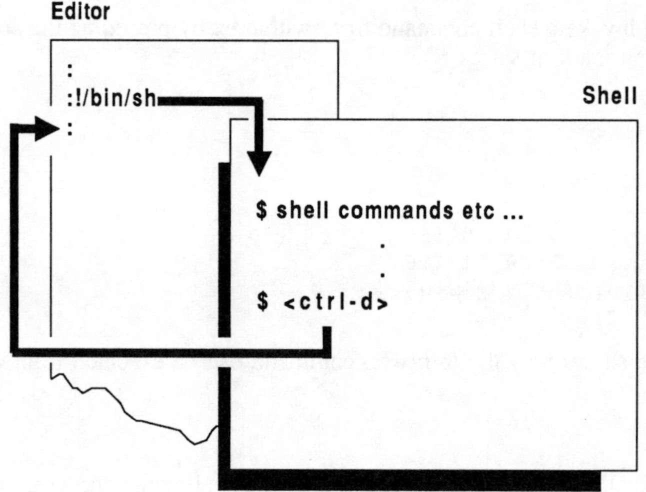

Figure 9.1 Creation of a shell from within the editor.

9.2.15 Summary of ex

ex is a *line-based* editor, i.e. it operates on one line at a time. A *visual* editor allows the user to work with a screenful of information at a time. The main editor under UNIX which provides these editing facilities is called **vi**. This is discussed in section 9.4, but before that, it is worthwhile taking a quick look at **ed**.

9.3 Ed

Ed is part of the 'standard' UNIX system. Whichever UNIX system you are using, whether it be Xenix or System V based, **ed** should be included (normally residing in the **/bin** directory). The facilities provided by **ed** are the similar to those of **ex**, but there are subtle differences. For a start, **ed** is more limited in its use of of regular expressions, whereas **ex** has an abundance of such expressions. If you now understand the concepts introduced in the previous sections, **ed** should not pose any problems.

9.3.1 Starting ed

Ed can be invoked by typing **ed** at the shell prompt with or without a filename. If the name of an existing file is specified, **ed** reads its contents into its buffer, in the same manner as **ex**, and tells you how many characters are in the file.

The **ed** command-mode prompt is a question mark (?). The examples below illustrate the creation of a new file, and the use of **ed** on an existing file.

Examples

Example 1

```
$ ed file_1
245
?
```

This shows how **ed** is invoked with an existing file (named file_1). The file is read into the buffer area and the number of characters in the file is displayed.

Example 2

```
$ ed file
? file
?
```

This shows the creation of a new file. ed queries the existence of the file by displaying a question mark followed by the filename. The interactive prompt (?) is **ed**'s way of telling you to enter a command. The most fundamental commands are that can be entered at the interactive level are shown in Table 9.5.

Table 9.5 Commands used with ed

Command	Action
a	Append text after the current line.
c	Change text on specified line.
d	Delete lines of text on specified line.
f	Rename the current file.
g	Global command (used in searches etc).
i	Insert lines of text before current line.
m	Move a group of lines to another line.
p	Print lines.
q	Exit from ed (need to q's to abandon work).
s	Substitute text.
u	Undo the latest substitution.
w	Write the contents of the buffer to disk.

As can be seen from the table, the majority of ed commands are the same as found in the **ex** editor; this is not unexpected because **ex** is a direct descendant from **ed**.

9.4 Vi

The **vi** editor is also part of the Berkeley tool set. It is a visual editor, allowing the user to work with a screen of information at any one time. All editors basically work in two modes, and **vi** is no exception. The first mode is the *command* mode (the interactive mode), and the second is the *edit* mode, where text is inserted into the current document. This section offers a comprehensive coverage of the most fundamental **vi** commands.

9.4.1 Vi and the terminal

Vi is very dependent on the capabilities of your terminal, mainly because it is a screen-based editor and therefore it must interpret specific control-codes and escape-sequences to allow you, the user, to perform the required tasks on the text being edited. The **/etc/termcap** file contains a list of available terminals and their capabilities. You may also find that some additional terminal names have been provided to specifically work with the **vi** editor on your UNIX system.

9.4.2 Starting vi

Vi is invoked at the shell level with or without a filename. If a filename is specified, the contents of the file are read in and displayed to you on the screen. **Vi** will, by default, display 25 lines of text on the screen to you. This portion of the screen can be *scrolled* upwards or downwards. The cursor plays a more active role in visual editing because of this. The command `$ vi file` results in the screen shown in Figure 9.2.

Figure 9.2 Creation of a new file

When a file is edited for the first time, **vi** displays the name of the file and a New File message on line 25 of the screen, as illustrated in Figure 9.2. The tildes (~) display the position of each empty line in the current screen; these disappear when text is entered into the blank line. The tilde symbols are non-printable characters, and therefore will never appear in any documents that are eventually printed. The last line on the screen (line 25) is termed the status line, and displays any messages to the user during a **vi** session.

Modes used in vi

Vi works in basically three modes – one *edit* mode (where text is inserted, amended or deleted etc.) and two *command* modes. The first command mode (the basic or screen mode) is used to move the cursor around the screen, or text, to the required location; and to enter the other two modes. No screen prompt is used with this basic mode, and when the commands are typed in, the response is immediate; they do not need to be entered by pressing the carriage-return key. Edit mode is entered by issuing the appropriate edit command (by using **i** – 'insert' or **a** – 'append' commands, for example). The second command mode (interactive mode) is used where additional processing is needed and it is similar to **ex**; it is accessed by pressing the **:** key to provide a **:** prompt and all the commands available to **ex** can be accessed from this mode. Pressing the **[ESC]** key returns you to the basic command mode from either interactive command or edit modes. The relationship between these three modes is summarised in Figure 9.3.

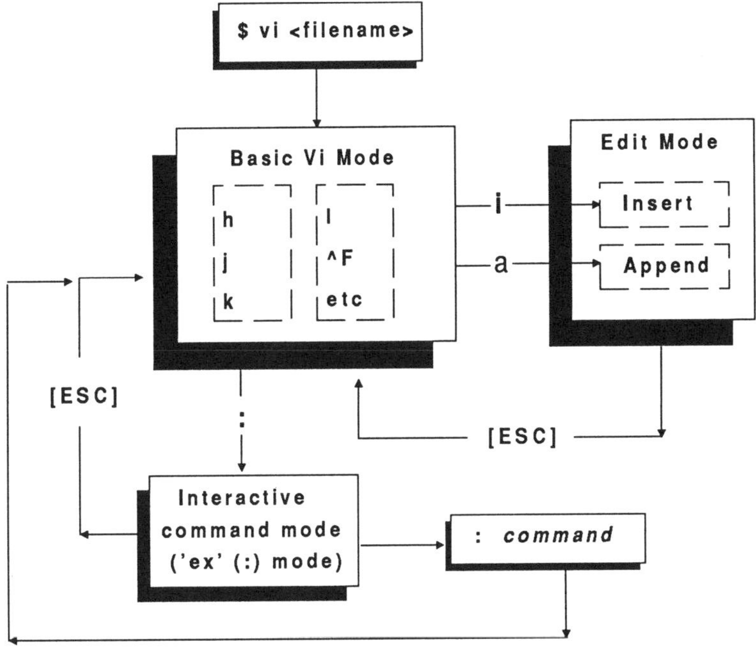

*Figure 9.3 Summary of **vi**'s operating modes*

9.4.3 Inserting text – the i command

Text is inserted at the current cursor position using the **i** (insert) command from the basic command mode. Assume we pressed 'i' to enter edit insert mode and typed:

```
UNIX was developed by Bell Laboratories in the late 1960s. Ken
Thompson, with support from people such as Joe Ossana, Doug
McIlroy, Rudd Canaday and Dennis Ritchie wrote a small time-
sharing system, which was then moved to a PDP-11 computer in 1970.
```

Figure 9.4 shows the screen display after the above text was entered using the insert option.

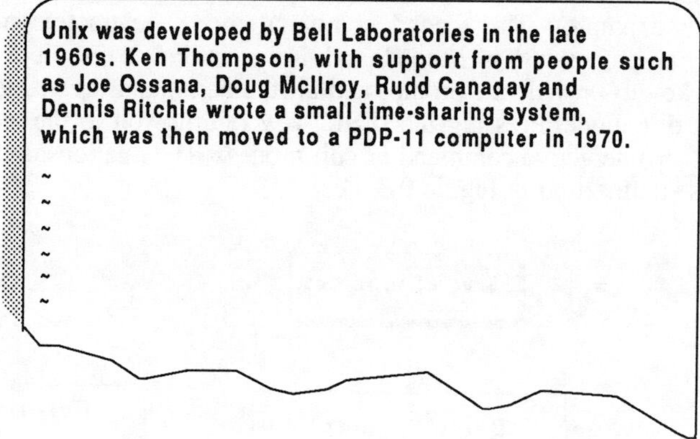

Figure 9.4. Insertion of a piece of text

Inserting and appending text (to be discussed shortly) into a document is rather clumsy in **vi**. For a start **vi** does not wrap words onto new lines, although it will wrap characters. **Vi** is a very simple wordprocessor, the user having to arrange the text neatly to their own specifications. For this reason it is wise to keep lines below the 80-column maximum that is imposed by the majority of VDU screens. However individual lines can exceed the 80-character maximum, up to a limit of 512 characters. However, the use of such long line lengths is not recommended because some **vi** commands are line specific, and manipulating a line that exceeds 80 characters can be extremely awkward.

Exiting edit mode

Once you have finished editing your text, you need to press the **[ESC]** (escape) key to return to the basic command mode. Without the use of an **[ESC]** key, the you are is effectively trapped in the insert mode of **vi**. This is where **/etc/termcap** is helpful, since it can include a definition of the correct code for the escape key on the particular terminal that you are using.

9.4.4 Appending text – the a command

The **a** (append) command allows text to be appended into the buffer. When a new file has been created (or a file contains no lines of text) the **a** command achieves the same action as **i**. When the **a** command is entered, from the basic command mode, the cursor moves one place to the right, ready for the new text to be appended into the current document. Press [ESC] to exit this mode.

9.4.5 Inserting blank lines – the o command

Blank lines can be inserted in one of two ways; either by editing in a series of blank characters (using the **i** or **a** commands, depending on where the line to be inserted must be placed), or by using the **o** command. This **o** (open line) command, opens a blank line immediately below the current line where the cursor is positioned. If **o** is the first command the user invokes, **vi** will place the cursor one line down from the top of the document. You need to press [ESC] before using the **o** command.

If the **o** command processes an unused line, indicated by a tilde (~) in its leftmost column, the tilde will disappear and a blank line will appear in the final document.

9.4.6 Saving and abandoning your work

When the task of typing a document is completed, the user must either save or abandon the work. Saving the current file involves writing the contents of the buffer to disk, while abandoning the current file means losing it for ever. To save or abandon a file it is necessary to enter vi's interactive mode, by pressing the colon (:). Once this has been done **vi** drops into the **ex** environment (note the : prompt in Figure 9.5), allowing the user to access the necessary commands to save or abandon the current buffer contents. The user has four options at this stage:

❑ Abandon the current document, and return to the shell

❑ Save the current document under the filename with which **vi** was invoked, and return to the shell

❑ Save the current document under a new filename and return to the shell

❑ Save the current document under a new filename, and resume editing.

Figure 9.5 illustrates the second command mode environment of the **vi** editor. Note the colon (:) in the status line (line 25 of the screen). This mode should always be used to issue commands to save your work and quit etc.

9.4.7 Abandoning your work

To abandon the current work which has been typed, enter interactive mode, by pressing ':', and then type **q** (the quit option). **Vi** then checks the state of the current document. If you have just loaded a file into the buffer, and **q** is entered, **vi** will exit gracefully, since no modifications have been made to the file, which would have been lost upon exiting. However, if the file has been altered in some way, using the **a** or **i** commands for example, before abandoning the file **vi** would warn you with a message similar to the one shown below:

```
:q
No write since last change (:quit! overrides)
:quit!
$
```

This message is telling you that the altered file has not been written to disk, and that the we cannot abandon it without specifying the command **quit!** (known as an absolute quit command – it can be abbreviated to **q!** if required). In the example above, the **quit!** command was specified, and **vi** returned us to the shell level. The contents of the file that we abandoned are now lost for ever.

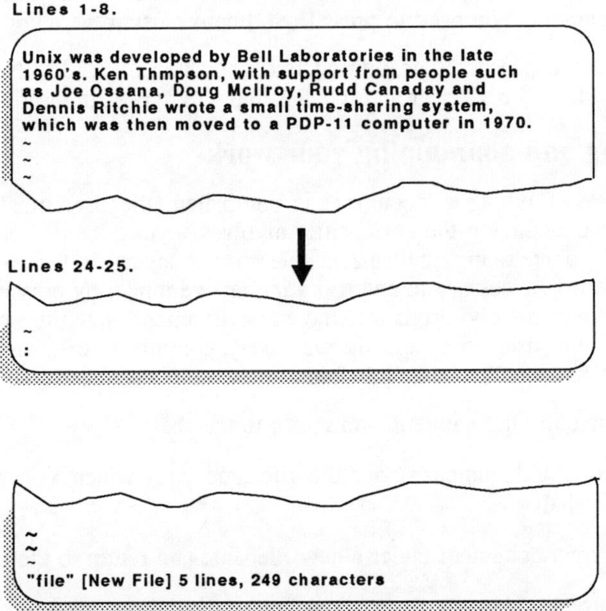

Lines 1-8.
Unix was developed by Bell Laboratories in the late 1960's. Ken Thmpson, with support from people such as Joe Ossana, Doug McIlroy, Rudd Canaday and Dennis Ritchie wrote a small time-sharing system, which was then moved to a PDP-11 computer in 1970.
Lines 24-25.
"file" [New File] 5 lines, 249 characters

Figure 9.5 The interactive/command mode of ***vi***

9.4.8 Saving your work under the current name

To save the contents of the buffer with the same filename as specified when **vi** was invoked, we use the **w** command, as follows:

```
:w[RETURN]
```

Once this command has been executed, **vi** displays some information about the file it has just saved to disk. Figure 9.6 shows a possible message.

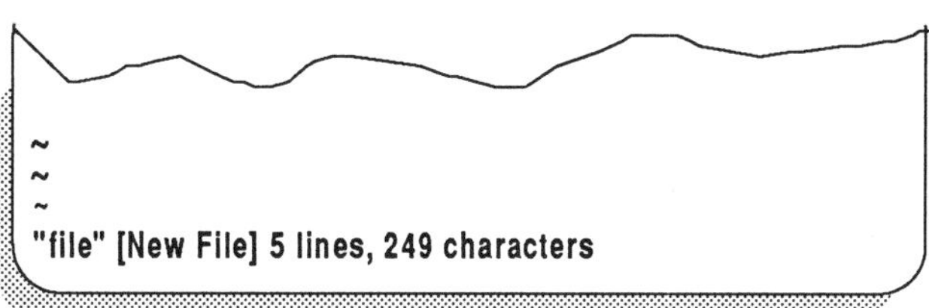
~
~
~
"file" [New File] 5 lines, 249 characters

Figure 9.6 status line after buffer is saved to disk

9.4.9 Saving your work under a new filename

To save the current buffer contents to a different file from the one you used to invoke **vi** with from the shell, the **w** command is again used, but an optional filename argument is supplied. The form of the command to save the buffer under a new name is:

```
:w [<filename>]
```

Overwriting files

If the **[<filename>]** specified in the last command already exists **vi** will warn the user of its presence, since saving the current buffer under this name will overwrite the existing file, a potential diaster, since the entire contents of the file will be irretrievably lost. In such an instance **vi** will ask you if you want to overwrite the file, in which case you should reply **y** (for yes) or **n** (for no – the default reply).

Absolute commands

If you are sure about the outcome of a command, for example, you are sure that you want to overwrite an existing file using the **:w [<filename>]** command, then you can make the command in question absolute. An absolute command is simply a command that will be carried out, disregarding the consequences. We have discussed this type of command already when abandoning the contents of a file using the **q** (quit) option. In this scenario **vi** issued the warning message **No write since last change (quit! overrides).**

The important part of the warning message is the **quit!** command, which is an absolute command to make **vi** quit from the editing session without saving the buffer contents to disk. In the context of saving the existing buffer contents to a new file, we could issue the command:

```
:w! <filename>
```

This command would ensure that the contents of the current buffer would be saved to the file **<filename>**, overwriting a file with the same name, if it exists, without issuing a warning message. Be warned, only issue an a absolute command if you are absolutely sure of the result of the operation that is being performed.

If you are worried about the possibility of overwriting a file, return to command mode and use a shell command i.e. **:! ls [filename]** to see if it exists. Note again, that the colon must be typed to enter the command mode.

Use of pathnames

When a file is saved with an unqualified filename (i.e. without a defined pathname), it is saved in the current working directory – the directory from which **vi** was initially invoked. However, the file held in current buffer can be saved to a different directory by preceeding the filename with a path, as shown below:

```
:w /usr/john/sales/data
```

This command saves the file named **data** in the directory **/usr/john/sales.**

9.4.10 Saving and exiting

To write the current document to disk and leave the editor, you can use the **[ESC]ZZ** command (note the case). Before **vi** exits back to the shell level, **vi** will display a message on the status line showing the name of the file and the number of characters and lines in the file, for example:

```
"file1" [New file] 18 lines, 763 characters
```

The **[New file]** message indicates that the file was created during the current **vi** session.

9.4.11 Moving around using the cursor keys

Now that we have discussed the fundamental commands to create a document, to enter some text, and to save the document to a file on disk, we will examine how you can move around your document while in the edit mode of **vi.**

All keyboards normally include cursor movement keys (the arrow keys). However, these cursor keys are not always interpreted by **vi.** To overcome this problem **vi** uses the four letters **h, j, k** and **l** from the basic command mode, to move the cursor in specific directions. These cursor directions are shown in Figure 9.7.

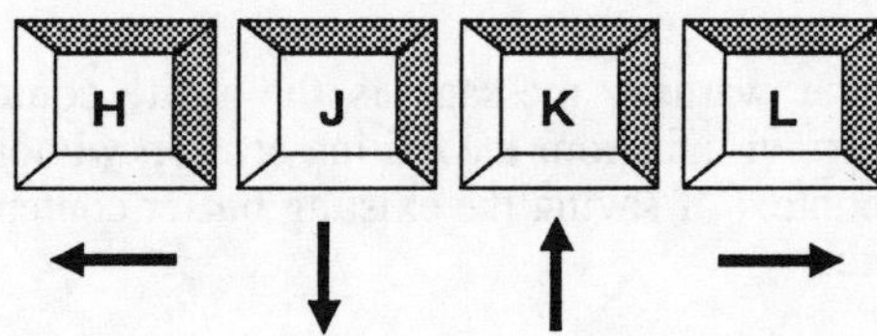

Figure 9.7 Vi cursor movement key letters

The terminal as a window

The terminal plays the role of a window while you are moving around inside a document. Any document longer than 25 lines cannot be seen in its entirety on the screen. The solution is to allow the user to scroll vertically through the document.

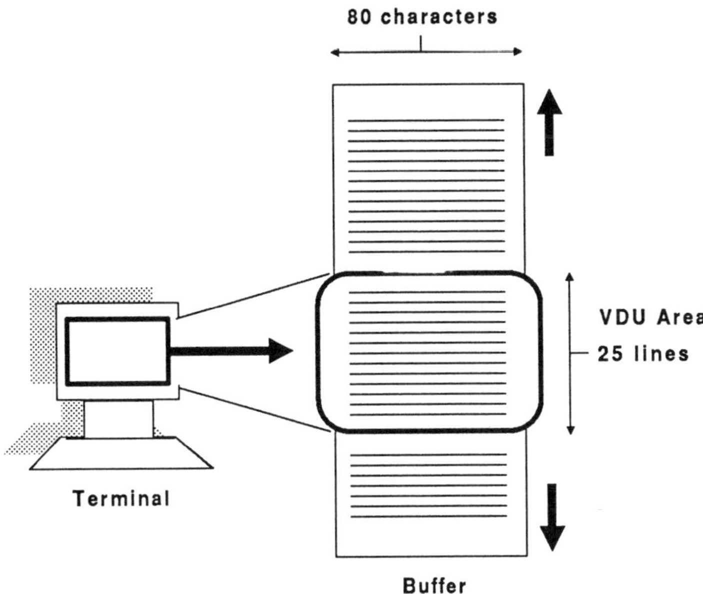

Figure 9.8 The terminal as a window

Specifying the number of lines/columns

The number of columns or lines through which the cursor is to be moved can be specified with the cursor movement keys. You need to press [ESC], to return to the basic command mode, and then type the number of lines/columns before the letter representing the direction required. The commands are as follows:

***n*h** Move cursor left *n* characters.
***n*j** Move cursor down *n* lines.
***n*k** Move cursor up *n* lines.
***n*l** Move cursor right *n* characters.

The only limitation with these commands lies in the numeric value that can be specified with each letter. For example, the user cannot specify more lines than actually exist in the buffer, and when specifying the number of columns, the number of remaining characters in the current line must not be exceeded.

Other movement commands

Don't forget that you can also use the interactive mode of **vi** (: mode) which opens up other addressing possibilities supplied by the **ex** editor, such as the ones given here:

+ Move to the next line and position cursor on first character of the line.

– Move back a line, and position cursor on first character of the line.

The only difference between these addressing techniques and those introduced previously is the fact that once these commands have moved the cursor to the specified line, they position it on the first character in the line; whereas, when the cursor movement letters **h**, **j**, **k** and **l** are used, the cursor goes to the previous column position on the specified line.

Screen movement

The **vi** editor includes many cursor movement commands, some of which are initiated through control-code sequences. Screen movement is more beneficial for the user since it is much faster, and it requires fewer key-presses. A screen in this context is 24 lines of text (1 line is reserved for the status line).

The control key (or **[CTRL]** in its abbreviated form) is used to invoke these commands by pressing the **[CTRL]** key and then while keeping it held down, pressing a single letter. The most important letters for screen movement are shown below (the ^ symbol is used to represent the **[CTRL]** key):

^F Move forward 1 screen.
^B Move backward 1 screen.

Screen movement is much faster than conventional scrolling, but it is not intended for individual line accuracy, for which scrolling should be used.

Scrolling

Scrolling in **vi** is rapid line-to-line movement and it is achieved through the use of the **[CTRL]** key and a single letter. The effect is accurate since the user can keep the keys depressed, and continue the movement through the document.

The two main scrolling commands in **vi** are:

^D Scroll downwards.
^U Scroll upwards.

Moving to a specific character

Vi can also be instructed to search for the occurrence of a particular character in a sentence. This is done using the **f**, **F**, **t** and **T** commands with the single character that you wish to find (notice that the *case* of the character is taken into consideration in such a search). Explanations of these character commands are overleaf. All are typed from the interactive command mode of **vi** i.e. at the '**:**' prompt.

f<character> Move cursor right to the **<character>**
F<character> Move cursor left to the **<character>**
t<character> Move cursor one character left of the **<character>**
T<character> Move cursor one character right of the **<character>**

Specifying physical units

The commands outlined in the previous section can also be executed with an explicit occurrence value. The general form of such a command is:

<occurrences><search command><letter>

Examples

Example 1

```
:2fM
```

This command will move the cursor to the second 'M 'on the current line. The **2** tells **vi** that we require the second occurrence of the letter, and the **f** is the <search command> to move the cursor onto the character that is matched, while the letter **M** is the search letter.

Example 2

```
:10Te
```

This command will move the cursor one character to the right of the tenth occurrence of the letter 'e' on the current line (i.e. the line where the cursor is currently located).

Homing the cursor – the H and L commands

The cursor can be placed in the first column of either at the top or at the bottom line of the current screen. The commands that perform these operations are **H** and **L** respectively. These commands are executed from the basic command mode, so remember to press **[ESC]** before using them.

Moving to a specific word

Vi can be instructed to move the cursor to a particular word within a line. The command structure for these commands resembles the one introduced for moving to a specific character, as follows:

<number>w Moves the cursor <number> words to the right. Note that punctuation marks are counted as words for movement flexibility.

<number>W Moves the cursor <number> words to the right. This command does *not* count punctuation marks as individual words.

<number>b Moves the cursor <number> words towards the left. Punctuation marks are counted as individual words.

<number>B Moves the cursor <number> words towards the left. Punctuation marks are *not* counted as individual words.

The **<number>** value represents the number of words that the cursor will be moved.

Moving to a specific line

Vi can also be instructed to move the cursor to a specific line within the current document, using the G command. This command can be used in two ways: with or without a line number. When used with a line number, the cursor is placed on the first character of the specified line, and the command takes the following form:

<line number>G

Used on its own, the G command places the cursor user on the first character of the *last* line in the current document.

Sentence and paragraph cursor movement

A *sentence* is defined as a string of characters (blank or non- blank) that end in ., ? or !, and are followed by either a new line (a carriage-return) or *two* spaces.

A *paragraph* always begins with of a group of characters following a blank line and ends with a new line. **Vi** also recognises a *section*, which is similar to a paragraph, in that it is a separate area of text. For example C programmers use the { and } characters to begin and end separate procedures in a program.

The (,), { and } commands are supplied especially for the movement of the cursor to the beginning or end of a sentence paragraph, or section. These commands are summarised below:

{ Move cursor to the start of the current section or paragraph.
} Move cursor to the end of the current section or paragraph.
(Move cursor to start of current sentence.
) Move cursor to the end of the current sentence.

9.4.12 Marking text

Line numbers, although a very useful addressing mechanism, do not always locate text accurately within a document, because line addresses may be continually changing owing to line insertions and deletions etc. A solution to this problem is to *mark* pieces of text in a document.

This is achieved using the **m** (mark text) command, which marks the current cursor position in the document, and hence we can refer exactly back to this point at a later time. The form of the **m** command is:

m<address letter>

The **<address letter>** is a single alphabetic character that is used to identify a position in the current document; thus by using different address letters, we can refer back to more than one position.

Returning to a specific address using '

Once we have marked a specific point in the document using **m** and an

<address letter> we can use the apostrophe (') immediately followed by the **<address letter>** to return to the marked position. For example:

```
'c
```

This command moves us back to the point we addressed earlier using the **<address letter>** 'c' (using the command **mc**). This command can be used from both basic and interactive modes.

9.4.13 Buffer manipulation

Vi makes nine buffers available to the user for the storage of temporary data. Buffers have many advantages, for example the user could delete a paragraph, store it in a buffer, and restored it again as and when required. **Vi** provides a total of nine delete (or auxiliary) buffers for the nine most recent deletions.

Vi also supplies the user with 26 insert buffers (also known as named buffers). An insert buffer is similar to a delete buffer, except that the text is normally deleted to them for movement to another area within the same document.

Buffer manipulation commands

Vi provides three main commands to manipulate the buffers. These commands are accessed from interactive command (:) mode, and include:

- ❑ The **d** (delete) command to move text into a delete buffer area.
- ❑ The **y** (yank) command to move text into an insert buffer area.
- ❑ The **pu** (put) command to move text from a delete or insert buffer area into the document.

9.4.14 The y (yank) command

When text is 'yanked' into an insert buffer area, the buffer area must be specified or named. The general form of the command is:

"<buffer name><number of lines>yy

where **<buffer name>** is a single, *lowercase* letter, and **<number of lines>** is the number of lines of text, starting from the current line (the line contiaining the cursor). Some examples will demonstrate the use of the yank command in action:

Examples

Example 1

```
"a7yy
```

This command yanks seven lines of text (beginning with the current line contining the cursor) into the **a** buffer area (the letter 'a' being an identifier for the buffer's contents).

The double quotation mark (") is used to tell **vi** to interpret the next character literally. In the example the quote before the **a** in the command **"a7yy** is very important, since without it, **vi** would invoke the append command. As a rule of thumb, *always* precede a buffer name with **"**.

Appending to a buffer

When text is written into an insert buffer area, the previous contents of the buffer are lost, that is, they are overwritten with the new text. To overcome this problem **vi** provides a second version of the yank command using uppercase letters for the buffer name, which appends the new text to the buffer, instead of overwriting the existing contents. The command has the following form:

"<BUFFER NAME><number of lines>yy

When the buffer name character is entered in UPPER CASE **vi** checks to see if a buffer with the same character name (in lower case) already exists, and if it does it will append the text specified by the new yank command to the same buffer area, rather than overwriting it. The next examples illustrate overwriting and appending:

Example 2

```
"c7yy
"c4yy
```

The last command in the example above shows how the text in buffer area 'c' can be overwritten.

Example 3

```
"c7yy
"C4yy
```

This command makes **vi** append the new contents of the 'c' buffer to the text that was previously stored within it (note the upper case letter C in the last command here).

9.4.15 The pu (put) command

The pu (put) command is used to place text from an insert or delete buffer into the current document. The form of the command is thus:

"<buffer name>pu

The **<buffer name>** is a single character that represents a buffer name letter i.e. a to z for any one of the 26 insertion buffers, or 1 to 9 for one of the nine deletion buffers.

Example

```
"apu
```

This command puts the contents of the **a** buffer directly below the line containing the cursor. The double quotes at the start of the command is used to make sure that **vi** interprets the 'a' literally (as a buffer), and not as the **a** (append) command. Always use the double quotes in such cases where a buffer name conflicts with a **vi** command.

9.4.15 The d (delete) command

Lines of text can be deleted, and placed in one of **vi**'s nine delete buffers, whereupon the deleted text can be restored to another part of the current document. The form of the command is:

<number of lines to delete>dd

Take the following example:

```
3dd
```

The first 'd' in this command is the **d** operator itself. The second 'd' must be specified if the command is to apply to whole lines.The three lines which have now been deleted are now placed in one of **vi**'s deletion buffers. If this deletion was the first, then the deleted text would be placed in delete buffer 1, and so on.

The deleted text can now be pasted back into another part of the current document using the **pu** (put) command.

```
"1pu
```

This command places the text from delete buffer **1** into the next line of the document. The cursor identifies the current line, and all the text that is pasted into position using **pu** is added below this line.

9.4.16 Summary of the delete, yank and put commands

The user can use both the delete and insert buffers to move text around within a document. Moving text using the delete buffers, involves deleting and putting.

Moving pieces of text can also be accomplished using the yank command which writes the required text to one of **vi**'s insert buffers (a compulsory buffer). This has added advantages since the user can store text in a wide range of named buffers (up to 26, named a to z). This is more flexible than using delete buffers which are not specifically named, and therefore cannot be referred to as easily as the insert buffers.

9.4.17 Copying lines of text

An alternative method to cutting and pasting text without using the buffer facilities is achieved through use of the **co** (copy lines) command. The general form of this command is:

:<start-line>,<end-line> co <destination-line>

Note that a colon (:) precedes the whole command which means that it must be entered from the interactive commnad mode. The **<start-line>** and **<end-line>** represent a range of lines to be copied. A range is implied because a comma (,) is used to separate the two values.

The **co** is the copy command itself, and the **<destination- line>** represents the line number which the copied lines will immediately *follow*. Also note the spaces before and after **co**. Some examples will demonstrate the movement of a range of lines in a document:

Examples

Example 1

```
:5,20 co 40
```

This command copies all the text from line 5 to line 20, to the line immediately after line 40 (line 41).

Example 2

```
:5,20 co 0
```

The destination line in this command appears to be invalid; however, this destination line represents the top of the document. Specifying line 1 is not correct because the copied lines will then appear on line 2, which is not required. To make a range of lines appear from line 1 onwards we have to specify the *zero* value.

Copying lines in this way does imply a temporary storage of the text (while we are deciding on a line location after which to place the copied text), although no buffers are explicitly stated in the command. You may prefer to use this command as an alternative to **vi**'s buffer manipulation commands, which tend to be more complex to operate.

9.4.18 Moving lines of text

To move a group of lines to a new location (thus erasing the text in the previous location) we use the **m** (move lines) command. The format for the command is similar to **co** in many respects:

:<start-line>,<end-line>m<destination-line>

WordStar users may think of this command as being the equivalent method to move text within the current document (using ^KB, ^KK and then ^KV), except that the lines to be moved are not physically marked (or highlighted as they are in the WordStar package). Note again that the **m** command is used from the interactive mode, so press ':' before starting the command.

Example

```
:3,10m20
```

This command moves lines 3 to 10 to line 21 (since the number 20 is the line after which the text is to be placed). The absence of spaces in this command is not important.

9.4.19 Cutting and pasting between documents

When **vi** is invoked at the shell level, a list of optional file name arguments can be specified on the command line. If more than one filename is supplied to **vi** as an argument, it will edit each one in turn, following the termination of the edit of the previous file in the command line list. Queuing files for editing in this fashion allows the user to cut and paste text between separate documents, as will now be demonstrated.

```
$ vi file1 file2
two files to edit
```

This command invokes **vi** on the files named **file1** and **file2** respectively. Assume that both **file1** and **file2** are new files and have yet to be created. Notice the message **two files to edit** which is self-explanatory. When **vi** is initially invoked we should see a screen display similar to that shown in Figure 9.2.

Vi is now awaiting us to enter some text. At this stage we could press either **i**, to insert, or **a**, to append, some text (both insert and append commands achieve the same result when a new file is created since there are no existing lines in the current document).

Switching files

Assume we entered the following text into the buffer:

```
Cutting and pasting between two different documents is achieved
by firstly supplying two filenames on the command line, and then
manipulating both files using vi's "mark" and "yank" commands.
```

Now that some text has been entered into this file we may want to switch to the next document specified in the command line. Before doing so, we must save this file in the current buffer using the **w** (write) command, which writes the contents of the current buffer to disk using the filename specified in the command line (file1). The **w** command allows us to save the contents of the buffer without exiting back to the shell. This is necessary in this case since we want to edit the next file that was initially invoked with **vi**. Don't forget that **w** must be entered from interactive command mode, so press '**:**' to obtain the interactive colon prompt.

```
:w
```

Once this file has been written to disk, **vi** will display some statistics on the saved file on the status line (line 25 of the screen).

Moving to the next file in the queue

Once the **:w** command has been executed, we can move on to the next file in the queue if we wish. This is achieved by using the **n** (next file) command. The **n** command is also used from the interactive mode:

```
:n
```

Vi should now display the name of the new file (file2). **Vi** should also display the [New File] message in its status line, since the file is newly created. If **n** is entered again, the message **no more files to edit** will appear in the status line, indicating that there all files have been edited i.e. all files that were specified on the command line when **vi** was first invoked.

Rewinding – the rew command

Once all the files supplied on the command line have been edited, we can rewind back to the previous file using the **rew** (rewind) command. For example, if, after issuing the **n** (next file) command, we were editing **file2**, then executing the **rew** command would return us to **file1**, for further editing etc. The **rew** command is issued from the interactive mode (**ex** mode) as follows:

```
:rew
```

9.4.20 Yanking text to another document

We are now in a position to explain how to yank text from document and place it in another. First we need to yank the required text into an insert buffer area (in the range a to z); once this has been done we simply switch documents using **rew** or **n** (depending on which document we are currently editing – use **rew** to go back to the previously edited document or **n** to go to the next document stated in the command line when **vi** was invoked). Take the following example:

```
$ vi file1 file2
```

This invokes **vi** with the two files: **file1** and **file2**. We assume **file1** contains the following text:

```
Cutting and pasting between two different documents is achieved
by firslty supplying two filenames on the command line, and then
manipulating both files using vi's "mark" and "yank" commands.
```

Now we need to yank this text into a buffer (insert buffer a, for example), move to **file2**, and then paste this text from line 1 onwards (assuming the **file2** was newly created). To achieve this we need to issue the following commands from **vi** (note that interactive commands have a preceding : sign and *comments* are displayed between the < and > brackets):

```
    <place cursor start of paragraph 'Cutting ...'>
"a4yy
    <place cursor on last line of paragraph>
:n
"apu
```

The first command in this example (**"a4yy**) places the four lines (starting from the line the cursor is on) into the **a** buffer, for future reference. The double quote(") in front of the **a** is used to make **vi** interpret the character literally, in this case as a buffer letter identifier, and not as the **a** (append text) command. The second command (:n – next file command) tells **vi** to move to the next file in the queue (**file2**). The third, and final command (**"apu**), is a **put** command telling **vi** to paste the text from buffer a (again, note the double quote (") before the **a**) to the current position. As we have moved into a new file (**file2**) the text is copied across between the two files.

Similarly we can reverse the direction of the cut and paste operation by copying text from **file2** across to **file1**. Note that in this case we would use **:rew** to go to the previous file in the queue in place of the **:n** (which moves on to the next file in the queue).

When not to use a delete buffer

When cutting and pasting text between documents, always use a named insert buffer (a buffer in the range a to z) because the contents of the nine delete buffers (also known as the auxiliary buffers) are lost when moving between different documents. So, always use the named buffers for the movement of text between files.

Repeating a buffer command

A single period (.) can be used to execute the most recent command altering one of **vi**'s buffers. The period must be entered from **vi**'s basic mode. The following example shows how this command can be used:

```
"a4yy
.
```

The first command in this example yanks the next four lines (starting from the line that the cursor is on) into the named buffer **a**. The next command is the single period, which tells **vi** to repeat the previous command that altered the contents of a buffer. Since the previous command altered the a buffer, the command **"a4yy** will be repeated, resulting in the next four lines of the document being written to the a buffer (thus overwriting it). Using **"A4yy** would append the lines to the same buffer.

9.4.21 Vi command summary

These commands (excluding those starting with a colon (:)) are invoked from **vi**'s basic commnad mode, so if you are using edit mode, or interactive mode, you must press the **[ESC]** key before typing any of these commands.

See overleaf for the command summary.

Table 9.6 Commands used with **vi. Key:** ^ [CTL] ~ [ESC]

Type of command	Command	Action
Cursor movement	**h**	Left cursor arrow
	j	Down cursor arrow
	k	Up cursor arrow
	l	Right cursor arrow
	^F	Forwards a screen
	^B	Backwards a screen
	^D	Scroll downwards
	^U	Scroll upwards
	[RETURN]	Next line
	$	Beginning of current line
	G	Beginning of the last line of the file
	***n*G**	Beginning of line *n*
Save and Exit	**~ZZ**	Save and exit
	:x	Save and exit
	:q	quit (if no alterations)
	:q!	quit (absolute)
	:w	Save and resume edit
	:wq	Save and quit
Text/line Insertion	**a**	Append text after current cursor position
	A	Append text at end of current line
	i	Insert text at cursor position
	I	Insert text at beginning of current line
	o	Open a line under cursor
	O	Open a line above cursor
Text/line Deletion	**x**	Delete at cursor position
	dw	Delete current word
	dd	Delete current line
	D or **d$**	Delete to end of current line
	p	Replace text after deletion
Miscellaneous	**~/<pattern>**	Search for <pattern> (Basic mode)
	:/<pattern>	Search for <pattern> (Interactive mode)
	~?	Continue search in reverse direction
	^L	Refresh screen
	^Y	Expose one more line at top of screen
	^E	Expose one more line (at the bottom of the screen)
	:	Enter interactive command mode (ex editor). Press [ESC] to exit. Automatic return to Basic mode following execution of an ex command.

9.5 Questions

1. What is the main difference between **ex** and **vi**?

2. What is the 'standard' UNIX editor?

3. Define and explain the three modes that can be used within the **vi** editor.

4. Which command is used to run a shell command from within the **ex** or **vi** editors.

5. Which key in **vi** is used to return to command mode?

6. Once inside **vi**, which command inserts text into the current document?

7. When a new file is created the insert and append commands perform the same action. Why is this?

8. How many insert buffers are there in **vi**?

9. What are 'insert buffers' and what can they be used for?

10. A delete buffer is not as 'powerful' as an insert buffer. Name the main reason for this?

11. Explain a method whereby text is moved into a buffer.

12. What is the rewind command used for?

13. Show how text can be appended to an insert buffer with the use of a simple example.

14. Explain the actions carried out by the following **ex** commands:

```
:/\<wombat
:/\<wombat\>
:g/[Ww]ombat/WOMBAT/p
:1,$s/Wombat/WOMBAT/p
```

10

UNIX Communication Facilities

10.1 Introduction

This chapter introduces many of the UNIX facilities provided for the distribution of electronic messages. UNIX includes an abundance of tools for the creation, distribution, and manipulation of such messages.

The first part of this chapter is dedicated to the Berkeley V4.2 **mail** system, which provides the user with an environment to create, send and read electronic-mail messages. **Mail** is a large communication system and therefore deserves an in-depth description. The other mailing tools that are available under UNIX, such as **biff**, **from**, **xget xsend** and **vacation** are also discussed in detail. Additional communication tools are discussed later in the chapter.

10.2 Mail

Mail is the standard intelligent mail processing system that is available on nearly all UNIX systems. Its command-line syntax is similar to that found in **ed** and **ex** - the UNIX editors discussed in the previous chapter. You can respond to the mail system at the interactive level only when there are messages awaiting your attention, as indicated by the **login** message 'You have mail'. **Mail** then needs to be invoked to examine these messages.

10.2.1 Invoking mail

Let us assume that some new mail has arrived and that the message 'You have mail' has been displayed at login time. Typing the command **mail** at the UNIX prompt would result in the display similar to the one shown at the top of the next page:

```
$ mail
mail version 5.2 6/21/85. Type ? for help
"/usr/spool/mail/jim": 1 Message 1 new
>N 1 jim Tue Feb 20 11:45 8/143 "hello"
&
```

From this dialogue we can establish first that mail is an interactive system, similar to the shell. Berkeley systems frequently use the ampersand symbol (**&**) as the **mail** prompt (and we will use this in our examples). The '?' sign is also common.

The above example also indicates the time and date that the message was sent, and from whom the message originated. The **>** symbol indicates the current message that is selected (by default this is the first message when **mail** is initially invoked). This shows that there is one new message for our attention, sent by user **jim** on February the 20th at 11:45 am. The subject heading in this example is 'hello' (see Chapter 10, section 10.4 for more details on headings). Commands to the mail system can be typed at the **&** prompt, shown on the final line of the example.

Incoming messages are commonly stored by the mail system in a file named **/usr/spool/mail/<your-name>**, where **<your-name>** is your username. Every user with incoming mail will have an entry in this directory in the form of a single file with your **login** name; for example the filename **/usr/spool/mail/fred**. Any unread mail is kept in the **/usr/spool/mail** directory until it is examined using the **mail** facility. Mail messages that have been read by the user (but not deleted) are stored in a file called **mbox**. The default protection attributes for the files in **/usr/spool/mail** should be set in such a way that other users cannot examine your incoming mail. You can look at your protection attributes using the command below:

```
$ ls -l /usr/spool/mail/<your-name>
```

For example we may type:

```
$ ls -l /usr/spool/mail/fred
-rwx------ 1 fred 76 Feb 19 13:01 fred
```

These protection attributes allow only the owner to examine the contents of the **mail** file. Similarly the **mbox** file that resides in your home directory should also have the same protection attributes as any file in **/usr/spool/mail** (see Chapter 12 - UNIX Security for more information).

10.2.2 Reading your mail - the t command

Mail messages are accessed using the **type** command, which can be abbreviated to the letters t or T. This command can be used repeatedly to make **mail** display each of the current mail messages in turn, until there are none left to display. However, it is common practice to specify the number of an individual message that you want to see, as shown below with **message 2**:

```
&t2
Message 2:
From: john (john brown) Wed Feb 10 12:06:29 1990
Subject: meeting
To: fred (fred smith)
Date: Wed, Feb 10 90 12:06:01 GMT
Cc: mark (mark bloggs)
Meet me at 10:30 at room 301 to discuss the new project.
&
```

This example shows all the information included in the message, as follows:

- the name of the user who sent the original message (**john**)
- the Subject: (the nature of the message)
- the Cc: (carbon copy) i.e. other users to whom the same message has also been sent (in this case there is only one user, namely user **mark**), and finally
- the message itself which appears below these details.

10.2.3 Replying to messages – the r command

You can directly reply to the message sender, (and coincidentally, all the recipients of the same message), using the **reply** command (or **r** for short). **Reply** can be used to respond to either all the messages that have been received, or to individual messages. When replying to individual messages the user must supply the message number following the **r** command, for example **r2** (or **r 2**) to respond to message number 2.

If **r** is used without qualification, **mail** assumes that the user wishes to reply to the message recently examined using the **t** (type messages) option. If the 't' option has not been used, then **mail** allows you to reply to each message individually. Once the 'r' option has been entered, **mail** invites you to supply a string of text for the subject of the reply (indicating its nature). After this **mail** reads from the standard input, and allowing you to enter your message. The **<ctrl-d>** keystroke is used to terminate the message, after which it is sent to the recipient.

If the recipient is logged in and using the **mail** facility, then they will receive the message **You have new mail** when they exit from **mail**. Incoming messages can also detect using the **biff** tool (see section 10.6). If the recipient-user is logged-out when the message is delivered, next time they log in the message **You have mail** will be displayed on their terminal. If a user is already using **mail** when an incoming message is received, they are notified. The second **Cc:** prompt shown in the example which follows, allows entry of further usernames, to whom a copy of the reply will be sent.

```
&t2
Message 2:
From: john (john brown) Wed Feb 10 12:06:29 1990
Subject: meeting
To: fred (fred smith)
Date: Wed, Feb 10 90 12:06:01 GMT
Cc: mark (mark bloggs)
Meet me at 10:30 in room 301 to discuss the new project.
&r
Reply to: fred
Subject: A reply
Thanks for the mail. I'll meet you as requested.
<ctrl-d>
Cc:<carriage-return>
&
```

The **r** option can also be used with multiple message numbers, for example:

```
&r 1 2 3
```

This results in the same reply being sent to messages 1, 2 and 3.

10.2.4 Replying only to the sender – the R command

To reply to the originator of the message alone (without including the other recipients of the same message) the R command is used (note the uppercase letter R). However, on Microsoft's Xenix version of the UNIX system, the R command returns a message to both the originator, and any carbon copy users. This difference should be noted.

10.2.5 Aborting replies – using <ctrl-c>

The user can abort a currently typed mail message by using the **<ctrl-c>** (interrupt) signal. You need to confirm this action by pressing **<ctrl-c>** a second time to kill the letter. The message can be continued after the first interrupt, if required, since two **<ctrl-c>** keystrokes in succession are necessary to kill the letter. Once a letter is killed it is dead and it is stored in the file **dead.letter**, which is created in your home directory by the mailing system. The **dead.letter** file will contain the message you were typing up to its termination. This file is also used to return a message to the sender if a problem is encountered when sending the letter (for example, in the case where the recipient-user does not exist). In the event of a nonexistent username etc., **mail** informs the sender. The example below illustrates the killing of a message.

```
&r
Reply to: fred
Subject: A reply
Thanks for the mail. I'll meet you as requested.
<ctrl-c>
(interrupt -- one more to kill letter)<ctrl-c>
Interrupt
&
```

This example illustrates the interruption and nullification of a message. Note the warning that **mail** issues when **<ctrl-c>** is pressed. The **dead.letter** file will now hold the contents of the message up to the point where the message was aborted.

10.2.6 Generating messages from the shell

The interactive level of both the shell and the mail system can be used for generating messages. However, it is important to realise that **mail** can only be invoked to examine messages that are already in the system, and so cannot be invoked primarily to *send* a message to a user; in this situation the shell must be used to initiate any new messages. An additional advantage of sending messages from the shell level is the potential to use input redirection, (which can either be a file, or the standard input device – the keyboard) as shown in the first example. The inclusion of the **-s** option allows the user to specify a subject heading for the message.

Examples

Example 1

```
$ mail -s greeting mary
... your text ...
<ctrl-d>
$
```

This example illustrates how **mail** can be used from the shell level (note the **$** prompt). In this mode **mail** reads from the standard input stream (by default, the keyboard device). The **<ctrl-d>** signal ends the message, and forwards it to the user (here called **mary**).

Example 2

The same information can be sent to several users by specifying them individually on the command line:

```
$ mail -s greeting mary mark paul
.... your text ...
<ctrl-d>
```

Example 3

As mentioned, a file can be used as input to the **mail** utility. This can be created using an editor and saves typing in the message directly from the keyboard.

```
$ mail -s greeting john < message
```

This command makes **mail** forward the data in the file **message** to user **john**. The **-s** option indicates the title of the message (a greeting). Note that if **-s** is included but a subject title is omitted, the mail system will assume that the next argument (in this context the username **john**) is the subject heading. Following an attempt to send mail to a nonexistent user, **mail** will return a message to the sender indicating that the required mail-message could not be delivered (the message being diverted to the ASCII file **dead.letter**).

10.2.7 Sending mail from inside the mail system

Once inside the **mail** system, you can use the **m** command to initiate mail to particular individuals from within the mail system. The syntax of the command is:

m <user-name, ...>

You can send messages to one or more users, by specifying their names directly; each user-name should be separated by (at least) a space. If a user-name argument is not supplied, many mail systems will default to your own user-name (thus sending yourself some mail).

Examples

Example 1

```
&m john
Hi john. Just a note to say that I can make the meeting
tonight at 5 pm. See you then.
<ctrl-d>
&
```

This allows mail to be sent to user john. Once we have entered the necessary user-name(s), the mail system drops into its 'compose' mode whereby the message you wish to convey to the recipients mentioned can be typed in from the keyboard.

Example 2

```
&m john fred
```

Likewise, this command will allow mail to be sent to the users john and fred simultaneously.

By default, the message compose mode is the standard input mode (directly from the keyboard). Thus characters are read from the keyboard until a **<ctrl-d>** signals the end of input (note that the **mail** system also has a *binary option* called 'dot' which can be set to allow composers of messages to use a single period or full stop (.) to signify the end of a message instead of **<ctrl-d>** – see section 10.16.1).

The obvious disadvantage of the standard input mode is the inability to correct a message. If a message is typed incorrectly, it should be abandoned using **<ctrl-c>** (two such signals will normally have to be issued in order to 'kill' the letter). However, the mail system can be set up to include a UNIX editor for composing messages. If the variable called **$EDITOR** (see sections 10.15.5 and 10.16.1) is assigned the name of a line-based editor such as **ex** or **ed**, this editor is loaded when the **mail** system is invoked, so that it is available when a message is to be composed. This in turn allows the user to compose the message in a more flexible environment.

The variable called **$VISUAL** is also available for use with a visual editor such as **vi** (see section 10.16.7). However, this editor is not loaded automatically when a message is composed, but can be called up using the **visual** command and used either to create a new message, or to edit an existing mail message, or group of messages. Use the actual message number(s) after the **visual** command when editing an existing message e.g. **visual 1** will edit **message 1**.

Both of these variables (**$EDITOR** and **$VISUAL**) can be defined in the file **.mailrc** (which should be located in your home directory – see section 10.15.5 under *Editor preferences*. Some mail systems will also allow these variables to be defined from files such as **.profile** or **.cshrc**, so check these files in your system for the following lines:

```
EDITOR=ex
VISUAL=vi
```

If they are absent, you may want to add these two commands to the appropriate file. If you compose a message, you will see the results of these new definitions. When the **ex** editor is invoked, you will see the colon (:) prompt in the usual way (unless your system automatically loads **append** so you can start typing you message directly). Chapter 9 examines the **ex** and **vi** editors in more detail.

The tilde commands **~e** and **~v** (see section 10.15.5) are also available to invoke the editors mentioned.

10.2.8 Deleting mail messages

The **d** (delete) command allows you to delete selected messages that have been received, and those which are stored in your **mbox** file. The **d** option can be used with a message list, or in conjunction with the currently active message (the message displayed on the screen using the **t** command).

Examples

Example 1

```
&t1
Message 1:
From: john (john brown) Wed Feb 10 12:06:29 1990
Subject: meeting
To: fred (fred smith)
Date: Wed, Feb 10 90 12:06:01 GMT
Cc: mark (mark bloggs)
See you at the conference tomorrow.
&d
```

This example deleted message 1 from the current list of mail messages (i.e. from the **mbox** file).

Example 2

The user can also delete several mail messages simultaneously by specifying the message numbers, separated by spaces, as shown in the next example:

```
&d 1 4 6
```

This command deletes messages 1, 4 and 6 respectively. Also note that the mail system does not inform you of the deletions, the whole process is carried out silently, without any feedback.

Example 3

A range of messages can also be deleted. This is done by specifying the starting message number, a hyphen (-) and then the ending message number, for example:

```
$ d 1-3
```

This command deletes messages 1, 2 and 3.

10.2.9 Exiting from the mail system – the q command

The user can exit from the **mail** system with the **q** (quit) command. This terminates the current session and writes any undeleted messages to the **mbox** file in the home directory. User **john** mayhave a file called **/usr/john/mbox** (depending on the user's home directory location). If new mail has arrived while **john** was in the **mail** system, You have new mail will be displayed on exit, but only if he has arranged for this to happen (this can be done using a command such as **biff** – see section 10.6).

The system mail file for a given user (the mail file in the **/usr/spool/mail** directory – known as the *post office*), is updated to reflect the messages that have been examined. Unread messages, such as messages not displayed using the **t** option, are kept in the post office file in the **/usr/spool/mail** until deleted, and the message **You have mail** will be displayed on logging in, indicating that new messages are awaiting attention.

Example

```
&t2
Message 2:
From: john (john brown) Wed Feb 10 12:06:29 1990
Subject: meeting
To: fred (fred smith)
Date: Wed, Feb 10 90 12:06:01 GMT
Cc: mark (mark bloggs)
Meet me at 10:30 in room 301 to discuss the new project.
&q
1 message(s) saved in mbox
$
```

The example illustrates that upon exiting from the mail system, one message was saved into the user's personal mail-box (the **mbox** file in the user's home directory).

The next time mail is invoked, the saved messages will be read in (in order of message number). Any new messages that are saved in the **mbox** file in the future will be saved alongside any existing messages (each message having a unique message number to identify it).

10.2.10 Exiting the mail system – the exit command

The exit (or **ex**) command can be used to leave the mail system without altering the user's system mail-box or local mail-box files:

```
&t1
Message 1:
From: john (john brown) Wed Feb 10 12:06:29 1990
Subject: meeting
To: fred (fred smith)
Date: Wed, Feb 10 90 12:06:01 GMT
Cc: mark (mark bloggs)
See you at the conference tomorrow.
&ex
$
```

The example display above illustrates the **ex** command in action. Note the absence of any messages when we exit. The state of any existing mail messages remains the same as when we entered the **mail** system.

10.3 Username aliases

We mentioned earlier that mail can be sent to groups of users by specifying them on the command line. This is a rather long-winded method, and the process may become a huge task if we have to send mail to a large group of users.

The answer to this problem is to create a *mail alias*, using the **alias** command. This command has the following syntax (when used under the C-shell **/bin/csh** – the default shell for many Berkeley UNIX systems):

alias <alias group-name> <alias list ...>

The **alias** command can be used from the shell level, but this defeats the object somewhat, since we want to end the process of typing in such lists. To overcome this problem we should edit such a command into a file called **.mailrc**, a hidden file that should exist in your home directory (or login directory). The **.mailrc** file is special, in that its contents are examined every time the **mail** system is invoked. Let us create a sample **.mailrc** file for future use with the mail system. In this example we are using the **ex** editor to create this file (see Chapter 9).

```
$ ex .mailrc
".mailrc" [New File]
:a
alias friends fred mary john
.
:x
$
```

The **alias** in this example has been set up under the name **friends**, using the C-shell (/bin/csh) syntax. We could now send mail using this alias name, so that we do not need to type the individual usernames **fred**, **mary** and **john**. We could enter:

```
$ mail -s friends < message_file
```

to send mail to three users by specifying one recipient name. The **Cc:** option can also be used to distribute mail to more than one user, but each username must be typed individually each time, because the alias cannot be used here.

The **alias** command (shell command) is not solely for use with the **mail** system, it can also be used from the shell level. The **alias** command works in different ways according to the shell that is being used.

10.3.1 Displaying the current alias definitions

The **mail** system also recognises a command called **alias**. In this context the alias command can be used either on its own, without any arguments (to display all currently defined aliases) or with an argument (an alias name definition). When used with more than one argument, an existing alias can be changed, or a new one created. This is summarised in Table 10.1.

Table 10.1 Mail system alias commands

Command	Action
&alias	Displays all aliases
&alias friends mary jim	Amends the friend's alias
&alias project john mark fred	Creates a new alias

10.4 Viewing mail headers – the from command

Among the other facilities that **mail** offers the user, there is one command which can be used to display only the titles of messages that have not yet been deleted (or read – whichever is appropriate). The command is called **from** (abbreviated to **f**), and it can be used on its own, or with a **message list**. The **from** command examines the current mail-box, and prints the message headers (or titles) from each message. An example illustrates using the **from** command on its own, as follows:

```
&f
> 1 jim Tue Feb 20 11:45 8/143 "hello"
> 2 mark Tue Feb 22 09:23 8/147 "greeting"
&
```

This example displays the headers from all the messages (two) that currently exist in the user's mail-box. The first message, from user **jim**, is entitled 'hello', while the second, from user **mark** is entitled 'greeting'. We can now read these messages at our discretion using the **t** (type) command.

10.4.1 Viewing a range of message titles

Because the syntax of the **f** command is actually

f [<message- list ...>]

we can supply a list of messages for which we require the titles.

Examples

Example 1

```
&f1-3
```

This command specifies the titles for a range of messages (1 to 3).

Example 2

The message-list can also be a single message.

```
&f2
```

This command requests the title of message number 2. If a message does not exist for the specified message number, **mail** will simply issue an error message such as **no applicable messages**, or words to that effect.

This command is examined in greater detail in section 10.19.1.

10.5 Selecting messages

Messages are most often selected or identified by message number. However, on some occasions you may need to select one particular message as the current message, or select specific messages for uses witn a particular command.

10.5.1 Selecting the current message

When you invoke the **mail** system, if there are several messages awaiting you attention, the first message (message 1) by default is the current message which can be displayed etc. To select a different message as the current one you can either specify the required message by number in a particular command (**t2** or **f3** for example) or move through the message list. Some of the keys that will allow movement between messages are shown in Table 10.2 below. The + and – movement keys need to be followed by the **[RETURN]** key.

Table 10.2 Message Movement keys

Command	Action
[RETURN]	The carriage return key moves forward to the next message.
+	Move forward one message, and display it.
-	Move back one message. Opposite of +.
-n	Move back *n* messages and then display the current message.
n	Displays message number *n*.

10.5.2 Using wildcards

The mail system recognises only a very limited set of wildcards, as follows:

* Addresses all the messages in the current **mail** session. For use in commands such as d and e etc. For example, the command d * would delete all the current messages. The command top * would thus print the top few lines of all messages.

$ As in the UNIX editors such as ex and ed, the $ wildcard matches the last message in the list. An example of its use could be d $ which would delete the last message in the current list.

To use the normal wildcard facilities when composing a message you are advised to use a standard UNIX editor such as **ed** or **ex**.

10.6 Deleting and printing messages in succession

The **t** (type) command has a twin command, called **p** (print) which works in exactly the same way as **t**. Both these commands can be combined with the **d** command (the abbreviated version of the delete command), to provide the commands **dt** and **dp**. Each of these deletes the current message and prints the next one. If the end of the mail-box file is reached the message **at EOF** (at end-of-file) is displayed. The example which follows demonstrates the **dt** command in action:

```
$ mail
mail version 5.2 6/21/85. Type ? for help
"/usr/spool/mail/John": 2 Message(s) 2 new
>N 1 John Mon Jun 20 11:56 8/156 "thursday"
>N 2 root Mon Jun 22 09:44 8/131 "new account"
&f
>N 1 John Mon Jun 20 11:56 8/156 "thursday"
>N 2 root Mon Jun 22 09:44 8/131 "new account"
&dt
Message 2:
From: root (Super-User) Mon Jun 22 09:44:29 1990
Subject: new account
To: fred (fred smith)
Date: Wed, Jun 22 90 09:44:01 GMT
Cc: admin
Your new Unix account has been raised. Please use the 'passwd'
command to allocate a password for yourself.
&f
> 2 root Mon Jun 22 09:44 8/131 "new account"
&q
1 message(s) saved in mbox
$
```

This long takes us from entry to the mail system, where we are notified that there are two new messages in our mail-box. The first is from user **John**, and the second is from user **root** (the super-user). This is confirmed using the **f** command. When we initially invoke **mail**, the current message number is set to **1**, so the command **dt** deletes the first message, and prints the next one, message 2, from **root**; note that user **root** has also sent a copy of the message to user **admin**. The final **f** command in the example demonstrates that the first message has been deleted, and that **message 2** remains. The **q** command at the end of the example returns us to the shell level, saving one message (message 2) in the **mbox** file.

10.7 Notification of incoming mail – biff

The UNIX mail system can notify users of incoming mail in a number of different ways. The most fundamental method of doing so is using the **You have mail** message at log in time. However the **mail** system can also be told to notify the user of any incoming mail using the shell command **biff**, which is part of the Berkeley tool set. It is used to notify users of incoming mail during the course of a UNIX session. **Biff** is used with one of two arguments:

i) the **y** (yes) argument which invokes biff and listens for any incoming mail that is addressed to the user, and

ii) the **n** (no) argument which disables this facility.

Biff is very useful, since incoming mail detected during the current UNIX session, can be inspected immediately. If **biff** is entered without any arguments, the current setting is shown. The default value for **biff** is **n** (do not detect incoming mail messages). The command **biff y** can be executed at the shell level, or from a file called .profile (Bourne Shell users), the contents of which are executed at login time (.login is the equivalent file for C-shell users). Entering this command into this type of file saves typing the command when logging in. Some examples will illustrate the use of the **biff** command in action:

Examples

Example 1

```
$ biff y
$ biff
is y
$
```

This first command in the example shows the **biff** option being enabled with the **y** argument. The second command makes **biff** display its current status (**y** in this case).

Example 2

To disable the notification of incoming mail messages, the **n** argument is used, as shown below:

```
$ biff n
$
New mail for John has arrived
----
From: Mark <Mark Johnson>
Subject: meeting
To: John (John Smith)
Date: Fri, 30 Mar 90 16:06:23 GMT
Don't forget the meeting tomorrow.
----
$
```

This example illustrates how an indication of some incoming mail would appear. When incoming mail is detected for a user, the current process being undertaken will be briefly interrupted while the status line and part of the message is displayed. On most Berkeley UNIX systems, only seven lines (or approximately 550 characters) of the incoming message are displayed. To see the message in its entirety the mail system would have to be invoked using the **mail** command. The **t** (type) or **p** (print) commands would then be issued, along with a message number (if applicable) to view the message(s) concerned. The only status lines shown in the notification message are commonly the **From:**, **Subject:**, **To:** and **Date:** lines:

```
From: Mark <Mark Johnson>
Subject: meeting
To: John (John Smith)
Date: Fri, 30 Mar 90 16:06:23 BST
```

This rather clumsy notification interrupting a session is typical for most UNIX systems.

10.7.1 Other notification messages

A different notification can appear while you are actually using the **mail** system. The message **New mail has arrived** is commonly displayed after the current mail session has finished, for example when the **quit** command is used. For example:

```
& quit
New mail has arrived
```

This message indicates that new mail arrived while you were using the mail system. Incoming mail can also be detected during mail system session, whereupon it can be examined immediately using the **t** (or **p**) command. It is advisable to use the **f** (display message headers) to see a list of the current messages when incoming mail arrives, since the message numbers are not displayed when the notification appears.

10.8 Saving mail messages – the s command

In addition to saving mail messages in the **mbox** file, the user can save a mail message in another location (another file) using the **s** (save) command. When **s** is used, the specified messages (complete with their header lines) are appended to the nominated file. The format for the save (**s**) command is:

s <message-list ...> <filename>

The **<message-list ...>** is simply one or more message numbers. The **<filename>** is a valid UNIX filename where the message is to be saved, which can contain partially or fully-qualified pathnames. When a message is saved to a file, the name of the file is echoed back to the user, along with the number of characters and lines that were saved. The following example illustrates the use of the **save** command:

```
& f
> 1 jim Tue Feb 20 11:45 8/143 "hello2
> 2 mark Tue Feb 22 09:23 8/147 "greeting"
&
& s 1 message1
"message1" 3 lines 458 characters
&
```

If you wish to save only the *body* of the message, without the header lines, see the **write** command, discussed in section 10.11.

10.9 Forwarding mail to other users – the f command (Xenix only)

On some occasions you may find that you need to send a copy of a particular message to another user on the system. A facility, only available on Xenix systems at present, allows the currently selected mail message to be forwarded using the **f** (forward) command. The format of the command is:

f <username>

The **<username>** is simply the login name the user to whom the current message is to be forwarded. Once a copy of the message has been forwarded, the original remains in the sender's root directory, in the **mbox** file. When the forwarded message is received, the recipient also obtains a few header lines to indicate the identity of the sender, and the time the message was sent etc. The command to forward message number 2 (assuming it exists) to a user called fred, would thus be:

```
& f fred
```

An example of a forwarded message that has been received, is shown below (assume the forwarded message has a message number of 1). Note how two groups of status lines are included in the message, the first telling the user the time and date and username of the person who sent this particular message, and the second (indented) group being the original header of the mail message that has been forwarded.

```
& t1
Message 2:
From: john (john brown) Wed Feb 10 12:06:29 1990
Subject: meeting
To: fred (fred smith)
Date: Wed, Feb 10 90 12:06:27 GMT
Cc: mark (mark bloggs)
    From: john (john brown) Mon Feb 8 11:21:46 1990
    Subject: meeting
    To: Jim (jim Brown)
    Date: Mon, Feb 8 90 11:21:44 GMT
    Cc: mark (mark bloggs)
    Please meet Susan at 12:30 pm on 23 february regarding the
    new project.
```

The whole of the forwarded message has been indented (commonly by a single **[TAB]** space) as a result of using the (lower case) **f** command. To avoid indenting the forwarded message in this way (in the case where the indentation may push the message off the right-hand side of the screen, for example) the **F** command should be used. An example of the same message forwarded using the **F** command is shown below. The > sign embedded in the left margin indicates the start of the forwarded message:

```
Message 2:
```

```
From: john (john brown) Wed Feb 10 12:06:29 1990
Subject: meeting
To: fred (fred smith)
Date: Wed, Feb 10 90 12:06:27 GMT
Cc: mark (mark bloggs)
>From: john (john brown) Mon Feb 8 11:21:46 1990
Subject: meeting
To: Jim (jim Brown)
Date: Mon, Feb 8 90 11:21:44 GMT
Cc: mark (mark bloggs)
Please meet Susan at 12:30 pm on 23 february regarding the new
project.
```

10.10 Transferring mail messages – the mb command

The **mbox** file (which contains all the messages that have been saved from your previous mail sessions) can be used as a storage area when transferring messages that have recently arrived, from your post office file. The **mb** (**mbox**) command can be used for this purpose. The format of the **mb** command is:

mb <message number ...>

This command transfers the specified message(s) (**<message number...>**) from the **/usr/spool/mail/<login-name>** directory (the user's post office file) into the user's own **mbox** file (local mailbox file). In effect, the transferred messages are deleted from main system mailbox (which holds all new incoming messages) and copied to the local mailbox (which stores any miscellaneous mail message files, which may be created when a **mb** or **q** command is issued, for example).

A typical command to move messages **1** and **3** to your personal **mbox** file would be:

```
& mb 1 3
```

If the **mbox** file already exists, the messages specified will be appended to the file. **Mail** does not actually remove the specified messages from the current session, this is carried out by the **quit** command i.e. the **mb** command does not take effect until you **quit** the **mail** system.

Ranges of messages can also be moved, by using this command in the following way:

& mb <start-message>-<end-message>

For example, the command:

```
& mb 1-4
```

will move messages 1 to 4 into the current user's **mbox** file. This command is synonymous with:

```
& mb 1 2 3 4
```

although this is rather long-winded when compared with the former command.

10.11 Saving the body of a message – the w command

Mail messages can be copied to other areas of the file-system, provided the appropriate write-permissions have been granted. We have already met the **save** command (see section 10.8), however another command, called **write** (abbreviated to **w**) is also available, which allows the user to save the *body* of a message, or group of messages, to another file. By the body we are referring to the message alone, and not to the status lines that the mail system provides. This option is useful for saving programs (such as shell scripts) since the status lines must not be included (because they will not be recognised by the shell as UNIX commands).

The format for the write command is thus:

& w <message number ...> <filename>

A **<filename>** can include pathnames (either fully or partly-qualified), so you can save messages to different areas of the file-system. Some examples illustrate the use of the **w** command in action:

Examples

Example 1

```
& w 1 /usr/john/oldmail
```

This command writes message number **1** into the file **oldmail** that exists in the directory **/usr/john**. A full pathname has been used here, because **/usr/john** is not the current working directory.

Example 2

If our current working directory was **/usr**, we could have issued the same command, but with a partially-qualified path name, as shown:

```
& w 1 john/oldmail
```

This command achieves the same as the first, assuming that **/usr** is our current working directory. We have not preceded **/john/oldmail** with a / sign, because that would specify a file called **/john/oldmail** to hold the current message, which may not exist (or may not have the appropriate write-permission).

Example 3

Assuming our current working directory was **/usr/john**, we could issue the command:

```
& w 1 oldmail
```

Example 4

Remember that you can submit a range of messages for storage in another location, as shown in the example below:

```
& w 1-3 oldmail
```

This example writes mail messages **1**, **2** and **3** to the file **oldmail**. If **oldmail** already exists, data will be appended to it; otherwise, it will be created.

10.12 Printing messages on the line printer

The **mail** system can also be instructed to print a message or group of messages on a line-printer, using the **lp** command. Many UNIX systems have a central printer available for all users. The **lp** command is used with a message list, as follows:

lp [<start-message>-<end-message>] [<message-number>]

As can be seen from the syntax description, the **lp** command can be used either with a single-message, or with a range of messages.

Examples

Example 1

```
& lp 1-4
```

This command example prints a range of messages (messages **1** to **4**) on the line-printer.

Example 2

```
& lp 1
```

This example prints only one message (message 1).

Example 3

Lists of individual messages can be submitted for printing, using a command such as:

```
& lp 1 2 4
```

This command prints messages **1**, **2** and **4** respectively.

10.13 Undeleting mail messages – the u command

After issuing a **d** (delete) command (or **dp** command etc.), you may find you need to undelete the message(s) concerned. The command **undelete** (abbreviated to **u**) is provided for this purpose. It is used with a message number in the following form:

u <message-number>

The **u** command can also be used on its own without a message number. In this mode the current message will be deleted i.e. the last message displayed or manipulated etc.

Examples

Example 1

```
& u 3
```

This command undeletes message number **3**.

Example 2

A range of messages can be undeleted using a command such as:

```
& u 1-3
```

Be sure to undelete the appropriate messages before exiting from the **mail** system, since deleted messages are irretrievably lost upon exit. Use **ex** to ignore any such deletions.

10.13.1 Holding mail

Messages can be held from deletion using the **ho** (**hold**) command. The **hold** command takes a message (or message list) and transfers the messages back to the system mailbox (your post office file) in the **/usr/spool/mail** directory.

When you invoke the **mail** system, any new messages in the system mail-box (the post office) that await your attention are read into memory so that you can view them. When you exist from the mail system, any messages (which have not been deleted) are normally written to your own **mbox** file. To avoid this, you can use **hold** (or **ho**) to send the messages back to the system mail-box (your post office file), so that they will be read in again next time you invoke **mail**.

10.14 Escaping from compose mode

The mail system provides a way for the user to escape from compose mode (used for typing in the mail messages) by using a *tilde escape* command. The ability to escape from compose or edit mode makes the **mail** system very flexible. For example, you might be typing in a message, and then require a list of the current users. To obtain this list you could use a tilde escape in conjunction with the **who** command. Both shell and mail commands can be accessed using tilde escape commands. They can also be used to change mail information such as the recipient names, subject headers etc. The tilde character (~) is used to initiate the command, and when it is to be included in a message always takes the form:

~<command>

The ~ (tilde) must be used before the command, in the first column of the current line, to ensure that the command is not interpreted as part of the message you are sending.

10.15 Tilde commands

The most common tilde commands, which allow the user to invoke **mail** or shell commands from compose or edit mode, are now examined.

10.15.1 ~! – Execute a shell command

The ! command is commonly used as a shell escape command. We have already met it in section 9.2.14 in Chapter 9 – UNIX editors. The ! command can be used to invoke a shell command, by typing the required command directly after the exclamation mark (!). In the context of a tilde command, the shell command following the exclamation mark will be executed as soon as the **mail** system interprets the tilde command. This can be demonstrated in an example; assume we are composing a message within the mail system, and we required a list of the current users. To obtain this list we would use the **~! who** command (a tilde escape command that invokes a shell process). Our session with the **mail** system would thus look similar to this:

```
$ mail -s users John
Meet on Thursday at 12.30 (Room 341) regarding the new
installation. See you then.
~! who
John tty01 Feb 10 11:58
jim  tty02 Feb 10 10:21
root tty09 Feb 10 08:46
fred tty10 Feb 10 10:27
mark tty11 Feb 10 11:02
john tty13 Feb 10 10:54
!
<ctrl-d>
Cc:
$
```

This example demonstrates how the **who** command can be invoked while you are composing a message. If we required a longer session with the shell we could simply type the command **~! sh** which would create a new shell process. This process would remain active until terminated using **<ctrl-d>**, whereupon we would return to the mail system. Note that the **mail** command **sh** can be used to invoke interactive shells.

10.15.2 ~b <user-list> – Blind carbon copy command

The **~b <user-list>** command is the 'blind carbon copy' (**bcc**) command. Issuing a **b** followed by one or more usernames, will ensure that the relevant message is forwarded to the user(s) in the **<user-list>**. The command is equivalent to the **Cc:** option, except that the usernames in the **Cc:** field will not be displayed. The command is thus called the 'blind carbon copy' command, because the recipient cannot see who else has been the message. The **<user-list>** can include one or more usernames, separated by spaces. An example using the **~b** command in a message is shown below:

```
$ mail -s greeting John
~b mark
Thanks for the project proposal. We'll meet on Monday to
discuss it further.
<ctrl-d>
Cc:
$
```

When this message is sent to user **John**, the **Cc:** line will be empty, even though user **mark** has been mentioned as a recipient of the message. When **John** reads his message, there is no indication of the carbon-copy users, as shown below when the message is typed out:

```
& t2
Message 2:
From: jim (jim smith) Wed Feb 10 12:06:29 1990
Subject: meeting
To: fred (fred smith)
Date: Wed, Feb 10 90 12:06:27 GMT
Cc:
Thanks for the project proposal. We'll meet on Monday to
discuss it further.
```

10.15.3 ~c <user-list> – visible carbon copy command

The **~c <user-list>** command is similar in use to the **~b** command, described in the previous section, except that the carbon-copy users *will* be displayed to the recipient when he receives the message. Take the example given in section 10.15.2, changing **~b** to **~c**:

```
$ mail -s greeting John
~c mark
Thanks for the project proposal. We'll meet on Monday to
discuss it further.
<ctrl-d>
Cc:
```

When user John reads this message, the **Cc:** line will be show the carbon-copy users which were included within the **~c** tilde command in the message. This is illustrated below:

```
& t2
Message 2:
From: jim (jim smith) Wed Feb 10 12:06:29 1990
Subject: meeting
To: fred (fred smith)
Date: Wed, Feb 10 90 12:06:27 GMT
Cc: mark (mark bloggs)
Thanks for the project proposal. We'll meet on Monday to
discuss it further.
```

10.15.4 ~d – include dead.letter file

The **~d** command specifies that the file **dead.letter** is to be inserted into the message that is currently being typed. This command can be very useful, especially when the **dead.letter** (the unsent message) is either very long or contains a large amount of detailed text that would otherwise have to be typed in again. Takc the example where you have typed a rather long message, and you want to send it to user **admin** (an administrative user on your UNIX system). By mistake, you type the name as **admim** and the **mail** system returns your message indicating that the user specified could not be found.

In this event the **mail** system would return your mail to you, with an indication of the error, and the file **dead.letter** would contain the unsent message. The long example which follows illustrates this:

```
$ biff y
$ mail -s quota admim
Would it be possible to increase my quota ? I am having
problems with the Ingres package when I try to save my work.
<ctrl-d>
Cc:
$
New mail for John has arrived:
----
From: Mail Delivery Subsystem <mailer-daemon>
Date: Fri, 30 Mar 90 16:06:23 GMT
Subject: Returned mail: User unknown
To: John
          ----- Transcript of session follows -----
... User unknown
----
You have mail
$ mail
mail version 5.2 6/21/85. Type ? for help
"/usr/spool/mail/John": 1 Message 1 new
>N 1 mailer-daemon Tue Feb 20 11:45 17/35 "Returned mail"
&t1
Message 1:
From John Fri 30 Mar 90 16:06:30 GMT
Date: Fri, 30 Mar 90 16:06:30 GMT
Subject: Returned mail: User unknown
To: John
          ----- Transcript of session follows -----
admim ... User unknown
          ----- Unsent message follows -----
Would it be possible to increase my quota? I am having
problems with the Uniplex package when I try to save my work.
&d1
&exit
$
```

UNIX operates with the **mail** system to ensure that mail is received and delivered to the appropriate users. It also validates mail messages, ensuring that a user actually exists etc. These tasks are carried out by the 'mailer daemon'. The previous example illustrated how the mailer daemon returned our message, indicating that user 'admim' does not exist, and hence the message could not be delivered. We could resubmit our message without retyping it using the tilde command **~d** in the following way.

```
$ mail -s quota admin
~d
Would it be possible to increase my quota? I am having
problems with the Uniplex package when I try to save my work.
<ctrl-d>
Cc:
$
```

This command makes use of the **dead.letter** facility. Rather than retyping the mail message, we simply issue the **~d** command to make the **mail** system read the **dead.letter** file from our home directory (its default location) into the current mail message. Now that the recipient name has been corrected, the mail should be forwarded without any further problems. If you are ever unsure about a username you can use **grep** to scan the **/etc/passwd** file for the name that you require, for example:

```
$ grep admin /etc/passwd
admin:gszsEC3cojrS6:0:1:Unix Operator:/:/bin/csh
```

This command ensures that user **admin** actually exists. If a user did not exist, then **grep** would return failure, and no matching lines would appear, for example:

```
$ grep admim /etc/passwd
$
```

This command uses **grep** to scan the **/etc/passwd** file for a user named 'admim'. No such user exists with that name and hence the shell prompt is simply returned indicating that no matches were found with the pattern supplied. Note also that we could send an unsent message using input redirection with the **mail** command, as in the example on the next page:

```
$ mail -s quota admin < dead.letter
```

This command provides a totally valid, rather slick alternative to the earlier tilde command example.

10.15.5 ~e and ~v – invoke editors on a message

The **~e** tilde command is used to invoke an editor while typing the message section of a mail-message. The default editor is normally **ed**, the standard UNIX editor, although any other UNIX editor can be specified (see Editor Preferences below).

When you enter **~e**, **mail** loads as much of the message body as you have typed so far, into the buffer area of the editor you are using. From this point onwards (until you exit the editor) you can compose your message in a more controlled way, ensuring that the message is satisfactory. All of the host editors facilities can be employed, so you can conduct searches, make replacements etc.

Editor preferences

The shell variable **$EDITOR** is used to store the name of the editor to be invoked when **~e** is used. The **~e** option normally invokes a line-editor, and hence there are a few choices that could be chosen here i.e. **ed** or **ex**, to name the most likely candidates. You can change the value of **$EDITOR** using the **set** command from within the **mail** system at the **&** prompt. An example is shown below on the next page, setting the editor to **ex** and then using it to edit a **.mailrc** file:

```
$ ex .mailrc
".mailrc" [New File]
:a
EDITOR=ex
.
:x
$ mail -s demonstration John
This text is about to be loaded into the buffer area by the
'ex' editor using the tilde escape command ~e.
~e
:1-3p
This text is about to be loaded into the buffer area by the
'ex' editor using the tilde escape command ~e.
:x
<ctrl-d>
Cc:
$
```

Similarly, we can use a visual editor (such as **vi**) to edit the body of our mail messages by typing **~v** while in compose mode (rather than using set **EDITOR=vi**).

10.15.6 ~p – print/view the current message

The one large drawback with **mail** (when you are not using an editor to create your messages) is the limited facilities available for checking that your message is satisfactory before you send it. **Mail** allows you to view your messages using the tilde escape command **~p** (or **~P** – same thing) to print the current message on the screen, up to the point that you made the request. The **~p** option also shows you the **To:** and **Subject:** fields of the current message (which coincidentally can also be changed while you are composing a message). The command can be useful when your message is unusually large e.g. when it exceeds a page etc. As a rule of thumb use a text editor such as **ex** or **vi** to edit large messages.

If you are in the middle of typing a long message and you must postpone your session, but do not want to send the current message, simply press **<ctrl-c>** twice to write the current message to the file **dead.letter**. You can then execute **mail** again at a later date and use the **~d** (read the **dead.letter** file into the current message) when in compose mode. Alternatively you can issue a command of the form:

```
$ mail username < dead.letter
```

It would also be advisable to rename the **dead.letter** file to prevent it being overwritten (for example, as found in the long example given in section 10.15.4) for example:

```
$ mv dead.letter last_message
```

10.15.7 ~h – edit header information fields

A header contains all the information pertaining to the sender and recipient of a typical mail message. When a message is being composed, the header will contain basic information such as the recipient's name i.e. as in the **To:** field; and the

Subject: field containing a title indicating the nature of the message that is to be sent. When you eventually send your message, the time and date is recorded and included in the recipient's header, along with the any carbon-copy users (and blind carbon-copy users) etc.

The **~h** command allows you to edit all of these fields, supplying new values where necessary. The old value(s) are displayed first, and you can either keep them (by pressing the **[RETURN]** key), or delete the current entry, using the **[DEL]** or backspace key, and type in a new value.

10.15.8 Editing the Subject and To fields – ~s and ~t

The **~h** command is useful, but you may only want to change one of the header fields in the current message. We have examined how to use the **~c** (add usernames to carbon-copy list), and the **~b** command (add usernames to blind carbon-copy list); however there are two other commands that are more likely to be used by the more casual **mail** user. These are **~s** and **~t** respectively.

The **~s** command allows you to change the **Subject** field of the current message. Simply type **~s** on a new line and **mail** will display the **Subject:** prompt. You can then enter a new subject for your message, or leave it blank to omit a subject header.

The **~t** option allows you to specify additional usernames (each separated by a space) to whom the current message will be sent. The command does not, however, allow you to delete the name of the original recipient. To erase that name you will have to interrupt the current message and recompose a new message with a different recipient name (or use the **dead.letter** file method described in section 10.15.4).

10.15.9 Reading miscellaneous messages using ~r

The **~r** tilde command is used to read a file into the current message. It can only be used while you are in compose mode, and you must have the necessary read permission on the file. You can also use pathnames to read in files from areas of the file-system other than the current directory. The format of the command is:

~r <filename>

Remember that files without a preceding pathname are assumed to exist in the current directory. If a file that is specified does not exist, an error message will be displayed and you will be returned to compose mode.

10.15.10 Requesting a receipt from a user

Another problem with the **mail** system is the actual message delivery. When a message is sent, it is not usually delivered to the recipient immediately. Try mailing a message to yourself, and make a note of the time interval. The delay in forwarding a message can be due to a number of reasons, but the most common is that the system is very busy at the time of sending the message.

The **~R** command is used to request a receipt from a user who has been sent a message. This ensures that the message has been delivered, and not lost somewhere. The format of the tilde command is:

~R <username>

The value for **<username>** should be the username of the individual from whom the receipt will be required. The **~R** command should be used near the end of your message, although it can occur anywhere in the current mail message. The receipt itself is a message that is placed in the recipient's mail-box file (the system post office in the **/usr/spool/mail** directory). When your message is sent, an additional header line is included which is named **Return-receipt-to:** on most systems, and it allows the recipient to know that the arrival of the message has been acknowledged.

10.16 Mail options

The operation of **mail** system can be controlled through the use of a series of environmental variables which can be set directly from within the **mail** system using the **se** (**set**) command. There are many options available, and you are advised to use the command **set ?** to display all the options available on your system.

Binary options (see section 10.16.1 below) can only be on or off, and never contain string values. An example of a *non-binary* environmental variable is **EDITOR=ex**, since the value of the variable **$EDITOR** is any string value that represents the name of a UNIX editor that is available on your system. Some of the binary options are described in the next few sections. They are turned on (enabled) using the **set** command and turned off (disabled) using the **unset** command.

10.16.1 Binary options

Default values for all options (binary and string options) are stored in the file **/usr/lib/mail/.mailrc**. These are normally examined every time **mail** is invoked. You will find the specific options for use with your personal mail sessions are located in your home directory under the name **.mailrc**. If the **.mailrc** file does not exist in your home directory, you can create one using your favourite editor. This **.mailrc** file should contain individual lines of the form **set <binary-option>** for binary options or **set <variable>=<value>** for non-binary options.

The most commonly used binary options are now examined in detail:

append

The **append** option ensures that all messages that are saved in your local **mbox** file are appended (i.e. placed at the end of the file, instead of at the beginning). If you examine your **mbox** file (for example, using the **cat** command), you may find that the most recent messages are stored directly at the top of the file. Using the **set append** command makes **mail** append the most recent message to the bottom of the **mbox** file, and not at the top. On version 7 UNIX systems the **/usr/lib/mail/.mailrc** file has this option set up, on a mandatory basis, so here it is common to find that the **set append** option has been set.

ask

The **ask** option causes mail to prompt you for a message *subject* title for each new message that you send. Pressing the **[RETURN]** key when prompted will leave the **Subject:** field blank. This option is nearly always set up by default in the system **.mailrc** file, so use **unset ask** to turn off the facility, if you do not require it. This option is system-dependent (see **asksubject** below).

askcc

The **askcc** option makes **mail** prompt you for additional carbon copy recipients when you terminate each message with a **<ctrl-d>** signal (or when a dot is discovered at the start of a line – see the **dot** option below) i.e. when compose mode is terminated. This option is nearly always set up in the system **.mailrc** file, so use **unset askcc** to override the system default.

asksubject

Similar to the **ask** option, in that **mail** will prompt you for a subject message before you start to compose a message. A system-dependent option (see **ask** above), Berkeley systems using **set ask**, while Xenix (and some System V systems) use **set asksubject**.

autoprint

The **set autoprint** option makes the **d** (delete current message command) act like a **dp** command (see section 10.6). When the **autoprint** option is enabled, pressing **d** will cause mail to delete the current message and display the next message in the list (if it exists). If there are no more messages, the message **at EOF** (at end of file) will be displayed. The normal default for the **autoprint** option is off, so use **set autoprint** in your local **.mailrc** file to override the system default.

dot

When **set dot** is enabled, **mail** will interpret a single period (.) in the leftmost column (column 1) to mean the termination of a message. The **<ctrl-d>** (**EOF**) signal is normally used to terminate a message, but most systems allow the detection by both methods i.e. **<ctrl-d>** and '.'. This facility has been carried over from editors which also use the dot notation to terminate edit or insert mode. The default setting in the system **.mailrc** file is normally off, so use **set dot** in your local **.mailrc** file to override the system default.

ignore

Enabling **set ignore** cause the mail system to ignore any user-generated interrupt signals i.e. **<ctrl-c>** signals. When an interrupt signal is invoked, the system normally displays a '@' sign, and ignores the interrupt. The usual default setting in the system **.mailrc** file is off, so use the **set ignore** command to invoke the facility. Note that you will not be able to kill a letter in compose mode if this option is set.

ignoreeof

The **ignoreeof** option (ignore EOF signal) is related to **dot** (see above). When enabled the mail system will not accept a **<ctrl-d>** signal as a message termination signal (or a **quit** signal from the interactive mail level), so **exit** (abbreviated to **ex** or **x**) or **quit** (**q**) must be used to exit the mail system. The system default setting is normally off, so you need to use **set ignoreeof** to enable the facility, and override the default setting.

metoo

When an alias contains the username of the sender of the message, that user is excluded from receiving the message. Using the **metoo** option makes sure that all the users who are included in an alias definition receive the same mail message. The default is normally off, so again, use the **set metoo** command to allow messages to be received by yourself if you are included in alias list that you are using as a group-recipient name. See section 10.3 for more information on alias lists.

nosave

When a message is aborted using the **<ctrl-c>** signal, the message, up to the point of the interrupt signal, is copied to the file **dead.letter**. When the **nosave** option is enabled, the **dead.letter** file is not created. The default for this option is normally disabled, and this is recommended, especially if you frequently compose long messages.

replyall

The **replyall** option, when set, reverses the sense of the **r** and **R** commands. That is, the **r** command, that normally replies to the sender and all the carbon copy users, will now only reply to the sender; and the **R** command, which normally replies only to the sender, will now reply to the sender and all carbon copy users that the sender specified in the original message. See sections 10.2.3 and 10.2.4 for more information on the **r** and **R** commands.

quiet

The **quiet** option suppresses the normal sign-on messages when mail is invoked i.e. the version number of the mail system being used etc.; on some systems (notably Xenix), the sign-on header message and message numbers are also cancelled. The default is normally off, so to override the system default you can include **set quiet** in your local **.mailrc** file.

verbose

When the **verbose** option is set, the delivery of mail messages is displayed on the recipient's screen. The option has the same effect as the command **mail -v** – which turns on *verbose* mode, but from the interactive level of the shell.

10.17 String options

The most commonly used environmental string variables that affect the **mail** system are discussed in this section. String variables, unlike the binary options which can only hold one of two values i.e. on (set) or off (unset), can hold more than two values which are assigned using **set** in the following way:

set <variable> = <value>

You can use **unset** to turn off a string option value for the duration of the current mail session.

10.17.1 $EDITOR

As discussed briefly in section 10.15.5, the **$EDITOR** variable is used for defining the line-based editor invoked using the **edit** and **~e** commands (but not **~v** which invokes the visual screen editor **vi**, see section 10.17.3). When setting the **$EDITOR** variable either from within the mail system, or by editing the **.mailrc** file, be sure to quote the fully-qualified pathname:

& set EDITOR=/bin/ex

If the value of the shell variable **$PATH** includes the directory containing the editor you want to use, the pathname may be omitted. For example you may want to set the value of **$EDITOR** to **/bin/ex**, but upon examination of **$PATH** (which defines the directories to be searched when an executable shell command is used) you may find that the **/bin** directory is already included. In such a case it is unnecessary to set the pathname in the **$EDITOR** variable. When the value of **$EDITOR** is not set, the system default is used. The common line editors include **ex** and **ed**.

10.17.2 $SHELL

The value of the **$SHELL** variable is the pathname of an executable shell to be used with the **!** command (shell escape command). The tilde command **~!** allows a shell command to be executed from compose mode (see section 10.15.1). A typical value, for example:

```
& set SHELL=/bin/csh
```

tells **mail** to use the C-shell for any shell commands, or shell sessions. If the **$SHELL** value is omitted, the mail system uses a default shell, commonly **/bin/sh**, the Bourne Shell.

10.17.3 $VISUAL

The **$VISUAL** variable is similar to the **$EDITOR** variable, but is used to specify the pathname of a visual editor, the most likely candidate being **vi**. When the value for **$VISUAL** is set, the tilde command **~v** can be used to invoke the visual editor on the current message body from compose mode.

10.17.4 toplines

The **toplines** variable is used in conjunction with the **mail** command **top**. The **top** command is used to display the first few lines of the either the current message, or each message specified by number on the command line. The actual number of lines displayed is defined by the variable **toplines**. If a value is not specified for **toplines** a default value will be used (as set in the system-wide .mailrc file – commonly 5 lines).

Examples

```
& set toplines=3
```

Set number of lines to be displayed to 3

```
& top 1-5
```

Show the first 3 lines of messages 1 to 5

```
& top 3
```

Show the first 3 lines of message 3

```
& set toplines=7
```

Redefine the number of lines to be shown

10.17.5 record

The **record** variable holds the name of a file which is to be used to save all outgoing mail messages. This facility can be useful as a reference for all the mail messages that are sent. Note that the pathname should be included, as shown below:

```
& set record=/usr/john/recordmail
```

This command names the file **recordmail** to be used to hold all the messages that you will eventually send. If the file does initially exist then it will be created when the next message is sent to a recipient.

10.18 Miscellaneous mail options

When the mail system is invoked from the interactive level of the shell, a number of options can be used which affect the way in which mail will operate.

10.18.1 -v – turn on verbose mode

The **-v** option has been mentioned briefly already (see section 10.16.1). It makes **mail** operate in its verbose (or talkative) mode. The main effect of the **-v** option will be to advise the user of the arrival of any mail message(s).

10.18.2 -n – ignore the local .mailrc file

The **-n** option can be very useful for when you want to invoke **mail** with the system defaults i.e. those which are defined in the **/usr/lib/mail/.mailrc** file (system defaults file) and ignore all your personal variable settings.

10.18.3 -s – subject title

The **-s** option is used when you are sending mail. The option signifies that the next string will denote the nature of the message that is being sent. For example:

```
$ mail -s greeting John
```

This command initiates the sending of a message to user **John**. The subject of the message is **greeting**. This text string will be inserted into the **Subject:** field of the recipient's message.

10.18.4 -f [name] – read contents of mbox file

The **-f** option is used to make the **mail** system read the contents of the **mbox** file into the current session, therefore allowing you to manipulate all of your old messages. The optional **[name]** argument allows you to supply a different filename if the messages you wish to use are not held in **mbox**.

This concludes the section on the fundamental use of the UNIX **mail** system. The next section examines some of the other tools that can be used in conjunction with the **mail** system.

10.19 Mailing tools

There are a number of tools that are specifically for using with the **mail** system. For example, we have already examined **biff** which notifies users of incoming mail. Further mailing tools are examined in the following sections.

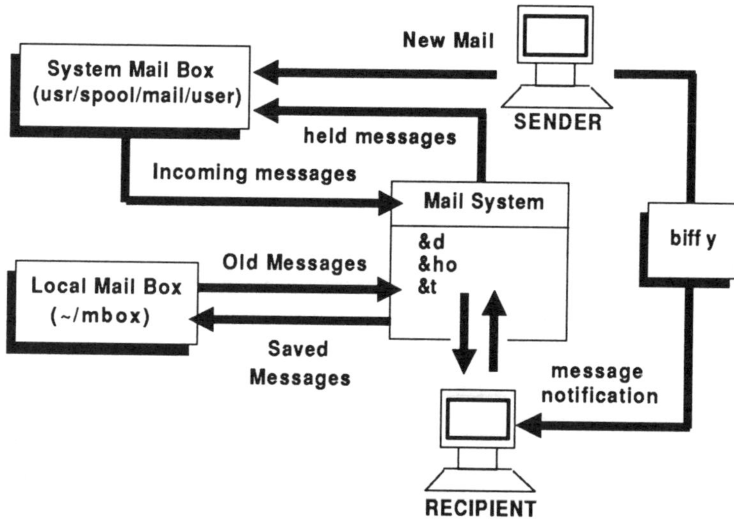

Figure 10.1 Diagrammatical view of the mail system

10.19.1 From – who is my mail from?

The **from** command, which is briefly examined in section 10.4, is part of the Berkeley tool-set. Basically it allows you to view the header information from your own system mail-box, or, if the necessary permissions are available, from another user's system mail-box. However, the default file permission characteristics of the mail files normally allow only the owner to examine the necessary files. The super-user is the only exception to this rule. The following syntax is applicable to the **from** command:

from [-s sender] [user]

The **[-s sender]** option specifies that only the header information for mail sent by the specified sender is to be printed. The optional **[user]** argument specifies that **mail** should examine the system mail-box of the person identified by the name **user**. When used without either argument, **from** will examine your own system mail-box, and print only the headers from messages.

Examples

Example 1

```
$ from
Message 1:
From: john (john brown) Wed Feb 10 12:06:29 1990
Subject: meeting
To: fred (fred smith)
Date: Wed, Feb 10 90 12:06:01 GMT
Cc: mark (mark bloggs)
Message 2:
From: mary (mary rice) Wed Feb 11 09:08:10 1990
Subject: reminder
To: fred (fred smith)
Date: Wed, Feb 11 90 09:08:00 GMT
Cc:
$
```

This example shows the use of the **from** command without any options or filename arguments, with the result that the header information from the current user's system mail-box is displayed. The default permissions on the user's system mail-box obviously allow read/write access.

Example 2

```
$ from root
/usr/spool/mail/root: access denied
```

This example demonstrates the error message that is generated when the system mail-box specified on the command line belongs to a user whose read permission is denied to the user making the request.

Example 3

```
$ from -s john
Message 1:
From: john (john brown) Wed Feb 10 12:06:29 1990
Subject: meeting
To: fred (fred smith)
Date: Wed, Feb 10 90 12:06:01 GMT
Cc: mark (mark bloggs)
```

This illustrates how the **-s** option (with a username) can be used to scan your mail-box for a specific sender. In the example the name **john** has been specified, therefore all headers which contain a **From:** field containing the name **john** are displayed. We could also use the command **from -s fred mary**. This would scan user **mary**'s system mail-box for any messages that **fred** has sent her. However, read permission on **mary**'s system mail-box would be necessary for this to work.

10.19.2 vacation – vacation indication program

The **vacation** command allows you to inform a user who has sent you some mail, that you are unavailable to read it, and thus respond. The facility requires you to create a file called **.forward**, which contains a single line in the following format:

\your-name, "|/usr/ucb/vacation your-name"

The name **your-name** is your login name. The character string **/usr/ucb/vacation** represent a pathname (fully-qualified) of the vacation program's location in the file system. You need to make sure that this pathname is correct for your system. For example if you have a vacation program in the **/bin** directory, put **\your-name, "|/bin/vacation your-name"**.

A file called **vacation.msg** holds your vacation message which is sent back to a user who sends you mail. The vacation message is sent via the **mail** system to the sender of the original message, so it should also include a normal header structure (although not essential). A **From:** line should not normally be included, since **mail** will be used to deliver automatic replies, and thus the name of the sender of the automatic reply will be included. A typical **vacation.msg** can be created with your favourite text editor. The example below illustrates the creation of the file using the **ex** editor:

```
$ ex vacation.msg
"vacation.msg" [New File]
:a
Subject: Sorry, I am on vacation
Delivered-by: The vacation program
I have received your mail, but I cannot respond to you until
the 30th April since I am away on business.
- Fred.

.
:x
"vacation.msg" [New File] 8 lines 199 characters.
$
```

The **vacation.msg** message will only be sent once a week to each individual sender. Two other files also exist which are created by the vacation program: **vacation.pag** and **vacation.dir**. Both are created by the vacation program when incoming messages are detected and they hold information pertaining to the message originators.

Vacation options

The vacation program has an initialisation option, commonly **-I**, which initialises the **vacation.pag** and **vacation.dir** files. The option should be used *before* the **.forward** file is modified in any way. It takes the following form:

```
$ vacation -I
```

This command initialises the vacation program, and thus invoke it. Don't forget that when you return from your vacation period you should disable the **vacation** program so that vacation messages are not sent back to the message senders reflecting your earlier absence. You can disable the vacation program by deleting the **.forward** file (or renaming it).

Some implementations of the vacation program include a **-tN** option that allows the user to change the interval time between repeat replies. The default, as mentioned, is one week, however different intervals can be specified used with this option. A trailing character (s, m, h, d or w) placed following the value of **N** scales N to seconds, minutes, hours, days or weeks respectively. For example **-t4w** instructs **vacation** send a reply to incoming mail once every four weeks.

Further notes on the vacation program

Some systems include an interactive vacation mode. It is invoked by executing the **vacation** program without any arguments. The interactive mode is useful since it will automate the automatic reply procedures. For example, it will check for the existence of the **.vacation.msg** file, allowing you to create one if it does not exist. The interactive mode also allows the user to enable or disable the vacation facility. The system automatically performs a **vacation -I** command to enable the facility, while disabling the facility involves the deletion of the **.forward** file.

The environmental variable **$SUBJECT** can be used within the **vacation.msg** file on many UNIX systems. It is used to substitute the value of the sender's **Subject:** field. For example you could create a **vacation.msg** file containing the following:

```
Subject: Sorry, I am on vacation
I received your mail regarding "$SUBJECT". I am on vacation
and will reply to your message after I return on the 20th.
- Fred.
```

10.20 Secret mail – enroll, xsend, and xget

The **mail** system that we examined earlier allows users to send plain-text mail to one another. By 'plain-text' we refer to pure ASCII messages. This does pose a slight problem of privacy since messages can be read by users with the necessary privileges i.e. by a nosy super-user!. As part of Version 7 UNIX (the first portable version of UNIX, which was released about 1978), a series of tools were provided for the distribution of secret mail. These tools provide a secure communications channel for the distribution of electronic messages. The recipient user must supply a password which is used to decipher the necessary message. This password is allocated by the sender of the message, and must be known by the recipient.

10.20.1 enroll

Before secret mail can be sent, the user must enroll onto the system, using the **enroll** command. **Enroll** is invoked, without any arguments, and then the system asks you for a secret key. This **key** will allow messages to be appropriately encrypted by the system. The **key** itself is also encrypted using the same mechanism therefore ensuring secrecy. The example below illustrates the use of the **enroll** command:

```
$ enroll
Gimme key:<your secret password>
```

Gimme key is the system's way of asking you to type in a password or **key**. The password is *not* echoed on the screen, so you need to take care when typing. Once you have typed in a password the system returns you to the shell level. Immediately after the key is supplied, the enroll utility creates a file in the directory **/var/spool/secretmail** (the commonly used directory name for Berkeley systems, but you may find the file in the **/usr/spool** directory on other UNIX systems). It contains the encrypted key that the you originally supplied when first enrolling. The filename is constructed from your username with the suffix '.key' e.g. **fred.key**. The file is owned by the user enrolling onto the system, so you have complete control over it. The file must exist if that secret mail messages are to be sent. If the file is deleted, the system will ask you for a new key the next time secret mail is to be sent.

10.20.2 xsend

The system will only allow secret mail to be sent to one named recipient at a time. Typing **xsend** without any arguments results in an appropriate error message, for example:

```
$ xsend
mail to exactly one person
```

So, to send some encrypted mail it is necessary to give the name of one user. Once this has been done, the system reads from the standard input stream, where you can proceed to compose your message (i.e. type it in). Press **<ctrl-d>** to end (or **<ctrl-c>** to cancel) the current message. For example:

```
$ xsend jim
This is an example of some secret mail. When this message is
finished the system will encode it. User jim will not be able
to read the message until the necessary password is supplied.
<ctrl-d>
```

The completed message is encoded and stored in the **secretmail** directory (under this user's username followed by an extension that consists of a single number in the range zero to nine). The mail system notifies the recipient with a message indicating that secret mail has been sent. This message will be sent to the recipient immediately if **biff** is set, or if the user is currently in the mail system (**mail** will notify the user upon exiting). In all other cases, the recipient will receive notification upon logging into the system with the normal message 'You have mail'.

A typical message that is delivered to a recipient who has been sent secret mail is shown below:

```
&t1
Message 1:
From: jim (jim smith) Wed Feb 10 12:06:29 1990
Subject: jim sent you secret mail
To: fred (fred forsyth)
Date: Wed, Feb 10 90 12:06:27 GMT
Your secret mail can be read using "xget".
```

The message contains the normal header lines, but notice how the system has altered the **Subject:** line, and the main message body tells the recipient to use **xget** to read the secret mail. Note that the normal mail system is not used in this process, it is purely used as a notification mechanism.

Note: the **user.key** file has been deleted from the **secretmail** directory, or you try to use **xsend** before enrolling, you will see the following error message, since **xsend** will not work until a key has been created.

```
$ xsend
addressee not enrolled
```

In this event, run **enroll** to create a (new) key (see previous section).

10.20.3 xget

Xget is used to examine any secret mail messages. It is invoked without any arguments, whereupon the system will ask you for the necessary **key**. Failure to supply the correct **key** will result in the system displaying the encrypted version of the message, i.e. a few lines of pure garbage. Supplying the correct **key** (as entered by the sender when enroll was initially used) results in the system displaying the deciphered message to the recipient. This is illustrated below:

```
$ xget
Key:<your secret password>

This is an example of some secret mail. When this message
is finished the system will encode it. User jim will not be
able to read the message until the necessary password is
supplied.
        ?
```

As mentioned, failure to supply the correct **key** results in garbage being displayed, for example:

```
$ xget
Key:<the wrong password>
0-;lwfgk' =ldf
   WoMbAtl.ksdhjfg v WE2sgbdbn jSEI =1572.
   03ef,34r 0-m,./dmf u943 rvg32FFR./ I
e5457ER=, ef dfEF .
   ?
```

The question mark (?) displayed in the previous example is a prompt that allows the user to interact with the secret mail system. A small range of fundamental commands is available to the user. These commands are summarised in Table 10.3:

Table 10.3 Xget Commands

Command	Action
q	Quit to shell, leaving any unread messages.
n	Read next message, and delete the current message.
d	Delete the current message and move to the next (same as n).
[RETURN]	Carriage-Return command. Move to the next message after deleting the current message (same as d or n).
!<cmd>	Invoke the shell command <cmd>, and then return to the xget ? prompt.
s[file]	Save the current message in the file named specifically after the s command, or by default in the current user's **mbox** file.

10.21 Direct communication facilities

The UNIX **mail** system is by definition a store and forward system. However, other tools exist that allow the direct communication between users.

10.21.1 Write – write to a terminal

In Chapter 7 (section 7.4.1) we examined how it is possible to write to a terminal using output redirection, such as:

```
$ who > /dev/tty/20
```

This command runs the **who** command and attempts to display the output on the terminal **/dev/tty20**. The command succeeds only if the necessary write-permission on the file **/dev/tty20** is enabled.

The **write** command works in the same way as this rather crude example. The main difference with the use of **write** is that the recipient user can **write** back and thus a two-way (full-duplex) communications link can be established between two users (see also **talk** – section 10.21.2). The syntax for the write command is:

write <user> [ttyname]

where **<user>** is the recipient user, and **[ttyname]**, is the name of a terminal that appears in the /**dev** directory. The syntax description of the **write** command shows that a username must be specified, and that an optional terminal code can be included, if required, for example when a user is logged in on more than one terminal. When you are trying to contact a user who is logged in on several terminals, **write** will establish contact with the terminal that the recipient user logged on to first.

When **write** is invoked, it reads from the standard input, so you simply type in your message, in the required format etc. You can end the session by pressing **<ctrl-d>**, and the message will be dispatched. The sender will be returned to the shell prompt. If the person whom you were contacting was in the middle of another task e.g. in an editing session etc., they will have to escape to the shell level to write back.

The **mesg** command (discussed earlier in 7.4.1) can be used in conjunction with the **write** command to stop incoming messages by simply removing the **write** permission from your terminal. However, if a user has contacted you and persists in annoying you by misusing the facility, past experience has shown that you will not be able to interrupt the message effectively, to invoke **mesg n** to disable incoming messages. The only solution is to log out, or seek administrative assistance.

One good method to employ is to place the line: **mesg n** in your **.profile** file. This file is executed at login time (by the Bourne Shell), hence no messages can reach you until you manually enter **mesg y**. But note that you cannot *send* messages when **mesg** is set to **n**; so the default value for **mesg** is normally **y** (messages enabled).

Examples

Example 1

This example shows the **write** command invoked with both the **<user>** and **[ttyname]** arguments:

```
$ who
John tty14 Jun 18 15:06
John tty18 Jun 18 15:55
$ write John tty18
Hi John, see you tonight at 7.30 pm.
<ctrl-d>
$
```

Example 2

If we tried to write to a user who was not logged in, we would receive an appropriate error message, as illustrated overleaf:

```
$ who
John tty14 Jun 18 15:06
John tty18 Jun 18 15:55
$ write wombat
write: wombat not logged in
$
```

Example 3

When you receive a message from a user, UNIX displays a one-line message indicating the name of the person who is contacting you, the terminal from which the message originated, and the date and time the message was sent. A small beep also accompanies the message to attract your attention:

```
$
Message from John (tty18) Jun 18 17:06:34 ...
Hi John, see you tonight at 7.30 pm.
$
```

Message indications, such as the one just illustrated, are not shown when you press **<ctrl-d>** (this is because you may wish for a two-way communications link) but appear the minute you press the **[RETURN]** after typing in the **write** command. Also note that messages are not displayed on the recipient's screen until you press **[RETURN]**.

A point of protocol

The **write** command, when used with a valid recipient name or terminal name combination, will interrupt whatever the recipient user is doing with the result that the recipient may find that the layout on his or her screen has been completely destroyed. Matters may appear even worse if the recipient was in the middle of a text editing session. But have no fear, since any messages that are written to a terminal while in an editing session will not alter the document in question. The best thing for the recipient do is to stop typing and save their document immediately, and then exit. They can then proceed to answer the message.

One slight problem with the **write** command is the absence of a screen-refresh option which would allow you to redraw the current screen to remove a message such as those generated by **write** or **mail** (especially when **biff** is set to **y**).

There may be the need to adopt some type of user protocol, whereby messages can be communicated more effectively. One approach is to use the letter 'o' to stand for *over* (a prompt for the other user to start typing the next piece of the current message), and 'oo' (for *over and out*). This final piece of notation would be used to terminate the write session.

There isn't any other sensible alternative when devising user protocol, apart from not using the system in the first place. After all it is very crude and it does tend to annoy some users. I would suggest that you use an alternative facility, assuming you have one. The **talk** command is a far superior tool, it has a screen refresh facility and the two parties who are involved in conversation have separate windows for sending and receiving messages. The **talk** command is described briefly in section 10.21.2.

Sending files with write

One useful facility provided by **write** is the ability to forward the contents of a file to a user. This allows messages to be created with an editor before they are actually committed for transmission. In this case the form of the **write** command is:

write <user> < <filename>

The method of input redirection that has been employed here is not a new approach. After all, the **write** command basically only writes the contents of the standard input (by default the keyboard) to a terminal device. We could send this file without using the **write** command at all, by using a command in the following form:

cat <filename ...> > /dev/terminal-name

This form of the command uses the **cat** (concatenate files) command to display a given file and direct the output to a terminal device. The disadvantage of using either **write** or **cat** to send files in this way is that the file is displayed on the recipient's screen and cannot be captured i.e. held in a file for later examination. The better approach is to use **mail** when you want a message to be stored for later examination.

Another disadvantage when using **write** or **cat** to send a file to a recipient is the problem of the size of the message. If the message exceeds 25 lines (the width of most terminal screens in 80 column mode) the message will shoot up the screen at an incredibly rapid rate. The way to sole this problem is to use a filter when sending a file. There are many UNIX filters that can be used in a pipeline to display only a certain number of lines in a stream. We have seen some already such as **tail** and **more**. The **more** command displays a screenful of information at a time; successive lines can be displayed by pressing **[RETURN]**; and a press of **[SPACE]** will display the next screen; for example:

```
$ cat file1 | more > /dev/tty20
```

This command is a much better solution, since it will allow the recipient to control the contents of the file more accurately.

10.21.2 talk

Talk is another command that is similar to **write** except that it includes a screen-refresh command, and it reserves a separate area of the screen for both the sender and recipient users (so that messages can be segregated). It also provides intelligent dialogue messages that accompany you through your session with the **talk** facility. The syntax for the **talk** command is exactly the same as the **write** command, so remember to use a terminal-name in the case where a user is logged in more than once. You can use **who** to find the user's terminal code.

The **<ctrl-l>** keystroke allows the current screen to be refreshed on most systems, although the facility does seem slightly redundant knowing that two areas of the screen are already allocated to both users. Nevertheless the facility is still useful, especially when other messages may interrupt the session i.e. mail notification messages, redirected messages, system messages etc. The **mesg** command can still be used to allow or prohibit incoming messages.

When **talk** is activated with a valid username or with a valid terminal name (or both), the current screen is cleared, and the sender's screen is divided into two areas, separated by a single line. The recipient user's screen, when he or she responds to the sender, will also be divided into two separate parts. The top half of the screen is where the sender will type a message to be sent to the recipient; this area will also contain certain system dialogue messages. Assume we had typed the following command:

```
$ talk John
```

This command would result in a screen display similar to that of Figure 10.2.

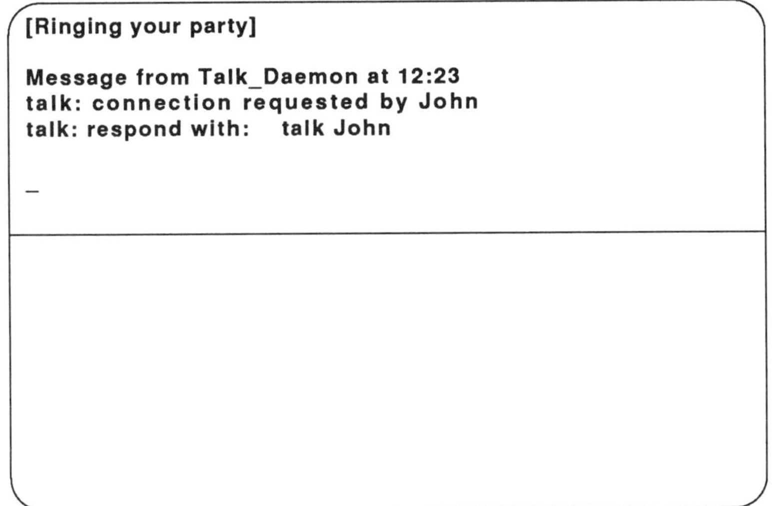

Figure 10.2 A typical screen when talk is invoked.

A two-screened window is opened, and **talk** contacts the recipient user, in this case user **John**. When **talk** is initially invoked, a message is displayed on the recipient's screen. This message can also be seen in Figure 10.2 and takes the form:

```
Message from Talk_Daemon at 12:23
talk: connection requested by John
talk: respond with: talk John
```

This message tells the recipient that somebody is trying to make contact, and that the recipient can respond with the command **talk John**. It is necessary for both the sender and recipient to each invoke the **talk** command (as with the **write** command).

The **talk** command also displays a series of intelligent dialogue messages to the sender user, for example 'Ringing your party' , which is self-explanatory.

When a connection with the recipient user has been established i.e. the recipient user has invoked **talk** with the sender's recipient name, **talk** displays the message **Connection established** and both users can proceed to type their messages (at the same time if required, since separate windows divide each party's messages). Figure 10.3 illustrates a typical conversation after a connection has been established between the sender and recipient party.

```
[Connection established]

Hello Jim, you haven't forgotten the meeting tomorrow at 8.30?

---------------------------------------------------------------

No. I'll see you there, but I may be slightly late.
_
```

Figure 10.3 Typical conversation using the talk command

To a conversation, the **<Ctrl-c>** (interrupt) or **<Ctrl-d>** key can be used to close the connection. Both the sender and recipient will then receive a message indicating that the connection has been terminated.

```
[Connection closing. Exiting]

Hello Jim,you haven't forgotten the meeting tomorrow at 8.30?
$
```

Figure 10.4 Termination of a typical conversation.

The part-screen display shown in Figure 10.4 illustrates the termination of a connection after the **<Ctrl-d>** (or **<Ctrl-c>** signal has been used. Note the 'Connection closing. Exiting' message which is displayed by **talk** when a conversation is being terminated.

Additional information for the recipient

When the **talk** command is invoked on a recipient user, it will keep trying to establish contact, by repeatedly displaying 'Message from Talk_daemon' about every 20-30 seconds. When the recipient receives the message, some systems have the alarming habit of making the shell prompt disappear. In such a case simply press **[RETURN]**, and the prompt should reappear. The recipient can then respond by using **talk** with the sender's name (which is usually quoted in the initial message to the recipient).

10.21.3 wall

Wall (write all) is similar in operation to the **write** command in that it writes a message on a recipients terminal, reading the message from the standard input. The main difference, however, is that wall delivers the message to all the users on the system (hence the name **write all**). Once the command has read the message from the standard input, it proceeds to write it simultaneously on every user's terminal.

The super-user normally uses the **wall** command to deliver important system messages and can override any **mesg n** setting (since the super-user can write to any terminal at any time whatever protection settings are in effect). An example of the **wall** command in action follows:

```
$ wall
Save and logout immediately, the system is going down in 5
minutes. Another warning will follow in 3 minutes.
<ctrl-d>
```

When this **wall** message is received by the users on the network, the message may take the form:

```
Broadcast message from 'root' 18 Jun 18:01:02
Save and logout immediately, the system is going down in 5
minutes. Another warning will follow in 3 minutes.
```

Since **wall** messages are broadcasted over an entire network, the header indicates this with the announcement 'Broadcast message'. The date and time of the broadcast are commonly included in the statement. The example above shows the sender's name as 'root', the super-user, therefore it will be delivered to all users on the network.

10.22 Questions

1. Which tool allows the user to stop incoming messages when commands such as **talk** and **write** are used?

2. Name an alternative method to stop incoming messages being written to a terminal.

3. What is the purpose of tilde-commands in the mail system?

4. Explain the action of the **~d** tilde command.

5. Which tilde-command can be used to invoke a new shell. Give an example of the command with a popular shell.

6. Taking the Berkeley UNIX for the purposes of this question, where are the system mail-boxes of each user stored on the system?

7. The **mbox** file should reside in the home directory of each user who uses the mail system. What does it contain?

8. Name two wildcards that can be used in the mail system.

9. Which editors can be used in conjunction with the **$EDITOR** mail-variable?

10. The **~v** tilde-command allows which type of editor to be invoked on a message?

11 How can the **~v** tilde escape command be told to use a different visual editor? Tip: variable.

12. What is the purpose of the **biff** command?

13. After reading a message in the mail system, which command is supplied to allow a reply to be sent back to the sender?

14. Shown below is a typical header from a mail message:

```
Message 1:
From: john (john brown) Wed Feb 10 12:06:29 1990
Subject: meeting
To: fred (fred smith)
Date: Wed, Feb 10 90 12:06:01 GMT
Cc: mark (mark bloggs)
```

Explain the purpose of the Subject:, To:, and Cc: fields.

15. Name the file that is used in conjunction with the vacation program to hold a message that is to be sent to any users in the event of your absence for a period of time?

16. Explain what the **set** command is used for, when used in conjunction with the mail system.

17. How can a range of messages be deleted from within the mail system? Give an example.

18. Name the command that prints a message or messages from within the mail system.

19. Messages that are being typed in compose mode are normally terminated with a **<ctrl-d>** (end of file) signal. There is an alternative to this method of terminating a message. What is it? Give an example.

20. How can the body of a message be saved to a file of your choice? Give an example of the mail command that does this.

The answers to these questions can be found in Appendix B.

11

Systems Administration

11.1 Introduction

Administration is a continuous process. At the highest level it will be carried out by a Systems Manager. If your system is large, then it is likely that a team of people will take responsibility for the administration process. At the lowest level the end-users will administer their own accounts and files on the system.

It is becoming popular for the smaller organisation to carry out some of the administrative tasks itself, while leaving the more complicated tasks to an trained engineer. There are numerous facilities available to the administrator of a typical UNIX system including utilities specifically tailored to their needs. If you have purchased a UNIX system recently, you will inevitably have to perform some administrative tasks. This chapter can help you with such tasks.

11.2 The Superuser

The superuser, as the name suggests, is the user who has the ultimate power on the system. Up to now you will have found that some commands and files cannot be accessed by certain users. The superuser can access *every* command or file on the system. Upon logging in with the username **root** (the superuser username), this user is assigned full privileges. Nearly all the examples in this section require root privileges. Every UNIX system must have a superuser, so that the administrative tasks of the system can be carried out.

11.2.1 How do we know who is a superuser?

The file **/etc/passwd** (the UNIX password file) lists all of the users who are registered on the system. When the UNIX system is first installed the username **root** is entered, along with other vital system information. Part of a typical **/etc/passwd** file is shown overleaf (yours will obviously be different):

```
root:IgHdHIL3Zqj0U:0:1:Superuser:/:/bin/csh
admin:gszsEC3cojrS6:0:1:Operator:/:/bin/csh
Paul:G8dfv85YU5ZcM:10:10:Paul:/home/STAFF/Paul:/bin/csh
Val:nHjUrdRkzMnbk:12:10:Val:/home/STAFF/Val:/bin/csh
Bruce:PFUjo6haxGUL2:14:10:Bruce:/home/STAFF/Bruce:/bin/csh
```

The first entries in the passwd file are for the administrative users. User **root** is nearly always listed first (although this is not absolutely necessary), followed by the other users of the system.

The important information of immediate interest in occurs in the third and fourth fields of the **passwd** file. As you can see from the example, the **passwd** file imposes a common structure for every entry held within it, the colons (:) in each line separating each particular field (or area) of data. The fields can be seen in Figure 11.1

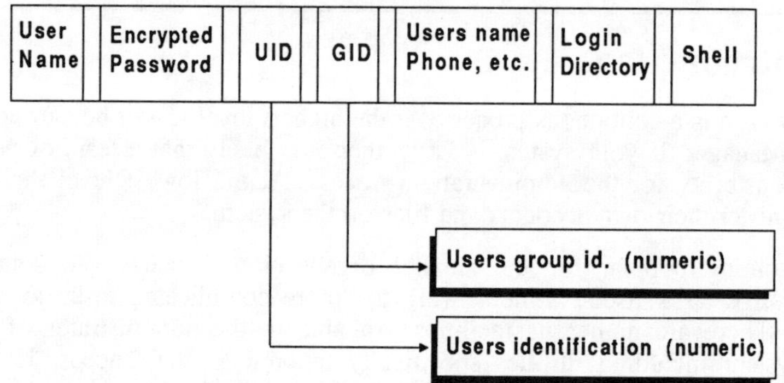

Figure 11.1 /etc/passwd fields

The **UID** (user identification code) is a numeric value representing the identity of the user. It is similar to the username that we have come to know, except that it is numeric. A user with a **UID** of zero is a superuser. This statement implies that more than one person can be superuser, which is correct. The **/etc/passwd** the previous example shows two users with a **UID** of zero, namely user **root** and user **admin**; both have superuser privileges. They can also log in under different names and acquire the same privileges.

The use of multiple superuser names is advantageous in the event of a superuser forgetting his password – another superuser can log in and reset it using the **passwd** command. Since UNIX passwords are encrypted by the system, a password cannot be decoded into its 'plain-text' equivalent, since for security reasons, no 'unencryption' facility exists. For this reason, operating a system with only one superuser is ill-advised because if the password for that superuser's account is lost, the system cannot be administered. If this should ever occur, the whole system will have to be reinstalled; a drastic but necessary solution.

The use of numeric UID values is convenient, since a superuser does not have to be referred to as **root**, but can use any name, such as 'john'. However, some UNIX systems use the **root** login name as the basis of a security check (built into the actual software), so you may find that a user called **john** (with a UID of zero) may not be able to access all the facilities available to user **root**. For example, some terminals may be used only by administrative users (such as console), and at login time the login program may check that the current username is **root**; if a different name is used, the user will not be allowed to log in on the current terminal. Other similar checks may be employed on your system.

11.2.2 Precautions

With superuser status, UNIX will execute any command that you specify, provided that command is valid. This means that performing everyday tasks with superuser privileges is not practical, and therefore not advisable. For this reason it is desirable to log in with normal user status, and then only request superuser privileges when they are needed to perform certain administrative tasks.

11.2.3 Temporary UIDs

UNIX allows users to acquire the identity of another user for a limited time. This is useful for administration purposes, allowing a user to log in as a normal user and only acquire **root** privileges when the need arises to undertake administrative tasks. We have already established that is bad practice to log in as **root** to undertake menial tasks. Once you have acquired the UID of another user, UNIX treats you as the user whose identity you have acquired, so if you choose the identity of the superuser (with a UID of zero) then you could effectively bypass the security of the whole system.

11.2.4 Acquiring a new identity – su

As far as UNIX is concerned you are only a number. The **su** command (substitute user command) is used to acquire the numeric **UID** code of another user temporarily, and then invoke a new shell. The syntax of the **su** command is:

```
su [-] [-f] [user] [-c command]
```

The first option (-) changes the environment to that of the user whose identity is being acquired. The user's environment contains several environmental variables such as **$PATH** , **$HOME** and **$SHELL** etc. so the – option is used in conjunction with the user argument. The Bourne Shell (**/bin/sh**) has two options **-su** which specify that either the user's **.profile** or **.cshrc** file should be executed at login time. They contain particular instructions that UNIX should execute upon logging in. When we temporarily log with a new identity using **su** we can specify for these files to be executed using the – option (which is synonymous with a **sh -su** command).

If either .profile or .cshrc file does not exist in the user's home directory, UNIX passes on the user's previous environment, with the exception of the variable **$PATH** which is set to **/bin:/etc:/usr/bin** if the user's name is **root**. The **-f** option specifies that the **.profile** or **.cshrc** files should *not* be executed upon logging in.

The optional **[user]** argument specifies the name of the user whose identity we want to acquire. If a username is not specified, the username of **root** is assumed. The final option **-c command** allows a shell command to be executed when logging in with the new **UID**.

Examples

A few examples of the **su** command in action are illustrated below:

Example 1

```
$ su
password:<superuser password>
#
```

This example illustrates the **su** command being used without any arguments, so UNIX assumes that we want to log in as **root,** and therefore the root password is required. The **password:** prompt allows us to enter the necessary password, and assume root's **UID**. The password is not echoed for security reasons. The # prompt is commonly used as the superuser's prompt. Our **$PATH** variable will be modified, and the console terminal will be notified of the **su** to user **root**.

Example 2

```
$ su
password:<invalid password>
Sorry
```

This example shows that we have failed to acquire the **UID** of user **root**. The message **Sorry** indicates failure i.e. an invalid **root** password.

Example 3

```
$ su - john
password:<johns password>
```

This example shows **su** being used with the – option. The environment of user whose **UID** we are acquiring will be set up just as if user **john** had logged in normally.

Special notes on using su

When **su** is used without any arguments (or options) the default user is assumed to be **root**, the superuser. UNIX normally only allows privileged users (those with a **GID** (group identification number) of zero) to **su** to **root**. Privileged users are discussed in the next section.

The **su** command is monitored by the UNIX system, using a file called **sulog** which resides in the **/usr/adm** directory. The **adm** (administrative) directory is used as a storage location for some administrative commands, and system audit files. It is discussed in more detail in Chapter 12 on UNIX Security. Some UNIX systems indicate on the system's console when user has successfully changed their identity to user **root**.

11.2.5 Privileged UNIX users

Privileged users are commonly used on some UNIX systems, to avoid the over-reliance on superusers, and they share the same **GID** (group identification number). The **GID** field is the fourth field in the **/etc/passwd** file, found next to the **UID** field. It is commonly expressed that superusers must have a **GID** of zero, but this is not the case for all UNIX systems. As far as UNIX is concerned, any user that has the same **GID** as **root**, is in the same group as the superuser (and is thus considered a privileged user). In the example below the root user has a **UID** of zero, and a **GID** of 1.

Using the value 1 for a **GID** is not always a good choice because some implementations of the **su** command only allow users who have a **GID** of zero to acquire **root**'s characteristics. The **su** command will also deny superuser power even if that user has the **root** password (simply because their **GID** is not zero). If you want to allow privileged users to acquire **root**'s power make sure you set one or more superusers **GID** to zero to match the **GID** of the user who wants to **su** to **root**.

Also remember that a password will always be required when performing an **su** command to acquire superuser privileges. There is only one exception to this rule, and that is when the superuser's password is blank (a potentially dangerous situation). The use of group identification numbers is a very useful concept when creating a privileged user. Users that belong to the same group can access each others files and utilities, depending on the setting of the permissions for the file concerned.

```
root:IgHdHIL3Zqj0U:0:1:Superuser:/:/bin/csh
admin:gszsEC3cojrS6:0:1:Operator:/:/bin/csh
Paul:G8dfv85YU5ZcM:10:10:Paul:/home/STAFF/Paul:/bin/csh
Val:nHjUrdRkzMnbk:12:10:Val:/home/STAFF/Val:/bin/csh
Jim:PFUjo6haxGUL2:14:1:Jim:/home/STAFF/Jim:/bin/csh
```

The portion of the **/etc/passwd** file shown here gives the details of five users. The first two users (**root** and **admin**) can be seen to share the **GID** of **1**. Both users also share the **UID** of zero, a rather rare situation that takes care of the situation where a superuser password has been lost. The last user in the **passwd** file above, user **Jim**, shares the **GID** of **1** with the superusers root and admin. Although not a superuser himself, user **Jim** can undertake administrative tasks that are normally undertaken only by **root** or **admin**.

User groups

Every user on a UNIX system must belong to at least one group. It has been known for a **GID** or **UID** to be left blank when modifying the **/etc/passwd** file, leading to a potential catastrophe in some situations. This is because there are many well-known bugs in the C source-code of certain utilities on the UNIX system (most of which are corrected by the systems programmers who are employed by the organisations who own the UNIX system concerned).

A user group can be defined as a number of UNIX users that share the same privileges, and it allows users with a common interest to share facilities. Take an academic scenario where staff, students and administrative users have access to a UNIX system. Figure 11.2 illustrates this.

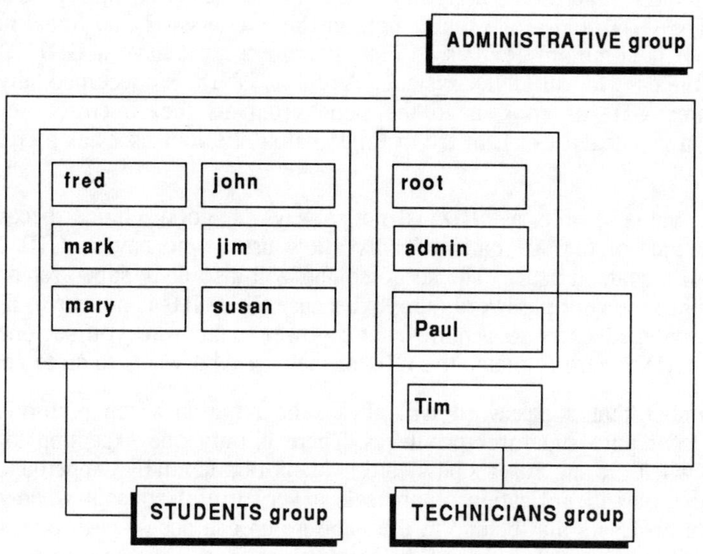

Figure 11.2 Typical group scenario

The organisation shown in Figure 11.2 consists of ten users, split into three distinct groups. However, the technicians group overlaps with the administrative group. In theory this means that user Paul belongs to both groups. Paul's default group will be the one he is assigned to in the **/etc/passwd** file when he first logs on to the system. Apart from the **/etc/passwd** file that stores an individual's default group and user identification numbers, an additional file **/etc/group** defines the members of each particular group on the system. The structure of this file is similar to that of the **/etc/passwd** file.

Some sensitive utilities, such as the **login** program (the program that checks and assigns user privileges at login time), have been known to assign superuser privileges (i.e. a **GID** or **UID** value of zero) to normal users upon finding that the **/etc/passwd** had null (empty) entries for a particular default **UID** or **GID** number (caused by the person who modified the **/etc/passwd** file). You can now understand why the structuring and ordering of the **passwd** file is so important. Returning to the subject of the **/etc/group** file, here is a typical group file for the users shown in Figure 11.2:

```
administrative::1:root,admin,Paul
technicians::10:Paul,Tim
students:3:30:fred,john,mark,mary,susan,jim
```

The first field of the **/etc/group** file is the group name. Their are three groups in this particular file – administrative group; technicians group and students group. The second field of the file (shown as empty in the example above) is normally for an encrypted password but most UNIX systems do not use this field, probably because a utility similar to **passwd** (for changing passwords in the **/etc/passwd** file) does not exist for changing passwords in the **/etc/group** file. The third field is the **GID** value. This corresponds to a user entry in the **/etc/passwd** file. The fourth and final field contains the usernames of members of this particular group, separated by commas.

Multiple group users

As shown in Figure 11.2, it is possible for users to belong to more than one group on a system. This is simply accomplished by placing a user in more than one group in the **/etc/group** file. Remember that the **/etc/passwd** file contains the default group and user-identification numbers for a user upon logging in. Figure 11.3 below illustrates the **/etc/group** and **/etc/passwd** file entries for the users in Figure 11.2.

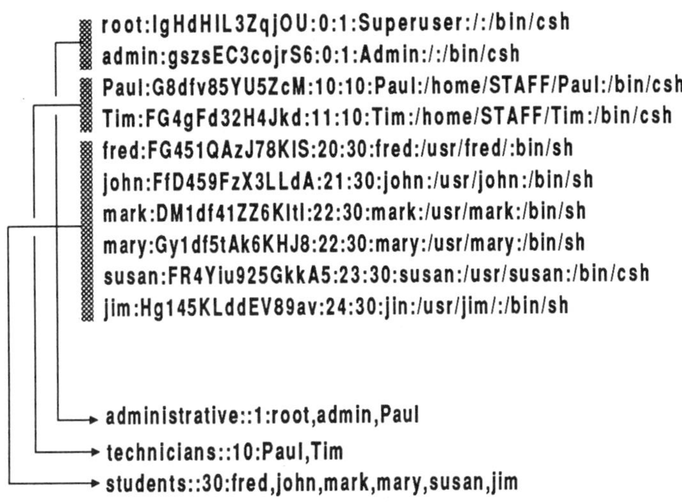

Figure 11.3 /etc/passwd (top) and /etc/group (bottom) files

The **/etc/group** file shown in Figure 11.3 illustrates how a user can belong to more than one group. This figure also shows that user **Paul** belongs to two user groups, the technicians group and the administrative group.

We have also established that the default group to which a user is assigned is stored in the **GID** field of the **/etc/passwd** file. We mentioned earlier that users who are members of the same group can share the same facilities, i.e. access each others' files. However, one member of the group can only access files owned by another member if the appropriate permissions have been set (i.e. so that permission is not denied). Being a member of a group does not mean that you will always want the other group members to access your files.

In Chapter 7, section 7.5.3, we examined the **ls** (list files) command. Used without any options or arguments this command simply lists the visible files in the current directory. When the **-l** option (long listing) is included, the **ls** command lists all the files, with the permission settings that are active on the files in the current working directory. It can also be used with a filename argument, for example:

```
$ ls -l Mail
-rwxrwx--- 1 jim 205457 Jun 18 09:48 Mail
```

This example uses the **ls -l** command to list only the file named **Mail**. This file exists and is listed with its information, which, in the first column, represents the protection settings for the user (the owner of this file), the group users, and lastly all the other users of the system. These protection settings are shown in Figure 11.4

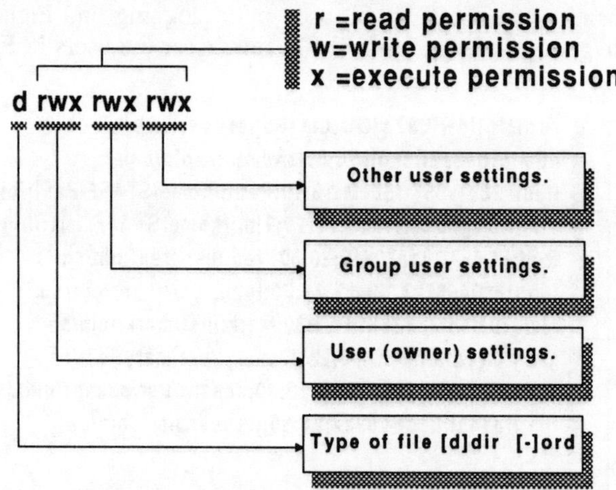

*Figure 11.4 **ls -l** file permissions (column 1)*

The group permissions (the fifth, sixth and seventh characters in the **ls -l** listing shown in Figure 11.4) directly relate to the other users in the group to which you belong to in the **/etc/group** file. It is also worth mentioning at this point the options **-lg** of the **ls** command will list the *group* permissions for files in the current directory.

In our example, user **jim** owns the file named **Mail**. The permission setting on this file is currently **-rwxrwx---**, which indicates that the owner (user **jim**) can read, write and execute the file (the normal settings for the owner). The group permission settings are also **rwx**, which means that the other members of **jim**'s group can also read, write and execute the file. The final three permissions are set to **---** which indicate that the read, write and execute permissions are denied any other users i.e. users who are not in the same group as the owner.

We could alternatively use **grep** to match the current users who are in the same group as **jim** (as opposed to **ls -lg**), and thus we can establish which users have been given read, write and execute permission on the file named **Mail**, or for that matter on any other file. The name **jim** (our current username) is used as a search pattern, as follows:

```
$ grep jim /etc/group
students:3:30:fred,john,mark,mary,susan,jim
```

Here, **grep** returns one match from the **/etc/group** file. We can establish that we (**jim**) are a member of the students group, and users fred, john, mark, mary and susan are also members of the same group. Our username can be seen at the end of the list. This effectively means that all these users can read, write and execute the file named **Mail** which we examined earlier.

Changing groups

A user who belongs to more than one group (such as user **Paul** illustrated in Figure 11.3) can change to another group using a command called **newgrp** (new group). The **newgrp** command is invoked with a single argument, namely a user-group name specified in the **/etc/group** file. An example would be for user **Paul** to type:

```
$ newgrp administrative
```

Once this command was entered, **newgrp** would check the **/etc/group** file to see if user **Paul** is listed under the group name 'administrative'. In our example as **Paul** is a member of the administrative users' group, he will be allowed to proceed, and thus will thus be given the extra privileges that are associated with that group. Recall that the **/etc/group** file in our example is:

```
administrative::1:root,admin,Paul
technicians::10:Paul,Tim
students:3:30:fred,john,mark,mary,susan,jim
```

User **Paul** is listed as being a member of the technicians group (his default group – as assigned to him at login time by the **/etc/passwd** file) and as a member of the administrative group. The administrative users' group has a **GID** field value of zero associated with it, the **GID** value of the superuser. User **Paul** is thus placed in the same class as **root** and **admin** (the superusers of this hypothetical system) and has file access that is associated with the administrative group.

Once **Paul** has changed to the administrative user group, his **GID** value becomes 1 (the **GID** value of the administrative users' group). However, the **UID** value associated with user **Paul** remains unchanged. The **su** command is used to change the **UID** of a user, and thus the user's identity (remembering that the numerical **UID** is how UNIX recognises each user).

11.2.6 Setting up a new user

If you are engaged in the creation of a new user account, the instructions below should help you in the process. Some UNIX systems such as Xenix, have special utilities that aid in the setting up of the new users (and the associated **/etc/passwd** and **/etc/group** entries). The following steps show you how to set up a new user account using the standard UNIX utilities.

Step 1. Log in as the super user (root) and supply the superuser password. You will need superuser privileges to create a new user account since write permission on some system files such as **/etc/passwd** and **/etc/group** is available only to the superuser.

Step 2. Choose a username for the new user. A username must be unique, and is commonly a christian name or surname (or a mixture of both). For example john, jsmith etc. Now check that the chosen username is unique by using **grep** to check the **/etc/passwd** file to make sure the name does not already exist. For example, if the chosen username is **simon**, use **grep simon /etc/passwd**. If **grep** returns a line with this username you will have to choose a different name and check again.

Step 3. The user must have a home directory area, a part of the file-system where user Simon can store his files etc. It is a convention on nearly all UNIX systems to have a directory called **/usr** (user directory) in which individual user directories are stored.

Examining **/usr** directory on your system may reveal a few existing files, which should all be directories (home directory areas for the users of the present system), for example:

```
$ ls -l /usr
total 1045
drwx------   1 fred     72568 May 15  22:05    fred
drwx------   1 jim     204911 Apr 10  11:48    jim
drwx------   1 john     62761 Apr 10  09:24    john
drwx------   1 mark     45136 Apr 10  09:58    mark
drwxrw----   1 mary     11346 Apr 11  10:21    mary
drwxrw----   1 Paul     22316 Apr 11  10:41    Paul
drwx------   1 susan   982313 May 15  22:17    susan
drwx------   1 Tim       3233 May 15  22:58    Tim
drwx------   1 fred     72568 May 15  23:05    fred
```

This directory listing shows that there are eight user directories, each of which corresponds to a user entry in the **/etc/passwd** (and **/etc/group**) file. Upon examination of the **/etc/passwd** file in our example (see Figure 11.3), we can see that all users have a corresponding entry in the **/usr** directory.

Step 4. The next step is to create a home directory area for the new user; assume you are creating a new account for a student user called **simon**. Since you have logged in as **root**, UNIX will allow you to create a directory anywhere that you specify, so it is important that you create simon's home directory in the correct place in the file system. If you wish to add this new home directory to those already existing, type **cd /usr** to make sure that you are in the correct directory. If you wish to put **simon**'s directory in a different directory, (which is perfectly valid), make sure the current working directory is the correct one. If necessary use **pwd** (print working directory) to verify your whereabouts. The **mkdir** command is used to make a directory *subordinate* to the current working directory.

Once you are inside the correct directory, type:

```
$ mkdir simon
```

This will make a new directory for user **simon** – it is not obligatory to employ the username for the home directory but it is a common convention, and one that we advise you to adopt. This will be **simon**'s home directory, the directory where **simon** initially will be placed when he logs into the system. You can list the files in the current directory to verify the existence of the new directory (we assume that the **/usr** directory has been used throughout this example):

```
$ ls -l
total 1045
drwx------   1 fred     72568  May 15  22:05   fred
drwx------   1 jim     204911  Apr 10  11:48   jim
drwx------   1 john     62761  Apr 10  09:24   john
drwx------   1 mark     45136  Apr 10 09:58    mark
drwxrw----   1 mary     11346  Apr 11  10:21   mary
drwxrw----   1 Paul     22316  Apr 11  10:41   Paul
drwxr-xr-x   1 root         0  Jun 28  13:01   simon
drwx------   1 susan   982313  May 15  22:17   susan
drwx------   1 Tim       3233  May 15  22:58   Tim
drwx------   1 fred     72568  May 15  23:05   fred
```

The directory listing reveals that the new directory was indeed created. However, there is a problem: a new directory is created, it is owned by user who created it. Since you logged in as root in order to create a home directory for **simon** in the **/usr** directory, UNIX makes **root** the *owner* of the directory. This is no use to **simon** since he will not be able to store any files in this directory. The current permissions have been set to be **drwxr-xr-x** and the owner is **root**. This means that only user root has read, write and execute permission on the directory; group users and other users (which currently include **simon**) have read and execute permission only, but not write-permission. Glancing at the earlier listing of the **/usr** directory you will see that each user owns their own directory, so that they can manipulate their own files, a logical set-up. The next step that we must perform is to change the ownership of this directory to **simon**.

Step 5. You have now created **simon**'s home directory area, and now you need to make sure that the file ownership permissions for **simon**'s home directory are all in order. Recall that you are logged in as **root** and that UNIX makes **root** the owner of all the files created by a superuser.

At this point we must introduce a new command called **chown** (change ownership) which is used to change the ownership of a file. Only the superuser can change the ownership of any file, which why you needed to log in as **root** to complete the whole task. When **chown** is used, we specify the user who is to own the new file first, followed by the name of the file itself. Normal users cannot change the ownership of any file which they do not own. The syntax of the chown command is:

chown <owner> <file>

The command you need to enter is therefore:

```
$ chown simon simon
```

This makes user **simon** the owner of his own directory (which is also called **simon**). As previously mentioned, it is imperative that a user owns their own home directory, otherwise they will not be able to access their own files. Remember that **simon** will probably want to create new directories within his home directory area (to structure the storage of his files).

This in turn means that he must have write-permission on his home directory (in which any new directories will have to be created in), otherwise access will be denied. Once the **chown** command has been issued, the **ls -l** command can be used to view the current directories to verify the new ownership:

```
$ ls -l
total 1045
drwx------   1 jim     204911  Apr 10  11:48   jim
drwx------   1 john     62761  Apr 10  09:24   john
drwx------   1 mark     45136  Apr 10  09:58   mark
drwxrw----   1 mary     11346  Apr 11  10:21   mary
drwxrw----   1 Paul     22316  Apr 11  10:41   Paul
drwx------   1 susan   982313  May 15  22:17   susan
drwxr-xr-x   1 simon        0  Jun 28  13:01   simon
drwx------   1 Tim       3233  May 15  22:58   Tim
drwx------   1 fred     72568  May 15  23:05   fred
```

This listing verifies that **simon** now owns his home directory area. Our next task is to update the group information for user **simon**.

Step 6. We are now at a suitable stage to amend the **/etc/group** file to include user **simon** in the students' user group (remembering our assumption that simon is a student in our example). There are two ways in which this can be achieved – either by using the **chgrp** command described in section 11.2.10, or by editing the **/etc/group** file directly using one of the standard UNIX editors, (such as the line-editors **ex**,or **ed**; or a visual editor such as **vi**. The **vi** editor is used for this example).

To edit the **/etc/group** file with the **vi** editor, you can simply invoke **vi** with the filename, by entering the following command:

```
$ vi /etc/group
```

Note that you must give the full pathname of the file you wish to edit because you have not yet moved into the **/etc** directory. If you prefer to use a line editor to edit the **/etc/group** (and who can blame you?), you are referred to Chapter 9, where the **ex** editor is explained in some detail. If you are using **vi** to edit the file, the top half of your screen should be similar to that displayed in Figure 11.5.

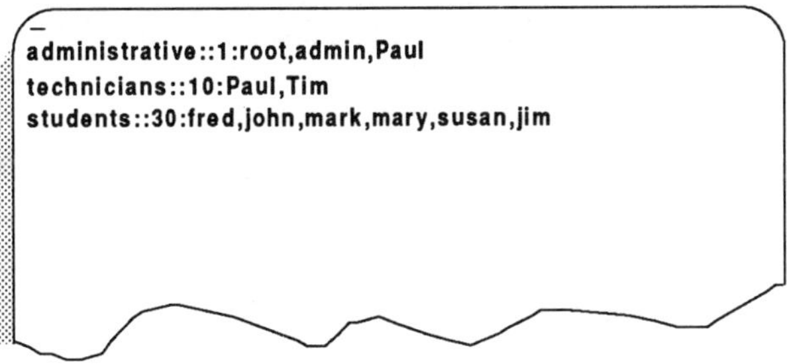
```
administrative::1:root,admin,Paul
technicians::10:Paul,Tim
students::30:fred,john,mark,mary,susan,jim
```

Figure 11.5 ***vi*** *part-screen when editing the* ***/etc/group*** *file*

The file you can see now is the **/etc/group** file as it currently stands. The user-group that we are interested in is the students' group and we must incorporate user **simon**, into this group by adding his username to the list of existing users. The position of his name in the list is unimportant, just as long as it is placed after last colon, so it is simplest to add the username **simon** to end of the list of usernames.

When **vi** is initially invoked from the shell level (as in our earlier example) the cursor is positioned in the top left-hand corner of the screen. You should now move the cursor to the end of the last line, directly after the username **jim**, and type a comma (,) followed by the name **simon** (remembering that the individual users in a particular user-group are separated by a single comma). If **vi** has been set up correctly to work with your terminal, you may be able to use the cursor keys (as are found on the numeric key-pad on all IBM or IBM-compatible personal computer smart-terminals) to move to the necessary position on the current screen. However, in case these keys are not available we will give full details of the **vi**-specific cursor-movement commands required to arrive at the correct position, as follows:

When **vi** is first invoked, it is in the basic command mode (see Chapter 9, section 9.4.2). This mode allows us to specify various cursor movement commands that act on the current text. So press the letter **j** (lower case) to move the cursor down one line; press it a second time to bring it to the third (last) line in the file. However, if you are editing your own **/etc/group** file, you may need to move the cursor further to the relevant line, so use as many **j** commands as are needed.

Now you need to move the cursor to the right to the end of this line, so that it is following the name **jim**. The **l** command (lower case 'L') moves the cursor one place to the right. You need to move 42 spaces to the right in the example. Rather than pressing 'l' 42 times, you can enter the **$** command to move the cursor to the end of the current line.

Once the cursor is in the correct position , press the letter **i** (lower case) to invoke **vi**'s insert mode, so that you can enter text at the current cursor position. Then you can type in a comma (,) followed by the name **simon**. Figure 11.6 illustrates the screen display after **simon** has been added to the students user group.

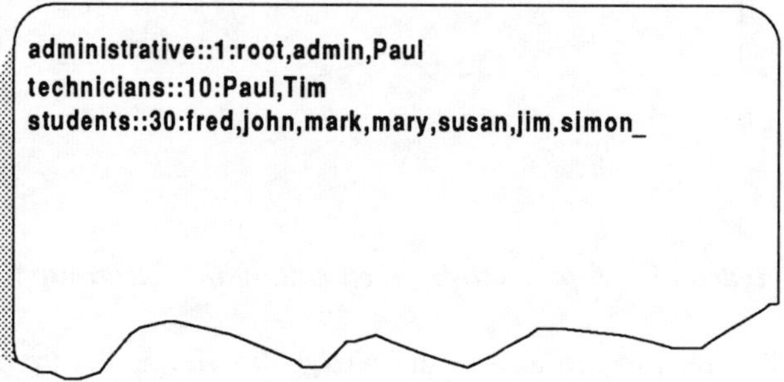
administrative::1:root,admin,Paul
technicians::10:Paul,Tim
students::30:fred,john,mark,mary,susan,jim,simon_

Figure 11.6 Entry of user simon into the students user-group

If you make a mistake typing the name, pressing the upper-case letter **X** deletes one character to the left of the current cursor position. Correcting mistakes is made easier if the **[DEL]** (delete) key is functional on your terminal (this can be used in place of the **X** command). If you press **[DEL]**, and **vi** cannot interpret the key, a nasty escape-sequence will be generated, which you will have to delete using **X**. (The generation of an escape-sequence in these circumstances indicates that your terminal is not properly configured for use with **vi**, the **/etc/termcap** file probably being the cause of the problem. Configuring your terminal is discussed in section 11.2.7 on user profiles).

One you have entered the necessary text, you can save the file and exit **vi**. The quickest way to do this is by employing the command **ZZ** (see Chapter 9 for more details). Because you are still in insert mode, you need to press the **[ESC]** (escape key) to return to **vi**'s command mode, before you can enter the **ZZ** command (note the Z's must be upper case). **Vi** will then save the file, informing you of its progress on the status line at the bottom of the current screen, and return you to the shell prompt (**$** in our examples).

Step 7. Now you need to put the new user in the **/etc/passwd** file. You may recall that this file holds the user's default group (**GID**) and user-identification code (**UID**) values. It also holds the pathname of the user's home directory, along with the pathname of the user's shell. The **passwd** file resides in the **/etc** directory. Change to this directory now using the command:

```
$ cd /etc
```

The next task is to edit the **/etc/passwd** file to include an entry for our new user. The **/etc/passwd** file was shown earlier in Figure 11.3. Every record in the file consists of seven fields, each of which is delimited with a colon (:). When creating a new user account we must allocate each of the following:

- Username
- Blank-password
- User-identification number (**UID**)
- Group-identification number (**GID**)
- Personal information e.g. phone number etc.
- Full pathname of this user's home directory
- Full pathname of this user's login shell.

We have already established a username in our example, although it is possible to create a new user account by adding an entry to the **/etc/passwd** file. This is not recommended, however, since the user may try to log in, only to find that either the home directory or login shell do not yet exist.

Some UNIX systems, upon finding that the user's home directory location is missing, place that user into the root directory (/) of the file-system. If a user does not have a login shell the system may assign a default shell (normally **/bin/sh**, the Bourne Shell). In some cases the system may immediately log the user out upon finding that the information in the **/etc/passwd** file is not complete, for example, the absence of a piece of information from one of the seven **passwd** fields.

Adding an entry to the **/etc/passwd** file is done in much the same way as with the **/etc/group** file, described in Step 6. The main difference here is that the entry for a new user must occupy a new line. Before we start editing the **/etc/passwd** file, we must firstly examine the existing file to ascertain a valid **UID** value for this new user.

UID values should always be unique (except in the case for users such as **root**, the superuser). Two users who sharing the same **UID** both have total control over the same files. While appropriate in the case of an administrative user such as **root**, it is not desirable for the other users of the system, since file security and integrity cannot be guaranteed. It is therefore necessary to control the structure of the **/etc/passwd** file so that such inadvertent duplications do not occur. Earlier, when we created the group details for our new user, it was mentioned that a username must be unique. This should also be the case for the **UID** values that are allocated to the ordinary users of the system. We cannot easily check for a unique **UID** value in the **/etc/passwd** file, so it probably best to take a look at the file ourselves (see next page).

```
$ cat /etc/passwd
root:IgHdHIL3Zqj0U:0:1:Superuser:/:/bin/csh
admin:gszsEC3cojrS6:0:1:Operator:/:/bin/csh
Paul:G8dfv85YU5ZcM:0:1:Paul:/home/STAFF/Paul:/bin/csh
fred:FG451QAzJ78k7S:1:30:fred:/usr/fred:/bin/sh
john:FfD459FzX3LLdA:2:30:john:/usr/john:/bin/sh
mark:DM1df41ZZ6kltl:3:30:mark:/usr/mark:/bin/csh
mary:GY1dfStaK6kHJ8:4:30:mary:/usr/mary:/bin/csh
susan:FR4Yiu925GkkAS:5:30:susan:/usr/susan:/bin/sh
jim:Hg145KLddEY89aw:6:30:jim:/usr/jim:/bin/sh
```

This hypothetical **/etc/passwd** file contains nine users and the **UID** values can be seen as the third field of each record. The ordering imposed in this particular file has adopted a simple numbering scheme whereby each **UID** is incremented for each new user. This is by far the simplest approach.

The last user in this file is **jim**. He has a **UID** value of 6. Keeping to the numbering scheme already implemented, the new unique **UID** value for our new user (**simon**) should be 7. We already know the **GID** value for our new user, the value 30 which corresponds to the students user-group. The following instructions use the **ex** line-editor to add an entry to the **/etc/passwd** file for the new user **simon**:

```
$ ex passwd
"/etc/passwd" 10 lines 878 characters
:a
simon::7:30:
```

This enters the username, a blank password, the **UID** and the **GID**. The password field must be left blank now as this entry will be generated later, either by the systems administrator or by the user who owns the account, using the **passwd** program. Passwords are encrypted by the system, and must *never* be edited manually.

It is not wise to leave an account unprotected by password since someone else could log in as this user. One possible solution to this problem is to allocate a password for this particular account, and operate a policy where new users must contact the systems administrator to obtain their initial password which allows them access to their account. This password can then be changed by the user upon logging in. This approach should ensure that misuse of the account does not take place.

The fifth field in the **/etc/passwd** file is used for personal details, such as the user's telephone number etc. Some administrators leave this field blank, but its use can have some advantages. In the current context for the purposes of the example, enter just the user's christian name (tools which can specifically manipulate this field are discussed below). The entry should now be:

```
$ ex passwd
"passwd" 10 lines 878 characters
:a
simon::7:30:simon:
```

This leaves the last two fields to fill, which are crucially important. They represent the user's login directory pathname, and the full pathname of the user's shell which will be executed when the user logs in. The user's home directory area, is the directory in which that user is placed once logged in. We can choose to place the user anywhere in the file-system, although it is a common practice to place them in their home, or login, directory (the root directory of their particular part of the file-system) in which their files are stored.

You have already created the new user's home directory using **mkdir** (make directory) and named it **simon** (after the user's christian name). Remember that the fully-qualified pathname of the user's home directory must be entered into this field, therefore you must plot a route from the root directory (/) down to user **simon**'s home directory area.

When creating **simon**'s home directory, you issued the command **mkdir simon** from within the **/usr** directory; this defines the fully-qualified pathname of **simon**'s home directory as **/usr/simon**. This can now be entered into the field, along with a delimiting colon (:) to give:

```
simon::7:30:simon:/usr/simon:
```

The last field which represents the user's login shell, can now be created for this entry. The superuser can assign any shell to the user by directly editing the appropriate part of the **/etc/passwd** file, however normal users are restricted in which shells they can choose. The user can normally choose **/bin/sh** (the Bourne Shell), or **/bin/csh** the C-Shell. Some UNIX systems may allow the user to choose the visual shell **/bin/vsh**.

The **/bin** directory is a common location for most system shells, since they are all executable (binary) files. In our example, we shall assign user **simon** the Bourne Shell (**/bin/sh**). This again, is a fully-qualified pathname. Note the absence of a final colon, which is not required. The final entry is thus:

```
simon::7:30:simon:/usr/simon:/bin/sh
```

The file can now be saved to disk. You need to return to command mode by typing a period in the first column (press the **[RETURN]** key to move to the first column after the user's login shell has been typed). The : prompt should then appear allowing you to use the x command to write the file to disk and then exit. The shell prompt will then appear.

```
$ ex passwd
passwd 10 lines 878 characters
:a
simon::7:30:simon:/usr/simon:/bin/sh<CR>
.
:x
$
```

The account can now be accessed by the owner (user **simon** can log in to his account). If you were to display the file (using **cat**) you should see:

```
$ cat /etc/passwd
root:IgHdHIL3Zqj0U:0:1:Superuser:/:/bin/csh
admin:gszsEC3cojrS6:0:1:Operator:/:/bin/csh
Paul:G8dfv85YU5ZcM:0:1:Paul:/home/STAFF/Paul:/bin/csh
fred:FG451QAzJ78k7S:1:30:fred:/usr/fred:/bin/sh
john:FfD459FzX3LLdA:2:30:john:/usr/john:/bin/sh
mark:DM1df41ZZ6kltl:3:30:mark:/usr/mark:/bin/csh
mary:GY1dfStaK6kHJ8:4:30:mary:/usr/mary:/bin/csh
susan:FR4Yiu925GkkAS:5:30:susan:/usr/susan:/bin/sh
jim:Hg145KLddEY89aw:6:30:jim:/usr/jim:/bin/sh
simon::7:30:simon:/usr/simon:/bin/sh
```

If you wish to insert an entry between two existing users, you will have to use a line address and the insert (**i**) command of the **ex** editor (see Chapter 9).

Remember that this account still has no password, so anybody can log in with the username **simon**. This can be rectified by using the command:

```
$ passwd simon
```

UNIX will then invoke the **passwd** program, allowing you to set a password for this user. This will stop unauthorised logins to the account from taking place but will also prevent the owner accessing his account. You must make sure the user contacts you so that you can pass on the necessary password.

Problems when editing the /etc/passwd file

The **/etc/passwd** file is one of the most important on the system, and it will be constantly updated as new users are added and old users are deleted. Some contents will have to be amended during the lifetime of the **passwd** file e.g. you may assign a different login shell to a user, or change a user's home directory location etc.

Backing-up this file (the process of making an exact copy of this file) is therefore very important. The process of backing up such files is discussed later in this chapter in section 11.12. Copying files to different media (commonly tape) allows files like the **/etc/passwd** file to be restored to their previous state in the event of corruption or destruction of the disk files. Tape files can also be stored in off-site locations, safe from risk of fire at the main computer site etc.

Data corruption is another problem. It has been mentioned already that multiple access to a file can corrupt it. If two superusers were to write different information to the **/etc/passwd** file simultaneously (a somewhat rare, but possible situation), the file could be badly damaged. Corrupting the **/etc/passwd** file would mean that access may be denied to some, if not all users, including the superusers of the present system.

Fortunately there is a tool that allows the **/etc/passwd** file to edited and locked. File locking ensures that only one user is allowed to modify a file at a time. Any other user that tries to modify the same file will be denied access. The **vipw** command, which is part of Berkeley UNIX, can be used by an administrative user (such as the superuser) to update the **/etc/passwd** file using the **vi** screen-editor (as implied by the name).

The appropriate locks are also set ensuring that corruption via simultaneous access to the **/etc/passwd** file cannot occur. The **vipw** command is entered on its own to invoke the facility, as follows:

```
$ vipw
```

If you are unfamiliar with **vi**, Chapter 9 explains all the relevant commands to enable you to edit the file. Note that **vipw can** only be run by user **root**, the superuser.

11.2.7 User profiles

Once a new account has been set up, it is common practice to create or copy the necessary skeletal profile files, that will be executed automatically when upon the user logs in, into the user's directory. The two most common profile files are **.profile** (executed by the Bourne Shell – /bin/sh) and **.cshrc** (executed by the C-Shell). They are both *local* profile files, that is to say that they are executed for each user of the system individually. Both files, which are hidden (note the period (.) at the start of each name) must exist in a user's login (or home) directory, for example **/usr/simon**, for them to be executed.

A system-wide profile file also exists on most systems, the **/etc/profile** file, which is executed for all users as they log into the system. This is useful to force the processing of vital instructions which apply to all users.

Personal profile files

When a user logs in, the system may assign default values to certain environmental variables such as **$HOME**, **$TERM**, **$USER** and **$PATH** etc. Some of these values will be correct for most users, however some may require changing, or 'personalising' at login time. Since the **.profile** file is automatically executed, it is an ideal location for all the necessary shell commands that need to be executed before starting a UNIX session. A **.profile** file taken from an administrator's home directory is listed below; it basically consists of a series of UNIX shell commands grouped together to form a shell-script.

```
echo 'who am i' >> /usr/admin/login_history
PATH=$PATH:/usr/admin/files
TERM=ibmpc
export TERM PATH
echo "Most recent users on system:"
tail -5 /etc/login_history
echo "  "
echo "There are ['who | wc -l'] users logged in."
```

The first command uses **echo** to redirect a substituted command into the file **/usr/admin/login_history**. The argument passed to **echo** has a shell command (**who**) with the argument **am i** (which makes UNIX echo the current username back on the standard output). The shell command argument is encapsulated in grave-accents ('), which means that the command substitution is taking place.

The first command will thus echo the current user's login name, and then redirect it to the file **/usr/admin/login_history**. The >> operator is being used, which means that the information being written to the file will be appended. If **>** was used the information would overwrite the existing file, a pointless exercise since we are interested in history of previous logins. The administrator of this system was making extra work for himself, since UNIX already maintains a login history of all users (in the **wtmp** file).

The second command sets up a value for the **$PATH** variable. This variable is set up by the login program on some UNIX systems, while on others it is left to the system-wide profile file to assign values for **$PATH** . In the example above, the command has extended the current pathname by resetting the value of **$PATH** to include itself plus an additional directory pathname. The single colon separates the new pathname from the existing definition. For example, if the initial default pathname for all users was set to **/usr/ucb:/bin:/usr/bin** the new definition for this particular user, as set by his local **.profile** file, would be **/usr/ucb:/bin:/usr/bin:/usr/admin/files**.

In the third command, the user has specified that the current terminal name be set to **ibmpc**. This definition should match an entry in the **/etc/termcap** file. Some UNIX systems set the terminal name automatically using a non-standard terminal enquiry program (such as **qterm** – the quiz terminal utility). This non-standard utility works out the emulation characteristics of the current terminal, and then alters the **$TERM** variable accordingly. This could be put into a **.profile** file using the command **TERM='qterm'**, for example. This would substitute the terminal name into the environmental variable **$TERM**. If **qterm** was unable to establish the emulation details for the current terminal, it may return a value such as **dumb**, a generic term that is used to define terminals with no special characteristics. This will also have to be defined in **/etc/termcap**. **Qterm** is used commonly on the larger UNIX systems where a wide range of terminals are in use.

The fourth command in the example **.profile** uses the **export** command, which is used to make a list of environmental variables available to any other shell environment that may be created. For example, a user may want to change the current shell to **/bin/csh** from **/bin/sh**. In such a case the old environmental variables would be lost, and new ones assigned. This may not be practical, especially where many variables have been changed in a previous shell. Exporting values such as **$PATH** and **$TERM** is advantageous since they are used so frequently by the user.

The fifth command uses **echo** to display a simple message telling the user that a list of the most recent users are to be displayed. It is used in conjunction with the next command, **tail** which prints the last five lines of the **login_history** file that was created at login time. Remember that **tail**, by default, prints the end of a file. In our context this is required, since the most recent logins are stored towards the bottom of the file (because they are appended to it).

The seventh command simply echoes a blank line, while the eighth uses **echo** in conjunction with a substituted command. This is **who** (the 'show current user's' command) and it is piped into the **wc** (word count) utility. The **-l** option that has been used with **wc** ensures that only the number of lines in the **who** listing are displayed. This value is echoed within the rest of the message on the same line. If we were to log in using this **.profile** in our home directory, the following would appear:

```
Most recent users on system:
john  tty14   Jun 8   16:01
root  tty13   Jun 8   13:03
mary  tty12   Jun 8   14:16
jason tty08   Jun 8   12:08
mark  tty04   Jun 8   11:51

There are [ 7] users logged in.
$
```

In summary then, we can say that the **.profile** file is used to execute commands that personalise the user's environment. Practically any UNIX command can be included within a **.profile** file, although keeping the number of shell commands to a minimum is beneficial because otherwise you may have to wait rather a long time before you can reach the interactive level.

System-wide profile files

System-wide profile files are used to perform commands for all the users logging into a system. The file **/etc/profile** is commonly used, although some systems have broken with tradition and opted for the creation of their own system-wide profile files. The commands that are included in the **/etc/profile** file are very similar to those found in a typical user's local **.profile** file. A typical **/etc/profile** file is shown below:

```
# System-wide profile file for all users.
stty erase "^h"
TERM='qterm'
PATH=:/usr/bin:/bin:/usr/etc
export TERM PATH
umask 022
```

This file contains six lines, five of which are commands. Two commands here have yet to be explained. These are **stty** and **umask.**

The first is a comment line. This particular comment declares the purpose of the file, the date it was last changed, and the user who changed it.

The second line uses the **stty** (set terminal modes and options) command to set up definitions for particular modes which have not been defined in the **/etc/termcap** file. **Stty** therefore allows the user to change the behaviour of the current terminal. The **/etc/termcap** file is used to describe the capabilities of various VDU devices. Individual control-character definitions can also be defined. However, **/etc/termcap** cannot physically alter a terminal's mode of operation, it can only alter the way in which it interprets this information. **Stty** is useful, since it can be used to override such modes and definitions and even to create new ones. The definition in the system-wide profile file in our example is:

```
stty erase "^h"
```

The keyword **erase** is used to define a key which is to be used to delete the previously typed character. The control-character in this context is <ctrl-h>, which can frequently be found defined within the **/etc/termcap** file for each terminal type.

Essential keys, such as the **[DEL]** key, may be interpreted differently by various machines. **Stty** can thus be used to redefine the necessary control-code sequences that a terminal recognises for a particular key-press. There are many other such keywords, most of which are binary. They are turned on by specifying them literally, and turned off by preceding the keyword with the "–" sign. For example we can turn off the process initiated with the keyword **echo**, which echoes characters on the screen, by using the command **stty -echo**. Similarly, to turn on the echoing back on again we would use the command **stty echo**.

The third line in this profile file uses the **qterm** facility discussed earlier. The values returned by **qterm** is a terminal name that exists in the **/etc/termcap** file. If your system cannot employ this facility, then you will need to set a default terminal name in this file for all users, and change each individual user's **.profile** accordingly. If your system uses a variety of terminals, you may have problems, since different emulations may be required for diverse screen-based applications. However, if only one type of terminal is used at your site, then there is no difficulty, since a single terminal name can be defined for all the users of the system using one command in the **/etc/profile** file. You should specify the terminal name literally in this case e.g. **TERM=vt200.**

The fourth line sets up a pathname definition which will be used whenever a user executes a command. The value for **$PATH** can be redefined locally in the users individual **.profile** file (as can all of these definitions).

This system-wide profile file (**/etc/profile**) should be owned by an administrative user such as **root** and the write-permission should be turned off for all users apart from the owner (and possibly the users in the same group as **root**, who may be privileged administrative users). This precaution will stop other users altering the default instructions held in this particular file. Every user's should own their individual **.profile** file, enabling them to alter their local instructions and definitions. The definitions for **$PATH** and **$TERM** are exported in line five of this profile file.

The final command is **umask** (user mask utility). This is used to assign as a set of access permissions to a file when it is initially created. The default value that umask is commonly assigned is 022. This is an octal value that corresponds to the permission settings for the owner, group and other users of a particular file.

Figure 11.4 depicted the file permissions that can be accessed using the **ls -l** commands. These permissions consist of three letters, namely r (read), w (write), and x (execute). They represent the type of permission that is currently set for a particular file.

Working out the correct **umask** code can be time consuming, and a knowledge of the octal numbering system is needed. A table of umask settings is by far a better approach for the calculation of such codes.

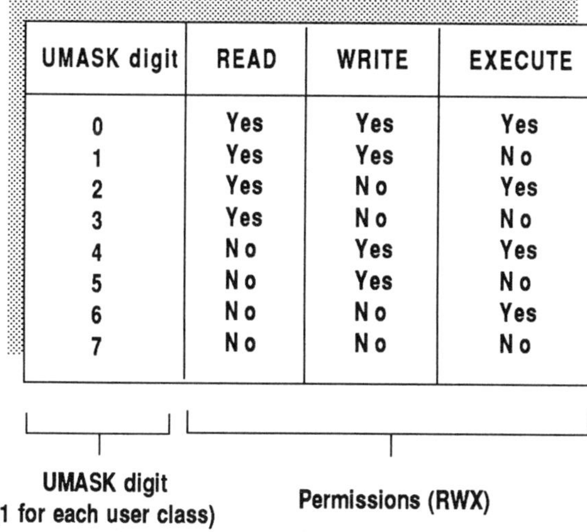

UMASK digit	READ	WRITE	EXECUTE
0	Yes	Yes	Yes
1	Yes	Yes	No
2	Yes	No	Yes
3	Yes	No	No
4	No	Yes	Yes
5	No	Yes	No
6	No	No	Yes
7	No	No	No

Figure 11.7 Umask settings table

Three **umask** digits need to be chosen, to represent the owner, group and other user permissions on a file. The code 022 thus translates to allowing read, write and execute permission for the owner, and read and execute (but not write) permission for the group and other users of the system. Remember that the value allocated to **umask** only effects new files, but not those already in existence. The protection modes for any existing file can be changed using the command called **chmod** (discussed in Chapter 12 on UNIX Security.

A **umask** code of 000 would therefore allow any new files to be read, executed or written to by any user of the system (not a recommended setting). The mode that gives sole access to the owner, and no access whatsoever to any other users of the system is setting 077. The common convention for most UNIX systems is to assign a **umask** setting of 022 (as a default) in the **/etc/profile** file, and then to allow each user to change their value of **umask** to suit their personal needs.

Creating a profile file for a user

It is not practical to type in a new personal **.profile** file for every a new account, once it has been created. A better approach is to copy a suitable **.profile** file across into the user's home directory area. You will have to be logged in as the superuser (**root**) in order to this, since write permission on the necessary directory will be needed. It is prudent for the administrative user to keep a 'miscellaneous' directory that contains standard files such as **.profile**, so that a new user's profile file can copied across quickly. Assume, for purposes of this example, that this directory exists in the superuser's directory (/), called **misc** that holds the necessary **.profile** and **.cshrc** files. Firstly you would need to make the new user's directory, the current working directory. In this example you would therefore type:

```
$ cd /usr/simon
```

Once inside the user's directory you should type:

```
$ cp /misc/.profile .
```

This copies the file from the **/misc** directory into the current directory (**/usr/simon**). You may remember that the **.** is a synonym for the current directory. It saves having to type **/usr/simon** as the destination directory. You can now verify that the file was copied by using the **ls** command, as below:

```
$ ls .profile
.profile
```

Other profile files – .login and .logout

The UNIX system recognises many other profile files in addition to the **.profile** file. The profile file that is selected for execution depends on the shell currently being used (as defined in **/etc/passwd**). The **.profile** file is used when logging in under with the Bourne Shell (**/bin/sh**) and is the only file executed automatically by this shell.

Another profile file, named **.cshrc** has also been mentioned as being used by the C-Shell in the same way as **.profile** to execute shell commands upon logging in. It should include personal commands such as **umask** settings, and any new environmental variable settings that are to be used. Two other files which emulate the characteristics of profile files called **.login** and **.logout** respectively, are also executed by the C-Shell. **.login** is executed after **.cshrc** when logging in to the system, and **.logout** file is used to execute various commands when the user logs out. For example, you could place the following command in a **.logout** file:

```
# My .logout file
echo "logging off ['tty'] on ['date'] ..."
```

This will make the system provide you with a more friendly logout message. You can also use **.logout** to carry out general house-keeping tasks.

11.2.8 Changing a user to a different group

The **chgrp** (change group) command is used to update the user group that is associated with a particular file. The syntax for the **chgrp** command is:

chgrp <group> <file>

The value for **<group>** is normally an alphabetic user group that exists in the **/etc/group** file, however it can also be numeric. in which case, the numeric value must correspond to a **GID** in the **/etc/group** (which refers to the group that you wish to use). The argument **<file>** is the file whose user-group name that we want to change. We would therefore type:

```
$ chgrp students simon
```

This command is analogous to **chgrp 30 simon**, where **30** is the **GID** value that identifies the students user-group. We can verify the new user-group setting for the directory **simon**, using **ls -lg** again, as shown on the next page:

```
$ ls -lg
total 1077
drwx------ 1 jim   students 204911 Apr 10 11:48 jim
drwx------ 1 john  students  62761 Apr 10 09:24 john
drwx------ 1 mark  students  45136 Apr 10 09:58 mark
drwxrw---- 1 mary  students  11346 Apr 11 10:21 mary
drwxrw---- 1 Paul  students  22316 Apr 11 10:41 Paul
drwxrwxr-x 1 simon students     32 Jun 28 13:01 simon
drwx------ 1 susan students  98231 May 15 22:17 susan
drwx------ 1 Tim   students   3233 May 15 22:58 Tim
```

This listing verifies that the change has taken place, and that all of **simon**'s files can be accessed by the students user-group (depending on the permission settings that are in force). The current permissions are drwxrwxr-x which indicates that the group users have read, write and execute permission on the directory. Remember also that permissions such as read, write and execute permission take on a slightly different meaning when applied to a directory file.

Read permission on another user's directory file stipulates that you can obtain a directory listing of that directory, write permission implies that files may be created or removed in that directory. Execute permission means that a user can access the directory using the **cd** command, that is to say that it may be made the current working directory.

In our context the other users of the user-group students can make **/usr/simon** their current working directory. They can also obtain a directory listing of this particular directory using **ls**, and can also read and write into the directory.

If we made **simon** our current working directory using the command **cd /usr/simon** (and the permission settings for the **simon** directory were drwxrwxrwx), we could effectively delete any file in the **simon** directory (and any files that may lie in lower directories levels in the **simon** directory). In general, a user's home directory should always have write permission turned off for all users apart from the owner (the user **simon** in this case) e.g. drwxr-xr-x, which dictates that the owner has full permissions over all files in the **simon** directory, the group users have only read and execute permission, as do the other users on the system. This is a safe and highly recommended set of file permissions.

11.2.9 Identifying and deleting a user

Deleting a user from the system is a typical administrative task. This process may be undertaken for a variety reasons; for example, a user may have left an organisation after accepting new employment elsewhere, or a user may have been dismissed (for crashing the system) etc. It may even be necessary to removed a user from the system simply because there is not enough disk-space. Monitoring the system's login activity may suggest that some users have not ever used the system, or that the requirement for access to the system is less than for other users of the system. The process is really the reverse of creating a new user, although there may be one or two extra clearing-up tasks that have to be performed in addition to this.

When permanently deleting a user from the system the following tasks need to be undertaken:

❑ Establish which user is to be deleted

❑ Delete **/etc/passwd** entry for the user

❑ Delete **/etc/group** entry for the user

❑ Delete the user's home directory, and all the files within it

❑ Perform clearing up tasks

When deleting the entry from the **/etc/passwd** file, it is essential that you remove the correct user. Similarities in names can be confusing (especially when upper and lower-case name combinations are used). It was mentioned earlier that the **passwd** file contains a fifth field for some personal information about the user. This field can be of great help when a user has to be deleted, since it can be used to hold the full name of the user, in addition to any other identifying information. If you are sure of the name of the user to be deleted, proceed to section 11.2 9. The following sections describe how to uniquely identify a user.

Assume there are two users on the system, one with the username **jenny** and the other with the username **Jenny.** Unless you actually created the accounts initially, and thus should know which username is to be removed, the task of identifying the correct user is not easy. A properly administered UNIX system will keep the full name of the user for identification purposes, in the fifth field of the **/etc/passwd** file, entered when the account for this user was initially set up (as described in section 11.2.6, step 7). A number of tools exist that allow direct manipulation of the fifth field of the **/etc/passwd** file. Two commands: **finger** and **chfn**, are now examined.

The finger command

Finger is a Berkeley command that examines the internal fields of the **/etc/passwd** file. It is the user information lookup program and therefore is useful to identify an individual user of the system. Using the **finger** command in this way requires careful preparation of the information in the **/etc/passwd** file. **Finger** has many options, many of which are discussed in the later section on system monitoring in Chapter 12 on UNIX Security. The simplest syntax is:

```
finger [name]
```

In the current context, it can be used to identify a user via the fifth field of the **/etc/passwd** file, and hence the use of the **[name]** argument will be required. The fifth field of the **/etc/passwd** file may contain an assortment of information and **finger** can be used with a variety of usernames or part usernames. For example, we could specify an account name (the most common name that is supplied), or the user's first or last name, as defined in the fifth field of the **passwd** file. This makes the process of user identification that much easier.

Coming back to the deletion of a user, we can use **finger** not only to make sure we are deleting the correct user, but also find out about the usage of the account, and whether it has ever been used. Considering the example, let us assume we want to delete the hypothetical user Jenny from the system. You may remember that there are two users in the current system with this name, although their login names are slightly different (Jenny and jenny – note the case). We could therefore type:

```
$ finger Jenny jenny
Login name: Jenny                      In real life: Jenny Taylor
Directory:/usr/STAFF/Jenny                 Shell: /bin/csh
Last login Thu May 3 12:42 on tty05
Extension: 456               Home phone: 555-1221
Project: Social Implications of Computers
No plan.

Login name: jenny                      In real life: Jenny Smith
Directory:/usr/STAFF/jenny                 Shell: /bin/sh
Never logged in
Extension: 456               Home phone: 556-2310
Project:
No plan.
```

Finger has now given us all the information we need about these two users. We can see that user **Jenny** has the full name Jenny Taylor, and that user **jenny** is in fact Jenny Smith. Also listed are the login shells for both users, taken from the last field of the **/etc/passwd** record for the respective users. Each user's fully-qualified home directory pathnames, taken from the sixth field of the **/etc/passwd** file, are also displayed.

Other information that can be obtained from the fifth field of the **/etc/passwd** file are the user's telephone and extension numbers. Each item of information in the fifth field (the user's full name, telephone details, etc.) is separated by a single comma (,). **Finger** has also informed us that user **jenny** has never logged in to the system, while the last login time, date and terminal code can be seen for user Jenny. The information for the users' project and plan are taken from those users' **.plan** and **.project** files that may or may not exist in the users' home directory areas. The **.project** file contains details of the user's current project and it may consist of many lines; however, only the first line is printed by **finger**. The **.plan** file can also be used to hold similar data, and **finger** prints all the lines of this file.

If the **finger** tool is not available on your system, it may be worthwhile making a note of the full details in the fifth field of the **/etc/passwd** file when a user is initially allocated an entry in the file. A tool such as **grep** could then be used to print the necessary information, for example:

```
$ grep -i '^jim' /etc/passwd
jim:Hg145KLddEY89aw:6:30:Jim Smith:/usr/jim:/bin/sh
jim2:edG23SzXr59XNmR:8:30:Jim Brown:/usr/jimmy:/bin/csh
```

Again, such a command relies on the fact that the fifth field of the **passwd** file contains the full identity of the user.

The **chfn** tool (discussed next) sets up the structure for the fifth field of the **/etc/passwd** file, to allow **finger** to examine it properly.

The chfn command

The tool that allows the user to access the information shown in the examples with the **finger** command is called **chfn** (change finger information). **Chfn** allows ordinary users to change the information that is stored about them in the **/etc/passwd** file. It is invoked with or without a single username, using the following syntax:

chfn [user]

If **chfn** is invoked without any arguments it assumes you want to change your own information i.e. the information held in your own entry in the **/etc/passwd** file. To change another user's details requires superuser privileges. When **chfn** is invoked it displays the current information divided into separate fields, and then prompts for new values for these fields, which include:

- ❑ The user's 'real-life' name
- ❑ Office room number
- ❑ Home phone number
- ❑ Office phone number (or extension).

The example below shows **chfn** invoked without any arguments. It displays a series of lines that prompt the user for the information categorised above. For example:

```
$ chfn
Name [Jenny]: Jenny Taylor
Room Number [ ]: none
Office Phone [456]: 554
Home Phone [555-1221]:
```

In the example here we can see that the existing values are displayed enclosed in square brackets ([ ]). These are default values picked from the current **/etc/passwd** file. To accept the current value inside of the square brackets the **[RETURN]** key should simply be pressed. To enter a null value (empty value) the word **none** can be used, as it has been on the line requiring a room number. In such a case, a blank value will be entered for this piece of information, which is indicated in the **/etc/passwd** record by two commas (,,).

Many users feel that insufficient information can be placed in the fifth field of the **/etc/passwd** file, and also that the information prompted by **chfn** may be irrelevant in many cases. A solution to this problem is to fool **chfn** into accepting the information that you are entering even though it may not be the correct information. For example, you could run **chfn** and in the place of the 'real-life' name you could enter different, but more useful information that you require. You may also be able to enter different information at the other prompts, but remember that **finger** may produce rather unusual results when it comes to displaying a user's details.

A similar command, **chsh** (change shell), may be available on your system. It is used to change your login shell as defined in the last field of the **/etc/passwd** file.

11.2.10 Carrying out the deletion of a user

When deleting a user, the relevant entries in the **/etc/passwd** and **/etc/group** files should be removed. This can be done using **vipw** if the system is being used extensively, or with **vi** or **ex** during a quiet system period.

The example below shows the deletion of the user 'fred' from the **/etc/passwd** file using the **ex** editor. Following the deletion the user will no longer be able to log in to the system with his particular username, although his files may possibly be accessed by another user by changing to the appropriate directory (depending on the file permission settings of the user concerned).

```
$ ex passwd
"/etc/passwd" 10 lines 878 characters
:g/^fred/d
:x
```

The **ex** command **g/^fred/d** is a global command (because of the initial **g**) that searches the whole file for the pattern **fred** occurring at the beginning of a line (notice the **^**). A global command has been used so we can apply another **ex** command once a pattern has been matched. The last command on the line is **d**, to delete the line which that has been matched. Hence, the whole command deletes all references to user **fred** from the file altogether. If you make a mistake simply quit from the current session without saving using the **ex quit!** command.

The final **x** command in the example saves the file and then exits **ex** back to the shell. If you would prefer to use the **vi** editor to delete the appropriate line, read section 9.4.15 on deleting text in Chapter 9.

Removing the user from the **/etc/group** file is fairly straightforward, except that the user will probably be deleted from within an existing group, so a whole line cannot be removed as in the case with a user entry in the **/etc/passwd** file. Deleting part of an existing line is a little difficult using a line editor such as **ex** or **ed**, so using a visual editor, such as **vi** may be more appropriate. The example below uses the **ex** editor to show you how to do it:

```
$ cat /etc/group
administrative::1:root,admin,Paul
technicians::10:Paul,Tim
students:3:30:fred,john,mark,mary,susan,jim
$ ex /etc/group
"/etc/group" 3 lines 101 characters
:g/fred,/s//
:x
$ cat /etc/group
administrative::1:root,admin,Paul
technicians::10:Paul,Tim
students:3:30:john,mark,mary,susan,jim
$
```

The global command in the example above searches for the pattern 'fred', (note the comma after the word **fred** which also needs to be deleted in this case, since **fred** is the first user in the group). Upon matching this pattern the s (substitute) command is invoked on the current line whereupon the matched pattern is replaced with nothing (note the // which substitutes nothing). This sort of substitution is practically the same as deleting the pattern **fred** from anywhere in the current file. Note that **fred** could appear in more than one group, and therefore global commands should be used to take care of any other occurrences that may exist. The example above also lists the **/etc/group** file before and after the deletion.

User **fred** has now been effectively removed from the system. All that remains is to delete the user's home directory from the file-system. If we assume all the user's home directories are stored in the **/usr** directory, we can simply issue the command:

```
$ rm -r /usr/fred
```

The **rm** command uses the **-r** option, which, if you can recall, recursively deletes all the files in a directory, including the directory itself. This is by far the easiest command that can be issued to delete a user's files, although you may want to move into the directory, using **cd**, and delete the necessary files individually. You may wish to consider backing-up some files in the user's directory (discussed later).

A note of caution

The **rm -r** command is very powerful and therefore great care should be taken when it is being used. The easiest way to avoid a potential disaster when deleting such files is to have a regular backup policy; there is no easier solution. A catastrophe is quite possible when using commands such as **rm** since you must be logged in as **root** to delete the necessary files to obtain the necessary write-permission on the required files or directories. You could even end up deleting the wrong person's files, bearing in mind that **root** has unrestricted access to everyone's files.

For example, supposing you press the **[RETURN]** key by mistake at the point where you have typed **rm -r /usr**. This would delete all the user files from the system. Take the even greater disaster if you press **[RETURN]** when only **rm -r /** has been typed. So be aware of what you are typing and make sure you are deleting the correct person's directory from the system.

A safer option to use with this type of **rm** command is **-i**, which allows you to confirm each deletion before it occurs, for example:

```
$ rm -ri /usr/fred
```

Clearing up tasks

The final clearing up tasks involve the removal of some other files that may have belonged to the user, but which occur in a different location in the file-system. For example, the user may have a system mail-box in the directory **/usr/spool/mail** directory, so this should be deleted using **rm**. In the current context the necessary command would be:

```
$ rm /usr/spool/mail/fred
```

The user may also have used the secret mail system, so the key files belonging to the user in the **/usr/spool/secretmail** (or **/var/spool/secretmail** directory on some systems) will have to be deleted in the same way.

11.3 Denying access to a user

Denying access to a user is a simple task to perform. It is an administrative task that requires superuser privileges and it involves manipulation of the **/etc/passwd** file.

A widely adopted approach consists of the alteration of the user's password field (the second field in the **/etc/passwd** file). Placing a single character or group of characters in this field will effectively deny access to that user. Deleting the user's entry in the **passwd** file is not recommended, since the entry will have to be reconstructed later (assuming only temporary denial to the system).

Note that the field should not be left blank, since this implies a null password. In such a case, any user could log in without a password. Altering the username is not a solution either, since read permission on the **/etc/passwd** is required for all user's because the system must be allowed to examine the user's password, home directory, and shell details. A user could thus gain access to the file and then log in. Take the single line **/etc/passwd** entry below for user Bruce:

```
Bruce:PFUjo6haxGUL2:14:10:Bruce:/usr/Bruce:/bin/csh
```

Denying access to this user can be achieved by deleting the user's encrypted password, and entering a character or series of characters into its place. The asterisk (*) character or the word NOLOGIN are commonly used to replace a password; the final choice is really up to you. Using the single asterisk notation you could modify this user's **/etc/passwd** entry to:

```
Bruce:*:14:10:Bruce:/usr/Bruce:/bin/csh
```

Editing the password can be done using your favourite editor. Using a substitution command with an editor such as **ed** or **ex** may be slightly laborious since you will have to enter the encrypted password as the basis for the replacement argument string.

Note also that the asterisk is a special character (a metacharacter) that has a different meaning to the editor. It will therefore be wise to remove its special properties by quoting it with the 3\ character. For example:

```
$ ex /etc/group
"/etc/group" 3 lines 101 characters
:g/PFUjo6haxGUL2/s/\*/
:x
```

Replacing the password field with this character does not mean that the user can use the character as a valid password. As mentioned already, the password field is generated by the system using the **passwd** utility. User Bruce, upon logging in and supplying his correct password, will be told that access has been denied to him. He may find this a bit bewildering, and he will probably attempt to log in again until finally going to see the Systems Manager.

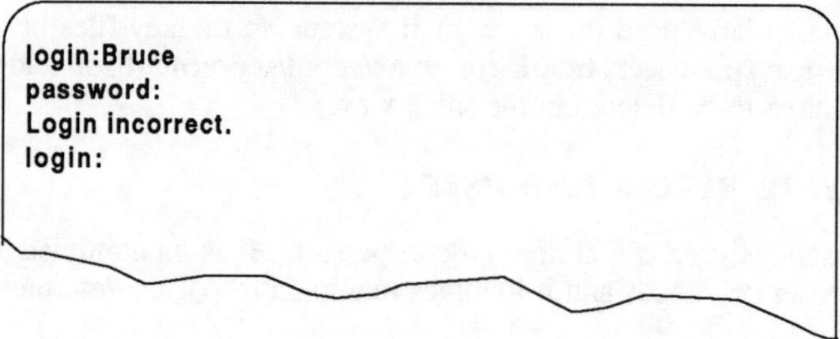
login:Bruce
password:
Login incorrect.
login:

Figure 11.8 A failed login

11.3.1 Tips

When blanking out a password to deny access to a user, it is suggested that you use a word such as NOLOGIN, since it can be more easily scanned using a tool such as **grep**. The command below counts the number of users with NOLOGIN entries:

```
echo "Banned users: `grep NOLOGIN /etc/passwd | wc -l`."
```

11.3.2 Notification of denied access

An alternative approach is to replace the user's shell by a notification of denied access. This has the added advantage of immediately informing the user of the fact that access has been denied to them. This method involves editing the seventh field of the **/etc/passwd** file, the user's shell, which is simply an executable file. The user's shell is simply replaced with the name of an executable file that notifies the user that he or she is being denied access to the system. This file can be a simple executable shell-script.

Some systems will require the user to be immediately logged out, but this is not necessary in most cases since the file in place of the user's shell will simply execute and terminate when it runs out of instructions. Hence the user will be cut off from the system once the file has completed its execution. The example below assumes this to be the case. You can experiment with your own system to determine its precise behaviour. The creation of a typical file is shown below. Assume that this file is being created in the administrator's miscellaneous (misc) directory:

```
$ ex /misc/deny_access
[New File] deny
:
# Tell user that he/she has been denied access.
echo You have been denied access to the system.
echo " "
echo Please contact your Systems Manager in order
echo that your account can be reinstated.
.
:x
$
```

Now the file has been created it must be made executable. This is because the shell must be instructed to interpret the file as a series of shell commands, and not just a series of plain text lines. So the executable mode of the file must be set using the **chmod** (change mode) command in the following way:

```
$ chmod o+x deny
```

This command gives execute permission on the file to all the other user's of the system i.e. to all those users who are *not* in the same group as the current user (**root** in this example). The **chmod** command is discussed in more detail in Chapter 12 on UNIX Security. We can now edit the **/etc/passwd** file and change the login shell for the particular user. Assume you are denying access to user Bruce. You need to remove the current shell definition, and replace it with the fully-qualified pathname of the file **deny** created previously. The final entry is thus:

```
Bruce:PFUjo6haxGUL2:14:10:Bruce:/usr/Bruce:/misc/deny
```

Note that the password field is still intact with this method. The user will be allowed to log in up to the point where the username and password are supplied. Directly after this the shell-script file **deny** will be executed and the user **Bruce** will be immediately thrown off the system (since a proper shell has not been allocated). This is shown below in Figure 11.9.

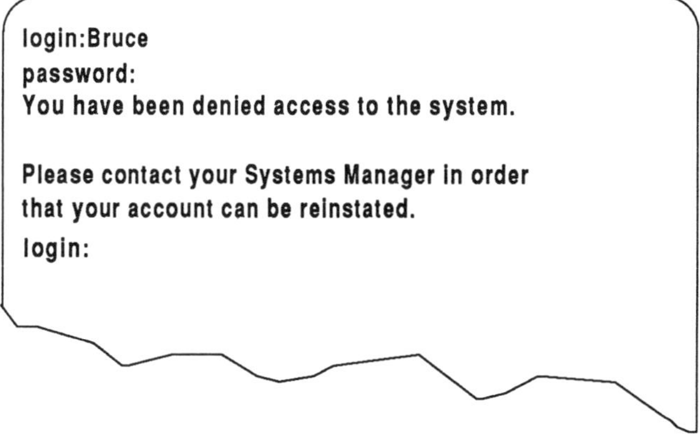
login:Bruce
password:
You have been denied access to the system.
Please contact your Systems Manager in order
that your account can be reinstated.
login:

Figure 11.9 An attempted login using the altered shell method

11.4 Reinstating a banned user

Any user that has been temporarily denied from accessing the system will have to be reinstated to the system at some later stage. The process of reinstating a user really only involves minor manipulation of the **/etc/passwd** file to restore its former state. For example, if you have replaced the user's password (as in the * or NOLOGIN technique described in section 11.3), you will have to remove the invalid characters from the password field, and then save the file. At this point the user's account is totally unprotected. You can tell the user to log in immediately, changing their password in the process, or you can assign a new password using the **passwd** command. In this case, the user will have to tell you their password so that it can be entered. The user can then proceed to log , in the normal way.

11.5 Installing a new user password

Users will often forget passwords. The login program is very particular in that it requires both a valid username and valid password. If either (or both) are incorrectly entered, then access is denied and the message shown in Figure 11.8 will be displayed.

Usernames always seem to pose a problem, and the spoken word does not always represent the name that the system recognises, because of case-sensitivity. Most users will associate a failed login with an incorrect password, when in fact it is often the username that has caused the problem. It is therefore wise to make sure that the user has actually entered the correct username. If you request them to enter their name and password, and the username format is valid, then the user must have genuinely forgotten their password. The tasks that are required to change a password are:

- Log in as the superuser (**root**)
- Execute the **passwd** command with the user's username as an argument
- Enter the new password and verify it.

The **passwd** command is a very useful tool, since it can be used to overwrite an existing password. When assigning a new password, the **/etc/passwd** does not require manual editing by the user because the **/bin/passwd** command actually overwrites the existing password with the new password that the user has chosen, but only when **root** is using it with a username argument. When a normal user employs **/bin/passwd** to change their password, the old password must be supplied.

11.5.1 Forgetting a superuser password

Forgetting a superuser password can be a minor problem or a massive catastrophe, depending on the provision made for dealing with this situation. This sort of problem can only be solved if preventative measures have previously been arranged, for example:

- Installing more than one superuser.
- Setting up privileged users

In order to reallocate a superuser password, one of the four main tasks listed below must be performed:

- Logging in under another superuser name (that has a **UID** of zero, as stored in the **/etc/passwd** file), and editing the **passwd** file to remove the forgotten encrypted password

- ❑ Asking a privileged user (who has write permission on the **/etc/passwd** file) to edit out the forgotten encrypted password
- ❑ At boot time (when the system is initially switched on) the system may allow the user to undertake certain administrative tasks within a superuser shell, but such facilities are highly system specific. If your system boots up with a single user-mode option, take this option and simply edit the password field as in the previous cases, as soon as you are given a shell
- ❑ If your system does not boot up in single-user mode, but instead boots into a mandatory multi-user mode, then you may have to reboot from an alternative device that allows the system to come up in single user mode. You can then proceed to edit the **passwd** file as in the previous examples.

The last two options require a little specialist knowledge of the system, although a large number of systems guide the user through a series of options from a simple menu. Starting up and shutting down a UNIX system is discussed later in this chapter. If none of the options listed above are available to you, you will have to completely reinstall your UNIX system, so it will be time to phone up the engineers!

11.5.2 Duplicate superusers

A good administrative technique is to have more than one superuser (see section 11.2.5 – Privileged UNIX users). A duplicate superuser is any user (other than **root**) who has a **UID** of zero in the **/etc/passwd** file. To reallocate a forgotten superuser password simply log in under an alternative superuser name (such as 'admin' in our examples) and then edit the forgotten password of the superuser in question. Beware that once the old password has been removed, any user can log in to the superuser's account, until a new password has been reinstated.

11.5.3 Privileged users

Another useful technique is the provision of privileged users who are allowed to undertake administrative tasks. A privileged user will need write-permission on the **/etc/passwd** file in order that the necessary password can be edited to allow the superuser to log in and choose a new password.

Privileged users should be placed in the same group as **root**, thus allowing them to use the **newgrp** command to gain administrative privileges. The **/etc/passwd** file will need to have write-permission set for the group users in this case, otherwise users in the same group as **root** will not be able to alter the file. The use of privileged users was discussed in some detail in section 11.2.5 earlier in this chapter.

11.6 Maintaining adequate storage space

The file-system that is provided by the UNIX system is entirely dynamic in structure, that is to say that it can expand until all the available disk space is exhausted. Allowing the file-system to become seriously congested with files is not a situation which should be allowed to develop. System performance times will begin to suffer as a result, and the system may eventually grind to a halt.

When administering a UNIX system, it is essential to monitor the disk space available to the system very carefully. UNIX provides many tools for the monitoring of the file-system with respect to the availability of disk-storage, some of which are now described.

11.6.1 Displaying disk usage statistics – du

The most common UNIX tool that can be used to monitor the amount of occupied disk space is the **du** (disk usage) command. This command can be told to report on the whole of the file-system or on a specific part of it. The syntax of the command is:

du [-a] [-s] [file ...]

The most frequently used options that are available on nearly all UNIX systems include **-s**, and **-a**. The **-s** option prints the total number of kilobytes occupied in the current storage area (whether it be a file or directory). All other measurements are in *kilobytes* (for each individual file). The **-a** option generates a listing for each individual file in a specified directory of the file-system. The two options are mutually exclusive.

Used on its own without any arguments, the **du** command reports on the current working directory (.), otherwise a filename argument can be supplied to obtain a report on an existing file or directory. When a directory name is specified as the file argument, **du** also searches for any subdirectories that may exist in that particular directory. **Du** is a useful tool to find excessively large files which, if obsolete, can be weeded out by deletion, or back-up followed by deletion. The examples below show the use of the **du** command:

Examples

Example 1

```
$ ls
file        dir1
$ du dir1
3    subdir1
5    dir1
```

This example illustrates when **du** is used with a directory filename argument, namely **dir1**. We can see that the file is a directory, since **du** has shown us that a subdirectory exists within it (named **subdir1**). The sizes of the parent directory and child subdirectory in kilobytes are displayed in the leftmost column.

Example 2

```
$ du -a dir1
1    dir1/file1
1    dir1/file2
```

```
1    dir1/subdir1/file3
2    dir1/subdir
5    dir1
```

This example illustrates the use of the **-a** option which requests that all the files in the specified directory should be individually listed. **Du** displays the number of kilobytes of disk-space allocated to each of the individual files of the directory specified, namely **file1** and **file2**. The file(s) in the subdirectory **subdir1** (**file3**) is also displayed. Finally it shows the total size (in kilobytes) of the actual subdirectory file (since individual directories also occupy disk-space), and the whole directory (which is simply the sum of all the kilobytes that have been listed up to this point).

Example 3

```
$ du -a subdir1
1    file3
```

This command makes **du** search for the file called **subdir1**. We already know that **subdir1** is a subdirectory that exists within the **dir1** directory. Once **du** has found the file (starting the search from the current directory location) the total number of kilobytes in that file are displayed. Since the file is itself a directory, only the files within it are displayed. One such file exists, namely **file3**, which occupies one kilobyte of disk-space. In the case where **-a** option is not specified, **du** would not list any nondirectory files specified as arguments.

Example 4

```
$ du -s dir1
5    dir1
```

Here we are using the **-s** option. It simply requests the total size of the specified file, instead of an individual file listing. The one argument passed to **du** in this example is itself a directory, and therefore a total of the files it contains are shown (note that this figure includes the size of the actual directory itself).

Special considerations

The **du** command should be available for use by any user of the system, so that anyone can find out the disk-space occupied by their own files. The systems administrator should run **du** with superuser privileges (such as those granted with the login name **root**), since **du** will only display information about files on which the user has read-permission. Without the necessary privileges the user will be locked out of certain files, for example:

```
$ du -a /usr/fred
/usr/fred : permission denied
```

This example illustrates a typical error message, which might occur if a user other than **fred** issued the above command, that informs us that permission to examine this particular file has been denied. This error basically means that read-permission has not been allowed to the other users of the system.

In the case where the **du** command is used on a directory that has a large number of linked files, the result may not be entirely accurate when reporting totals. Such an example can be seen below where the individual entries for a group of files does not match with the final total. This is simply because some of these files are linked to other directories within the file-system. When **du** searches through the file-system it includes every linked file in the process and so may include some files in more than one directory total, where in reality only one such file actually exists. The final total therefore is actually smaller than the total obtained when each file is added up manually.

```
$ du -a /usr/staff
411  /usr/staff/east
312  /usr/staff/west
102  /usr/staff/north
901  /usr/staff/south
21   /usr/staff/misc
1642 /usr/staff
```

When invoking **du** on an entire file-system the / argument should be used. Most listings tend to be very long, especially if your file-system is large, and contains many individual directories and subdirectories. It is therefore wise to run a command that captures the output from **du**, and places it in a file. This could be run as a background process, thus freeing the terminal for other interactive commands while the list is being constructed. A command to achieve this might be:

```
$ du -a / > du_list &
```

Remember that **du** can be used with a specific part of the file-system. For example **du** could be used to list all the files and their individual sizes for the **/usr** or **/bin** directories only. Such a listing would take a significantly shorter time to process that listing an entire file-system.

11.6.2 Available disk-space

The availability of disk space and the actual disk usage of a system are related, disk usage referring to the amount of storage space that is already allocated while the available disk space indicates the amount of storage space that is presently unused on a storage device. The UNIX operating system is hungry for disk-space. It is one of those systems that creates and maintains a multitude of files throughout the entire file-system.

The number of files that are maintained on your particular UNIX system will depend the activities performed. The number of users who need access to the system, the number of devices that are supported, and the amount of accounting information stored on your system will also determine the amount of disk-space that is required.

Many administrators tend to underestimate the amount of disk- space required when operating a UNIX system because it is so file-orientated, and relies on the existence of many files for its smooth running.

Because UNIX has a very flexible file-system, users tend to put the system to its full paces, creating large and elaborate miniature file-systems in their own directory areas. Users also tend to accumulate a large volume of files which then become redundant. Of course, there is nothing wrong with the use of the file-system to manage such information, and indeed users should be encouraged to organise their files in such ways, although for the administrator, the increased use of the file-system in such a manner can cause problems in the long-run.

There is no accepted guideline for the amount of disk-space that should be kept available on a particular storage device, although many administrators believe that at least a quarter of the storage device should be available for use.

11.6.3 The physical file-system

A typical UNIX system will have one or more storage devices, the most common being a hard-disk device, which is used at *bootstrapping* time (that is unless the system is being booted from a removable disk device). The root file-system, which may contain directories such as **/bin**, **/etc**, is nearly always held on the booting device. Some UNIX systems mount the rest of the file-system onto the existing **root** file-system from different devices, while other systems go the whole way and mount an entire file-system from one device.

All disk devices must have at least one file-system in which the users can store information. The file-system can be as large as the device containing it, although common practice is to create a series of file-systems on a single storage-device particularly on a hard-disk system.

An underestimation of the number of files that are to be stored on a particular storage device often results in disk-space being unavailable, even when total capacity of the device is considerably more than the total sum of the files stored on it. This is because every file in the system has an individual i-node holds critical file information (such as access permissions and other details – the time and date of the most recent modification to the file, etc.). A finite number of i-nodes (and data blocks) are specified for the file system when it is initially created. When the number of i-nodes on the system is nearly exhausted the system will probably enter a state of confusion, and then when all the i-nodes have been used, the system will then crash. Therefore an adequate number of i-nodes (or files) should be allocated to a system to prevent it from running out of disk-space.

Section 6.4.3 in Chapter 6 describes the problems of allocating i-nodes and data blocks to a storage device (and how specifying the correct amount is only achieved through experience). Section 11.9 examines how a file-system can be constructed from scratch.

11.6.4 Examining quotas – quot

To prevent the system from exhausting the available disk-space, and thus crashing, it is common practice to set a threshold limit, after which action can be taken to rectify the situation. Normally at least a quarter of the entire storage device should be available, and a danger threshold could be set in the region of one-tenth of the storage device's capacity e.g. 10%.

Two common administrative terms are the *hard* and *soft* limits. Both are threshold values which can be examined by the system. A hard limit, normally higher than a soft limit, suggests potential disaster when exceeded; whereas a soft limit that has been exceeded carries a warning.

To examine the available space in a file-system, UNIX provides a command called **quot** (which normally resides in the **/etc** directory). The **quot** command displays the number of blocks in a named file-system, for each user. Using **quot** allows the administrator to examine the system's disk space usage, and thus make decisions regarding its appropriate usage.

The difference between **du** and **quot** lies in the display. **Du** commonly shows the number of kilobytes used taken up by a series of files, whereas **quot** displays the number of disk blocks. The relationship between these two numbers obviously depends on the current block size used by the system. When provided with a file-system argument **quot** scans for the specified file-system; alternatively, **quot** can be used to give a user-by-user breakdown of block usage. The syntax of the quot command is:

quot [options] [file-system]

Most versions of the **quot** command have about three options, some of which may not be available on your system. Two common options are now examined. The most widely used option is **-f** which prints the number of files and the space occupied by these files for each user.

Another option, **-c**, instructs **quot** to display a three-column statistical listing. The first column lists the file sizes (in blocks); the second gives the number of files of each block size, and the final column lists a cumulative total of the number of blocks. If an argument (file-system name) is not specified, **quot** simply lists information for the current file-systems. A typical example of the **quot** command with a single device name argument is shown here:

```
$ quot /dev/root
7633 root
1043 bin
2581 sys
1121 uucp
```

Upon finding that a user, or indeed a file-system has an abnormally large amount of blocks taken up, the appropriate action can be taken. This action can involve deletion or the backing-up of files. Before deleting any files, you should check to see if they need to be backed-up first. The backing-up and archiving of such files is discussed in section 11.12.

Files without an owner

It is common for commands such as **quot** to display a single numerical figure in the place of a username, when it is used with an option such as **-f**. This is because the owner of the file has been removed from the system, but the file has not been deleted. **Quot** obtains user information (such as usernames) from the **/etc/passwd** file, so if it cannot find the owner of the file, it simply displays a single numeric value, commonly zero on some UNIX systems. When this occurs, any such files should be deleted.

This eventuality is not a a large problem since, any files still remaining on the system after the deletion of their owner, can be easily spotted (refer also to section 11.2.9).

11.6.5 Other quot related commands

A number of other commands, similar to that of quot also exist. These are the commands **quota**, **edquota**, **quotacheck**, **quotaon** and **quotaoff**. A brief explanation of each of these can be found in the following sections.

11.6.6 Quota

The **quota** command may be available on your system. It is used by the systems administrator to display a user's disk usage and limits. The syntax of the command is:

quota [-v] [user ...]

The **-v** option makes **quota** display a user's quota on a file system where storage is not allocated. If no option is specified **quota** reports on users that have exceeded their disk **quota** limit (discussed later).

From the syntax description, it can be seen that arguments to the **quota** utility consist of individual usernames. Where more than one user is specified, simply separate each username with a space. The **quota** command can only be used by the superuser when examining other users' quota limits. One point to note is the fact that the superuser (**root**) does not have any quota limits. Note also that users can only examine their own quotas, for example:

```
$ quota -v root
no disk quota for root (uid 0)
$ quota -v john
quota: Paul (uid 10): permission denied
```

11.6.7. quotacheck

The **quotacheck** command examines a specified file-system to check that file-systems quota limit is consistent with the disk quota file that is associated with a particular file-system. If inconsistencies are found i.e. disk usage in a particular file-system is excessive, then **quotacheck** updates the quota file for that file-system.

While **quotacheck** is running, it constructs a table of the current disk usage, and compares this against the existing quota file for the file-system being examined (called *quotas*). This is how any inconsistencies are found. The constructed current disk usage table (the table of incorrect quotas) is also updated in the process, but only if the file-system is active. The syntax of the command is:

quotacheck [-v] [-a] <filesystem ...>

The **-a** option makes **quotacheck** check all the file-systems that are stored in the file **/etc/fstab** (the file-system table). This allows only a certain set of file-systems to be checked, which may be more practical in many situations. The **-v** option makes **quotacheck** print the changed disk quota amounts for each user on a particular file-system. **Quotacheck** will expect each file-system to have a quota file, named *quotas*, that exists in that file-systems root directory area. If this a file is absent, then the file-system is simply ignored by **quotacheck.**

Special considerations

The best time to run **quotacheck** is directly after booting the system. The UNIX system has a series of configuration files (discussed later) which are examined at bootstrapping time, and which can initiate actions at certain time intervals during the day. Enabling the **quotacheck** utility from a configuration file should be done before the **quotaon** command is used to enable the disk quotas.

Quotacheck accesses the raw storage device (stored in the **/dev** directory), therefore it is wise to ensure that any file-system that is being checked is inactive.

11.6.8 Quotaon

Quotaon allows the systems administrator to enable or disable file-system quota checks. The syntax of the command is:

quotaon [-v] <filesystem ...>

or

quotaon [-v] [-a]

The **-a** (all) is a toggle option that enables or disables all checks for all file-systems that are listed in the **/etc/fstab** file which are marked read/write with quota checks (see the example **fstab** file in section 11.7). This option is normally used at bootstrapping time to enable quota checking.

The **-v** option prints a diagnostic message for each file-system where quotas are enabled or disabled. Without the **-v** option the command performs more silently. **Quotaon** expects to find a file named *quotas* in the root directory of each specified file-system on which quotas are to enabled (or disabled).

When **quotaon** is executed it updates an options field in the **/etc/mtab** (mounted file-systems table file) to indicate when quotas are on and off for each file-system concerned. Individual file-systems can be controlled using the **<filesystem>** argument. Simply include the file-system name literally on the command line. Multiple file-system name arguments can also be specified.

Examples

Example 1

```
$ quotaon /user1
```

This command turns on quota checking for the **user1** file-system that resides in the root directory.

Example 2

```
$ quotaon -a
```

This command (if used the first time), turns on quota checking for all file-systems that are specified in the **/etc/fstab** file.

11.6.9 quotaoff

The **quotaoff** command, as the name suggests, disables quota checking for one or more specified file-systems. Remember that **quotaon -a** can also be used to toggle on or off the checking of quotas for all the file-systems that are specified in **/etc/fstab**.

11.7 The structure of the /etc/fstab file

The **/etc/fstab** file describes the file-systems used by the local UNIX machine. The file can be modified with a text editor such as **ex** or **vi**. The **fstab** file is read by a number of different commands that manipulate file-systems, such as **mount** and **umount** (discussed in section 11.9). The **/etc/fstab** file contains single line entries of the form:

<file-system name> <dir> <type> <options> <freq> <passno>

The **<file-system name>** is the name of the storage device on which a file-system is contained e.g. **/dev/dk01b** (a disk storage device). **<dir>** refers to the fully-qualified directory name of the required mounted file-system. An example is **/tmp**, the temporary directory used on nearly all UNIX systems.**<type>** makes direct reference to the **<options>** and **<file-system name>** arguments. It is used to ensure that these two options are the **fstab** file are correctly interpreted. The options are system specific, and therefore you are advised to check your own system to find out the precise values can be placed in the **<type>** field. Some common options that can be found on some Berkeley UNIX systems are: **ignore**, **4.3**, and **swap**. When the **ignore** option, is specified, the current entry is completely ignored. This option is useful to show disk partitions that are not currently in use. The **4.3** option is used on Berkeley BSD 4.3 version systems only. It corresponds to block devices, such as a disk storage device that stores data as individual blocks (see Chapter 6 *the Physical File Structure of UNIX* for more information on block devices). If **swap** is specified, the device in the same entry will be used as a swap partition.

The values placed in the **<options>** field refer to the protection attributes assigned to the current file-system. Multiple entries can be included, separated with commas. The default protection setting is **rw, suid** (read/write and set user identification). The **suid** protection allows non-privileged users access under a temporary **UID** value (see Chapter 12 on UNIX Security). The protection options that are valid on all file-systems are listed in Table 11.1:

Table 11.1 Fstab file protection options

Protection	Effect
rw	Read and write from the file-system
ro	Read only from the file-system
suid	Set-uid identification allowed
nosuid	No set-uid allowed
swap	Allows partition to be used as a swap area

Other options that relate to the enabling and disabling of file-system quota checking (specific to the **4.3** file-system option) include:

quota - Check quotas for this file-system
noquota - Do not check quotas for this file-system

The **<freq>** field is used to determine how often the file-system partition is backed up using the **dump** command. This field will only accept numeric values, which correspond to the number of days that must expire between consecutive dumps. A common, and indeed safe, option is 1, so that the file-system partition is backed up daily.

The final field, **<passno>**, is used in conjunction with a consistency check program called **fsck** (file-system consistency check). The numerical value in this field determines on which pass the file-system is to be checked. So all file-systems with a **<passno>** value of 1 are checked simultaneously on the first pass; then all file-systems with a value of 2, on the second pass, and so on. It is common to give the root file-system a **<passno>** value of 1, and then arrange for one file-system on each available disk-drive to be checked on each following pass until all have been checked.

11.7.1 The swap area/partition

The UNIX system employs a memory management technique known as *swapping*. This is a method of moving a process from the computer's main memory to a reserved area of the disk, known as the swap area, and back again. Swapping does not increase the *performance* of the overall system, since time is consumed while processes are swapped from disk to memory, and vice-versa, which in turn reduces the time that is actually available for process execution. Swapping is commonly employed because it allows a UNIX system to run more processes simultaneously that could otherwise be handled by the memory of the computer. The alternative to swapping is to deny execution to some processes, which is by no means an adequate solution.

If a UNIX system becomes overwhelmed, because too many processes are running simultaneously, so that the system is finding it difficult to allocate each process a part of main-memory, swapping can impede the overall performance of the system, since a high percentage of time is spent swapping. Solutions to this problem are normally expensive; for example, purchasing new memory or moving users to another machine.

UNIX normally uses a dedicated area of a disk as the swap area, so system efficiency is increased. An exact copy of each process is made in this area, and the copy is updated each time it is swapped out to memory. When a process is completed its image is removed from the swap area by the system, thus making room for more processes. If you are running a small UNIX system, you may find that no allowance was made for the provision of swapping when the system was initially configured.

11.7.2 Boot drive swap partitions

The swap area on many UNIX machines is commonly a separate (high-speed) disk drive on to which processes are copied. Some systems assume that there is a default swap partition on the boot drive of the current system.

If an entry in the **/etc/fstab** is for the boot drive swap partition, it should not be used. A common entry in the **fstab** file for such a partition consists of the disk device mentioned twice, as the **<file-system-name>** and the **<dir>** name, and with the word *swap* in both the **<type>** and **<options>** fields. The swapping process can also be controlled manually the **swapon** command.

The swapon utility

Swapon is a Berkeley UNIX command used to specify additional devices for swapping activity. Its syntax is:

swapon [-a] [-f]<name>

The **-a** option causes devices marked as swap areas in the **/etc/fstab** file to be made unavailable. This option is useful when a disk-device used for swapping is being repaired or replaced etc. The **-f** option forces the device specified by **<name ...>** to be a swap device even if it is not marked as being eligible for swapping in **/etc/fstab**.

When a typical UNIX system is booted, swapping is normally configured to take place on only one device. In the case where one disk-device is being used to swap files and store mounted directories etc. a swap partition on the same disk may be used.

The **swapon** command is commonly placed in the UNIX system configuration file **/etc/rc** (discussed later in this chapter in section 11.10).

Examples

Example 1

```
$ swapon -a
```

This command makes all swap devices (as marked in the **/etc/fstab** file) available.

Example 2

```
$ swapon -f /dev/dk0b
```

This command causes the disk device **/dev/dk0b** to be allocated as a swapping device, even though it is not mentioned as being a swap device in the **/etc/fstab** file.

11.7.3 A typical /etc/fstab file

A typical **/etc/fstab** file can be seen below. it consists of five entries, four of which are for file-systems, and one for a swap area. Notice how the swap area has no dump frequency time or file-consistency settings.

```
/dev/dk0a/          4.3   rw,noquota  1  1
/dev/dk0b /tmp      4.3   rw,quota    1  3
/dev/dk0c /usr/src  4.3   rw,quota    1  4
/dev/dk1a /usr/local4.3   rw,noquota  1  2
/dev/dk1b /dev/dk1b swap  swap
```

The first line contains an entry for the root file-system. The file-system type is **4.3**, and the protection settings are **rw** (read and write). There is no quota checking on this file-system as shown by the word **noquota** in the options field. The file-system is also dumped every day, and the pass number for consistency checking is **1**, indicating it is checked first.

The second entry is for the file-system **/tmp** (the temporary directory). This file-system is also type **4.3**, and it has read and write permission settings. Quota checking is enabled (note the **quota** keyword), and this file-system is dumped every day. When a file-system has quota checking enabled (as set in the **/etc/fstab** file) a file named **quotas** must exist in that file-system's root directory, **/tmp** in this case, so that quotas can be checked by the system. This type of file is updated by the system when the disk-usage in the file-system is changed i.e. increased (as new files are created) or decreased (when existing files are deleted). If we issued an **ls** command on the **/tmp** directory in our example, we may see a listing resembling:

```
$ ls /tmp
man1236 man1245 man2322 quotas
```

This example shows the existence of the file named **quotas**, which (as discussed above) is required to check disk-usage levels in the current file-system.

11.7.4 Reporting quotas – repquota

Reporting quotas for each user on the system can be performed using a command named **repquota**. This utility is a Berkeley tool that summarises the quota allocations for a given file-system. The syntax for the **repquota** command is:

repquota [-v] <filesystem ...>

or

repquota [-v] -a

The **-a** (all) option causes **repquota** to report all the quota allocations for all the file-systems as recorded in the **/etc/fstab** file (as discussed in the previous sections). The second common option, **-v**, requests **repquota** to display a small diagnostic message for each file-system that has its quota enabled. Such file-systems can be recognised by examination of the **/etc/fstab** file for entries containing the word **quota**.

Repquota, as well as printing the individual quotas for users, also gives a summary of the disk-usage for the file-systems concerned. For each user, the current number of files and amount of disk-space, in kilobytes, is printed, along with any quotas that have been created using the **edquota** command (edit user quotas – discussed in section 11.7.5). As an administrative command, only the superuser should be able to use **repquota**. However, it may be useful for individuals to have execute access on the command so that they can examine their own and group quotas etc.

Repquota examines the quotas file in each file-system (where quotas have been enabled) so that the necessary statistics can be displayed. For example:

```
$ repquota -a
User            Block Limits            File Limits
                used  soft  hard        used  soft  hard
fred      --    91    2500  4000        52    1000  9999
john      --    232   2500  4000        37    1000  9999
susan     --    2144  2500  4000        329   1000  9999
```

This small example illustrates a hypothetical listing for three users. The first user, **fred**, owns 52 files which have used 91 blocks. User **john** has used 232 blocks, and has created 37 files. The last user in the listing, user **susan**, has used 2144 blocks, and this disk-space is occupied by 329 individual files.

From the example it can be seen that **repquota** divides up the listing into block and file limits. Users can therefore have restrictions put on the number of files they can create. This is also the case for the number of disk blocks. A soft limit and hard limit is allocated for both blocks and files. When a soft limit is exceeded, the systems administrator can see if a particular user is monopolising the system with unnecessary files, or perhaps the user has a genuine need for a large amount of disk-space e.g. in the case of a large project etc. The administrator will need therefore to investigate the user to ascertain the nature of the actual disk-usage.

When a hard-limit is exceeded that user can no longer create any more files (thus occupying more blocks on the disk device concerned). A warning will be generated by the system when a hard-limit is exceeded.

11.7.5 The edquota command

The **edquota** command is used by the systems administrator to assign quotas to individual users. The syntax of the command is:

edquota [-p proto-user] <user ...>

or

edquota -t

The **-p** options allows duplication of user quotas for a user known as the prototypical user. This is the most common option chosen when group quotas have to be allocated. The **-t** option is used to edit the soft limits for each file-system.

Edquota is used to manipulate and update the quotas file, that should be stored in each file-system where quotas are to be allocated, with the standard UNIX editors, as defined by the **$EDITOR** variable. If the **$EDITOR** variable is not set, **vi** is commonly used as the default editor that will be invoked on many systems.

One or more individual users can be specified on the command line when **edquota** is invoked. A temporary ASCII file is created for each user whose quotas are being changed, and the editor is used to allow it to be updated etc. On leaving the editor, the temporary ASCII file is used to update the quotas file (which itself is a pure binary file, and thus cannot be edited using the standard UNIX editors).

11.8 Making a file-system – mkfs

Up to now we have discussed file-systems, and how they can be assigned quota limits etc., but we have not mentioned how to actually create a new file-system. We explained in Chapter 5 that a file-system is simply a hierarchical tree-like structure to organise our files, and indeed this simple definition is perfectly adequate. However, a true file-system is not initially made using tools such as **mkdir** and **rmdir**; this would be too simplistic. File-systems are created in such a way that the flexibility of the system is ensured, using the **mkfs** (make file-system) command. The syntax of the command is:

mkfs <device> <size> [number of i-nodes]

To make a file-system therefore, the administrator needs to specify:

- The name of the disk-device on which the file system is to be created e.g. **/dev/dk08**
- The size of the file-system (in blocks)
- The optional number of i-nodes that are to be allocated to the file-system i.e. the number of individual files.

For more general information on mounted file-systems and removable disks etc., you are referred to the section entitled *Removable disks and mounted file-systems* in Chapter 5 (in section 5.8.3). A typical **mkfs** command could thus be:

```
$ mkfs /dev/dk01 9000
```

This command makes a file-system on disk device 1, which will be allocated 9000 blocks. The number of i-nodes in this file-system has been omitted (this value is optional) and the system will allocate a default number of i-nodes, a system specific value which depend on the block size of the system etc.

11.8.1 Mounting a file-system

We have mentioned the considerable flexibility of UNIX many times already. Another flexible feature is the mounting and unmounting of file-systems at the discretion of the administrator. The users view of the file-system hierarchy can be changed at any point by mounting or *grafting* new file-systems on to the existing file-system.

The root file-system (/) is always mounted automatically by the system. Any new file-systems will be joined to this part of the system when one needs to be mounted. Similarly, a file-system will be separated from the root file-system when an unmount operation takes place.

UNIX can be instructed to mount and unmount file-systems at specific times using a special configuration file that contains the required times and instructions. A background process (a daemon) checks the stored times and mounts the file-systems when specified. Alternatively, the systems administrator can mount file-systems at any time by using a direct command called **mount**. Unmounting a file-system is done using the command **umount**.

The mount command

The **mount** command commonly resides in the **/etc** directory, although it may be found in **/bin** on some systems. It is used to mount a file-system on to an existing directory. When mounting any file-system, the name of the directory where the new file-system is to be mounted must be specified, with the name of the disk device that contains the file-system to be mounted. File-systems can be mounted from a variety of devices, thus files can be stored and manipulated across a wide range of individual disk-devices. As a result, a complete file-system can be constructed on a separate disk (using **mkfs**), and can then be mounted on to the system from a separate device. The syntax of the command is:

mount [options] <filesystem>

Mount has many options some of which may be system specific. The **-a** option is used to make **mount** attempt to mount all of the file-systems that are described in the **/etc/fstab** file. (The fstab file contains enough information i.e. devices names and directory locations for the mount to take place.)

The **-p** option causes mount to print a list of all the file-systems that are currently mounted. The list may be produced in structure suitable for the **/etc/fstab** file.

The **-o** option is also common on some UNIX systems. It is used with keywords (some of which are listed in Table 11.2 below) which control the way in which the named file-system is mounted.

Table 11.2 Keywords to define how a system is to be mounted

Keyword	Effect
rw	Read and write allowed
ro	Read only allowed
suid	Set user-identification allowed (see section 11.8.1)
nosuid	Set user-identification not allowed (see section 11.8.1)
noauto	Do not mount this file-system automatically (used when the **-a** option is specified).

Several keywords can be used in a single command, provided each one is separated by a comma. The default value for all mounted file-systems is **rw, suid**. Keywords must be specified following the **-o** option.

Another option, **-v**, also exists on many systems. It specifies that a file-system should be mounted in verbose mode, which means that UNIX will inform users of the file-system that is currently being mounted.

When used without any parameters, **mount** prints all the file-systems that are currently mounted.

Examples

Example 1

```
$ mount -a
```

This command makes **mount** attempt to connect all the file-systems described in **/etc/fstab** on to the main root file-system. The word 'attempt' is used because file-systems that are mounted from different devices may fail simply because a disk-drive is not ready or missing etc.; an error message will inform the user of any file-systems which could not be mounted.

Example 2

```
$ mount /dev/dk02 /usr
```

This command forces a direct mount by specifying the name of the device where the file-system is located, and the directory (**/usr**) to which it is to be joined. Assuming that disk-device **/dev/dk02** is a removable disk that stores the three directory files **sales**, **profits**, and **debts** (and any files that are contained within these three directories) and that the **/usr** directory contains no files, then following the mount operation the user can access the files **/usr/sales**, **/usr/profits** and **/usr/debts**, whereas previously the only accessible directory was **/usr** itself, and that was empty. This type of mount operation is known as a *local* mount operation.

Example 3

```
$ mount -p > /etc/fstab
```

This command uses the **-p** option to save the current mount state by redirecting it into the file **/etc/fstab**. The existing **/etc/fstab** will be overwritten, as it should be otherwise multiple entries would be stored in the **fstab** file which would cause considerable confusion (e.g. a file-system may try to be mounted twice). Do not use this command unless you wish to overwrite the **fstab** file.

Example 4

```
$ mount -o ro /dev/dk02 /
```

This command uses the **-o** option to mount a local disk and connect the file-system contained on it to the root-file system (/). The file-system (i.e. the files within it) may only be read, and not written to, therefore no information will be allowed to be saved within this file-system (on disk **dk02**).

A disk that is physically write-protected by the user (i.e. by using a write-protect tab) must be mounted using the read-only option if this type of command is used, otherwise problems may arise when the system tries to write access times etc. to the disk (whether or not any explicit write operation is attempted). Alternatively the **-r** option, which accomplishes the same as a **-o ro** option (and is a shorthand notation to mount read-only disks) can be used in this situation.

Using suid and nosuid

These use of the **suid** and **nosuid** settings will depend on your security consciousness. When a file-system is mounted, the superuser can ensure that any **suid** programs (see Chapter 12 – UNIX Security) are run with the **UID** of the user executing them. Executable files owned by **root** with their **suid** bits set are dangerous if execute-permission is accidentally given to another user group. The **nosuid** option therefore enforces this course of action by making files lose their **suid** characteristics. The **suid** option should be used if it is believed that a file-system contains loosely protected **suid** programs i.e. the use of **suid** files will be enforced.

Quota Checking

Quota checking can also be used in the case of **4.3** type file-systems (see section 11.7) by using the **quota** and **noquota** keywords with the **-o** option when using the **mount** command. For example:

```
$ mount -o quota,rw /dev/dk02 /
```

This command mounts a local disk with read and write operations and quota checking enabled. The listing overleaf illustrates a typical display when the mount command is used without any arguments.

```
$ mount
Filesystem kbytes  used   avail  capacity  Mounted on
/dev/dk01  20015   17895    118  99%       /
/dev/dk02  95583   73166  12858  85%       /usr
/dev/dk03  71711   53534  11005  83%       /staff
/dev/dk05  49759   36747   8036  82%       /data
```

This listing shows the number of kilobytes originally allocated to the file-system; the number of kilobytes that have been used, and the number still available (which, when added together equal 90% of the original allocation); and the capacity used, shown as a percentage. The space available and the capacity are both useful indicators to watch when disk-space in a file-system is running low. As the capacity nears 100%, so the available disk- space becomes less and less. In the example it can be seen that the file-system **/dev/dk01** is the root file-system and it has nearly used up all of its allocated disk space, the capacity level being 99%.

11.8.1.3 umount

The **umount** command (unmount a file-system) is used to remove a named file-system on from the root file-system. The syntax of the command is:

umount [options] [host-device]

Note that only a host-device, along with any options, is specified and the file-system name is omitted. The two most common options for this command are now described. The **-a** option is used to unmount all the currently mounted file-systems; these are held in the **/etc/mtab** file (discussed in the next section) so unmounting will remove them from this file. The second most common option is **-v**, the verbose option, which causes **umount** to print a diagnostic message indicating the file-system(s) that have been unmounted from the system (as each unmount operation takes place).

Examples

Example 1

```
$ umount /dev/dk02
```

This command separates the file-system stored on the local disk-device **dk02** from the root file-system. If applied to the second example in section 11.8.1. the file-system attached to **/usr** (the directories **sales**, **profits** and **debts**) would all disappear from the root file-system.

Example 2

```
$ umount -a
```

This command attempts to unmount all of the file-systems specified in the **/etc/mtab** file (since **mtab** holds the names of all mounted file-systems – see next section).

The /etc/mtab file

The **/etc/mtab** file contains a list of all the mounted file-systems. The file is similar in structure to **/etc/fstab**, but whereas the **fstab** file indicates all the file-systems which have been created on the system, **mtab** only lists those which have been mounted. A typical **/etc/mtab** file is shown below:

```
/dev/dk0a /           4.3   rw,noquota  1  1
/dev/dk0b /tmp        4.3   rw,quota    1  3
/dev/dk1a /usr/local4.3   rw,noquota  1  2
```

This listing indicates that there are three file-systems currently mounted, as follows:

i) the root file-system (/), which is always mounted by the system,

ii) the **/tmp** file-system, and lastly

iii) the **/usr/local** file-system.

A comparison of the **fstab** and **mtab** files indicates which file-systems are not currently mounted.

Notes on mount and umount

Great care should be taken when mounting or unmounting a file-system. For example, unmounting a file-system while it is still being used is a potential disaster, and should obviously be avoided. Mounting a file-system that contains nothing but garbage could possibly crash the entire system, while file-systems that are listed in the **/etc/fstab** file should never contain linked files, because this may confuse the mount program during the mounting process. If a directory on which a file-system is to be mounted is itself a symbolic link, then the file-system will not be mounted on this directory where the link is specified, but on the directory to which the link refers. Linked files can also lead to mistakes in disk-usage amounts in some cases.

11.9 System configuration

The following sections discuss the most common configuration procedures which can be undertaken by someone in an administrative capacity. Superuser privileges are needed for all of these configuration activities.

11.9.1 The /etc/rc and /etc/rc.local files

The **/etc/rc** and **/etc/rc.local** files contain instructions that are carried out at bootstrapping time when the system is first started. The **/etc/rc.local** file stores instructions that are site specific. It is started from within the main **/etc/rc** file. The main duties of the **/etc/rc** file normally include:

❑ Starting up swap partition devices

❑ Starting daemon (background) processes

❑ Mounting file-systems

❑ Enabling system accounting routines etc

❑ Performing clean up tasks.

Since the **rc** and **rc.local** files are executable, the file(s) on your system may include other commands which have not yet been explained. these commands and constructs are explained in Chapter 13 on Shell Programming. The administrator can add whatever shell commands are required into the **rc** files, although commands which are site specific, and which have been personally added by the administrator should be placed in **rc.local.** For example, you may wish to mount a personal file-system when the system is initially started, or you may wish to exclude certain file-systems at boot time.

Any of the commands which have already been discussed in the previous sections, such as quota checking and file-system mounting and unmounting can all be included in the **rc** or **rc.local** files, as can any shell commands that are valid under UNIX. Any invalid commands will simply be ignored by the system when they are read from the file.

The best way to test any new commands added to either of the files is to reboot the system. This can either be done by performing a hard reboot i.e. by turning the system off and on again (which I do not advise without first performing a proper shutdown procedure – see section 11.15), or by performing a soft reboot entering the command **reboot**, which is discussed in section 11.14. A typical **/etc/rc** file is shown here:

```
# /etc/rc file - executed once every boot time.
echo "Staring /etc/rc ..."
HOME=/;export HOME
PATH=/bin:/etc; export PATH
# Mount file-systems
echo "Mounting file systems ..."
/etc/mount -av
echo "Starting standard daemons ..."
/etc/update
/etc/cron
echo " "
echo "Making swap partitions active ..."
/etc/swapon -a
# Invoke local rc.local file
sh /etc/rc.local
# Clean-up tasks
echo "Deleting any files in /tmp ..."
/bin/rm /tmp/*
# Exiting rc
echo "Exiting /etc/rc ..."
date
```

This is a fairly small **/etc/rc** file. First it sets the **$HOME** and **$PATH** variables, and exports them to the outside world. All the file-systems in **/etc/fstab** are then mounted using the **-a** option, which mounts all the named file-systems, and the -v option which enables the verbose mode so that a series of diagnostic messages will appear after every file-system is mounted. This is useful, since any problems will be immediately reported. Mount will update **/etc/mtab** showing all the successfully mounted file-systems.

The standard *daemons* (background processes) are then started. The most common is probably **cron**, the clock daemon that executes events to occur at regular intervals (see section 11.11.1). The update daemon is used on some systems to ensure that the superblock is updated correctly (see Chapter 6 on the Physical File Structure of UNIX).

The command **swapon -a** enables all the swapping devices. These will also be specified in the **/etc/fstab** file. The **swapon** command has been used with the **-a** option in our example to ensure that *all* swap partitions are activated, and not just the default ones.

Specific devices could be mounted at this stage by including the necessary command(s) in the **rc** or **rc.local** file. The next command to be activated is the **/etc/rc.local** file. It includes any site-specific tasks or personal commands that may need to be executed e.g. starting local daemons, reporting disk-usage etc. Many administrators leave the **rc.local** file empty and only use the **/etc/rc** file. A shell is spawned for the execution of the **/etc/rc.local** file, and when any commands that may be in the **rc.local** file have been executed, the system returns control back to **/etc/rc** (the calling program) which goes on to execute the next instruction.

In the example, the next assignment is the clean-up tasks. It is common to find that nearly all **/etc/rc** files delete the contents of the scratch directory **/tmp** (the temporary directory). The option **-r** should *not* be used here because this would also delete the **/tmp** directory entry itself (not a wise thing to do because the system expects it to be there).

The final command in the **/etc/rc** file is **date** which simply prints the current date and time. Note the generous use of comments (#) throughout the file; these are invaluable, especially if a certain command is complex and needs a bit of explaining. Comments also assist other users who may need to amend these files in the future. Also note the many echo statements that have been used throughout the file, which chart the progress of the execution of the file. These commands help personalise the **/etc/rc** file, and reduce its otherwise unexciting nature. It is also helpful to put an **echo** statement, with a simple message, at the start and end of the **/etc/rc** file so that its entry and exit points can be monitored.

It is emphasised that invoking commands such as **mount** etc. with their verbose options enabled (i.e. **-v** options set), although not essential, nevertheless can provide an invaluable source of system generated feedback (let the system do the work for you). The more complex **/etc/rc** files are made up of shell programming constructs that can, for example, cause the failure of one particular command to trigger the adoption a certain course of action. A complex question and answer session could even be set up allowing the selection of certain options i.e. asking which file-system is to be mounted, or whether or not the swapping partitions are to be active etc.

Programming constructs that can be used in the **/etc/rc** file are discussed in Chapter 13 on Shell Programming.

The bootstrapping procedure

At this point it may be worthwhile to explain the bootup procedure, and what is involved. When the system is switched on (known as a hard or cold boot), it starts four UNIX utilities in sequence. These utilities change the single-user system to a multi-user system, thus allowing other users to log in at their own terminals.

The first utility executed by UNIX is known as **init** and it initialises the system (hence the name), preparing it to accept user logins. **Init** is relevant to the previous section, since it reads the **/etc/rc** file, and executes it. Another file, **/etc/inittab** (initialisation table), is also read in and this contains certain instructions that an administrator can alter to allow specific application-processing to take place at boot time.

A number of **init** states occur when **init** is executed. Most systems support only two states: the single-user state, and the multi-user state. The single-user state is used for system maintenance (normally undertaken on the system console). When the system is booted it may be possible for the user to undertake administrative tasks with a superuser shell. This facility normally requires a password to be supplied, although some systems do not (a potential security loophole). Additional **init** states can be configured (by modifying the **/etc/inittab** file) so that only parts of the system can run within certain times of the day etc.

When the single-user mode is exited (or the option to enable single-user mode is not taken) the system attempts to go multi-user. This again involves the **init** utility which spawns an individual *child* process (the *parent* being **init** itself) for each terminal. Each of these child processes then executes another utility called **getty**. This utility displays the familiar **login:** prompt and waits for a user to supply a username and password. **Getty** then executes the **login** utility which verifies the user's username and password against the **/etc/passwd** file, and then executes a shell for this user. Possible shells include **/bin/sh** – the Bourne Shell, and **/bin/csh** – the C-Shell. This shell will remain active until the user logs out, whereupon **init** is called to allow another user to log in. Figure 11.10 illustrates these steps diagrammatically.

More notes on init at bootup time

The **init** utility is invoked from inside the operating system as the last step in the bootstrapping procedure. Some systems may run a file called **/etc/rc.boot** which is similar to **/etc/rc** in that it contains a series of shell commands. The commands in **rc.boot** normally check the file-system prior to the system being brought in multi-user mode following the execution of **/etc/rc** and **/etc/rc.local**.

Whenever a single-user shell is created the **init** program demands a superuser password, and the system is running as a secure system (depending on the system configuration – UNIX gurus can consult the 'issecure' page in their UNIX manual). This stops normal users from logging in and therefore circumventing system security. Logging out of this shell makes the system go multi-user. The option of a single-user shell allows the administrator to undertake administrative activities before the system is made available to the other users of the system.

The **/etc/ttytab** file is also read by the **init** utility. This file contains the necessary instructions to carry out a new process, most commonly to execute the **getty** program. Each **init** process will wait for its spawned shell to terminate (as in the case of a user logging out), whereupon it will remove the user's entry from the **utmp** file (which records the names of all the currently logged in users), and then updates the **wtmp** file (which records the details of all users who have logged in).

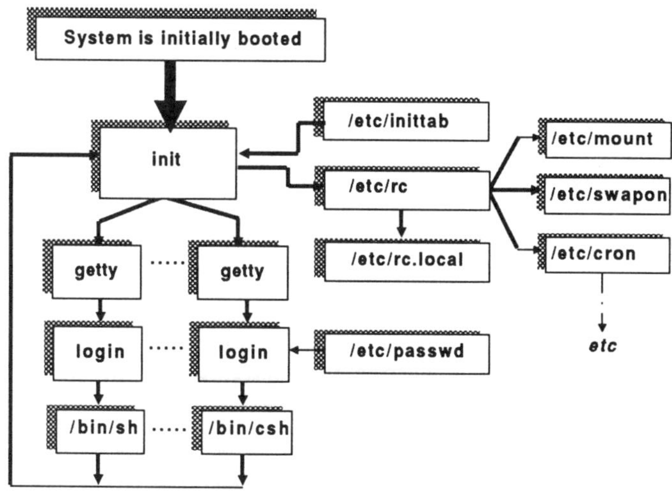

Figure 11.10 UNIX bootup sequence

The /etc/ttys file

The **/etc/ttys** file merits explanation at this stage. This file is examined at the last stage of the **init** procedure (before **getty** is invoked). The file basically contains a list of terminal names each occupying one line of the file. The file allows the system to identify which procedure is to be invoked for each person using a particular terminal. Individual entries in the **/etc/ttys** file consist of a two-digit number immediately followed by the name of a terminal connected to the system, such as **tty03**. A typical entry could be:

```
14tty03
```

The first number (character 1) must be either one or zero. Zero (0) indicates that **init** should take no action on this terminal, thus users will not be able to use it for logging in; this action is reversed when this first digit is one (1) (i.e. **init** can use the terminal for users to log in). The second character (in our example, 4), provides information about the baud rate; the digit is interpreted by the system, and the actual value is system-dependent. On some System V and Berkeley UNIX systems, the digit represents the actual baud rate of the terminal.

Init is one of the most critical processes on the whole system, and if killed, the system will normally reboot itself automatically. If the **init** program cannot be located at bootstrapping time, the system will print an error message on the system console, and then panic!

11.9.2 Editing the /etc/rc file

Since the **/etc/rc** and **/etc/rc.local** files are stored in a plain ASCII format, they can be edited with any of the UNIX line editors, such as **ex** or **ed**, or with a visual editor such as **vi**. You can simply add in the commands that you require at the necessary point in the file. It is a good idea to try out the command(s) beforehand to see that they actually work before putting them into the **rc** or **rc.local** files.

11.10 Daemons

Daemons are processes that are normally executed in the background (although not specifically using the **&** technique). They perform a variety of tasks, such as looking after printers and executing commands at certain times of the day etc. A number of daemons are described in this section, starting with **cron** the clock daemon. Such daemons are nearly always started from the **/etc/rc** or **/etc/rc.local** files.

11.10.1 Cron

Cron executes commands at a specified dates and times according to the instructions in the files **/usr/lib/crontab** and **/usr/lib/crontab.local** (used for local events). These names are system specific, so you will need to check your system to find out the names used. Each entry in the **crontab** file is contained on a single line and consists of seven fields. The first five fields are integer patterns that specify, in order:

❑ Minute (0-59)

❑ Hour (0-23)

❑ Day of month (1-31)

❑ Month of the year (1-12)

❑ Day of the week (1-7, where 1 is Monday)

Each of these patterns may also include:

❑ Two numbers (separated by a hyphen), indicating an inclusive range of values to be used.

❑ A list of numbers (separated by commas) indicating that any of the mentioned numbers are to be used.

❑ An asterisk (*), that indicates any valid value.

The sixth field contains the username of the person executing the actual command, which is included in field seven. Remember that the command to be executed could be an executable shell-script, which in turn may execute a series of other commands, so you are not necessarily limited to a single command.

The **cron** daemon examines the **crontab** (and **crontab.local** file) every minute so that time-specified events can be invoked. An example **crontab** file can be seen below; lines that begin with a hash (#) are comment lines. These can be useful for certain comments, such as the actual field values. Note that times are in a 24 hour format.

```
# Format:
# <Min> <Hours> <DOM> <Month> <DOW> <User> <command>
5 14 1 * * root /usr/adm/utils/cronscripts/monthly
0 22 * * * root /usr/adm/utils/cronscripts/latenight
0 7 * * 1 root /usr/adm/utils/cronscripts/weekly
5 10 * * 1-5 root /usr/adm/utils/cronscripts/weekday
30 14 * * 1-3 root /etc/mount -v /dev/dk06 /usr/games
30 16 * * 1-3 root /etc/umount /dev/dk06
```

This **crontab** file translates into the times, dates and actions shown in Table 11.3.

Table 11.3 Translation of example crontab file

Time	Day of the Month	Month	Day of the week	Command(s)
2.05 pm	1st	Jan-Dec	1 to 7	Monthly commands
22.00 pm	all	Jan-Dec	1 to 7	Nightly commands
7.00 am	all	Jan-Dec	1	Weekly commands
10.05 am	all	Jan-Dec	1 to 5	Weekday commands
2.30 pm	all	Jan-Dec	1 to 3	Mount the games directory
4.30 pm	all	Jan-Dec	1 to 3	Unmount the games directory

This example **crontab** file executes a series of files stored in the **/usr/adm/utils/cronscripts** directory. This directory, which we stress is system specific, contains a series of executable shell scripts that hold the necessary instructions to be carried out. Such an arrangement allows the use of **cron** to be made more flexible when used frequently, since certain times periods are confined to a series of individual files.

Problems with dates

There are always the inevitable problems with dates when using the **crontab** facility. If you want a certain command to be activated at the end of a month, do not enter 31 as the maximum value, since **cron** will leave out all months which do not have 31 days, such as February etc. The solution to this particular problem is to perform the operation on the first day of the month with an entry such as:

```
5 14 1 * * root /usr/adm/utils/cronscripts/monthly
```

A partial solution to this problem is to include a day of month entry such as 28,30,31.

This solution may not be preferred since some commands will be performed three times in months that have 31 days, and twice for months that have 30.

11.10.2 Update

Update is a daemon found as part of the Berkeley tool set. It is program that periodically updates the system's superblock area. It issues a command called **sync** approximately every 30 seconds. This is done to keep the file-system up-to-date in case a system breakdown occurs. The **update** command should not be executed directly, and is most commonly started as a daemon from the **/etc/rc** file. However, the **sync** command can be entered directly, and it is common for some systems to have an **/etc/passwd** entry of:

```
sync::1:1::/:/bin/sync
```

This entry will allow the **sync** program to be executed by typing the username **sync** at the **login:** prompt. It means that the executable file **/bin/sync** has replaced the normal login shell. No user can thus log in under such a username, but it allows the command to be run simply by issuing its name. However, it should be mentioned that *any* user can run this command, since it is not executed upon logging in, but is executed when a user issues the particular-user name/command (note the absence of a password in the second field). There are no protection settings in force at this stage either.

This technique is also commonly employed with commands such as **who** and **finger** to allow any user to see the current system user-load without having to actually log in to the system.

11.10.3 Lpd

Lpd is the line-printer daemon. It controls the handling of print requests from users. It is nearly always invoked from the **/etc/rc** file whereupon it listens for such requests. Any terminated print requests are also normally handled by **lpd**. The **spool** directory for print jobs is commonly the **/usr/spool** directory on many UNIX systems.

A file called **lock** is placed in the **spool** directory and is used to prevent multiple daemons from becoming active simultaneously. After the daemon has set the necessary **lock** file, it scans a series of configuration files. These files specify the necessary actions to be carried out i.e. for a file to be printed out etc. These printer configuration files are commonly stored in the directory **/usr/spool/lpd**.

11.10.4 Miscellaneous daemons

Many UNIX systems have their own daemon processes that take care of system operations, such as network communications. Many other daemons exist, the majority of which are specific to different UNIX systems. Daemons can be identified using the **ps** (processor status command), which is examined in more detail in Chapter 12 on UNIX Security.

11.11 Backing up a UNIX system

Now we come to one of the most important administrative tasks, backing up the files on a UNIX system. Backups are taken as a preventative measure against the loss of information through system breakdown, accidental erasure or corruption of data.

A backup copy of a file is simply an exact copy of that file. A backup can even be a copy of a complete file-system, or at least part of it. An archive copy is used to represent the state of all or part of the system at a given time in the past, and are used to restore a system to a previous state. The key point to remember is that backup copies are not really intended to capture the working state of the system at a specific time, they are taken so that data can be restored up to the time that the backup was taken.

11.11.1 When to backup your files

If your system is used extensively, for record keeping, for example, it is paramount that backup copies are taken every day, preferably just before the system is shut-down, so that system performance does not suffer during peak hours.

One procedure that seems to be a good preventative measure against the loss of information involves the backup of each day's work on one storage media item (e.g. a tape or disk). This will result in a large number of backups, one for each day of the working week, each occupying a separate disk or tape etc. This way the system is regularly backed up, allowing the system to be restored for any day in the previous week (a type of mini-archive, although the latest copy will be, in the true sense, a real backup copy).

A true archive copy could be taken at the end of each month, to ensure that the state of the system during any previous month existed for reference purposes. If your system needs to be audited regularly, a more frequent archive copy may need to be taken i.e. fortnightly etc.

Of course, taking so many backup and archive copies may become a problem due to the sheer number of disks or tapes that are needed, and which then have to be stored. One answer to this problem is to have a strict policy to delete the backups after a defined period. Another important point to consider is the storage of backup and archive copies offsite. This approach is a commonly used precaution against the irreplaceable loss of data through fire or other catastrophe.

The UNIX system is rich in backup and archive facilities. The commands to be examined in the next few sections include **dump**, **restor** and **tar**. All of these commands originated in Version 7 UNIX, and are still used in the most modern UNIX systems, notwithstanding a few enhancements.

The dump command

Dump is one of a pair of commands that is used to backup (or 'dump') files from a system disk to portable storage media such as floppy disk or tape cartridges etc. Data backed up using the **dump** command can be restored to the system (the whole purpose of taking such a dump) using the **restor** command (described in the next section).

When using the **dump** utility it is necessary to understand the concept of *dump-levels* which allow incremental backups to be taken. Ten dump levels (0-9) exist in nearly all implementations of the **dump** utility, each of which defines the extent of the dump being taken.

At level 0 the entire file-system is dumped. The use of **dump** then becomes quite complex if any other level is specified. The extent of any dump operation specified with a level number greater than 0 is dependent on the level of any previous dumps.

Where previous dumps have a level of zero or a level greater than that specified for the current dump, only those file which have altered since the latest level zero dump operation will be copied. If a dump operation is carried out in which the level number is the same as the most recent dump operation, or which is higher than the previous one, then only the files which have altered since the last dump at the same level will be duplicated. For example, if we started by making a dump at level zero, the whole file-system would be copied accordingly. To restore the system we would now have to restore from this level 0 copy. If our next dump was at a higher level, say at level 5, dump will copy only the files which have changed since the previous level 0 dump (whenever that was). Restoring the system will now involve the use of two backup disks or tapes etc (one for the level zero and one for the level 5 dump). If we now made a dump at level 6, dump will only process files that are have altered since the last level 5 dump. Three disks or tapes will thus have to be used to restore the entire system (the ones that hold the level 0, level 5 and level 6 dumps). Careful use of the **dump** command ensures that a minimum amount of disks have to be used to restore the system. For example, we previously mentioned that three disks (or tapes) would be needed to restore the system when a level 6 dump was invoked. If we missed out the level 6 dump, but used a level 4 dump, only the files since the last level 0 dump will be processed. This in fact means that only two disks or tapes would have to be used to carry out a complete system restoration.

Dumping in such a way can be done on a day-to-day basis. It is common practice for an administrator to take a complete file- system backup (a level 0 dump) at the end of each working week. During the period of the following week, a dump could be taken at level 4 (on the first day of the week, Monday), decreasing each following day by one dump level i.e. Tuesday would be a level 3 dump, Wednesday a level 2 dump, and Thursday a level 1 dump. By Friday we will arrive back at a level 0 dump (an entire file-system dump).

As mentioned, two dumps are only needed in order to restore the entire file-system. Dumping files is a time-consuming process, especially if a large file-system is being backed up and a large number of files are being copied. An alternative method to that above is to **dump** all the files at the same level as the previous day. This method ensures that only the most recent file alterations will be taken account of, therefore reducing the amount of files to be dumped. Restoration though is a problem with this method. Such a dumping method normally involves a large number of restoration operations.

The syntax of the dump command is:

dump [dump-level] [options] [file-system]

The **dump** command has many options. The ones which are described in this section include **s<amount>**, **u**, and **f <device>** (note the absence of any hyphens in front of the options).

If you are using a tape cartridge, the **s**' option is used to set the length of the tape (in feet). The actual amount is placed directly after the **s** option. The **dump** command expects a default value for the tape length (system specific). If the default amount is not appropriate, the **s** option must be used. The **u** option is used to append a record to a file that records each dump operation. The **/etc/ddate** file is commonly used to store these records.

The **f <device>** option is used to force a dump to a non-default device. The name of the device follows **f** option (see the example below). Default dump devices are specific to individual UNIX systems. A typical **dump** command could therefore take the form:

```
$ dump 4f /dev/crt04 /dev/dk05
```

This command makes a level 4 dump of the file-system that is stored on the disk-device **/dev/dk05**. The dump will be written to the tape cartridge device **/dev/crt04**, a removable data storage media item. The **f** option forces the dump to the non-default device – **/dev/crt04**, a removable tape cartridge device.

The restor utility

The **restor** command, as the name suggests, is used to restore data from a disk or tape etc. on to a system disk. The syntax of the command is:

restor [options] [device] [filename]

The most common options are **x** and **r** which instruct **restor** to restore single and multiple files respectively. The **f <$device>** option allows restorations to be carried out on to non-default devices.

Examples

Example 1

A typical command could be:

```
$ restor r /dev/dk05
```

This command restores multiple files (note the **r** option) from the system's default device (which is not specified literally in the command) on to the disk-device **/dev/dk05**. If you do not know which is your system's default device, you can specify the name of the device literally (see the next example).

Example 2

If a default device is not being used to restore information, the device to which information is to be restored from must be specified using the **f** option (followed by the name of the device). A typical command would thus be:

```
$ restor rf /dev/crt04 /dev/dk05
```

This command forces a new restoration device using the **f** option followed by the device name concerned. The **r** option specifies that multiples files i.e. a complete or partial restoration is to take place. The information will be restored to the (hypothetical) system-disk **/dev/dk05**.

Example 3

The optional **[filename]** argument allows single files (using the **x** option) to be restored, for example:

```
$ restor x /usr/dirl/filel
```

This command assumes that the system's default restoration device is to be used. The **f** option and device name should be used to force a non-default device. Note that the full pathname of the file in this example is to be restored. Assuming that the directory **/usr** is in fact part of the root file-system (and that the **/dir1** directory was mounted under the **/usr** directory) this particular file will referred to as **/dir1/file1** and not the filename **/usr/dir1/file1**.

The dumpdir utility

Another utility that may be useful is called **dumpdir**. It is used to list the named of dumped files. It can be used to verify the names of all the files on a particular device before a restoration takes place.

The tar utility

The **tar** command restores and saves multiple files on a single storage media item and although **tar** stands for tape archive, it can also be used with disk media. The **tar** command's operation is controlled through the use of its many options. The actual copies of files cannot be controlled on an incremental basis through dump levels as with the **dump** command, but **tar** is useful since it backs up files according to their position in the file-system hierarchy. It traces a through a directory, and any files within it, and makes a copy of either the entire, or part of, the file-system.

Tar can also be used to restore the archived information. This is done using a specific restore option. The syntax of the **tar** command is:

tar [key [options]] [file ...]

Only one key can be specified, and this determines how **tar** operates – whether to make copies of files, or extract existing files etc. The most common keys used are listed, with their functions, in Table 11.4.

Table 11.4 Keys used with tar

Key	Function
c	Creates a new tape or disk.
r	Appends files to the end of a tape or disk.
t	Lists the names of files each time they occur on a tape or disk. If filename arguments after the **t** option are not specified all names are listed by default.
u	Adds the named files from the tape or disk.
x	Extracts the named files from the tape. If filename arguments are not given following the **x** option, the entire tape or disk is restored.

Common options used with **tar** are listed in Table 11.5.

Table 11.5 Options used with tar

Option	Action
f	This option causes **tar** to force the backup on to a different device (other than the default device). The default device for use with tar is **/dev/rmt?** or **/dev/mt?** (for example **/dev/rmt1** or **/dev/mt3** etc). If a single hyphen is given as a name, **tar** reads the standard input.
h	This makes **tar** follow symbolic links just as if they were normal files or directories.
l	This option is used sometimes in conjunction with the **h** option. It causes **tar** to print a series of error messages for linked files that could not be processed.
m	This option is sometimes used with the **x** key (see Table 11.4). It specifies that the modification times of files will simply be the time the files were extracted from a tape or disk. When files are being moved from system to system this option should be used.
p	When **tar** restores files it normally abides by the protection settings set by the current **umask** setting. The **p** option makes **tar** restore files to their original modes ignoring the current **umask** setting.
v	This option causes **tar** to print the name of the current file being processed, preceded by a key (as listed in Table 11.4). If this option is specified with the **t** key the protection modes of the file are displayed on some systems. This option is also known as the *verbose* mode of **tar**, and allows feedback to be given by the program.
w	This option specifies that the interactive mode of the **tar** utility should be invoked. In this mode **tar** waits for a keypress when processing a file (according to the options that **tar** has been invoked with). Pressing the letter 'Y' results in **tar** processing the file.

It should be mentioned that the **tar** utility comes in many forms and that some of the options described here may be unavailable on your particular system. Typing **tar** on its own may make it tell you the options that are valid. If not, consult your own system documentation. Some examples of **tar** in use are illustrated below along with simple explanations.

Examples

Example 1

```
$ tar cf /dev/fp4 /usr/adm/misc
```

This command uses the **c** key with the **f** option (note the absence of any hyphens before the options here). The **c** key stipulates that **tar** is to create a new backup tape/disk thus overwriting any files on this storage device. The disk being used is not the default device, because the **f** (force a new device) option has been given on the command line. When the **f** option is given, it must be followed by the name of the new device, in this case, **/dev/fp4** (a floppy disk-drive).

The files in directory **/usr/adm/misc** will be copied on to the floppy disk (**/dev/fp4**) without changing the hierarchic structure currently in place, so any directories in the **/usr/adm/misc** directory will also be copied onto the disk.

Example 2

To restore the files from the floppy disk in the previous example, you could issue the command:

```
$ tar xf /dev/fp4 /usr/adm/misc
```

Here the fully-qualified pathname is specified to restore the file(s) to their previous location in the file-system.

Example 3

If the pathname specified for the restoration directory is not fully-qualified, then the **tar** utility simply restores files to the current working directory. For example:

```
$ tar xf /dev/fp4 file1
```

This command restores the file **file1** into the current working directory. To restore the file to the correct location in the file-system, it is necessary therefore to change the current working directory (using **cd**) to the correct directory before such a command is issued.

Example 4

```
$ tar c /usr
```

This command specifies that a new tape or disk is to be prepared (erasing any previous files on this tape or disk), and that the files in and below the **/usr** directory are to be copied to the default storage device.

Example 5

```
$ tar xvmf /dev/fp3 /usr/adm
/usr/adm/file1
/usr/adm/file2
/usr/adm/dir1
/usr/adm/dir1/file1
/usr/adm/dir1/file2
. . . .
. . . .
```

This command uses the key **x** to extract files from a device (here the non-default device **/dev/fp3** using the **f** option). The files on this disk will be extracted up to the **/usr/adm** directory. The **v** option turns on the verbose mode of **tar**, making it show the name of each file in turn as it processes them (as shown in the example). The **m** option ensures that all the extracted files have their modification times and dates updated to reflect this latest modification – their extraction.

Example 6

The **tar** command uses rather a strange syntax. From the initial syntax description it can be seen that the key letter, option letters and filename arguments are all optional. Without the **[file ...]** argument, the **tar** command can be told to examine a device (such as a tape or disk device) to report on a particular storage media item.

```
$ tar tv
rw-rw-r-- 20/5 1911 Feb 5 13:01 1990 file1
rw-rw-r-- 20/5 6911 Feb 9 13:34 1990 file2
```

The command in this example stipulates that **tar** should examine the default device (note the absence of any device name) and report on all the files on that disk or tape etc. Here, **tar** lists the filenames (in accordance with the **t** key letter), along with each files permission settings and modification times (such additional information is provided by the **v** option).

11.12 Checking file-systems – fsck

During bootstrapping it is a common procedure for the system to check a number of file-systems for any inconsistencies that may have occurred in them. These inconsistencies are caused in many ways, including power-loss while the system is up and running, or a rushed shutdown procedure

A utility named **fsck** (file-system check) is used to detect and correct any such inconsistencies. You need to know how the file-system is physically constructed before you can understand the inconsistencies that can occur, therefore you are referred to Chapters 5 and 6 which cover the physical file-system of UNIX.

Fsck repairs a specified set of file-systems or, by default, those mentioned in **/etc/fstab** (the file-system table file). It is commonly invoked from the **/etc/rc** file (see section 11.9.1) when an automatic reboot is in operation. This happens in some systems when power loss occurs, or when a critical process such as **init** is killed off. When **fsck** is invoked it makes a series of passes through each file-system as defined in the **/etc/fstab** file (see section 11.7.3 for more details on the internal structure of the **/etc/fstab** file). The root file-system is normally checked on pass 1; other root file-system partitions are checked on pass 2, and other small file-systems are checked on separate passes (pass numbers 3 and 4). Pass number 5 is commonly used to check larger file-systems. A pass number of zero (0) in the **/etc/fstab** file prevents **fsck** from checking that particular file-system. Similarly, file-systems that do not have **rw, ro** or **rq** mount permission settings are not checked either (since they are not recognised as having a valid permission access setting). The syntax of the **fsck** utility is:

```
fsck [option] [file-system ...]
```

A common list of options are given below. It must be stressed though, that some of these options are system specific, and you should consult your system documentation. Table 11.6 gives the options available for the Berkeley version of **fsck**:

Table 11.6 Options used with fsak (Berkeley version)

Option	Effect
-n	Assume a *no* response to any questions that **fsck** may ask the user.
-p	Repairs file-systems with those inconsistencies mentioned in section 11.12.1. Normally used in the **/etc/rc** files to automatically repair such systems.
-y	Assume a *yes* response to any questions that **fsck** may ask the user.

11.12.1 File-system Inconsistencies

There are only a few minor inconsistencies that normally can occur (except when software or hardware failures take place), which include:

- ❑ Unreferenced i-nodes
- ❑ Missing blocks in the free-list
- ❑ Link counts in the i-nodes are too large
- ❑ Blocks in the free-list are also in individual files
- ❑ Counts in the superblock are incorrect.

These are the only inconsistencies that can be corrected by most versions of the **fsck** utility when the **-p** option is used on the command line. If one of the inconsistencies listed above is not recognised, then **fsck** aborts its operation. When each file-system inconsistency is found and corrected, **fsck** lists the name of the relevant file-system with a message indicating the nature of the inconsistency.

After **fsck** has completed the correction of an entire file-system, it prints the number of files found, along with the number of available blocks, in that particular file-system. If the **-p** option is not used, **fsck** interactively repairs the file-systems specified on the command line, or those included in the **/etc/fstab** file (when no particular file-system name is nominated).

When **fsck** finds an inconsistency is found in the file-system, the system prompts the user for a *yes/no* response to carry out the necessary course of action to attempt to repair the inconsistency (when **-p** has not been used). Here the **-y** and **-n** options are useful, freeing the user from entering the necessary responses manually. Only *yes* or *no* is available as an answer, and once either of these option has been specified by the user it will remain in effect for the duration of the command.

If the user, who invoked **fsck** from the command line, does not have write permission on the specified file-system, the system will not normally allow *yes* answers (to correct inconsistencies in the file-system) to be entered, and will default to a **-n** action. It is always wise, therefore, to log in as **root** when running **fsck** to repair such file-systems.

A more complete list of inconsistency checks that can be found and repaired by **fsck** include:

- ❑ Blocks claimed by more than one i-node or the free-list
- ❑ Blocks claimed by an i-node or the free-list that lie outside the boundary of the file-system
- ❑ Incorrect link counts in a file-system
- ❑ Bad i-node formats
- ❑ Blocks that are not accounted for
- ❑ File(s) that point to unallocated i-nodes
- ❑ I-node numbers that are out of range
- ❑ More blocks for i-nodes than actually exist in the file-system being checked
- ❑ Bad free-list block format
- ❑ Total free block and/or free i-node count errors.

Fsck also checks for *orphan* files, those files which are allocated but are unreferenced within the system. When found, these files are placed in the directory called **lost+found**, if the **-y** option is set or the operator chooses *yes* when operating in interactive mode.

11.12.2 The lost+found directory

If the link count in a particular i-node is not zero, but no links were found by **fsck**, it is possible that a directory entry has been located for a file that is unrelated to that particular i-node. Such an entry (known as an orphan file) is placed, via a special link, to the directory **/lost+found**. This directory is provided to be used with the **fsck** utility, and it should not normally be created by simply issuing a **mkdir** command (unless no provision for its creation has been provided – see section 11.12.3). Some systems install an executable shell-script called **mklost+found** which should be run to create the directory.

The reason why the **lost+found** directory should not normally be created using **mkdir** is because of allocating the size of the directory. The **lost+found** directory must be large enough to hold any orphan entries that are to be placed in it by the **fsck** utility. When a directory is initially created using the **mkdir** command, the size of the directory is simply the entry itself and when files are created inside it, the directory expands accordingly (as links to the other files within the directory are created, and the files themselves take up disk-space). A parent directory, such as **lost+found**, is significantly increased in size by having directory files created within it, but when any of these files are deleted, the parent directory remains the same size. The spaces allocated to the deleted files are sometimes referred to as 'empty slots'.

Utilities such as **mklost+found** carry out the process of making the **lost+found** directory with multiple directory entries within it, which are then removed leaving the parent directory sufficiently large in size so that it can accommodate orphan entries.

11.12.3 Making a lost+found directory

A procedure for making a **lost+found** directory without a utility such as **mklost+found** is possible, although very laborious. It involves making a directory file in the root directory named **lost+found** and then creating a series of files (such as a group of directory files), and then simply deleting them. You may not have to make a **lost+found** directory in some cases because the **mkfs** program carries out this task when a new file-system is created. The commands shown below show just what is involved when initially creating the **lost+found** directory manually:

```
$ cd /
$ mkdir lost+found
$ cd lost+found
$ mkdir dir1
$ mkdir dir2
. .
. .
$ mkdir dir12
$ mkdir dir13
$ mkdir dir14
$ mkdir dir15
$ rm dir??
```

As can be seen from the example, you can create the directory using **mkdir**, move into it using **cd**, and then create a series of directory files (here named **dir1 ... dir15**) using **mkdir** again. The files are then deleted using **rm**. Note the wildcard **dir??** which ensures only the files we have just created are deleted (assuming no existing files will be matched under the same name). The number of files that actually need to be created is debatable, although around 15 to 20 should be enough for most needs, remembering that the **lost+found** directory will only contain orphan files.

If **fsck** runs out of space when attempting to place an orphan file in the **lost+file** directory, the file may be irretrievably lost. It is recommended that the **lost+found** directory is emptied after **fsck** is run, any files that have been placed in it being moved to another location in the file-system, or deleted.

11.12.4 Fsck phases

When **fsck** is executed it undertakes a series of phases to check the file-systems concerned. **Fsck** accesses the actual disk-storage device when checking the necessary file-system, so superuser permission is needed to use **fsck**. A file named **/etc/checklist** exists on some UNIX systems, and is used by **fsck** to determine which devices to check. This file contains a list of all the mounted devices when the system started up. Some systems use the **/etc/fstab** for the same purpose.

When running **fsck**, it is advisable to make sure the system is running in single-user mode. This is partly why the system invokes **fsck** when it initially starts up (before going multi-user). **Fsck** runs best in a single-user environment because changes to the file-system while it is running will result in errors during its execution. This is because **fsck** checks the consistency of the file-system against the data that is currently held in it, and therefore such information must remain static while **fsck** is in use.

If **fsck** is being run in a multi-user environment, which will be necessary in some cases where it is impractical to perform an automatic reboot (see section 11.12.5), make sure the file-system is not being used for the period while **fsck** is in use.

This can be done by unmounting the necessary file-systems, or as mentioned previously, by placing the system in single-user mode, which is also necessary when checking the root file-system, because this can never be unmounted.

The five basic phases of the **fsck** program are now briefly examined:

Phase 1

Phase one involves a check of every i-node file in the file-systems specified. Remember that if no file-system name argument is specified, all those in the **/etc/fstab** file will be checked. On some systems the file **/etc/checklist** will be used for the default file-system check list. Each disk block that points to the various i-node entries will also be validated in this phase. If incorrect i-node data is found, an error message indicating **BAD INODE** may be given.

If a disk block is allocated to a particular i-node which has already been claimed by another, an error message such as **DUPLICATE INODE** or simply **DUP** may be displayed. The message **PARTIALLY ALLOCATED INODE** may also be displayed when **fsck** checks i-nodes. You will be able to clear such i-nodes later during the phase. Directory files are also scanned during phase 1. If any size inconsistencies are found in a particular directory file entry, the error message **DIRECTORY MISALIGNED** will be displayed.

The system will require you to clear any duplicate i-node entries by pressing the letter

Y (yes) to indicate the action should be carried out. If your system includes the **-y** option and it has been set, this will done automatically by the system. A procedure may allow you to save such information before it is cleared. Clearing such i-nodes can lead to a potential loss of data, and should be approached with care.

Serious error messages that may require **fsck** to be aborted include **FILE SIZE ERROR** or **MISALIGNED DIRECTORY**. These errors may be corrected at a later phase, although if not undertaken you will have to perform a manual repair. **Fsck** should tell you the names of the offending files, in which case a manual repair would involve the backing up of the files concerned, the deletion of the file, and then the re-invocation of **fsck**. If **fsck** does not report any error diagnostic messages the second time around, simply restore the files back to the necessary directories, if they are still needed by the system.

Phase 2

Phase 2 starts by checking the i-node entry for the root directory. If a discrepancy is found here a potential disaster looms, since a reinstallation of the entire UNIX system may be required. A message similar to **ROOT INODE ENTRY NOT DIRECTORY ... Fix? (y/n)** will be displayed.

If a positive reply is given now, then there is a greater chance of system errors at a later stage. In some cases it may be easier to reinstall the system's root directory area. During the second phase the user will also be given the choice of clearing the duplicate or corrupted i-node entries that were detected in the first phase.

Again, clear only such information if you have saved the data associated with these problem i-nodes through an earlier option. Answer **N** (no) in any other situation, unless of course the potential loss of data is inconsequential (assuming you are using the interactive **fsck** mode).

Phase 3

During phase 3 directory files in all the file-systems are scrutinised for erroneous values. Such directories are known as unreferenced directory files. If such a file is found **fsck** will ask you if you want to reconnect the file, which involves using the **lost+found** directory. Upon answering yes, the system makes a link between the unreferenced directory and the **lost+found** directory, where sufficient space must exist to ensure the necessary file(s) are properly saved (see section 11.12.2).

Phase 4

During phase 4 an i-node count takes place. The earlier phases accumulate i-node information which is used as the basis of a comparison here. In phase 1 the number of links for a particular i-node is set to the number of links for the actual physical file. This count is known as an 'i-node reference count'. During the next two phases the i-node reference count is decremented when a valid link for the relevant file is located. When phase 4 is invoked the i-node reference count should be zero. Thus an inconsistency is detected if a file does not have an i-node reference count of zero. If no links for a particular file were found, at the user's discretion (unless the **-y** option is being used), the file is reconnected and placed in the **lost+found** directory.

If the user chooses for the file not to be reconnected, a message similar to **CLEAR UNREFERENCED ENTRIES? (y/n)** will be displayed. Answering yes at this stage is advisable since you have already chosen not to reconnect the orphan file(s). If any further problems are found with i-node entries in the file-system, an error message similar to **FREE LIST INODE COUNT WRONG IN SUPERBLOCK. FIX? (y/n)** may be shown. Answering **Y** (yes) to this question is advisable.

Phase 5

In the last phase, **fsck** checks the free-list, the list of blocks that are free to be occupied with data. A message similar to **BAD FREE LIST. SALVAGE (y/n)** will be displayed if there are any duplicate blocks, or if there are discrepancies in any of the blocks in the free-list.

The answer given at this stage should again be **Y** (yes). **Fsck** will then reconstruct the free-list. No actual investigation of the file-system takes place upon answering yes to the salvage option, and the process is normally completed in a very short time.

11.12.5 Fsck – Rebooting the system

After stage five has been completed, **fsck** will reboot the system automatically. It is worth pointing out that the reboot takes place without a **sync** operation (see section 11.10.2). This is because the system has a different conception of the file-system from that which actually exists following the changes made by **fsck**, and issuing a **sync** command would write the old image of the previous file-system to disk, thus corrupting any changes. The system therefore reboots without operating a **sync** command, and this will be notified to the user during the final moments of the **fsck** process. If no changes were made (as in the case of a **-n** option) the system may take a different course of action.

11.13 Preen

The preen command may be available on your system. Basically it performs the same function as the **fsck -p** command although it can operate much faster. This is because **preen** operates **fsck** in a parallel manner. The syntax for preen is:

```
preen [options]
```

The most common options are **-o** and **-n**. The **-o** option makes **preen** check the root file-system only while the **-n** option makes preen check everything *except* the root file-system. **Preen** tries to keep all the system's disk-drives busy, whereas **fsck** tends to leave such disk-drives inactive for a small period of time. Without any options **preen** checks the root partition, and then tries to keep one **fsck** program executing on each disk-drive in the system. When all file-systems have been checked, **preen** terminates.

Since **preen** calls **fsck** to actually perform the checking of disks, the same environment as discussed in section 11.12.4 earlier is in effect. Some versions of **preen** cannot be used on specific file-systems (see syntax), and therefore the existence of a file such as **/etc/fstab** is needed in order to provide file-system and device information. **Preen** is commonly used in the **/etc/rc** file during automatic rebooting.

11.14 Rebooting a UNIX system – reboot

Many UNIX systems have a **reboot** command that can be used to restart the system in the same way as starting it by switching it on. The **reboot** command is commonly used in files such as **/etc/rc** to perform an automatic reboot after a file-system consistency check (using tools such as **fsck -p** or **preen**). The syntax of the **reboot** command is:

```
reboot [options]
```

The most common options are **-n** and **-q**. The **-n** option is used to avoid issuing a **sync** command. As explained in section 11.12.5, a newly modified file-system (modified using **fsck -p** etc.) will not be consistent to the current view of the file-system held by the UNIX system in memory. **Fsck** caters for this problem, and in the case where a **sync** command would corrupt the newly configured file-system, it reboots the system without issuing a **sync** command. The **reboot** command can also be used with this option because the default operation automatically issues a **sync** command.

On some UNIX systems it is common to run the **/etc/rc** file, before the system proceeds to multi-user mode, to check the file-system for inconsistencies using the **fsck** or **preen** tools, for example. If the file-system has been modified, it is common for **fsck** or **preen** to return an *exit code* (see section 8.2.5) that indicates this modification. A shell-script can be programmed to test for this particular exit code, and then reboot the system without issuing a **sync** command, hence the need for a **-n** option. If the file-system has not been modified, there is no need to reboot the computer because the system's memory will not require resetting. In this situation the system can simply continue to the next set of instructions in the **/etc/rc** file.

The **-q** option can be found on some UNIX systems. It is used to reboot the system quickly without issuing a **shutdown** command (discussed next). The file **syslog** is sometimes maintained to record the details of such reboot activities. The login accounting file **wtmp** is also updated with a shutdown record. These two actions are not performed if either of the **-n** or **-q** options are specified.

11.15 Shutting down the system – shutdown

Shutdown allows the administrator to close down the system, either immediately or at the end of a given time. The procedure provided by **shutdown** is usually automated on most UNIX systems, and facilities are provided to warn users of the impending action. The syntax of this command is:

```
shutdown [time] [warning-message]
```

There are many configurations of the **shutdown** command. Nearly all of them allow the administrator to provide a time interval before the system is actually shut down. This is done using a [**time**] argument.

11.15.1. Specifying a shutdown time

The [**time**] argument commonly accepts three formats. The first allows the number of minutes to be specified before the shutdown operation is performed. This particular format uses an addition sign (+), which is placed on front of the numeric argument. For example:

$ shutdown +60	- Shuts the system down in 1 hour
$ shutdown +3	- Shuts the system down in 3 minutes.

The second format uses a hour:minute notation to specify a particular time for the shutdown operation, commonly using the 24-hour clock. A single colon (:) separates the hours and minutes. For example:

$ shutdown 11:30	- Shuts the system down at 11:30 am.
$ shutdown 15:00	- Shuts the system down at 3 pm.

The third and final format uses a *word* notation. Special keywords are used to specify the shutdown time; for example **now** shuts down the system immediately. Other keywords such as **noon** and **midnight** exist on other UNIX systems. Check your documentation to find out the valid keywords for your system. For example:

```
$ shutdown now
```

This command will shut the system down immediately. When a specific time or time interval is included, as in the first two formats, **shutdown** displays a series of messages on each user's terminal warning of the impending shutdown. It is common practice for **shutdown** to disable logins five minutes before the specific shutdown takes place, (or immediately if the shutdown period is less than five minutes).

A file called **/etc/nologin** is created by the **shutdown** utility to disable user logins when a shutdown operation in taking place. The normal login process checks for the existence of this file, and if it is found, its contents are displayed. The actual contents of the **/etc/nologin** file are not important, but the administrator can put a message in the file telling users the reason why they cannot log in. **Login** will then print this message held in **/etc/nologin** when a user attempts to log in during a shutdown. The warning-message to be placed in the **/etc/nologin** file is itemised in the syntax description; the time and date of the shutdown operation may also be included in the file by the system.

The **/etc/nologin** file is removed just before the system is shut down. The **init** process (see section 11.9.1) is then sent a termination signal that brings the system into single-user mode. Basically, the machine can then be turned off. However this method does gloss over some of the more fundamental steps that need to be taken. The **/usr/adm/shutdownlog** file is maintained on some UNIX systems which holds the time and date when a **shutdown** command was issued, along with the name of the user who invoked the command, and the warning message that is placed in the **/etc/nologin** file. Some examples can be seen below:

```
11:52  Mon   Sep 11, 1990.  Shutdown: System problems (root)
18:40  Wed   Sep 17, 1990.  Shutdown: System reconfig. (root)
10:59  Thu   Sep 30, 1990.  Shutdown: Engineers working (root)
```

11.16 A more orderly shutdown procedure

Closing down a system must be done methodically, since many file-system inconsistencies may be caused by rushed or improper shutdown procedures. Firstly, we must not forget the users of the system. It is their information that will be lost if proper warning of the shut down procedure is not given. A verbal warning may suffice, although a tool such as **wall** can be used to warn all users, for example:

```
$ wall
   The system is shutting down in 5 minutes ...
   SAVE all work and log out NOW!
   <ctrl-d>
```

Many **shutdown** utilities also warn users of the impending shutdown operation by displaying a message on the terminal of each user who is logged in. Before the system is shut down, it is essential to check that there no users are still logged in. The **kill** command can be used to kill any user processes, however, as **init** is always the primary process (being the first process started by the system when processing user logins), the command **kill -1 1** will kill the **init** process, and effectively reduce the system to single user mode. (This option is system-specific, so check your system documentation to be absolutely sure.) Following this, the system's console terminal should be the only machine left running (with a single-user shell in operation). The **ps** – processor status command, (discussed in Chapter 12 on UNIX Security) can be used to find out what the user is doing on a particular terminal device.

Bear in mind that some users may need more time to save their work; you can use **ps** to view their activities and allow them more time to log out if they need it, otherwise you may become rather unpopular in certain quarters.

11.17 Starting up a UNIX system

Having discussed the procedures that need to be undertaken when shutting down a UNIX system, it may be worthwhile briefly describing the start-up procedures. Unfortunately, there is no standard start-up procedure. There are, however, a series of steps that are common to nearly all UNIX systems. These are:

- ❑ You turn the machine on
- ❑ The operating system kernel is loaded into the computer's memory from disk
- ❑ The file-system is checked for inconsistencies
- ❑ The system eventually goes from single-user mode into multi-user mode.

11.17.1 The bootstrapping procedure

Bootstrapping (also known as 'booting' the system) is the most common procedure associated with starting up a UNIX system; this is also called the initial Program Load, or the **IPL** procedure. Many UNIX systems, especially the smaller installations, boot up from a single device. However, booting the system from a separate secondary storage device can be advantageous, since a breakdown in the normal booting device would otherwise prevent the system from being used.

The disk normally used to boot the system, uses block 0 as the boot area. Block 0 is not a part of the normal UNIX file-system but is provided for the dedicated operation of bootstrapping the system. When the system is initially switched on, block 0 area is read into memory commonly using either a special shell-script, or a UNIX command such as **dd** (not described here), which is a file copy and transformation program.

The next process depends very much on the particular system in operation. However, by some means or other, the UNIX kernel will be loaded; for example, some systems may ask the user to supply the name of a boot program , while in others the system may even load it automatically. The executable kernel is sometimes referred to by the names **/unix** or **/vmunix**. The second stage, or supplementary booting program (if it exists), is named **/boot** on some UNIX systems.

Once the executable kernel has been loaded, the system checks main memory to establish its present size. The **init** process is then started by the system, ant it will normally start up a single-user shell (sometimes referred to as a superuser shell) on the system's console terminal. This allows the administrator to make certain checks on the system, for example using **fsck** or **preen** to detect and repair file-system inconsistencies, before it transfers to multi-user mode.

Some systems prompt for a superuser password, once the single-user shell has been started on the console. When this has been entered, the user can proceed to the interactive shell with superuser privileges. Systems without this facility risk a circumvention of system security.

11.18 Keeping in touch with users – /etc/motd

If file-system maintenance needs to be carried during user time, you should make use of the system's facilities to warn users. The **/etc/motd** file is displayed when a user logs in to the system, except on systems where the file **.hushlogin** exists (which quietens down the login process). You can place simple ASCII messages in the **/etc/motd** file to warn users of system backups, archives and file-system maintenance, or any other activities which cause delays in system resources for the users.

11.19 Questions

1. What is the purpose of the **fsck** program?
2. Explain the purpose of the **update** daemon.
3. Give three typical operations that would be included in the **/etc/rc** file.
4. What is the purpose of the **/etc/rc.local** file?
5. What do the letters **IPL** stand for?
6. Explain the purpose of the **lost+found** directory.
7. List three file-system inconsistencies that **fsck** will recognise.
8. Why is the use of the **preen** utility said to be more beneficial than the **fsck** utility?
9. Explain the use of the **du** command.
10. Show how a hypothetical file-system can be mounted with read/write operations and with quota checking enabled.

12

UNIX Security

12.1 Introduction

This chapter introduces the security aspects of the Unix operating system, starting with routines that are fundamental to any secure system, such as file protection mechanisms and monitoring commands which include **ps**, **finger**, **last**, **lastcomm** and **who**. UNIX was not designed with security in mind, but a UNIX system can be made secure if the correct procedures are adopted. This chapter describes these procedures, and explains how they can be implemented by the administrator or the casual user.

12.2 What is wrong with UNIX's security?

The problem of security lies in UNIX's flexibility as an operating system. Its versatile file-system structure allows users to browse extensively through many of the system's files. It is also commonly found that non-privileged users have access to administrative tools simply because no one has bothered to set the correct access permissions on the relevant files.

UNIX provides nearly all of the facilities to implement and monitor system attacks and yet it is a lack of education and awareness that leads to many security problems. In the majority of cases the facilities that are made available to the user and administrator are not appreciated or understood. Inevitably this leads to gaps in system security.

12.3 File security - chmod

Most breaches of UNIX security take place at the file level, because access permission settings are not set correctly when the system is initially installed. In addition, the file permission settings will inevitably be changed at times for various reasons, and failure to reset the permissions correctly can lead to all sorts of problems. New files that are created will also need their access permission settings set to reflect the desired access.

The **chmod** (change mode) command is used to alter the access permission settings (

or modes) of a particular file, or group of files. The syntax of the **chmod** command is:

chmod [options] <mode> <file ...>

The permission settings can be supplied in one of two ways. The first uses an octal number code to represent the access settings for the user, group, and other members. The second method, the symbolic form, uses the letters u, g, o literally, with the necessary access permissions, which are the read (**r**), write (**w**) and execute (**x**) permissions respectively. This mode also employs the signs '+', '-' and '=', as follows: the '+' sign adds the permission to the file's mode, the '-' sign removes the permission, and the '=' sign assigns absolute permission for the file (resets all permissions). Each class of user is separated by a single comma, and multiple user classes can be handled.

The options available for **chmod** vary from system to system, although common options include **-f** (which suppresses the warming message given by **chmod** if it fails to change a particular mode of a file) and **-R** which makes **chmod** recursively descend directory arguments setting the appropriate mode for each file. Linked files are not processed.

12.3.1 Symbolic file permissions

When assigning symbolic access permissions to files, a knowledge of the **/etc/group** file is required. This file contains the necessary information regarding the various user groups needed when you assign file permissions for various people in your particular user group. The **/etc/group** file can also be used to determine any users who are not in a particular group, and to whom the other (**o**) file permission will be granted.

Examples

Example 1

```
$ chmod g+r file1
```

This command assigns read permission, for all group members, on the file named **file1**. To discover exactly which users are affected, find your own username in the **/etc/group** file, and then note the other users in the same group as yourself. These are the users to whom you have granted read permission on this particular file.

Example 2

Similarly, to deny read access to this file to all group user members, simply type:

```
$ chmod g-r file1
```

Example 3

To give everyone read access to the file named **file1**, we would type:

```
$ chmod a+r file1
```

Example 4

As mentioned, we can mix such user keywords by bundling them together.

```
$ chmod go+rw file2
```

This command grants read and write permission to the file named **file2** to all the users who belong to the current user group, and also to those users who do not. Remember that such access means that the file could also be deleted by any users with this file permission setting.

Example 5

When a file of shell commands is to be made executable, the **x** letter is used with the grant (+) symbol.

```
$ chmod +x prog1
```

This command will be used extensively when you come to write programs in the language of the shell (see Chapter 13).

12.3.2 Using ls to view file permissions

The **ls** command with the option **-l** can be used to list the current permission settings for files. The first nine characters represent the permissions assigned to a file. The first three characters of these nine represent the user (owner) settings, the next three represent the group settings, and the final three represent the other users of the system. **Ls -l** can be used to verify any permission changes that we make to our files. The **ls -l** command can also be used to view the permission settings of other users' files. For example:

```
$ ls -l /usr/John/file1
-rw-rw-rw- 1 John 1086 Feb 13 14:01 file1
```

Assuming we were user **John**, issuing the command **chmod g- rwx,o-rwx** would result in the new listing shown below:

```
$ chmod g-rwx,o-rwx /usr/John/file1
$ ls -l
-rw------- 1 John 1086 Feb 13 14:01 file1
```

The file permission setting now stipulates that only the owner of the file named **file1** can read and write to it. No other user has the necessary permission (except the superuser).

12.3.3 Octal file permissions

Octal file permissions use the numbers in the range zero to seven (0-7) for setting access permission settings (unlike the denary number system that employs the numbers zero to nine (0-9)). When using octal permissions you will need to remember the following:

❑ Read permission is represented by the value 4

❑ Write permission is represented by the value 2

❑ Execute permission is represented by the value 1

	USER	GROUP	OTHER
READ	4	4	0
WRITE	2	0	0
EXECUTE	0	0	0

Figure 12.1 Octal permission code 640 represented in a table

In order to assign an octal permission, it is helpful to construct a simple table representing the permissions, and the user classes to which they are to be applied, as shown in Figure 12.1. This gives a table that shows a permission setting giving the owner read and write permission, the group users only read permission, and the other users no permissions at all. Each column is summed to give the final octal code. This octal code is used on the command line as the actual protection setting. This octal protection setting (640) is equivalent to the symbolic setting in the command **chmod u+rw,g+r,o-rwx.**

12.3.4 Directory permission settings

Another important point to remember that permission settings on an ordinary file are treated somewhat differently to a directory file. If read permission is granted on a directory, that directory can be examined using **ls** for example. Write permission on a directory effectively means that files can be created and deleted from that directory using command such as **rm**. Output redirection into the directory is also possible using the > or >> redirection operators.

Execute permission on a directory file is changed to become search permission. This means that a user may make that directory file the current working directory, using a command such as **cd** (the change directory command). When protecting individual files against deletion by other users, remember that it is only necessary to deny write permission on the directory that holds these files. Protection on a directory takes precedence over any individually write-protected files that are held within that directory.

12.4 The SUID protection-setting

The **SUID** (set user identification) protection is a very important development, and has wide security implications for UNIX. The use of the **SUID** setting allows users to temporarily acquire the **UID** of the owner of a file. Considering the utility **/bin/passwd** which allows nonprivileged users to change their own passwords. Examination of the protection settings for the **/etc/passwd** file reveal that only user root has read and write permission. Since changing a password involves writing to the **/etc/passwd** file, how is it possible that a person without superuser privileges can accomplish such a task?

The answer lies in the use of the **SUID** protection. If you examine the protection settings of the **/bin/passwd** file you may see the following:

```
$ ls -l /bin/passwd
-rwsr-xr-x 1 root 4316 Jun 12 12:09 passwd
```

Note the letter **s** that replaces the normal **x** for this particular file. The file is still executable, except that during its operation, the **UID** of the person running the program is temporarily replaced by the **UID** of owner of the file, **root** i.e. the ordinary user running the program temporarily acquires superuser powers. This in turn allows that user to write to the **/etc/passwd** file when the new password is chosen. At the conclusion of the program, the **UID** returns to the original **UID** of the person executing the file.

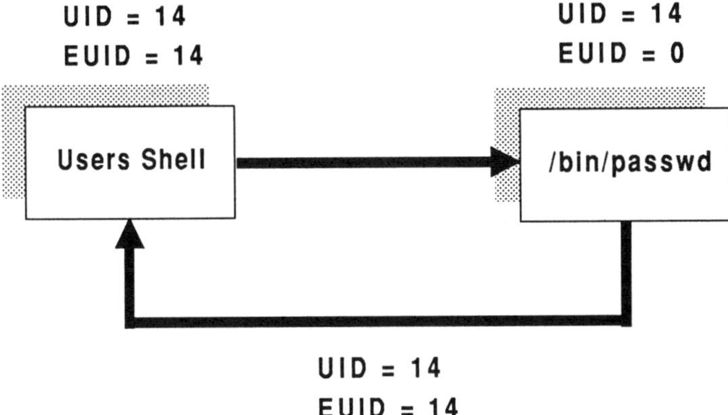

*Figure 12.2 **UID** and **EUID** settings*

The **EUID** is the effective user identification number. It is a numerical fingerprint used by the system to determine what a user may or may not do. When a user executes a file belonging to another user, the owner's **UID** is sought in the **/etc/passwd** and is checked against the **EUID** of the person executing the file. If both match, the file will be executed; however, if the **UID** and **EUID** do not match, the file will not be executed. One can think of this operation as being a temporary replacement of the user's **UID** (after all **SUID** means to set the current user's **UID** to that of the owner of the file being executed).

The effective user and group identifications codes are allocated to the user upon logging into the system, and the default values are stored in the **/etc/passwd** file, in the third and fourth fields. A user with a **UID** value of 224 would therefore also have an effective user-id (**EUID**) of 224. A **UID** value can be temporarily changed using the **su** (substitute user) command, which is covered in Chapter 11, section 11.2.4.

SUID protection settings are another cause for concern with regards to the security of a UNIX system, since an incorrect setting can lead to chaos if in the hands of a malicious user. For example, take the entry below which corresponds to the **/bin/rm** command. Such an entry is a potential disaster, since it means that any file on the system could be deleted, simply because the user executing the file gains the temporary powers of **root**, the superuser (note that execute permission is needed only on a file that has the **SUID** permission set for an owner such as **root** in order to gain superuser privileges).

```
$ ls -l /bin/rm
-r-sr-xr-x 1 root 8216 Mar 01 13:58 rm
```

Fortunately utilities such as **rm** check user permissions, including the current user's **UID** and **EUID** values. This checking is carried out by many shell utilities that create and delete files, such as **mkdir** and **rmdir** etc. These utilities need to ascertain whether or not a user is allowed to create or delete a file in a particular part of the file-system.

12.4.1 Checking file SUID settings

A well-known loop-hole in the UNIX system involves the potential system penetrator trying to find an executable program (owned by **root**) which has the **SUID** bit set, and which has a shell escape or command facility.

Shell commands can be invoked from many UNIX tools, especially the editors such as **ed** and **ex**, and the mail system (e.g. using the **!** command). These tools are nearly always owned by **root**, and should not have their **SUID** permission set. If the **SUID** protection is set for a program that allows the user to temporarily escape (using of a shell command facility, for example) then there is a chance that this user will exit with superuser status, an administrator's nightmare.

12.5 Seeking out SUID files - find

Programs with **SUID** permission set should be sought out using a command such as **find**. This command is extremely powerful in that is recursively descends entire file-systems searching for specific attributes such as a filename, or more relevant to us, a permission setting. The **find** command has a complicated syntax, and we endeavour only to explain the options which are relevant to this particular section and topic. The basic syntax is:

find <pathname> <primaries>

Both arguments are compulsory and must be stated. The **<pathname>** tells **find** the part of the file-system where the search is to be initiated. The **<primaries>** argument is expanded to be specific about the type of data we are seeking. The most common primaries of the **find** command can be seen in Table 12.1. Of most interest in this context are the primaries named **-perm**, **-name** and **-print**. Note that any arguments, such as the username etc. are placed following this primary in question, leaving at least one space to distinguish the two. Also note that such primaries can be bundled together on one line to make up multiple conditions.

Table 12.1 Primaries used with the find command

Primary	Action
-name	Matches a filename as specified on the command line enclosed in double quotes (") after the actual option (see examples).
-perm	Searches for a specific permission, as specified on the command-line (see examples).
-print	Prints out the pathnames of matching files (see examples). This has no argument.
-user	Prints the names of users who own a particular file that is found. The numeric **UID** of a user can also be included.

Some examples will illustrate the use of the **find** command.

Examples

Example 1

```
$ find /   -name "who" -print
/bin/who
```

This command searches the entire file-system (note the / pathname setting) for the file **who**, and if it is found, the full pathname location of the file is printed. In the example, find has printed the pathname **/bin/who.**

Example 2

```
$ find /  \(-perm 4000 -a -perm 0011\) -user 0 -print
```

This command searches the entire file-system (a wise choice) to search for any files that are owned by **root** and which have the **SUID** permission set. The command also searches for execute permission on the files that are matched for the group or other users of the system. All of these conditions must be met for the file to be matched and displayed. Note how the two **-perm** conditions are bracketed. The \ signs are used to take away the special meaning of the brackets from the shell because we want the shell to interpret the brackets without any special consideration. All shell metacharacters must also be quoted in this way. The **-a** option in the previous example stands for a logical **AND** operator, and allows multiple conditions to be specified for a particular file. A logical **OR** (**-o**) can also be specified, if required.

The two conditions here use the **-perm** primary twice to search for the **SUID** permission on a file owned by root (**-perm 4000**) and which has execute permission for group or other users of the system (**-perm 0011**). The **-user 0** ensures that only files owned by root are sought.

Example 3

Similar **find** commands can be executed and a list of the file pathnames (printed using the **-print** option) placed in a separate file using output redirection, for example:

```
$ find / -name 'e*' -print > e_files
```

This command finds all files beginning with the lower-case letter 'e' (or files that are just named **e** remembering that the * metacharacter matches zero occurrences as well). Note how the * character pattern is quoted with single-quotes, so that the shell does not interpret the metacharacter literally. All such files (or rather, their pathnames) will be placed in the file named 'e_files' which can then be referred to.

Example 4

```
$ find / \(-name "ex" -o -name "mail"\) -print
/bin/ex
/bin/mail
```

This command uses the logical **OR** operator, that specifies that either of the two conditions here must be true for the file to be displayed. Thus only the pathnames of files named **mail** or **ex** will be printed, as shown in the example.

Problems associated with the **SUID** permission and shell escape facilities can be solved if access to program source-code is available. Many commercial suppliers of UNIX systems so not provide source-code, in which case you may have to consider taking away execute permission for all users of the particular file, apart from the owner (which we assume is a superuser such as **root**). This solution may not be appropriate in the case where the file is an editor (such as **vi**) or a mailing system (such as **mail**) because they are used so frequently. In such cases you are advised to consult your supplier to amend the source-code, or rely on the fact that the problem will hopefully remain undiscovered!

12.6 Fake logins

Many security breaches tend to revolve around the persistence to obtain user details entered at log-in time. Fake or pseudo logins have been mentioned in many articles on UNIX security.

Because UNIX is so flexible, it can be used to emulate existing system procedures. A *pseudo-login* program is a small shell-script which simulates the login process. It provides a prompt for a username and password, and then stores this information away in a part of the file-system ready for examination by the perpetrator. The program is left running on a terminal awaiting unsuspecting users. Upon using the fake program, the user would then be told that the system was unavailable, for example, or the program may continue to tell the user that a wrong password has been supplied (some actually invoke the real login program).

Such programs are very easy to program, and only a small knowledge of the shell and a few programming constructs are needed. The program below uses shell constructs that have not yet been explained. You can refer to Chapter 13 - Shell Programming, to learn the full meaning of these constructs.

```
# Fake login program
while :
do
   clear
   echo "login:"
   read username
   echo "password:"
   stty -echo
   read password
   echo $username > .user_data
   echo $password > .user_data
   echo "----------------------------" > .user_data
   stty echo
   echo "Login incorrect."
done
```

These commands could be entered using a editor such as **ex** under the name 'fakelogin'. Then the command **chmod +x fakelogin** would be entered to make the file executable, so that the shell can interpret the file as a series of executable shell commands.

Before a listing of the program in action, let us take a few moments to explain what is actually happening in the program. The first line is simply a comment. The shell commands between the **while** and **done** constructs are repeated until a certain condition becomes true. This is known more commonly as a *loop*. The condition is always specified after the while command, and in this example it is a single colon (:). The colon is a built-in shell construct that is used in loops to make them iterate forever. The condition is therefore not directly specified in this example and the program will thus loop forever until interrupted using **<ctrl-c>** or until the process is terminated, using the **kill** command.

The first command in the loop, **clear**, clears the terminal screen. The next command, **echo**, requests the user to enter a username at a simulated login: prompt. Note the use of the **-n** option with the **echo** command that ensures that the username is entered on the same line (without a carriage-return), as occurs in a genuine login program.

The next command is **read** which allows a value to read from the keyboard into a shell variable. The shell variable in this case is called **USER** and will hold the current user's username. After the user has entered the username, the **[RETURN]** key will be pressed allowing the password to be entered. The second **echo** statement is used to prompt the user for a password, but note the command following this. The **stty** (set terminal type and characteristics) command has been used to turn off the echoing of characters to the screen, an essential feature to build into a fake-login program since the real program does not echo user passwords either. The argument - option turns off echoing of characters, but it must be done after the **password:** prompt has been displayed. Echoing is enabled again afterwards to allow the 'Login incorrect' message to be displayed (and any subsequent echo statements also).

The next command (**read password**) reads the users password and stores it in the shell variable **PASS**. Both the username and password (stored in the shell variables **USER** and **PASS**) are then immediately written to a hidden file named **.user_data**. Note the use of the redirection command **>** which appends data to a file. Using a single **>** symbol would mean that any new users that use the program would overwrite any existing data in the **.user_data** file. A dividing line is also written into the **.user_data** file to divided up individual username and password entries.

The next command uses **stty** again, but this time to enable the echoing of characters to the screen so that the next statement can be displayed. The final shell command is an echo statement that issues a small message telling the user that an invalid password has been entered. This series of instructions will be carried out until the program is interrupted. The actual program is shown below, followed by a listing of the file **.user_data**, the hidden file that was used to capture the users' input.

```
login:Jason
password:
Login incorrect.
login:Fred
password:
Login incorrect.
<ctrl-c>
$
$ cat .user_data
Jason
wombat
----------------------------
Fred
secret
----------------------------
$
```

Access to the real source-code of a UNIX system can also be a problem. Users can browse for potential bugs, or can copy and amend code (note though that the original ownership is reset and thus copied program(s) will not run with superuser status). Where source-code is available to users, it may be worth considering denying access to the more 'sensitive' program source-code, such as **login** and **passwd**.

12.7 Monitoring and Accounting Utilities

Many of the problems outlined up to this point can be prevented by paying careful attention to the processes that are running on the system. This section examines some of the popular monitoring commands such as **who, finger, last, lastcomm** and **ps**.

12.7.1 Last

The **last** command examines the **/usr/adm/wtmp** file that stores the login and logout activity of all users on the system. The syntax of the command is:

last [options] [username] [keyword] [tty]

The most common options are **-<number>** and **-f <file>** on Berkeley systems. The **-<number>** option allows the number of user entries to that indicated by the value **<number>** which is specified directly after the hyphen (-).

The **-f <file>** option allows the user to specify an alternative accounting file (other than **wtmp** file, that is). The **wtmp** file is the default accounting file. The **[username]** is useful when specific information about certain users is required. The **[tty]** option allows the login and logout activity of a certain terminal to be checked, a very useful option. Terminal names can normally abbreviated to the terminal number, for example the command **last 7** examines terminal login/logout activity for **/dev/tty7**.

The **[keyword]** allows the user to specify additional information such as the times of system reboots, and the system administrator's (**root**'s) activities. The keyword **reboot** examines any system bootstrapping entries in the **wtmp** file, and the keyword **root** examines all root (superuser) logins and logouts, along with any activity undertaken from the console terminal. With no arguments, **last** will list all the login and logout activity for all users. If **last** is interrupted (using **<Ctrl-C>**) its display tells the user how far the search into the **wtmp** file went. The control keystroke **<Ctrl-\>** makes **last** declare the current extent of the search (into the **wtmp** file) and then continues the listing.

Example

```
$ last John tty08
John tty08   Thu  Dec 14  10:13 still logged in
John tty08   Thu  Dec 14  08:02 - 10:14 (02:12)
John tty08   Sat  Dec 11  08:30 - 15:58 (07:27)
```

This example shows a small entry for user **John**; note that the terminal named is specified. The login and logout messages help identify the duration of each session with the system. The final message indicates that user **John** is still logged in and thus the record for this user cannot be completed until his session ends. The numbers in brackets indicate the total number of hours and minutes spent logged in. The **who** command can also be used to examine the **wtmp** file, by specifying it as a **who-file** command-line argument (see section 7.3.14 for more details).

12.7.2 Lastcomm

Lastcomm is one of the most useful monitoring commands. It lists the commands that were invoked by a particular user. The time and date of each command is also given, along with the terminal device on which it was executed (the actual content of the **lastcomm** listing varies from system to system). The syntax of the command is:

lastcomm [command] [username] [tty]

Lastcomm examines the accounting file **/usr/adm/pacct** which records all the facts about the commands users have invoked up to the present time.

The [**command**] argument allows the user to specify a particular command that is to be sought, which has been used either by the user specified with the [**username**] argument, or, if no user is specified, the current user. **Lastcomm** then lists all the commands executed by that user in reverse order (starting with the most recent entries). The [**tty**] argument allows a particular terminal to be specified. It is normally used alongside the [**username**] argument, although it can be used without it if required, to list information about the current user. A typical listing from a **lastcomm** command is given below. It has been invoked without any arguments, therefore the system prints information regarding the current user, who executed the command.

```
$ lastcomm
sh   John   tty08   0.00 secs   Thu Dec 14 12:57
date John   tty08   0.09 secs   Thu Dec 14 12:57
cat  John   tty08   0.11 secs   Thu Dec 14 12:56
grep John   tty08   0.03 secs   Thu Dec 14 12:56
who  John   tty08   0.05 secs   Thu Dec 14 12:56
who  John   tty08   0.05 secs   Thu Dec 14 12:55
ls   John   tty08   0.09 secs   Thu Dec 14 12:54
mail John   tty08   0.12 secs   Thu Dec 14 12:54
```

Some **lastcomm** programs list additional information regarding the execution of the command, as if a command was executed with superuser status, or terminated etc. Such circumstances are provided on some systems by supplying an additional column that indicates a single letter alongside the command. Typical entries are **S** for a command that run with superuser status and **X** for a command that was terminated. Note also from the listing that command options are not listed. The fourth and fifth columns indicate the amount of CPU time used by each command (in seconds).

The last four columns show the time and date that a particular command was executed. Note how **lastcomm** prints the latest command that was executed, and continues in a descending order chronologically.

12.7.3 Finger

The **finger** command has been examined briefly already. It is particularly useful since it can monitor the *idle time* of users. The idle time of a user refers to the amount of time that has passed since a physical interaction with the system. To monitor idle times of users the **-i** option is used, for example:

```
$ finger -i
Login    TTY       When                 Idle
John     *tty09    Mon Jun 4 10:53      19 minutes
Jim      tty10     Mon Jun 4 11:01
Susan    *tty12    Mon Jun 4 12:14      1 hour 30 minutes
Mark     tty20     Mon Jun 4 12:56      12 seconds
```

This listing illustrates the idle times for four users. Users with a blank idle time column have no idle time and are therefore constantly interacting with the system. Notice how **finger** also displays an asterisk (*) next to some terminals and not others.

This indicates which terminals are protected with a **mesg n** command (which does not allow incoming messages, such as those generated with **talk** or **write**, to interrupt that user's session). Only the superuser can bypass this protection, since write permission to a device in the **/dev** directory is needed (remembering that **mesg n** simply removes write-permission from a user's terminal device for the group and other users of the system). Other information displayed by **finger** includes usernames, terminal names, and the time and date each user logged on to the system.

12.7.4 Ps

Ps displays the status of user processes. By default, without any options, it displays information about processes that have the same **UID** as the present user. It is possible to display information about other user processes, hence it is beneficial as a monitoring command for an administrator. The fundamental syntax for the **ps** command is:

ps [options]

The **ps** command is one of those UNIX commands that has a myriad of options. This section looks as only a few of these, which are the most relevant and useful for monitoring purposes. The **-a** option is used to display process information that belongs to the other users of the system. This option is useful since it shows system-wide process statistics. Another option, option **-g**, makes **ps** display *interesting* processes (those which are process group leaders); without it **ps** will only display uninteresting processes. This option thus eliminates those processes waiting for users to log in on free terminals, for example.

Examples

Example 1

```
$ ps
PID  TT   TIME    COMMAND
2901 08   0:05    -sh (sh)
3043 08   0:06    ps
```

A typical listing from the **ps** command invoked without any options makes **ps** display process information that concerns the current user. As can be seen, the fundamental process is the shell itself (here **sh** the Bourne Shell), and the current **ps** command which is being executed. The four columns that **ps** returns in the example are:

PID the system allocated process identification number

TT the terminal device on which the process is running

TIME the elapsed time for the process, and

COMMAND the actual process itself, or rather the UNIX command being executed.

Example 2

Combining -a and **-g** allows the user to see a detailed list of all the system processes:

```
$ ps -ag
PID  TT   STAT TIME   COMMAND
42   con  S    25:02  -csh (csh)
763  con  IW   0:03   /etc/update
143  10   I    0:00   -sh (sh)
143  10        0:06   vi file1
201  09   I    0:00   -sh (sh)
342  08   I    0:09   -sh (sh)
231  08   I    0:09   ps -ag
231  07   S    0:00   -sh (sh)
```

This extended listing has an additional **STAT** column. Many of the letters that can be found in this column are illustrated in Table 12.2 below:

Table 12.2 ps command STAT letter codes

STAT Letter	Meaning
S	Processes sleeping for less than 20 seconds (approx.)
I	Processes that are idle, such as those sleeping longer than 20 seconds (approx.)
W	Process is being swapped out
T	Processes that have been stopped
N	Process priority has been reduced
<blank>	Process is loaded into memory

Notice that the **ps -ag** listing shows the processes that are currently being run by the user invoking the **ps -ag** command (on terminal **tty08**). Process information, especially the **PID** number, is useful to the administrator since unwanted processes, for example, those which have locked up terminals, or those which have been idle for a long time, can be identified and killed, and removed from the system.

The kill command

The **kill** command can be used in the case of a locked-up terminal, where it may be necessary to terminate the offending process:

kill [-signo] [PID]

The value for **signo** depends on the severity of the **kill**, and the type of process being terminated. The **PID** value (process identification) is obtained using tools such as **ps**. Users can only kill processes that they own, so administrative users must have superuser privileges (typically **root** privileges) in order to delete other processes on the system. Two **signo** values are commonly used:

i) the **-9** signal number is used to ensure the process is killed. This signal gives the process no time to clean up, it is immediately killed off. The **-9** signal code is known by the name **SIGKILL**, the sure kill signal.

ii) some processes can catch or ignore certain signals (**SIGKILL** being the exception to this rule). The **-3** signal number can be used to kill specific background processes i.e. those started specifically with **&**. The most common signal number is the interrupt signal number (known as **SIGINT**) which is generated by **<Ctrl-C>** or the **[DEL]** key on some UNIX systems. It is used to terminate a process that is running in the foreground. An example is the mail system, which processes the **SIGINT** signal when you press **<Ctrl-C>** to interrupt the current message that is being composed.

A useful signal process number to remember is zero. If the command **kill 0** is issued, all the current user processes are killed except the login shell, so you are still left logged in to the system.

12.8 Security of mounted file-systems

Mounted file-systems bring forward new security problems that must be considered. More and more UNIX systems now use floppy disks that can easily be transported by users. Such disks could penetrate the security of an existing UNIX system, simply by installing administrative commands on a floppy disk and then mounting it on to part of the existing file-system. The user could then, upon logging in, access these commands and circumvent security.

An example of such illegal utilities are those that have the **SUID** bit set for a root-owned utility which has execute permission set for the user who brings in the disk. Of course, such a breach in security can easily be avoided by making sure access to the hardware component is restricted to authorised administrative staff of the system concerned.

12.9 Security of administrative files

Weaknesses in the access permissions to certain administrative files, such as **/usr/lib/crontab**, must be ensured. **Cron**, the clock daemon, is a special case since it runs with superuser status. Therefore every command in the **crontab** file will be attempted by the system regardless of the person running it.

The **crontab** file should be checked regularly, for it contains instructions that are be carried out with superuser status. Manipulation of the commands in the **crontab** file will allow a would-be system penetrator to acquire superuser privileges. For example, an entry in the **crontab** file could be entered which would give a particular user access to modify the **/etc/passwd** file at a certain time of the day. Take the following **crontab** entry:

```
00 14 * * 2 root chmod 777 /etc/passwd
30 14 * * 2 root chmod 444 /etc/passwd
```

This entry translates into the following:

> "Every Tuesday (2) at 2.00 pm (00 14) on any day of the month (*) on any month of the year (*) remove all protection on the /etc/passwd file, and then on the same day, but at the time of 2.30 pm (30 14) put back the previous protection settings"

This entry places a deliberate trap-door into the system (for half an hour each day between the hours 2.00 and 2.30 pm) to allow a user to modify the **/etc/passwd** file. This user could thus modify the appropriate entry assigning a zero **UID** value to him or herself thus gaining superuser privileges. At 2.30 pm **cron** would change the settings their previous values.

Of course, the user could do this earlier since that user has superuser privileges. Proper protection of the **crontab** file will ensure that such problems do not arise. Some sites also have **crontab.local** files, so the protection of these needs to be checked as well. The thing to remember is that no user (apart from the privileged) should have write permission on any confidential files.

Similarly you should make sure that the **/etc/rc**, **/etc/rc.local**, and on some systems, the **/etc/rc.boot** files, are all write-protected since corruption of this file may create havoc at bootstrapping time. The **umask** command should be used from a file such as **.profile** or **.cshrc** to ensure that any files created by an administrator have default file protection settings assigned to them. This reduces the risk of any sensitive files that are created by a privileged user being unprotected (see section 11.2.7 for more details on **umask**)

12.10 System-wide login files

System-wide login files can also be used to improve security. The **/etc/profile** file is an prominent candidate. The environment of a UNIX system can be controlled by ensuring that only certain people have access to various terminals in a network. For example you may wish to deny terminal access to certain people according to their status in an organisation. Denying access to certain users can be done in a number of ways, although controlling which terminal a user can log in to is slightly harder. It can be done through a shell-script that executes from the **/etc/profile** file.

Assigning user classes can be done through use of the **/etc/group** file, although direct checking of usernames is easier, using the **/etc/profile** file. The script on thje next page assumes a knowledge of shell programming constructs. You can read Chapter 13 for more information on programming constructs.

```
# /etc/profile file. Called for all users on the system
# Makes sure that users cannot log onto terminal tty15
# which we will assume is an administrative terminal.
# Assume that users are using /bin/sh (Bourne Shell).
trap "" 1 2 3
if [`tty` = tty15] && [$USER = root ]
  then
    echo "Welcome to the system on 'date'."
  else
    # The terminal may be tty15, but user is not root
    # therefore deny access to this terminal.
    clear
    echo "\n\07\07\07\07\07"
    echo "You are not authorised to use this terminal."
    # we assume exit logs user out. Some systems use logout
  exit
fi
```

The strange notation used with the **echo** statements on line 14 makes the terminal bell sound (**07** is the ASCII code to sound the terminal's bell) and thus acts a warning sound. Note that this facility is not available on all terminal devices and is dependent upon the particular emulation being used. The **trap** command is discussed in section 13.9.

12.11 Questions

1. The **ps** command is useful since it allows a user to obtain **PID** information. What other command is the **PID** used with when processes have to be terminated?

2. Why is the **crontab** file a likely candidate for malicious alteration by a system penetrator?

3. What is the main difference between the **last** and **lastcomm** commands?

4. Which file does the **last** command examine? Name another command which can be used to examine the same file.

5. Explain the concept of the **SUID** permission setting.

6. Why is a file such as a UNIX editor (that has the **SUID** permission for **root** set and execute permission set for the group and other users) a potential security problem?

7. Give an example of a find command that searches the **/usr** directory (and the area below this directory) for any files that are owned by the user with a **UID** of **0**.

8. Explain the **perm** option of the **find** command.

9. The **SIGINT** signal can be caught or ignored. Which signal cannot be caught or ignored? Give an example of a command using this particular signal.

10. Give an example of a command that can show the idle time of each user that is currently logged in.

13

Shell Programming

13.1 Introduction

This chapter introduces the main concepts that you will need to write programs in the language of the shell. Two popular shells are examined throughout this chapter: the Bourne Shell (**/bin/sh**) and the C-Shell (**/bin/csh**).

The actual syntax of shell programs written under each of these two shells differ to a certain extent, so examples and descriptions for each shell are given. A fundamental shell program is simply a series of individual shell commands grouped together in a file which is then made executable and run from the shell in the same way as a standard shell command is invoked. The more complex shell programs use what are known as shell control structures. These control the execution and flow of control within a program. Such structures allow conditions to be tested, whereupon the necessary action(s) can be taken. These structures play a large role in this chapter and there are many shell-script excerpts for you to type in and try. Writing shell programs allows you to create your own tools from the existing UNIX tool set. These programs can then be used to automate everyday functions which would otherwise involve considerable work at the interactive level.

13.2 If-then-else-fi

The first control structure we are going to examine is known as the **if .. fi** structure. The **if** command allows certain conditions to be tested for and then appropriate actions to be invoked depending on the result. The syntax of the constructs for the two different shells is shown in Table 13.1.

The **<test-conditions>** argument allows the user to specify one or more conditions to be attached to the if statement. These are discussed in more detail in the next section. If the condition is true, then the actions following the **if** statement are carried out, otherwise the actions following the **elif** (else-if) component are executed. This allows **if** statements to be nested which makes the selection process more powerful (**then** statements are used to execute the statements following each **elif** because they also follow the **<test-condition>**). The **elif** and **else** components are optional and can be removed if desired. The **fi** statement closes the whole construct, and must be included.

Table 13.1 if .. fi constructs for the Bourne Shell and the C-Shell

Bourne Shell	C-Shell
if <test-conditions>	if <test-conditions>
then	then
[actions ...]	[actions ...]
elif [actions ...]	else
	[actions ...]
then [actions ...]	fi
else	
[actions ...]	
fi	

The final **else** statement is used when a condition is not satisfied, to executes the necessary actions in this situation. Note that if a condition is met using the **elif** structure, then the **else** statement will be skipped and the action(s) beneath it will not be performed. The **[actions ...]** themselves can be shell commands or further ('nested') **if-then** structures.

13.2.1 Conditions

A conditional test is used within an **if-then** statement, and the result is either true or false. Tests are structured in one of the following ways according to the shell used:

Bourne Shell	C-Shell
if [<operator>=<value>]	if (<operator>=<value>)
if [<Shell-command>]	if (Shell-command)

The **<operator>** used here could be a shell variable, or something more complex like a shell command. Note the second line above that indicates that a valid test condition is simply a shell program that ran successfully.

Shell commands return exit statuses that indicate whether the command ran successfully (true) or not (false). This is the basis used for most test conditions in the shell. Also note that the Bourne Shell uses square brackets ([ ]) to encapsulate tests conditions, whereas the C Shell uses parentheses (the brackets (and) respectively). The Bourne Shell is used as a basis for the examples in this chapter. A **<value>** can be any numeric or alphabetic value. We can now demonstrate a series of shell condition statements.

Examples

Example 1

```
if ['grep John /etc/passwd']
   then
      echo 'John exists in the /etc/passwd file.'
else
      echo 'John does not exist in the /etc/passwd file.'
fi
```

This construct uses an **if** statement to detect the presence of the user named John in the **/etc/passwd** file. Command substitution is used in the test condition. **Grep** returns a true or false exit status depending on whether it found the search pattern in the named file (here **/etc/passwd**). Grave accents (‘) must be used in this way when using shell commands as test conditions.

The actions in this example are echo statements that display a short messages informing us of the user's existence in the **/etc/passwd** file.

Example 2

```
if [$USER = JOHN]
   then
      echo 'Yes, you are called John'
fi
```

This example shows how the shell variable **$USER** can be used in test condition. The equals sign (=) tests whether the shell variable **$USER** is equal to the value 'Jason'. If they match, the echo statement is executed. Note the absence of an **else** statement here. In this case the possibility of the condition not being satisfied is not tested for, which is perfectly valid. When programming in the shell, sometimes we are not interested in conditions which are *not* satisfied (and vice-versa), thus we leave out the optional **else** part of the construct.

13.3 The test command

The **test** command is provided to make the testing of conditions easier to implement. A number of options are provided by the command which allow the user to test for simple and complex conditions. The **test** command can be used directly from the shell prompt, although it is mainly used in shell-scripts in test-conditions for **if** statements.The test command can be used according to the two following syntax descriptions:

i) test <expression>
or
ii) [<expression>]

Note that in the second syntax description, the square brackets do not denote an optional clause in the syntax, and should be typed in literally around the <expression> clause. The <expression> clause to which we are referring can be made up of two things, namely: i) string patterns (including user/shell variables); and ii) filenames.

The **test** command alters the **$?**, the Bourne shell exit status variable (some UNIX systems, such as Ultrix, use the variable **$STATUS** instead of **$?**) after performing a test. If the value of an <expression> is true, the test command returns a zero (0) exit status, otherwise it returns a non-zero status. The actual condition we teat for is determined according by the following options (shown in Tables 13.2 and 13.3).

Table 13.2 Common file-based test options

File Option	Test condition
-b	File is a block-special file
-c	File is a character-special file
-d	File exists and is a directory file
-f	File exists and is an ordinary file
-g	File has the set group-id permission set
-r	File is readable i.e. read permission set
-u	File has SUID permission set
-w	File is writable i.e. write permission set
-x	File is executable i.e. execute permission is set (not version 7 UNIX).

The alteration of the exit-status code is useful, since we may want to evaluate whether or not a particular command was successful (this would be done directly following the particular command, since sucessive commands would alter the exit-status value).

Note that the actual command-name **test** can be excluded according to the syntax description; this acts as a type of shorthand notation for the **test** command, and will be demonstrated in the later examples.

Table 13.3 Common string-based test options

String Option	Test Condition
-n	String has a non-zero length
-z	String does have a length of zero
=	Equality of two strings
!=	Inequality of two strings
-ne	Not equal (similar to !=)
-gt	Greater than operator (>)
-lt	Less then operator (<)
-le	Less than or equal to operator (<=)
-ge	Greater than or equal to operator (>=)
!	NOT operator
-o	OR operator
-a	AND operator

Examples

Example 1

The **test** command can be run from the shell interactively with a filename argument.

```
$ ls File1
file1
$ test -f File1
$ echo $?
0
```

In this example we are testing whether the file named **file1** exists and if it is an ordinary file. No output is provided. Recall that **test** only alters the shell exit status variable (**$?**). The value returned by **test** is zero which is the *true* status. Any non-zero value (typically 1 or -1) would have been returned if the file was not readable and was not an ordinary file.

Example 2

```
if [test -r File1]
   then
      cat File1
else
   echo 'File1 is not readable.'
fi
```

This **if-then** programming example tests whether or not the read-permission is set on a file using the **-r** option. If the file is readable, it is displayed using the **cat** command on the standard output. If the file is not readable a suitable message is displayed using the **echo** command to inform the user. The expression in this particular example is:

```
test -r File1
```

An equivalent expression would have been:

```
if [ -r file1 ]
```

which omits the keyword **test** from the expression, even though the test command is still being used. All the other file options listed in Table 13.2 above are used in exactly the same way.

Example 3

String-based expressions are formed using the same rules as for the file-based expressions. For example, the **!=** operator can be used to test whether any differences exist between two variables (which may have been input previously by the user, employing some **read** commands) in the following way:

```
if [ test $STRING1 != $STRING2 ]
   then
      echo $STRING1 "is not the same as" $STRING2
else
      echo $STRING1 "is the same as" $STRING2
fi
```

Example 4

The small shell-script below can be used to scan the current directory and give a report on the status of the file(s) in that directory, indicating if they are readable, writable, or executable. (The **for .. done** construct is examined in section 13.5).

```
# Examine all files in current directory for R, W or X.
# make this file executable using "chmod +x this_file"
for FILE in *
do
   echo $FILE:
   if [ test -r $FILE ]
      then echo 'readable '
   else
      if [ test -w $FILE ]
         then echo 'writable '
      else
         if [ test -x $FILE ]
            then echo 'executable '
         else
            echo 'Not R, W or X'
         fi
      fi
   fi
   echo # blank line for next file
done
echo
echo 'All files have been examined.'
```

Example 5

The existence of a shell variable value can be tested by quoting the variable literally (with double quotes) in the following way:

```
if [ "$MAIL" ]
   then
      echo "MAIL variable is defined":$MAIL
else
      echo "MAIL variable is not defined."
fi
```

This tests the **$MAIL** variable to see if it holds a value. If it does, then the user is informed of the value. In the case where a value is not allocated (a null variable), the user is also told. Any shell variable can be used in string test conditions of this type.

Obtaining User Input

The problem with our small shell programs so far is that no user interaction has taken place. All the values for our test conditions have taken place as 'hard-coded' instructions inside of the program. To obtain user input we need to use the **read** command, which enables the user to type input directly from the keyboard. The syntax of the read command is:

read <variable-name>

When a value has been read, a new shell variable is created to hold it, which can then be accessed by prefixing the variable name with a dollar ($) sign (see example below). Shell variables are discussed in more detail in Chapter 5. The **read** command, as usual, can be run directly from the shell level. For example:

```
$ read NAME
Fred Bloggs
$
$ echo $NAME
Fred Bloggs
```

This example shows how a value is read from the keyboard into the variable **NAME**. **NAME** (using the **echo** statement here) is accessed by preceding the variable with a **$** sign, as explained earlier.

Putting this into a program

Now that we have a rough idea of how the **if** command functions, it may be worthwhile explaining the whole procedure that is involved when creating a program. The program below accepts the name of terminal device as input. This is stored in the shell variable called **NAME**. The value of **NAME** is then examined against the entries in **/dev**, whereupon the program informs the user whether the device is a block- or character-special device.

Programs should always contain comments (by using the # character at the beginning of a line, normally followed by the comment). Commands, such as **clear**, can be used to clear the terminal screen allowing the program to start with a fresh screen display. If you discover any errors when executing the program, correct them by re-editing the file. Firstly we invoke an editor to allow us to create our program. Assume that we are using the **ex** editor in this example.

```
$ ex program1
[New File]
:a
# Program 1: Enter a device name and program tells the user
#       whether the device is character or block.
clear
echo -n 'Enter the name of a device :'
read NAME
# Test if the file exists first
if [ -r /dev$NAME ]
   then
   echo 'This device does not exist (or is not readable).'
fi
# Test for block device
if [ -b /dev/$NAME ]
   then
      echo 'That device is a block-special device.'
fi
```

```
# Test for a character device
if [ -c /dev/$NAME ]
   then
      echo 'That device is a character-special device.'
fi
.
:x
'program1' 27 lines 675 characters
$
$ chmod +x program1
```

Now that the file has been entered and saved we have to make it executable, i.e we need to inform the shell that we want this file to be interpreted as a series of shell commands, and not as an ordinary text file. The **chmod +x program1** takes care of this. To run the program we would simply enter its name on the command line. This is shown below, with the program listing as it executes:

```
$ program1
Enter the name of a device:tty10
That device is a character-special device.
$
```

Running the program with an invalid device name results in the following display:

```
$ program1
Enter the name of a device:Fred
This device does not exist (or is not readable).
```

The program also detects block-special devices. A listing to meet this condition is shown below:

```
$ program1
Enter the name of a device:dk04
That device is a block-special device.
```

Explanation of Program 1

The program starts by clearing the screen. This is done using the **clear** command (not illustrated in the example runs). The program then requests the user to enter the name of a device. This is done with an **echo** command usinſ the **-n** option which specifies that a carriage-return is not to be printed after the **echo** has executed. This allows us to read the user input on the same line as the echo, which looks more readable. Try taking out the **-n** and see what happens. The **read** command is then invoked with the variable **NAME**, which is used in a series of if statements, the first of which tests if the file is readable i.e. if it exists. This allows an error message to be displayed when the user enters the name of a device that does not exist in the **/dev** directory (or that cannot be read).

The program does not have to be executed from within the **/dev** directory (note how the pathname **/dev/$NAME** has been used). The value of **$NAME** is substituted into this line, so a fully-qualified pathname will be constructed by the program. For example if we entered **tty10** the program would test for the file **/dev/tty10**. Note that if a user enters **/dev/tty10** as input, the program will check for the device **/dev/dev/tty10** which will obviously not exist.

The program then uses two similar **if-then** statements to scan for the file to see whether it is a block-special or character-special device. You will have noticed that the previous program made use of quite a few **if-then** statements. This can be avoided through use of a new control structure, is known as **case .. esac** (or simply as a case statement) under the Bourne shell, or **switch .. endsw** under the C-Shell (or simply as a switch statement).

13.4 Case and switch

The **case** (Bourne Shell) and **switch** (C-Shell) constructs offer alternative structures for testing values. The syntax descriptions for these two structures is shown below in Table 13.4.

Table 13.4 Constructs used for Case and Switch

<table>
<tr><th>Bourne Shell</th><th>C-Shell</th></tr>
<tr><td>case <$variable> in</td><td>switch (<$variable>)</td></tr>
<tr><td>value1)</td><td>case value1:</td></tr>
<tr><td>[actions ...]</td><td>[actions ...]</td></tr>
<tr><td>;;</td><td>breaksw</td></tr>
<tr><td>value2)</td><td>case value2:</td></tr>
<tr><td>[actions ...]</td><td>[actions ...]</td></tr>
<tr><td>;;</td><td>case value3:</td></tr>
<tr><td>value1|2)</td><td>case value4:</td></tr>
<tr><td>[actions ...]</td><td>[actions ...]</td></tr>
<tr><td>;;</td><td>breaksw</td></tr>
<tr><td>*)</td><td>default:</td></tr>
<tr><td>[default actions ...]</td><td>[default actions ...]</td></tr>
<tr><td>;;</td><td>breaksw</td></tr>
<tr><td>esac</td><td>endsw</td></tr>
</table>

As can be seen both forms of the construct are similar. The main differences between the two lie in the use of colons (:) following a condition value in the C-Shell version, and the use of a right bracket in the Bourne Shell version. The C-Shell version of the construct allows multiple value to be represented by simply repeating a case statement, whereas Bourne Shell version uses the pipe character (|) to separate possible values.

Double semicolons (;;) are used to end a series of statements in the Bourne Shell version, whereas the word **breaksw** is used in the C-Shell version of the construct. A default value (a value not matched in any earlier condition) is represented by an asterisk (*) in the Bourne Shell construct, whereas the C-Shell version uses the word

default:. The only other noticeable differences are the construct names themselves e.g. **case ... esac** and **switch ... endsw**.

The example below illustrates the use of the Bourne Shell version of the construct in a simple program that checks the current value of the **$TERM** variable to see if it contains a **vt100** emulation. If the terminal is set up with this emulation, then the **vi** editor is invoked to edit a file, the name of which is supplied by the user. If the **vt100** value is not found in the **$TERM** variable, it is set by the program and **vi** is invoked.

```
# Program 2: Uses case .. esac to obtain a file name,
#        set terminal type and edit file. Assume
#        the user file exists in current directory.
echo -n "Enter the file you want to edit:"
read FILE
# See if user's file actually exists
if [ -r $FILE ]
   then
   case $TERM in
      vt100|vt)
      echo "Terminal recognised as vt100 ..."
      echo
      vi $FILE
      ;;
      *)
      echo "Terminal not recognised, setting to vt100 ..."
      echo
      TERM=vt100
      vi $FILE
      ;;
   esac
else
   echo "I cannot find that file."
fi
```

Notice how the **case .. esac** construct in this program is embedded within an **if .. fi** construct. This effectively means that if the file that the user requests to edit does not exist, the file will not be edited i.e. the **case .. esac** statement is skipped over and the **else** statement of the **if** statement is invoked. The action following the **else** statement is a simple **echo** statement that tells the user that the filename supplied could not be found.

The reason why **case .. esac** and **switch .. endsw** are preferred to the **if .. fi** construct is a matter of both performance and flexibility. The **if** statement runs a command when testing data (which is the actual condition being tested), whereas the **case** statement performs the matching of patterns directly in the shell itself, without having to call any external commands as found in the **if** statement. Some UNIX systems have the **test** command built into the shell itself, but then again some systems do not. Where the **test** command is part of the shell, an **if** test statement will perform as quickly as a **case** statement. However, where the test command is an external command, the **case** statement should be used instead of an **if**, except for testing files (i.e. whether they exist and have read permission set etc.) when the **case** statement cannot be utilised easily; in this situation the **if** statement, used in conjunction with a test, is probably the most convenient solution.

13.5 Looping - for and foreach

Looping is the process of iteration within a program. When programming the shell we constantly find a need to process some information more than once. The shell provides a number of constructs for iterative processing. The first two constructs are **for** (Bourne Shell) and **foreach** (C-Shell). These constructs allow looping to take place through a series of actions. The syntax for both shells is given here:

Bourne Shell	C-Shell

for <var> in <var 1> ...
do
   [actions on <var> ...]
done
	foreach <var> <var 1> ...
	      [actions ...]
	end

The value for **<var>** is an arbitrary variable name. The values for **<var 1> ... <var n>** are normally names of individual files. The **in** part of the Bourne Shell version is optional, thus a loop can be performed over each file, allowing processing to take place on each pass of the loop. The program below uses the **for .. done** construct to loop over every file in the current directory (using the * metacharacter which matches all files) giving the user the chance to delete the file if required.

A **case** statement is used to allow the yes/no confirmation to delete the current file. The name of each file is shown on each pass of the loop. Note that the variable file has a preceding $ because it is a variable, and to be referred to it must have this dollar sign. The value for **$file** will be replaced on each pass of the loop by the next file in the current working directory. When the file list is exhausted the loop will terminate.

```
# Program 3: Loop through each file in current directory
# allowing user to delete the file if required.
for file in *
   do
      echo -n "[" $file "] Delete this file (y/n) ? :"
      read yesno
      case $yesno in
         y|Y)echo "I have deleted the file [" $file "]."
            echo
            rm $file
            ;;
         *)echo "Keeping [" $file "]."
            echo
            ;;
      esac
   done
   echo "All files processed."
```

Notice how the program will not delete a file when a reply is not recognised (using the default option). Also note the use of the matching pattern (**y|Y**) which matches both upper and lower-case letters. The shell notation **[Yy]** can also be used.

A no (n or N) response is matched by the default option. This saves having to put another group of lines to test for the condition. Notice that only yes (y or Y) options are processed in this particular program. When the program is executed an output similar to that below is displayed. Assume the file is named **program3** and has been made executable using the command **chmod +x program3**. Also assume a hypothetical directory exists which contains the three files: **file1**, **file2** and **file3**. The program will be executed in this context:

```
$ program3
[file1] Delete this file (y/n) ? :y
I have deleted the file [file1].

[file2] Delete this file (y/n) ? :z
Keeping [file2].

[file2] Delete this file (y/n) ? :N
Keeping [file3].

All files processed.
$
```

After the program has executed, the file named **file1** has been deleted, while the files: **file2** and **file3** were not processed (note that the reply obtained for the second file was **z**, and the reply for the third file was **N**, which were both caught by the default option within the program).

13.5.1 File processing with for

The **for** construct has additional properties that allows it to process a file of data. Take the following example, where a plain ASCII file containing the names and phone numbers of a group of people have been placed in the file **phone_book**. A typical file can be seen below:

```
Fred Bloggs    219   0091
John Smith     452   2573
Mark Smith     981   7710
```

If we now created an executable file named **phone** and placed the command below in it, we would effectively have a small program that searched for a particular phone number using the first argument that we supplied as a person's name:

```
grep $1 phone_book
```

This command uses **grep** to search the **phone_book** file, using the search pattern **$1**. The **$1** variable is a positional parameter representing each part of the command line (see section 7.2.2). The value of **$0** is thus the command name - **phone**. The value of

$1 could therefore be an argument to the program allowing us to search for a person's phone-number. The value of **$2** would be the file **phone_book** in our example.

When we run the program a value must be supplied. This value will simply be an item of data in the file, which will be referred to within the program as positional parameter **$1**. Its value will be passed to **grep**, which in turn will search for that value in the file **phone_book**. Some examples demonstrate this:

```
$ phone Fred Bloggs
Fred Bloggs    219 0091
$ phone Fred
Fred Bloggs    219 0091
$ phone Smith
John Smith     452 2573
Mark Smith     981 7710
```

Grep returns the whole line when a pattern is matched so we obtain the person's name and phone-number. Notice how entering just the surname **Smith** results in **grep** returning two lines of information. This example will allow us to move on to see how a for construct can be used in conjunction with a file of data.

13.5.2 Iterating over positional parameters

This section briefly discusses how a for construct can be used to loop over all the current positional parameters that have been set on the command line. Take the example below. This short piece of code works through all the positional parameters which have been allocated values on the command line, using each one in turn. It could therefore be used to scan the command line for more than one data item as the basis of a search pattern in a file such as the **phone_book** file.

```
for n
   do
      grep $n phone_book
done
```

Assume that we saved this file under the name **phone2** and made the file executable. We could now enter commands such as:

```
$ phone2 Fred John
Fred Bloggs    219 0091
John Smith     452 2573
```

Here we are using two names, and not one as in the older version of this program (which only searched positional parameter **$1**). This program searches the positional parameters **$1** upwards. Notice though, that the command line can only hold a set number of positional parameters. The **shift** command must be used to access positional parameters that extend **$9**. The **shift** command was explained in section 8.3.2.

We can also scan multiple files using the **for** command by simply making the loop iterate over each file in succession. This was demonstrated in section 13.5. Assume we created a new program called **phone3**, and entered the following:

```
for n in phone_book address_book
  do
     grep $1 $n
done
```

This small program allows us to scan two files matching a single patterns that is specified on the command line, and which occupies positional parameter **$1**. The **n** variable loops over the two files **phone_book** and **address_book** applying the **grep** command with the search pattern held in **$1** to these two files as it proceeds (these filenames are held in the variable **$n** on each pass of the loop). Assume the file **address_book** holds the data:

```
John Smith     28 Cherry Blossom Lane Wimbledon SW19
Fred Bloggs    72 The Drive Raynes Park SW20
Mark Smith     12 Circle Gardens Wimbledon SW19
```

A limitation of this program is that it can only accept one positional parameter (**$1**) as the search pattern on the command line. A typical command would be:

```
$ phone3 John
John Smith     452 2573
John Smith     28 Cherry Blossom Lane Wimbledon SW19
$ phone3 Smith
John Smith     452 2573
John Smith     28 Cherry Blossom Lane Wimbledon SW19
Mark Smith     981 7710
Mark Smith     12 Circle Gardens Wimbledon SW19
```

The previous example demonstrates how two files can be searched successively for data. Notice how the name **Smith** makes **grep** return two entries from each respective file.

13.6 Looping - while and until

The **while** (both Bourne and C-Shells) and **until** (Bourne Shell only) constructs provide another looping mechanism, albeit slightly different to the **for** and **foreach** constructs introduced earlier. The syntax for these constructs can be seen below:

Bourne Shell	**C-Shell**

while [<command-list>]
do
   [actions ...]
done
	while (<expression>)
	   [actions ...]
	end

While loops are useful since they execute until some condition is set true. The exit status of a command can thus be used to control the iteration of a loop. **For** loops iterate for a more specific duration, such as over a list of files etc., whereas the iteration duration of a **while** loop is less definite, since the outcome of a shell command (if used) may be less certain.

Both the **while** and **until** loops depend on the exit status of a command in order to control the loop-body. This can be thought of as the instructions between the **do** and **done** (Bourne Shell) or the **while** and **end** statements (C-Shell). Take the following example:

```
while [ 1 ]
do
   who | grep John
   sleep 300
done
```

This small program uses a single value as the command list. The existence of a value (such as **1**) will be recognised as a true condition, thus the loop will execute infinitely. The body of the loop contains the command **who | grep John** which runs the **who** command to check if the user named John is currently logged in.

The **sleep** command suspends execution by a predefined number of seconds, here 300 (or 5 minutes). This will stop the program continually to print the **who** entry for the specified user. If user John is logged-in, a single line entry from the **who** line will be displayed for him (unless he is logged in more than once, in which case one line for each entry for this user will be displayed). Assuming that we have placed the previous piece of code in a file and made it executable. A typical listing when the program is executed is illustrated below. Assume we have named the file **watch**:

```
$ watch
John tty14 Jun 8 16:01
```

Since the loop is infinite, the shell prompt will not be returned. You will have to interrupt this foreground program by pressing **<Ctrl-C>**. This program could probably be run better as a background process, for example:

```
$ watch &
2346
John tty14 Jun 8 16:01
```

This time the shell prompt has been returned. In its present form the process may be slightly disruptive since it is running as a background process, and therefore will periodically interrupt you. The terminal may also appear to be processing your commands more sluggishly than normal. This is because you have set a running program active as a background process. To stop the program, type **ps** and find the process id-number (**PID**), by identifying the program name against the **ps** listing, and then terminate it using **kill**.

Infinite loops can also be invoked using the single colon (**:**) in the **<command-list>**. The colon is a built-in shell command that simply does nothing but return a true condition. Two commands named **true** and **false** also exist on nearly all UNIX systems. They return true and false exit status codes. The colon is more efficient since it does not execute a command from the file-system. Take the following example:

```
while :
do
    who | grep John
    sleep 300
done
```

Note the absence of any square brackets in the **<command- list>** in this example. These are not required since, as mentioned earlier, the colon is a built-in command.

13.6.1 Using commands in the <command-list>

It was mentioned earlier that a shell command could be used in the **<command-list>**, and indeed this has been demonstrated previously with the use of the built-in shell command :. Any shell command that returns an exit status can be used as the basis of a condition to keep a **while** loop iterating. Take the example below:

```
while who | grep tty01
do
    sleep 120
    echo 'User on tty01.'
done
```

This program will process the instructions in the body of the loop only while a user is logged on to the terminal **tty01**. When a user is found, an entry for the terminal is displayed, and the program sleeps for a minute. Remember that the loop body is executed just as long as the command **who | grep tty01** returns a true exit status.

If the user is still logged in on **tty01** after another two minutes, the user is informed again. The program will stop when terminal **tty01** is no longer being used i.e. when **grep** returns a non-zero exit status because it could not locate the search string **tty01** in the output supplied by the **who** command. The program has many disadvantages. For a start the program will continue to display output until the user logs out from **tty01**, and if a user is already logged in on this terminal you may have to wait two minutes before finding out.

A better approach involves the use of the **until** construct which is normally only available under the Bourne Shell. Take the example below where the same program is implemented using an until construct:

```
until who | grep tty01
do
    echo 'No user on tty01 yet.'
    sleep 120
done
```

In this program the main body of the loop is repeated until the command **who | grep tty01** command returns failure. Thus an entry is only printed once, where the user using **tty01** is found upon execution of the program. The program will iterate in the case where somebody is not using the terminal **tty01**.

13.7 Commands to exit and continue loops

Two important commands that can be used within loop control structures allow the loop to be either terminated or continued. These are **break** and **continue** respectively.

The **break** command can be used anywhere within the loop body to terminate the current loop. When a **break** statement is scanned, control is passed to the next statement after the end of the loop body, which will be the next statement after the **done** statement (or end statement if using the C-Shell). Nested loop structures can be constructed, whereby control can pass from an inner loop to an outer loop, using strategically placed **break** statements. If no statements lie outside of the loop body, the program simply terminates. Figure 13.1 illustrates the logic flow of the **break** statement. The arrow lines indicate the flow of control within the program.

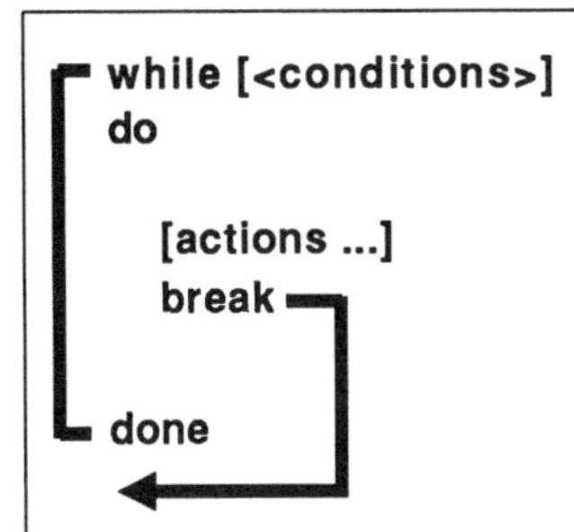

Figure 13.1 ***Break*** *statement logic*

The **continue** statement is useful when processing must resume without any actions being carried out. Such conditions arise in **if-then-else** constructs (notably around the area after the **else** statement). Including a **continue** statement ensures that the current loop is reactivated.

Figure 13.2 illustrates the logic of the **continue** statement. Notice how its use is beneficial in **if-then** statements where there is no need to carry out any type of processing. In such cases the current loop can be continued immediately.

13.7.1 Explicitly repeating commands - repeat

The C-Shell also has a command named **repeat** that can be told to explicitly repeat a particular command for a number of times. For example:

```
$ repeat 20 who
```

This command will run the **who** command 20 times.

13.8 Other looping commands - xargs

The **xargs** command is a clever little tool that takes a line from the standard input and then executes a named command, substituting the standard input where specified on the command line. The **xargs** tool is useful for executing one type of command (in a similar way to the **repeat** command briefly discussed in section 13.6.1) on a group of one or more files. The fundamental syntax of the **xargs** command is:

xargs [-n amount] [command]

A typical command using **xargs** could therefore be:

```
$ ls | xargs -n 10 cat
```

This short command will make **xargs** use **cat** to display the contents of the first ten files in the current directory. Notice also how **xargs** has been used as a filter in this example, and that it takes its standard input from the **ls** command to obtain a file list.

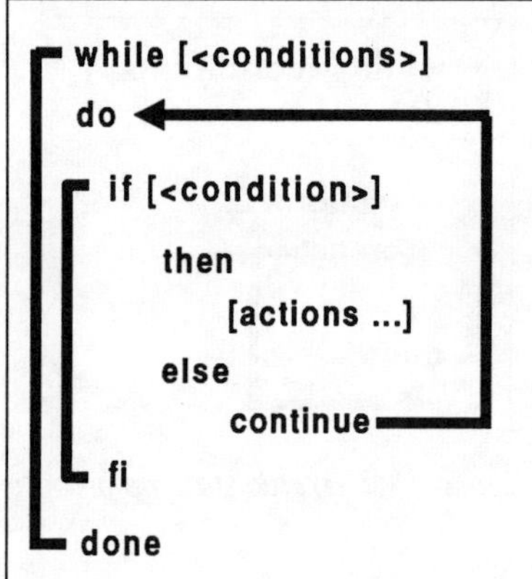

Figure 13.2 ***Continue*** *statement logic*

13.9 Catching interrupts - trap

During the time that a program is executing you may want to disable, or even process, any interrupt signals that may occur. The **trap** command allows many signals to be caught and evaluated, whereupon a series of actions can be taken. An example of a common interrupt that can be scanned for is **SIGINT**, generated by pressing **<Ctrl-C>**, the interrupt key.

Trap allows us to set up a sequence of commands that are to be executed upon detecting a signal. Signals can even be ignored (with the exception of **SIGKILL**) effectively preventing a program from being interrupted by the user. The syntax of the trap command is:

trap <commands> <signals ...>

When using **trap** it is necessary to specify the signal number that is to be trapped. The commands to be executed, when the particular signal has been detected, may need to be quoted because they are included as a single argument. Multiple commands can be inserted using the ; character and by bracketing the commands. A list of the most common shell signal numbers are listed in Table 13.5 below:

Table 13.5 Shell signal numbers

Shell signal	Meaning
0	Shell exit (Any cause)
1	Hangup (Normally <Ctrl-D> signal)
2	Interrupt (The <Ctrl-C> signal or DEL key on some systems).
3	Quit signal (Normally <Ctrl-\> signal)
9	Sure kill (cannot be caught or ignored)

A typical program that makes use of the **trap** command is given below:

```
# Small program to read the /usr/adm/wtmp file (System V
# uses /etc/wtmp). If program is interrupted etc., the
# interrupt is trapped, and a small message is printed.
trap 'echo Program interrupted' 0 1 2 3
echo -n 'Enter a username: '
read USERNAME
echo
cat /usr/adm/wtmp | grep $USERNAME
```

This program uses a simple **trap** statement to handle the shell **exit**, **hangup**, **interrupt** and **quit** interrupt signals. The program scans the **wtmp** file to look for all usernames that match the user-supplied value, stored in the shell variable **$USERNAME** (obtained using **read**). Executing the program, assuming we named it **finduser**, would produce a listing similar to the following:

```
$ finduser
Enter a username: Fred
Fred  tty01   Jun 13   16:45
Fred  tty01   Jun 13   17:56
Fred  tty04   Jun 16   11:05
Fred  tty04   Jun 16   16:21
<Ctrl-C>
Program Interrupted
$
```

During the time that the program was executed, the user pressed the interrupt key **<Ctrl-C>**. The program detected this user interrupt through use of signal number **2** (the shell interrupt signal).

Multiple commands can also be invoked when an interrupt is detected. This is done by bracketing the commands together and separating them by semicolons (;), as illustrated below:

```
trap (clear; echo Program terminated) 1 2
```

Trap can also be used interactively. Take the following example which invokes a command which runs for a long time, and stops it from being interrupted by the user accidentally logging out. The command is executed as a background process because of its long execution duration.

```
$ (trap '' 1; cat /usr/adm/wtmp | grep Fred > file) &
```

Notice the null **<commands>** list in this example. This has the effect that nothing is carried out where signal **1** is generated (which is the **hangup** signal). The use of single-quotes and double-quotes must be taken seriously depending on the type of processing that takes place in the **trap** command.

Trap commands are normally read twice, once when the program starts, and once again when a predefined signal is generated, and recognised, by the **trap** statement. If shell variables are used within the **trap** statement, use single quotes to protect their integrity. Double quotes can be used in null **trap** statements, as they have been with the **/etc/profile** shell-script in section 11.13. Again, abide by the rules laid down by the shell when the interpretation of various commands is taking place (see section 7.5.5 for more details on quoting conventions).

13.10 Updating data

Updating files involves adding, changing and deleting any information. Simple update programs can be written in the language of the shell, although there are dedicated shell utilities that allow files to be updated in the ways mentioned. Throughout the examples in this section we will use the two files **phone_book** and **address_book**. The contents of these files are summarised below:

```
$ cat address_book
John Smith     28 Cherry Blossom Lane Wimbledon SW19
Fred Bloggs    72 The Drive Raynes Park SW20
Mark Smith     12 Circle Gardens Wimbledon SW19
$
$ cat phone_book
Fred Bloggs    219 0091
John Smith     452 2573
Mark Smith     981 7710
```

13.10.1 Deleting data - grep and mv

Deleting a record from one of these files can be done simply by using a few of the standard UNIX tools such as **grep**, **mv** and the redirection symbol **>**. First, it will be necessary for the user to enter a string of text which will used to identify the record to be deleted. This string may be a phone-number or the name of a person etc.

The program you are about to see achieves the deletion of a record by prompting the user to enter a string, and then uses **grep** with the **-v** (invert search) option to redirect the all entries but the one required to a new file. This has the effect of creating two files, the original version, and a new version without the string that was specified by the user.

The new file is placed is given a unique temporary name (using the value of the **$$** - shell id variable). This file is then written over the original file using the **mv** command. The old file is thus overwritten, effectively deleting the original entry the user specified. The program that does this is shown below:

```
# Delete a record from address_book. Uses grep -v
# to get all records except the one specified by
# the user.
echo -n "Enter the name of a person to delete :"
read PERSON
grep $PERSON address_book
case $? in
   0) grep -v $PERSON address_book > temp $$
      mv temp $$ address_book
      echo "Record for this person has been erased."
      ;;
   1) echo "This person does not exist"
      ;;
esac
```

The initial **grep** command is used to verify that the person being deleted actually exists. The **grep** command thus searches the **address_book** file, whereupon the **$?** variable (exit status of last command) is tested in a **case** statement. This determines whether the deletion can go ahead or not.

A zero (**0**) exit-status means that the **grep** command has found the pattern specified by the user, and thus the program proceeds with the deletion using the method already explained. A non-zero exit status (here tested as **1**) means that the initial **grep** command failed, that is, it did not match the pattern specified, which in turn means that the deletion cannot go ahead. The user is informed in a simple **echo** statement and the program terminates.

Running the program (assume the file has been named 'delete') results in the following listing:

```
$ delete
Enter the name of a person to delete :Fred
Record for this person has been erased.
$
```

If we now examined the **address_book** file we would find that the entry for Fred Bloggs has been deleted:

```
$ cat address_book
John Smith     28 Cherry Blossom Lane Wimbledon SW19
Mark Smith     12 Circle Gardens Wimbledon SW19
```

Running the program with a nonexistent name results in the following display:

```
$ delete
Enter the name of a person to delete :Tom
This person does not exist
```

13.10.2 sed

Sed is a powerful command that copies the specified files (the standard input is the default) to the standard output, edited according to a list of commands on the command line. The fundamental syntax for the **sed** command is:

sed [options] [file ...]

Options include **-e <commands>** which allows the transformation commands to be applied. The **-f <file>** option allows these editing commands to come from a file rather from the keyboard. The **sed** command can be used with many options; those we are specifically interested in substitute text and allow us to update fields. Updating fields is a difficult process and involves the manipulation and substitution of individual patterns in files.

Substituting and updating data

To substitute a string of text within a file, **sed** would be used in the following way:

```
$ sed -e "s/SW19/SM4/" address_book > address_book
```

Because **sed**, by default, writes its results to the standard output device, we have to use output redirection to capture any new changes. The changes that have taken place in the previous file are simple substitutions, as follows: all occurrences of the post-code value SW19 will be changed to SM4 in the file **address_book**. The changes will also be written back to this file, effectively updating the file (which is the facility that we initially required).

The statement **s/string1/string2/** causes the substitution to take place - **string1** being replaced by **string2** in the named file. This allows us to update various field values in a file with relative ease. This notation is similar to that found in **ex** and **ed**, the UNIX editors, and indeed the substitution commands are very similar.

The result of the previous **sed** command on the file **address_book** can be seen below (taking into account any previous alterations on the file):

```
John Smith     28 Cherry Blossom Lane Wimbledon SM4
Mark Smith     12 Circle Gardens Wimbledon SM4
```

We can update individual fields with null (empty) values by leaving out the second replacement string, for example:

```
$ sed -e "s/SM4//" address_book > address_book2
```

This would replace all occurrences of the pattern SM4 with nothing. Thus the **address_book2** file would now look like this:

```
John Smith     28 Cherry Blossom Lane Wimbledon
Mark Smith     12 Circle Gardens Wimbledon
```

Deleting data items

Deleting individual records (whole lines) of information from within a record can also be achieved using **sed**. This is done employing the following form of the command:

/string/d

The letter **d** at the end of this line indicates that the pattern named string is to be searched for in a line, and that line is then to be deleted. The command to delete every occurrence of the surname Smith would thus be:

```
$ sed -e "/Smith/d"
```

Multiple deletion operations can be included on the command line as follows:

```
$ sed -e "/Wombat/d" -e "/wombat/d" a_file > file
```

Note here that each editing expression must be preceded by the -e option. Multiple substitutions can also be formed using this notation. The **-f** option allows a series of **sed** commands to be read in from a file. A typical file can be created with an editor such as **ex**. This is shown below:

```
$ ex commands
[New file]
:a
s/unix/Unix
s/shell/Shell
/UNIX/d
.
:x
"commands" 3 lines 31 characters
$
```

Now that a series of **sed** commands have been inserted into a file we can invoke **sed** with the **-f** option, as illustrated below:

```
$ sed -f commands document1 > newdocument1
```

This would invoke **sed** with its instructions arriving from the file **commands**. The file to which these instructions will be applied is named **document1**. Any alterations will be written to the file **newdocument1** leaving the older version of the file intact.

13.11 Awk

The **awk** utility comprises a whole language of its own. Such is its size that only the main concepts are explained here. **Awk** is a pattern scanning and processing language, which works in much the same way as **sed**, although using **awk** is similar to programming in the shell. The most useful **awk** programs should be placed in files for convenience, and then executed. When used from the interactive level, the syntax description of **awk** is as follows:

awk '<program>' <file 1 ... file n>

Used in a program, **awk** takes the following form:

awk <pattern> {action}

When **awk** is executed it reads its input from the input files **file1 .. filen**, one line at a time. The lines in these files are compared with each **<pattern>** in turn. If the pattern matches the line, then the corresponding **{action}** is performed. Any output produced by **awk** does not go to a file unless output redirection is employed by the user. The input files used by **awk** are also left untouched during processing, so remain unaltered.

Each **<pattern>** can be a regular expression, as found with tools such as **egrep** (extended **grep**) (see section 7.5.4 for more information on egrep). Some simple examples of **awk** in action may aid our understanding:

Examples

Example 1

```
$ awk '/Wombat/' { print } file1 file2
```

This command searches the files named **file1** and **file2** for the pattern **Wombat**. If the pattern is matched in either of the files, the line containing that pattern is displayed (in much the same way as the **grep** family).

Example 2

The print statement allows unformatted text to be displayed. Without the pattern (or regular expression), **awk** can be used to concatenate files in much the same way as the **cat** command:

```
$ awk '{ print }' file1
```

This command simply prints out, line-by-line, the file named **file1** on the standard output. Printing text in this way is the default action.

Example 3

Awk instructions can also come from files, as found with **sed**. Again, the **-f** option is used for this purpose.

```
$ awk -f commands file1 > file2
```

This command makes **awk** take its commands from the file named **commands**. The actions in this file are applied to the file named **file1**. Any results are placed in the file named **file2** using output redirection.

13.11.1 Field processing with awk

When **awk** runs, it divides each input line into a series of fields which must normally be separated by at least one or more spaces (such as a **TAB**) so that they can be distinguished from each other. Take the **who** listing which we have used in numerous examples up to now. The listing supplied by **who** can be thought of as five field columns:

```
$ who
Doug        tty08    Jun 16    12:07
Pauline     tty10    Jun 16    11:56
```

If we were using **awk** and wanted to refer to these fields, we would use a notation similar to that of the positional parameter. The notation **awk** used is:

```
$1 ... $NF
```

Note the absence of a **$0** field. **$0** still exists in **awk**, although it is not used to refer to individual fields. The variable **$NF** is maintained automatically by awk and is equal to the total number of fields. In the case of the **who** listing the value of **$NF** would be **5**. Now that we know how to refer to individual fields from command listings we can manipulate any shell command whose output is divided into separate columns. For example:

```
$ who | awk '{ print $1 }'
Doug
Pauline
$
```

This uses **awk** as a filter, whose input is arriving from the **who** command. As the data arrives, **awk** divides it up into fields and carries out the command(s) within the braces ({}), **print $1**. This makes **awk** display only the first field of its standard input which contains the names of all users who are currently logged in. Multiple fields can be printed in any order by listing each field separated by a comma:

```
$ who | awk '{ print $1, $5 }'
Doug        12:07
Pauline     11:56
```

This example prints column 1 and 5, the username and time of login for each respective user.

13.11.2 Using different field separators

We mentioned earlier that **awk** assumes that individual fields are separated by one or more spaces. Using spaces as field separators may not be useful when processing data whose fields are delimited by different characters. Take the **/etc/passwd** and **/etc/group** files where the fields are separated by colons (:). **Awk** can be instructed to interpret a different field separator using an option, commonly **-F<field separator>** which allows us to specify a visible character as a field separator (the default being one or more spaces).

Examples

Example 1

```
$ awk -F: '{ print $3, $4, $5 }' /etc/passwd
```

This **awk** command uses the **-F:** option to use colons as field separators. It then projects the third, fourth and fifth fields of the **/etc/passwd** file, which are the **GID**, **UID** and **User** information fields respectively. **Awk** also recognises a series of various operators which can be used to test field values. The most important **awk** operators are summarised in Table 13.6.

Table 13.6 Awk operators

Operator	Action
==	Equality (equal to)
!=	Not equal to
>	Greater than
<	Less than
++	Increment
--	Decrement

Example 2

The equality (==) operator is frequently used to check field values. The next example takes the **grep** command to check if a user has a password:

```
grep '^[^:]*::' /etc/passwd
```

Example 3

Scanning for an empty password field using **awk** involves typing the command:

```
awk -F: '$2 == '""' /etc/passwd
```

The null (empty) password string which we are seeking is represented by the expression "", an empty string. The other operators can be used in similar ways.

Example 4

```
$ awk -F: '{ $1 != "Doug" }' /etc/passwd
```

This command will find all users who are not named Doug.

13.11.3 BEGIN {} and END {} constructs

Awk provides the constructs **BEGIN** and **END** which allow actions to be performed before the first line of input has been processed, and after the last line of input has been processed. Take the short **awk** excerpt which follows:

```
awk -F: '
      BEGIN {print All users in /etc/passwd file
         print
         }
         { print $1 }
      END{ print
         print End of file
         } ' /etc/passwd
```

This code (which should be included in an executable file, i.e. a shell-script) uses the **BEGIN** statement to print a simple heading, and then a blank line (a **print** command on its own) followed by a list of each username (**field 1**) in the **/etc/passwd** file.

The **END** statement ensures that a short message is printed when processing finishes. Note how the single quotes are placed strategically right at the start and at the end of the file. The file to be processed appears outside the quotes at the end of the program. When **BEGIN** and **END** are used, the **awk** instructions to be carried out must be placed inside the braces { and }. Both **BEGIN** and **END** are optional, and either can be used without the other if necessary.

13.11.4 Regular expressions

Awk also handles regular expressions. A search string (or pattern) must be delimited by / slashes, as follows:

/string/

The tilde (~) is used to match a regular expression, and the operator **!~** inverts the matching process. These are used in the examples below. Assume we are using the **address_book** file introduced earlier.

Examples

Example 1

```
$ awk '$1 !~ /John/' address_book
Mark Smith 12 Circle Gardens Wimbledon SW19
```

This command will make **awk** search for all entries where the first field (**$1**) does *not* match the pattern **John**.

Example 2

Similarly **awk** can be used to match patterns within certain fields of a file using the tilde on its own:

```
$ awk '$2 ~ /Smith/' address_book
John Smith     28 Cherry Blossom Lane Wimbledon SW19
Mark Smith     12 Circle Gardens Wimbledon SW19
```

Example 3

Regular expressions can be formed by using the standard metacharacters.

```
$ awk '$3 ~ /../' address_book
John Smith     28 Cherry Blossom Lane Wimbledon SW19
Mark Smith     12 Circle Gardens Wimbledon SW19
```

This command uses the **.** metacharacter to match single characters. Two dots have been specified, therefore only the third field of the **address_book** file which has two characters will be matched (which is both records in the example).

13.11.5 Conditional expressions - if

Awk can also be instructed to carry out selection operations using an **if** construct. The syntax for the **if** statement under the **awk** utility is:

```
if (condition)
    [statement1]
else
    [statement2]
```

Notice that when the **if** statement is used under **awk,** it has no **fi** component. The **else** is an optional component also. A typical statement could therefore be:

```
awk 'BEGIN {n=0}
   { if ($2=="Smith")
   n++
   }
   END { print n }' address_book
```

This **awk** shell-script excerpt counts the number of people in the **address_book** file who have a surname of Smith. The **BEGIN** statement has been set up to initialise a counter variable (called **n**) to zero. This counter will be used to keep track of the number of Smiths that are counted. The **if** statement tests the value of field **$2** (the persons surname field) with the value **"Smith"**. The equality sign (==) checks for a match. If a match is made, the **n** variable is incremented (increased by one). Incrementing a value is done using the operator ++ (which has been carried over from the C language).

This shell-script excerpt is not very user-friendly and the output is not formatted. The **printf** statement can be included to format (or 'pretty print') such output (see next section).

13.11.6 Formatting text - printf

The **printf** command is used to present formatted text. Such text can be displayed according to a format conversion definition supplied by the user within the **printf** statement. The positioning of values within textual strings is also possible.

When using **printf** the text to be displayed must be enclosed in brackets and double quotes (see the example below). Variables are placed at the end of the statement following the last double quote. A comma is inserted before the variable name to separate it from the text string. The position of the variables is defined using a series of output format definitions. These take the form of a percentage sign (%) followed by single letter. A **%3d** definition therefore allows a three-digit wide decimal variable (numeric data), whereas **%s** defines the positioning of a string of characters (alphanumeric data).

Expanding our previous shell-script, we could add the new **printf** statement to format its output, as follows:

```
awk 'BEGIN {n=0}
   { if ($2=="Smith")
      n++
   }
   END { printf ("There are %2d people named Smith.",n)
      }' address_book
```

Note how the **printf** statement is structured, mixing both a textual string and an output definition for a variable at the necessary position. The variable itself appears at the end of the line (and note that this is not the output position for the variable). Assuming we had put this **awk** code into an executable file (using **chmod +x**) named 'findsmith', a typical program run would be as follows:

```
$ findsmith
There are 2 people named Smith.
```

Without the formatted string (as in version 1), the output would have simply been:

```
$ findsmith
2
```

13.11.7 looping - for

The **awk** tool allows the user to incorporate iterative constructs in the form of a **for** statement. The syntax of this construct is:

```
for (expression1; condition; expression2)
   statement
```

Take a look at the following **awk** extract:

```
awk '{ for (n=NF; n > 0; n--)
   printf ("%s",$n)
   printf ("\n")
   }' address_book
```

This program prints the contents of the **address_book** file in reverse, by successively moving through each variable on the input line. The value of **n** must be greater than zero for the body of the loop to continue executing. The value of **n** becomes equal to the number of fields in the current input line (**8**). It is decremented (**--**) on each pass of the loop. The value printed by **printf** is a character string (**%s**) followed by the value for **$n**, the value of a field in the current input line.

Note that the fields will be printed in reverse order in this example, because **NF** starts with the value **8**, and then works downward. Therefore **$8** is printed first, followed by **$7** and so on until **$1** is printed, when **n** will be zero, and the loop will terminate. To print out the file exactly as it appears, we would use the following program:

```
awk '{ for (n=1; n < 9; n++)
   printf ("%s",$n)
   printf ("\n")
   }' address_book
```

This program starts with **n** as 1, and then increments **n** on each pass of the loop. The value for **$n** is thus **$1, $2 .. $8**. The condition in this piece of code is **n < 9** which stipulates that the body of the loop will only execute while **n** is less than 9. The value 8 is the highest valued candidate which meets this condition, and is correct for the number of fields in the file being examined. The **printf ("\n")** prints a new line (carriage-return), and is executed after each variable is printed.

13.11.8 looping - while

There is also a **while** construct included as part of the **awk** language. It is directly equivalent to the **if** construct. Its syntax description is:

```
expression1
while (condition) {
            statement
            expression2
            }
```

In context to our previous example, we could therefore construct the following piece of equivalent code:

```
awk 'BEGIN {
   n = 1
   while (n < 9) {
            printf ("%s",$n)
            printf ("\n")
            }
      }
   END { printf ("%s",$n) } ' address_book
```

We can customise our shell-script to display any file using a simple **read** statement, as shown below:

```
echo -n "Enter a filename to display :"
read FILE
# check that file exists
if [ -r $FILE ]
awk 'BEGIN { n = 1
   while (n < 9) {
            printf ("%s",$n)
            printf ("\n")
            }
      }
   END { printf ("%s",$n) } ' $FILE
else
echo "I cannot find the file :" $FILE
fi
```

13.12 Questions

1. Why is the colon (:) command more efficient when programming an infinite loop using a **while .. done** construct?

2. Show a typical **sed** command that replaces all instances of the word UNIX with the two words Operating System.

3. Explain the purpose of the **trap** command.

4. Show how a **trap** command can be used to process the **SIGINT** signal. Assume we want the screen to be cleared and the message "Interrupted" to be displayed when the **SIGINT** signal is detected.

5. Which command can be used to exit from a **while .. done** construct?

6. Write a small shell-script to count the number of users who are currently logged-in.

7. How can a default value be captured in a **case .. esac** construct?

8. The **test** command uses a series of options to test certain conditions. What does the **-r** option test for?

9. How can a variable be tested to see if it holds a value? Give an example of a typical command.y

10 Show how a loop can be used to loop over each file in a directory specified by the user, and then allow each file, at the discretion of the user, to be backed-up by copying that file to the same directory but with a filename extension of **.bak** e.g. **file1** becomes **file1.bak** etc.

APPENDIX A

Glossary of Terms

accounting The process of keeping records or an audit of system activity.

alphanumeric Characters consisting of either letters or numbers or both. Letters can be upper and lower case. Punctuation symbols such as %, & and ! etc. are not normally included.

ASCII An acronym for American Standard Code for Information Interchange. A coding system for each letter, digit and other characters. An ASCII file is a file of ''plain-text''.

attenuation The gradual loss of a signal over distance and time.

baud rate The baud rate is the speed of serial data transmission. The word serial refers to the fact that data is transmitted sequentially i.e. one piece of data after the other. The name arose from the engineer Henry Baudot.

Berkeley The University of California in Berkeley pioneered the popular Berkeley UNIX system.

binary image A binary image (of a file) is also sometimes referred to as an executable file or executable image.

bit A binary digit, either 0 or 1.

bootstrapping The process of starting-up a computer, which normally involves the loading of the operating-system. Synonymous with boot and boot-up.

bps Bits per second. A measurement for the number of binary digits transmitted in one second.

buffer A buffer is a place of temporary storage. It could be part of computer memory, although the meaning is normally applied to smaller, temporary, areas of storage space which are used to hold information. Buffers are commonly used to slow down the amount of information transmitted to a device because one device is much faster than another.

bus A transmission route where electronic signals are passed backwards or forwards. A bus is frequently used in many computer systems to link devices together. Common in networking.

byte A unit of data measurement, which is most commonly 8 bits in length. A byte is therefore a series of binary digits that represent a piece of information, normally a single character of information. In the ASCII code a character is represented by one byte.

C language A high-level computer language that is used to make the computer perform a series of instructions. The C language is very flexible and in many ways emulates the facilities of a low-level language.

command pre-processor The program that accepts commands from the user and then carries out these commands. In UNIX, the command pre-processor is the Shell. In MS-DOS and PC-DOS the command pre-processor is an executable program with the name COMMAND.COM. Command pre-processors normally contain resident or internal commands that are executed much faster than those which are stored in a computer's file-system.

compiled A program is compiled into a machine-code language so that it can be executed more quickly by the computer. Languages which are not compiled are called interpreted languages. Interpreted languages do therefore not have executable binary images (q.v.) as a result, and hence execute more slowly.

contention The struggle or competition for the transmission of data over a network. A contention based system is normally one in which access across a network is hectic and where collisions can occur as a result.

control-code A control-code is a code or signal generated most commonly through the use of the keyboards CONTROL (Ctrl) key. The control key is used to allow additional commands to be issued from the keyboard. Control-keystrokes are found in many computer applications packages to invoke various commands etc. The Ctrl key is held down and a single letter (or combination) of letters is simultaneously pressed to invoke the desired action.

CRC Cyclic Redundancy Check. A method whereby errors can be detected in transmitted data.

device A device is an item of equipment in a computer system. It could be a terminal or a storage-device. Some devices are also known as peripherals. In UNIX, devices are categorised into the two main classes *block special* and *character special*.

directory In the context of UNIX, a directory is an area of the file-system in which files are stored (including further directory files). This allows the UNIX file-system to adopt a hierarchical structure.

E-mail An electronic mail system is a system that allows users to send electronic messages to each other in a networked situation.

escape-sequence An escape sequence is a series of codes that are commonly used in the display of terminal screen characteristics. An escape-sequence code could therefore be included in a command to print some data on a VDU screen.

Ethernet A specification that a describes a manner by which computers can be connected together (using a form of cable) in a networked environment.

executable An executable file or binary image. Normally program files.

file-name extension A string of characters appended to a file-name. The extension acts as a means of identifying the contents of a file. For example, the file-name FRED.LET may indicate a letter to Fred, while FRED.BAK may mean that this file is back-up copy of the original FRED.LET file. The file-name and extension are separated most commonly with a single period (.) or full-stop.

file-system The collection of files on a disk or a specific part of it. Under UNIX, the file-system is modelled hierarchically in a tree-shaped structure.

fixed-length As the name suggests, the length of a record which is fixed in size. May be seen as a limitation where variable-length record sizes are available.

full-duplex A system in which the user and the computer system can communicate backwards and forwards at the same time. A full-duplex system, more generally, is one in which simultaneous two-way communication is possible. A half-duplex system is one in which two way communication is available but not at the same time. The UNIX system is a full-duplex system.

housekeeping There are two definitions which are valid here. One is the set of transparent actions undertaken by the computer system which ensure its overall performance. These include such functions as memory and disk management. The second definition of housekeeping is the collection of general day-to-day tasks that have to be performed on a computer system i.e. the deletion of old and obsolete files and general clearing-up tasks.

i-node The UNIX systems file description mechanism. An i-node is allocated to each file in the UNIX system. The i-node holds critical information about the file to which it is allocated such as the files modification time and dates, and protection attributes etc.

intelligence Intelligence of a device etc. means that device has the ability to receive information and make sensible decisions regarding the processing of that particular item of information. Node intelligence is frequently found in network topologies. For example, a star network has central node intelligence for the routing of information from the outlying nodes in the network.

kernel The part of the operating system that is used to communicate with external programs. Normally is the system dependent part of operating systems because it is tied to the architecture of the computer system. The kernel is responsible for the allocation of memory and time to individual processes, and for handling communication functions.

LAN An acronym for Local Area Network. A LAN is a network that connects a number of devices together in a relatively small geographical area, and thus a much smaller configuration to a WAN (q.v.) network.

lock-up The event when a device, commonly a VDU or keyboard will not respond to the user. This may happen as a result of an operating system error or a program error.

MCDB An acronym for Manchester Coded Digital Baseband. A signalling technique used in LAN systems whereby a transition takes place at the centre of every time slot when a signal is transmitted.

mount The operation performed when the contents of a disk (or other storage media) are made available to the users of a computer system. In UNIX, a disk is mounted by joining its contents to the existing file-system.

MS-DOS An acronym for Microsoft Disk Operating System. A standard operating system for all non-IBM personal-computers. MS-DOS is a 16 bit operating system.

multi-user A multi-user system is one on which allows more than one user to access the facilities of the host computer system. A time-slice is allocated to each user in quick succession thus giving the impression that each user has the sole use of the computer system, when in fact attention is being paid to every user on the system. UNIX is a multi- user system by definition.

nethack A game available on UNIX machines and some personal-computers. The scenario is a level of mazes, which the user has to find their way through in order to accumulate a higher score.

network drive A disk-drive that holds a vast amount of information (typically upwards of 350 Megabytes on many systems. The drive can normally be accessed centrally by many users. The NFS system allows users to use network drives to access their information. They tend to be much faster than conventional disk-drives, like those found on personal-computers.

packet A set of data bits transmitted over a network. The packet is a structure that stores the destination address of the packet, the actual information in the packet along with any additional information such as error check digits, or CRC fields.

PDP-7 An older minicomputer, used for the first port of the Multics operating-system which then led to the UNIX operating system. The computer is manufactured by DEC (Digital Equipment Corporation) who are also the manufacturers of the VAX computers.

pipeline A mechanism introduced in the UNIX operating-system which is used to take the output of one command and use it as the input to another. Pipelines allows "new" UNIX commands to be constructed by manipulating the output of existing commands.

pointer A term used in computing to describe the physical linkage of data items. The pointer is simply an address of a particular data item, although in diagrams the linkage via addresses is shown by a a physical line or ''pointer''. Pointers or pointer techniques are used extensively in the C programming language.

poll To constantly interrogate a device to see if it needs attention. Normally done by the computer system's CPU and used extensively in networked environments. Extremely time consuming process, and considered to be resource-wasting since the polled device may not need attention, and thus CPU time is wasted.

port Refers to the interface on a computer i.e the type of port. On personal-computers ports are parallel and serial. In UNIX, porting is the moving of one UNIX system to another machine. UNIX is said to have a high portability factor because of the fact that it is written in the high-level language C.

process A much-used term to describe an event in a computer system. A process can be a program in execution, or a more long-term process such as a user who is logged-in to a computer system. In UNIX, processes are referred to extensively, and they ''live'' and ''die'' at periodic intervals.

prompt A prompt is an indication to the user that the system awaits a command or some type of instruction(s) from the user. In UNIX the system prompts the user for a reply with a dollar prompt ($) which is found on many UNIX systems. All interactive systems, such as UNIX and Pc/MS-DOS all have such prompts.

protocol A group of computing rules. Protocols are used extensively in data transmission over networks.

shell A working environment in which the computer system accepts commands from the user, and which then goes away and processes them. A number of different shell environments are available under the UNIX system.

shell-script A series of commands placed in a file, which are then executed by the computer system. In UNIX a shell-script is a series of internal and external shell commands that are executed in succession.

source-code The actual instructions that form the software product. The source-code may be written in a high-level or low-level language.

SunOS The version of the UNIX operating-system manufactured by Sun MicroSystems. The system is based around Berkeley UNIX.

superblock A UNIX term referring to a physical area of the file-system. The superblock is an area of the disk that contains all the information about the disk itself i.e. its size, and the total number of data-blocks. It also contains information about the data-blocks that are allocated to individual i-nodes, and the address of the free-list (an area on the disk that contains the addresses of all the unused data-blocks). The superblock is one the most critical areas of the disk and if damaged may cause irreparable damage to the file-system.

System V A standard UNIX system, piloted by AT&T (the equivalent of British Telecom in Britain). It is currently running in its fourth version. Version four incorporates three main UNIX systems, namely Berkeley UNIX, Xenix and SunOS. Version four is supposed to be the new industry standard.

terminal A device used to make contact with the central computer-system. A *dumb terminal* is a terminal that has no additional processing power and is merely used as a contact device. An *intelligent* or *smart* terminal has local intelligence, and can download data from the main computer-system on to local storage such as a hard-disk etc. An *intelligent terminal* may also have additional circuitry thus adding to its overall power i.e. additional memory etc.

time-sharing A system that allows multiple users to access a computer system, and which allocates a time-slice to each user.

toggle A command or action which is used both to enable and disable a particular operation. The operation is thus toggled on and off using the same command or action, rather like a light switch.

transceiver A device used to make connections in a cable (in a network) do that devices can be linked into the network.

UID An acronym for User Identification Number. UNIX uses the UID as a numerical identity of a user. Each registered user must have a UID as far as the UNIX system is concerned.

Uniplex An integrated applications package that incorporates E-mail, database and word-processing functions along with other facilities such as diary and calendar management. The package is used on UNIX machines.

VAX A range of computers manufactured by DEC (Digital Equipment Corporation). VAX is an acronym for Virtual Address eXtension, which arises from its virtual memory capabilities.

VAX VMS An operating system that runs on the VAX range of machines. VMS is an acronym for Virtual Memory System, a system that allows a disk to be used as memory, thus allowing large programs to run on relatively small machines.

VDU An acronym for Visual Display Unit, the primary device used for output in a computer system. A VDU Screen typically consists of 23-25 lines, and 80 columns (where one column is one character).

VT100 An industry standard terminal manufactured first by DEC (Digital Equipment Corporation). VT is an acronym for Video Terminal, and many manufacturers emulate this terminal through VT100 clones, or through different terminals that support a VT100 emulation.

WAN An acronym for Wide Area Network, a network that is spread over a wide geographical area. See LAN.

Xenix Microsoft version of the UNIX operating system. Popular on personal-computers and has enabled UNIX to access smaller computers.

APPENDIX B

Answers to Questions

Chapter 3

1. The two principal types are reliable stream sockets (SOCK_STREAM), and unreliable (SOCK_DGRAM) sockets.

2. This term has a number of different meanings. Basically, it is a set of rules that allow processes to communicate with one another.

3. The seven layers are (in order): Application, Presentation, Session, Transport, Network, Link and Physical.

4. YP map: an ordered collection of key and value pairs. These are replicated across YP server machines, thus increasing the availability of the service.

   YP client: a process requiring a naming service i.e. a mapping from an IP address to a machine name through the /etc/hosts file.

   YP server: a machine running a naming service, and which is contacted by a YP client. Each YP server runs a service that a YP client can access.

5. Could have had: Error, Event, Request or Reply.

6. There are a number of concepts, although the main ones include:

   ❑ Access to remote file-systems (via mount style request) i.e PC UNIX server machine;

   ❑ Near-transparent access to files;

   ❑ Access to more than one operating system i.e. data transfer between DOS UNIX is possible, etc;

   ❑ Concept of client and server used heavily.

7. Both adopt a layered approach, and similarity between actual layers. For example: OSI transport layer is roughly equivalent to the TCP network interface layer.

8. A set of service primitives (to access services), and a set of protocol specifications (how a service will be provided i.e. the rules or protocol).

9. Bitmap: A pixmap with a depth of one (one bit per pixel). Used to represent small shapes such as cursors etc.

   Pixmap: A rectangular raster area onto which an application can draw. They are not visible until copying them into a window (or drawable).

   Window: An area into which text or graphics (such as pixmaps can be drawn.

10. Could describe: Bridge, Transceiver cable, Terminator Ethernet controller device, or Coaxial (Ethernet) cable itself.

Chapter 5

1. The name parent file is used in context to the hierarchical nature of the UNIX file-system. A parent file is simply the directory file which lies above the current working directory.

2. The parent of all files is the root directory, since it lies at the very top of the file-system.

3. Nothing. Note how the second path-name ends with a / sign. UNIX assumes that a fully qualified path-name that does or does not end with a / sign is the root directory of that particular directory (assuming we are talking about directory files and not ordinary files).

4. The three main categories of user classification when setting access protections are user (or owner), group (the members of the user-group in which the owner is also a member) and other (all those users who are not in the same group as the owner).

5. A mount operation involves a new file-system being joined to the existing file-system, whereas an unmount involves the opposite operation i.e. the mounted file-system is detached from the main file-system.

6. Any of those in section 5.8.3.3, such as problems of security (since a user could mount a file-system containing tampered administrative utilities that allow that user to run applications without super-user status etc). Another problem concerns the increasing use of removable disk media, and the pressure on users to mount their own file-systems in order that certain applications programs will work.

7. A file-system is all the files (ordinary and directory etc) that reside on a disk (or part of it). In UNIX the file- system is mapped as an upside-down tree structure. This is hierarchical structure is possible since UNIX makes use of directory files, which themselves can contain further directories at lower levels.

8. A Major number is a number given to a special file i.e. a device. It is used to encode that particular device, whereas a Minor number is used to indicate all the possible instances of the device concerned.

9. The /dev directory.

10. The /tmp directory is the directory whose contents are commonly deleted at start-up time (hence the name temporary directory).

11. A path-name is a list of directories (linked together using / as a separator) which leads to an individual file (or group of files).

12. A fully qualified path-name does not take into account the user's position in the file-system with respect to that user's current directory. The path-name is thus 'full' in the sense that a path is followed from the root directory (/) to the file(s) concerned. A partly qualified path-name takes into account the user's current file-system location with respect to the current working directory.

13. The current working directory is the directory that the user is currently placed within inside the file-system.

14. Simply, an i-node is a unique piece of information that is attached to each file in the file-system. It is unique in the sense that the i-node has a unique i-node number which identifies that particular file. I-nodes contain other additional information such as a files protection attributes etc.

15. A character device is a device from which characters are read or to which characters a written. Typical character devices are terminals and printers. A block device is a device which deals in blocks of information. A block device cannot be written to in the same way as a character based device, and requires special input/output requests. A typical block device is a disk-storage device.

16. The root file-system is the file-system that is always mounted. It contains the necessary information to allow a UNIX system to be successfully started-up. It is to this file-system that any mounted file-systems will be attached.

17. Three access attributes that can be assigned to a file are the read, write and execute access permissions respectively. Execute permission becomes search permission when referring to a directory file.

18. The special notation for a parent file is double-dot (..). These refer to the directory immediately above the current working directory. This notation is invalid if the current working directory is / (the root directory), although some UNIX systems will not complain, since the root directory is simply a link to itself.

19. Any of the features mentioned in section 5.2, such as a files dynamic structure, the concept of a structureless file, the hierarchical nature of the file-system and the access permissions and security of files.

20. Files are said to be structureless since the file-system imposes no real internal structure on a file. A file is simply a sequence of bytes.

Chapter 6

1. The main advantage is performance. Since a 1024 block system is twice as large as a 512 block system, double the amount of information can be handled at any one time thus decreasing the number of disk input/output operations that have to be performed by the system.

2. Some Berkeley systems can be, and are, configured with a 4096 byte block size.
3. Indirect blocks are used because the number of data blocks may be fully allocated, and thus a certain amount of indirection has to be used in order to address other data blocks on the system.
4. An indirect block is a structure which either points to other indirect blocks or to the data blocks themselves. The concept of triple, double, and single addressing is used in order to address a disk. Indirect blocks facilitate this by allowing large disk areas to be addressed in this way.
5. Files are termed 'dynamic. because they can expand or grow as large as is required (within disk limitations that is). There is therefore no limit as to the size of a file.
6. The maximum size of a UNIX file-system is simply the size of the disk itself.
7. The four regions are: i) the boot block; ii) the super-block; iii) the i-list; and iv) the free-list. Note that the ordering is not important in your answer.
8. The superblock is block 2 of the disk file-system. It is used to store information regarding the entire disk file- system. It typically contains information regarding the size of the disk, the amount of blocks that make up the device, and the amount of free space on that device.
9. Any of those in section 6.5, such as owners GID, owners UID, the file type, protection information, date of files creation, date of most recent access or modification of that file, or the pointers to indirect blocks or data blocks.
10. An i-node is a structure that stores critical information about a file. Every file has an i-node, that stores allows the system to locate the file, and identify its protection settings etc. The individual i-nodes are stored in an area of the disk known as the i-list.
11. The most significant fact about the boot block that we have mentioned is the fact that it resides on the first block of a disk (block zero).
12. Non-contiguous disk-storage refers to the fact that a file or group of files are not stored side-by-side, but are in fact scattered over an area of a disk.

Chapter 7

1. A metacharacter is a character that has a special meaning to the shell, and is thus interpreted differently.
2. The single quote notation can be used to encapsulate an argument to deprive the interpretation of a metacharacter such as the command ls **'d*e'** which makes **ls** search for a file named literally as d*e ignoring the special metacharacter. The single-quote can also be used to encapsulate multiple patterns when passed to utilities such as grep thus allowing a multiple worded pattern to be treated as a single pattern i.e. grep 'John Smith' /etc/passwd would make grep search for the whole name John Smith and not the two separate names John and Smith.

3. As mentioned in the answer to question 2, to make **grep** use one argument consisting of individually (spaced) patterns.

4. **Grep** differs from fgrep in that **fgrep** cannot deal with patterns that use metacharacters, that is to say it can only deal with "fixed" strings i.e. Jon not Jo*n etc. The **fgrep** utility is also programmed to be more faster.

5. The standard input file is a stream associated with all input arriving from the keyboard (by default) or from a another command when used in a pipeline. The standard output file or stream is normally (by default) the screen although it can be made to be a file using output redirection. The standard error stream is also (by default) the screen. This stream displays any errors that may have occurred while a command was being processed.

6. A pipeline is a group of shell utilities, the input of one file coming from the output of the previous utility. The symbol | is used to join commands together. The standard input file is manipulated frequently since the input to a command will come from another Shell command and not from the keyboard (default device).

7. The shell command is **`who | grep 'tty[^234]'`**

8. The **touch** command is used to change a files modification time and date to that of the current time and date, as set by the system.

9. The shell command is: **`who | sort +4`**

10. Use the command **ls -a.** A 'hidden' file is any file whose file-name starts with a period, for example `.profile`.

11. The **tail** command displays lines from the end of a file. By default tail will display 10 lines of a file.

12. Command (a) and command (b) are exactly the same, since the argument +1 in command (b) prints all lines of the who command from line 1 (as normal). Command (a) does the same, hence the | **tail +1** part of the command in command (b) is unnecessary.

13. The **-i** option tells **grep** to ignore the case of a pattern, For example JOHN and john are treated as one and the same.

14. The secondary prompt is supplied by the Shell when a command is incomplete (and thus the Shell needs more information). A command to invoke the secondary prompt could thus be: **echo 'hello.** Since the second single quote is absent the shell would display the following:

```
$ echo 'hello
> '
hello
$
```

Typing the second single-quote at the secondary prompt completed the command, and it was executed accordingly. The primary prompt is then returned.

15. The command needed is **cp file? sales.** The directory sales is mentioned partially qualified because the current working directory is /usr/john, and hence we need not mention the fully qualified version **/usr/john/sales.** The **?** wildcard has been used to copy those files which match the pattern file and then a single character i.e. file1 and file2. Other valid commands include:

    cp file1 file2 /usr/john/sales
    cp file1 file2 sales
    cp file* /usr/john/sales
    cp file* sales

    Note that we assume only the files named **file1** and **file2** exist to be copied. If other files are named similarly, care will have to be taken when using wildcards.

16. The **-r** option of the **rm** command is dangerous since it is used to recursively delete a directory and all of the files that lie in that directory. Therefore all lower level directories would be deleted along with any files that resided within them. Take the command **rm -r /** which if accidentally typed by a super-user would be disastrous.

17. The **mkdir** command issued to make a directory file that is subordinate to the current working directory. The **rmdir** command is used to remove a directory file.

18. The tree structure is as below:

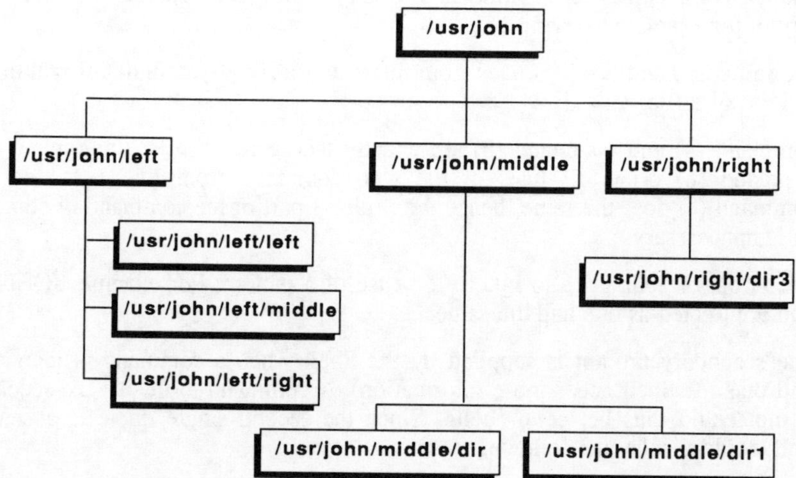

19. The directory **/usr/john/right** cannot be deleted because the directory file dir3 exists within this directory.

20. These include: a) file-name does not exist; b) directory is not empty; and c) a directory is trying to be deleted when the use is not in a higher level (or parent) directory or if the user is inside of the directory trying to be deleted.

Chapter 8

1. The **export** command is used to allow shell variables to be made available to any other shells that may be invoked. When a new shell process is created the environment (by default) is renewed, and it will ignore any previous variable settings. The **export** command solves this by making available such variables.

2. The **$PATH** variable contains a list of directories that will be searched (delimited by a :) whenever a command is executed from the command-line. The common directories include **/bin** and **/usr/bin** for the normal shell utilities. Each directory is scanned in the order it was mentioned in the **$PATH** variable.

3. The shell process-id is held in the shell variable **$$.**

4. The effect of this command would be to overwrite the current value of the **$PATH** variable, thus nullifying it i.e. erasing it.

5. Typing **who** would involve the system running the **who** utility (executable file) which is normally stored in the **/bin** directory. Since there is no **PATH** setting, the system will not find the who file and will return an error along the lines of ''file not found''.

6. The syntax is: <Shell command> <Variable>=<value>

7. The first command executes the who command and sends the standard output to the **grep** utility which attempts to locate the pattern **fred.** If **grep** is successful i.e. fred is in the **who** listing the **&&** metacharacter ensures that the **who** command is executed again. The second command does the opposite i.e. the second who command is only executed if user fred is not logged in. Hence **&&** works only if an true exit status is returned, and || if a false exit status is returned.

8. The command **cd $HOME** is equivalent to using **cd** on its own, since the default operation of **cd** is to return the user to his or her home directory location.

9. The **/etc/termcap** file is the terminal capabilities file. It stores the screen display characteristics (escape-sequences and control-codes) of a variety of terminal devices, and tells the system how a particular terminal should interpret cursor key movements and other signals etc.

10. The equivalent notation is \c.

Chapter 9

1. The **ex** is a line-editor and the **vi** editor is a screen- based editor.

2. The standard UNIX editor, that is, the editor most frequently found on the majority of UNIX systems is **ed,** the line-editor.

3. The three modes are: a) Edit mode - where text is entered; b) command mode 1 - where the **ex** prompt is available for additional processing i.e. pattern matching; and c) command mode 2 - this has no prompt and is used for such tasks as cursor movement etc.

4. The **!** command is used to run an external shell command.

5. The **<Escape>** key.

6. The **i** key is used to insert text once inside of **vi,** although the **a** (append) text achieves the same action when a new document is created (see below).

7. Simply because there is no text in the current document, and therefore i (insert) will insert text at the current position as will the **a** (append) command.

8. 26.

9. Insert buffers are used to allow deleted text to be moved (or pasted) to another part of a document. Very similar to a delete buffer in operation.

10. This is because cutting and pasting cannot be done between different documents using a delete buffer.

11. To move text into a buffer, the y (yank) command can be used to yank text to a buffer, for example:

    ```
    ''a7yy
    ```

    which yanks seven lines (beginning at the current line) into the insert buffer named a). The **d** (delete) command can also be used to delete text and place it in a delete buffer, for example:

    ```
    3dd
    ```

    which deletes three lines and places them into a delete buffer.

12. The rewind (abbr. **rew**) command is used to move back to a previously edited file when a number of files have been mentioned on the command-line for editing. Each file will be edited in succession in such a case. The rewind command allows the previously edited file to be reloaded.

13. A typical command is of the form:

    ```
    ''c7yy
    ''C7yy
    ```

    The first command appends 7 lines to the c buffer and the second command does this again, but appends the contents to the c buffer instead of overwriting it. Note the case of the buffer-letter. This is the key to the appending process. An upper-case buffer-letter indicates an append operation is to take place.

14. The first command searches for the string 'wombat' at the start of a word. The second command will search for the string 'wombat' within any position on a line. The third command performs a global operation (on an entire file) whereby the patterns 'Wombat' or 'wombat' are matched and then replaced with upper-case word 'WOMBAT'. The p command ensures that the lines (in which the patterns were located) are printed.

Chapter 10

1. The **mesg** command.
2. Change the mode on the terminal using the **chmod** command so that write permission to all users apart from the owner is denied (same as **mesg** although the **chmod** command is not literally used).
3. Tilde commands allow the user to escape from "compose mode" and are thus able to perform external commands. These commands may be shell commands or other mail commands.
4. The **~d** tilde command makes the mail system include the contents of the **dead.letter** file in the current message.
5. The **! /bin/sh** command could be used as could the more efficient command **sh.**
6. Mail boxes for each user are normally stored in the **/usr/spool/mail** directory.
7. The local users **mbox** file contains all the saved messages that have ever been read by the user. messages are saved to the **mbox** file upon the user exiting (assuming the user had not deleted any such messages from within the mail system).
8. Two wildcards are * and $.
9. Any of the UNIX editors, such as **ex** and **vi.**
10. The ~v tilde escape invokes the **vi** (visual) editor.
11. Change the **VISUAL** variable.
12. The **biff** command notifies users of any incoming mail while they are logged in.
13. The **r** command can be used to reply to the sender (and recipients), or the **R** command can be used to reply to just the sender of the original message.
14. The **Subject:** field holds the subject heading for the message. It may indicate the nature of the message, i.e. warning or greeting etc. The **To:** field stores the name of the person to whom the current message is addressed. It may contain a single user-name, or an alias name, to which you belong. The Cc: field is the carbon copy field. It indicates the other users who were sent the same message by the original sender of the message.
15. The file is named **.vacation.msg.**
16. The set command used within the mail system is used to create and manipulate the mail systems environmental settings.
17. The - (hyphen) can be used to indicate a range, and used in conjunction with the **d** (delete) command, for example:

    ```
    d 1-4
    ```

    will delete messages one to four.

18. The **t** command. For example: **t*** types all messages, **t1** will type message number one, and **t 1-5** will type the first five messages.

19. The environmental variable **dot** should be set using the command **set dot.** The **<Ctrl-D>** control-code will then not be recognised, and a single period in the first column of a composed message will end the current message. For example:

```
& se dot
& m fred
Subject:hello
Hello fred, how are you doing?
.
Cc:
&
```

20. The **w** command should be used. For example:

```
& w 2 /usr/fred/mail
```

This command writes the body of message one to the file **/usr/fred/mail.**

Chapter 11

1. The **fsck** utility is used to check and repair file-system inconsistencies.

2. The update daemon is used to make sure the systems superblock area is up-to-date by writing the contents of it in memory to disk. A **sync** command is used for this purpose. **Update** is run every 30 seconds.

3. Three typical operations are: a) mounting file-systems; b) turning on swapping operations; and c) deleting the contents of the **/tmp** directory. Others include the invoking of system accounting routines and the execution of the **rc.local** file.

4. The purpose of the **rc.local** file is to invoke procedures that are only specific to a certain site i.e. personal commands and procedures that have been devised, and which are not part of the main start-up procedure.

5. Initial Program Load.

6. The **lost+found** directory exists as a special directory that is used in conjunction with the **fsck** utility. It acts as a storage place (temporary) for orphan files i.e. files that are not linked to an i-node entry for some reason.

7. Any of those in section 11.13.1 such as bad i-node formats, bad free-list format, blocks claimed by more than one i-node, incorrect link counts in a file-system.

8. **Preen** runs **fsck** in parallel on a number of disk devices at the same time, thus speeding up the time taken to check for file-system inconsistencies. When **Preen** detects an error, it uses **fsck** to try and fix it in its ''repair mode''.

9. The **du** command is used to display disk usage statistics. It can be used to monitor the amount of disk-space in a file-system whereupon the necessary action can be taken.

10. A typical command is of the form:

```
$ mount -o quota,rw /dev/dk02 /
```

Chapter 12

1. The **kill** command.
2. The **crontab** file is a likely candidate for malicious alteration since the instructions within the file are carried out with super-user privileges. If the file is left unprotected, a user can grant him or herself extra privileges thus allowing that user to circumvent system security.
3. The last command lists the login times and dates of a user, and the **lastcomm** command lists the commands invoked by a particular user.
4. The **last** command examines the **wtmp** file which records all the login and logout activity of the system. The **who** command can also be used to examine this file, although the display may be slightly irregular.
5. The **SUID** permission settings allows a non-privileged user to temporarily acquire super-user powers so that a particular task requiring such powers can take place. Execute permission on a command must be available to the user in question, and the command must be owned by root and have the **SUID** permission enabled for the owner.
6. This is dangerous since such utilities have shell escape facilities i.e. a ! command. This means that a user may be able to temporarily exit the utility and acquire super-user privileges since the program is executing with **SUID** permission set.
7. An example command is:

   ```
   find /usr -user 0 -print
   ```

8. The **perm** option allows the user to search for a file that has a particular permission access setting i.e. execute permission for all group users etc.
9. The **SIGKILL** signal cannot be caught or ignored. It is the ''sure kill'' signal. The command:

   ```
   kill -9 762
   ```

   will terminate the process with the **PID** of 762 by sending it a **SIGKILL** signal.
10. The command needed is:

    ```
    finger -i
    ```

    The **-i** option shows the idle time of each user logged in.

Chapter 13

1. The : (colon) is a in-built shell command and is therefore more efficient to use in infinite loops, because it does not involve the execution of a file from the file-system. Commands such as true and false return true and false exit status codes respectively. Because these are commands which exist in the file-system

they must be searched for and executed accordingly. This process obviously takes longer than the timer taken to execute a command that is built into the Shell.

2. A typical command that would do the job is:

```
sed -e 's/UNIX/Operating System/' file > file
```

where file is a hypothetical file to be examined and updated. Remember that sed does not update the contents of a file so it is left to the user to redirect the output to "file" in order to capture any changes.

3. **trap** is used to catch and process interrupts. A signal number is provided that corresponds to a certain interrupt signal, which can then be processed.

4. The trap command we need is as follows:

```
trap (clear; echo Interrupted) 2
```

Signal number 2 is the user interrupt (the **<Ctrl-C>** keystroke) which interrupts a foreground process.

5. The command is called **break.** It is used to break out of the current active loop (returning control to the next statement after the **done** part of the construct.

6. The shell-script needed is as follows:

```
# This script counts the number of users who are
# currently logged into the system.
clear
echo "Number of users logged in [" 'who | wc -l` "]"
```

7. A default value can be caught in a **case .. esac** construct using the asterisk notation *). This matches any of the inputs not matched already in the case statement. For example:

```
case $TERM in
vt100) echo "Terminal is VT100"
;;
vt200) echo "Terminal is VT200"
;;
*) echo "Terminal not known."
;;
esac
```

8. The **-r** option tests for a file that is readable (i.e. which has read permission set for the user trying to read the file). For example:

```
echo -n "Enter a file-name :"
read FILE
if [ -r $FILE ]
then
echo "That file is readable."
fi
```

9. To test to see if a shell variable has a value we simply use an if .. fi construct, and simply use the name of the variable encapsulated in double-quotes, for example:

```
# Test $TERM variable to see if it has a value
if [ "$TERM" ]
then
echo "TERM variable is set, and has value of: " $TERM
else
echo "TERM variable is not set."
fi
```

10. The program is as follows:

```
# Loop over files, allowing user to back up each
# file if required. Assumes that a non-yes reply
# is an error or means no.
echo -n "Which directory (full path-name) to examine: "
read DIR
cd $DIR
for file in *
do
  echo -n "[" $file "] backup (y/n) ? :"
  read yesno
  case $yesno in
  [yY]) cp $file $file.bak
       echo "File backed up."
     ;;
     *) echo "File not processed."
     ;;
  esac
done
```

Index